MARLOW AND MISS HARDCASTLE
"I'm called their agreeable Rattle."

THREE ENGLISH COMEDIES

SHE STOOPS TO CONQUER

THE RIVALS

THE SCHOOL FOR SCANDAL

EDITED WITH NOTES, LIVES OF GOLDSMITH AND SHERIDAN
A DISCUSSION OF LONDON LIFE AND DRAMATIC
LITERATURE AND AIDS TO THE STUDY
AND ACTING OF THE COMEDIES

BY

A. B. DE MILLE, A.M.

SIMMONS COLLEGE

SECRETARY OF THE NEW ENGLAND ASSOCIATION
OF TEACHERS OF ENGLISH

1947

ALLYN AND BACON

| BOSTON | NEW YORK | CHICAGO |
| ATLANTA | SAN FRANCISCO | DALLAS |

Personal Book Shop
1.17
9-20-48 cdm
9-27-48 cdm

Norwood Press
J. S. Cushing Co. — Berwick & Smith Co.
Norwood, Mass., U.S.A.

FOREWORD.

THE attendance at our public schools is so large that the problem of reference-books and of library facilities in general is not an easy one to solve. The present edition of *Three English Comedies* meets this problem by bringing together in convenient form the equipment necessary for a careful study of the plays. The material is planned to satisfy the requirements of the College Entrance Board and the Board of Regents of the State of New York, while at the same time it is adapted to the needs of the general reader.

A full and informative body of notes has been prepared. The Appendix contains, besides biographies of Goldsmith and Sheridan, a sketch of London life in the eighteenth century, an outline of dramatic writing during the same period, and a brief account of the principal London Clubs and Coffee-houses. A special section is devoted to a discussion of acting the comedies in school. The illustrations are of unusual value. Twenty-four pictures have been provided. Of these seven have been drawn especially for this book; the others are all reproduced from authentic photographs or from famous contemporary paintings. In several instances well-known actors are shown in the various rôles.

Questions on the text are included in the notes, and a list of topics for oral or written work will be found at the

Foreword.

end of the volume. The emphasis throughout has been placed on the study of the plays as plays, rather than as literary exercises.

A. B. DE MILLE.

SIMMONS COLLEGE,
BOSTON.

CONTENTS.

LIST OF ILLUSTRATIONS.

SHE STOOPS TO CONQUER

OR

THE MISTAKES OF A NIGHT.

A COMEDY BY OLIVER GOLDSMITH

AS ACTED AT THE

THEATRE-ROYAL, COVENT-GARDEN

[First printed in 1773]

DEDICATION

TO SAMUEL JOHNSON, LL.D.

Dear Sir,

By inscribing this slight performance to you, I do not mean so much to compliment you as myself. It may do me some honour to inform the public, that I have lived many years in intimacy with you. It may serve the interests of mankind also to inform them, that the greatest wit may be found in a character, without impairing the most unaffected piety.

I have, particularly, reason to thank you for your partiality to this performance. The undertaking a Comedy, not merely sentimental, was very dangerous; and Mr. Colman, who saw this piece in its various stages, always thought it so. However, I ventured to trust it to the public; and, though it was necessarily delayed till late in the season, I have every reason to be grateful. I am,

Dear Sir,
Your most sincere
Friend and admirer,
OLIVER GOLDSMITH.

PROLOGUE.

BY DAVID GARRICK, ESQ.

Enter MR. WOODWARD, *dressed in black, and holding a
Handkerchief to his Eyes.*

Excuse me, Sirs, I pray — I can't yet speak —
I'm crying now — and have been all the week.
' 'Tis not alone this mourning suit,' good masters:
' I've that within ' — for which there are no plasters!
5 Pray, would you know the reason why I'm crying?
The Comic Muse, long sick, is now a-dying!
And if she goes, my tears will never stop;
For as a play'r, I can't squeeze out one drop;
I am undone, that's all — shall lose my bread —
10 I'd rather, but that's nothing — lose my head.
When the sweet maid is laid upon the bier,
Shuter and I shall be chief mourners here.
To her a mawkish drab of spurious breed,
Who deals in Sentimentals, will succeed!
15 Poor Ned and I are dead to all intents;
We can as soon speak Greek as Sentiments!
Both nervous grown, to keep our spirits up,
We now and then take down a hearty cup.
What shall we do? — If Comedy forsake us!
20 They'll turn us out, and no one else will take us.
But, why can't I be moral? — Let me try —
My heart thus pressing — fix'd my face and eye —

With a sententious look, that nothing means,
(Faces are blocks in sentimental scenes)
Thus I begin — ' All is not gold that glitters,
Pleasures seem sweet, but prove a glass of bitters.
When ign'rance enters, folly is at hand: 5
Learning is better far than house and land.
Let not your virtue trip, who trips may stumble,
And virtue is not virtue, if she tumble.'

   I give it up — morals won't do for me;
To make you laugh, I must play tragedy.   10
One hope remains — hearing the maid was ill,
A Doctor comes this night to show his skill.
To cheer her heart, and give your muscles motion,
He, in Five Draughts prepar'd, presents a potion:
A kind of magic charm — for be assur'd,   15
If you will swallow it, the maid is cur'd:
But desperate the Doctor, and her case is,
If you reject the dose, and make wry faces!
This truth he boasts, will boast it while he lives,
No pois'nous drugs are mix'd in what he gives.   20
Should he succeed, you'll give him his degree;
If not, within he will receive no fee!
The College you, must his pretensions back,
Pronounce him Regular, or dub him Quack.

DRAMATIS PERSONÆ.

MEN.

Sir Charles Marlow	*Mr. Gardner.*
Young Marlow (*his son*)	*Mr. Lewes.*
Hardcastle	*Mr. Shuter.*
Hastings	*Mr. Dubellamy*
Tony Lumpkin	*Mr. Quick.*
Diggory	*Mr. Saunders.*

WOMEN.

Mrs. Hardcastle	*Mrs. Green.*
Miss Hardcastle	*Mrs. Bulkley.*
Miss Neville	*Mrs. Kniveton.*
Maid	*Miss Willems.*

Landlord, Servants, &c., &c.

ACT I.

SCENE I. A CHAMBER IN AN OLD-FASHIONED HOUSE.

Enter MRS. HARDCASTLE *and* MR. HARDCASTLE.

Mrs. Hard. I vow, Mr. Hardcastle, you're very particular. Is there a creature in the whole country but ourselves, that does not take a trip to town now and then, to rub off the rust a little? There's the two Miss Hoggs, and our neighbour Mrs. Grigsby, go to take a month's 5 polishing every winter.

Hard. Ay, and bring back vanity and affectation to last them the whole year. I wonder why London cannot keep its own fools at home! In my time, the follies of the town crept slowly among us, but now they travel 10 faster than a stage-coach. Its fopperies come down not only as inside passengers, but in the very basket.

Mrs. Hard. Ay, your times were fine times indeed; you have been telling us of them for many a long year. Here we live in an old rumbling mansion, that looks for 15 all the world like an inn, but that we never see company. Our best visitors are old Mrs. Oddfish, the curate's wife, and little Cripplegate, the lame dancing-master; and all our entertainment your old stories of Prince Eugene and the Duke of Marlborough. I hate such old-fashioned 20 trumpery.

Hard. And I love it. I love every thing that's old: old friends, old times, old manners, old books, old wines; and, I believe, Dorothy (*Taking her hand.*), you'll own I have been pretty fond of an old wife.

5 *Mrs. Hard.* Lord, Mr. Hardcastle, you're for ever at your Dorothy's, and your old wives. You may be a Darby, but I'll be no Joan, I promise you. I'm not so old as you'd make me, by more than one good year. Add twenty to twenty, and make money of that.

10 *Hard.* Let me see; twenty added to twenty makes just fifty and seven.

Mrs. Hard. It's false, Mr. Hardcastle; I was but twenty when I was brought to bed of Tony, that I had by Mr. Lumpkin, my first husband; and he's not come to 15 years of discretion yet.

Hard. Nor ever will, I dare answer for him. Ay, you have taught him finely.

Mrs. Hard. No matter. Tony Lumpkin has a good fortune. My son is not to live by his learning. I don't think 20 a boy wants much learning to spend fifteen hundred a year.

Hard. Learning, quotha! a mere composition of tricks and mischief.

Mrs. Hard. Humour, my dear: nothing but humour. Come, Mr. Hardcastle, you must allow the boy a little 25 humour.

Hard. I'd sooner allow him an horse-pond. If burning the footmen's shoes, frightening the maids, and worrying the kittens be humour, he has it. It was but yesterday he fastened my wig to the back of my chair, and when 30 I went to make a bow, I popt my bald head in Mrs. Frizzle's face.

8

Mrs. Hard. And am I to blame? The poor boy was always too sickly to do any good. A school would be his death. When he comes to be a little stronger who knows what a year or two's Latin may do for him?

Hard. Latin for him! A cat and fiddle. No, no, the 5 ale-house and the stable are the only schools he'll ever go to.

Mrs. Hard. Well, we must not snub the poor boy now, for I believe we shan't have him long among us. Any body that looks in his face may see he's consumptive. 10

Hard. Ay, if growing too fat be one of the symptoms.

Mrs. Hard. He coughs sometimes.

Hard. Yes, when his liquor goes the wrong way.

Mrs. Hard. I'm actually afraid of his lungs.

Hard. And truly so am I; for he sometimes whoops like 15 a speaking trumpet — (TONY *hallooing behind the scenes*.) — O there he goes — a very consumptive figure, truly!

Enter TONY, *crossing the stage.*

Mrs. Hard. Tony, where are you going, my charmer? Won't you give papa and I a little of your company, lovee?

Tony. I'm in haste, mother, I cannot stay. 20

Mrs. Hard. You shan't venture out this raw evening, my dear. You look most shockingly.

Tony. I can't stay, I tell you. The Three Pigeons expects me down every moment. There's some fun going forward. 25

Hard. Ay; the ale-house, the old place; I thought so.

Mrs. Hard. A low, paltry set of fellows.

Tony. Not so low neither. There's Dick Muggins the exciseman, Jack Slang the horse doctor, little Aminidab

9

that grinds the music-box, and Tom Twist that spins the pewter platter.

Mrs. Hard. Pray, my dear, disappoint them for one night at least.

5 *Tony.* As for disappointing them I should not so much mind; but I can't abide to disappoint myself.

Mrs. Hard. (*Detaining him.*) You shan't go.

Tony. I will, I tell you.

Mrs. Hard. I say you shan't.

10 *Tony.* We'll see which is strongest, you or I.

[*Exit hauling her out.*

Hard. (*Solus.*) Ay, there goes a pair that only spoil each other. But is not the whole age in a combination to drive sense and discretion out of doors? There's my pretty darling Kate! the fashions of the times have al-15 most infected her too. By living a year or two in town, she is as fond of gauze and French frippery as the best of them.

Enter Miss Hardcastle.

Hard. Blessings on my pretty innocence! drest out as usual, my Kate. Goodness! What a quantity of 20 superfluous silk hast thou got about thee, girl! I could never teach the fools of this age, that the indigent world could be clothed out of the trimmings of the vain.

Miss Hard. You know our agreement, Sir. You allow me the morning to receive and pay visits, and to dress 25 in my own manner; and in the evening I put on my housewife's dress to please you.

Hard. Well, remember I insist on the terms of our agreement; and, by the by, I believe I shall have occasion to try your obedience this very evening.

MR. HARDCASTLE

"Ay, there goes a pair that only spoil each other."

Miss Hard. I protest, Sir, I don't comprehend your meaning.

Hard. Then to be plain with you, Kate, I expect the young gentleman I have chosen to be your husband from town this very day. I have his father's letter, in which he 5 informs me his son is set out, and that he intends to follow himself shortly after.

Miss Hard. Indeed! I wish I had known something of this before. Bless me, how shall I behave? It's a thousand to one I shan't like him; our meeting will be so 10 formal, and so like a thing of business, that I shall find no room for friendship or esteem.

Hard. Depend upon it, child, I never will control your choice! but Mr. Marlow, whom I have pitched upon, is the son of my old friend, Sir Charles Marlow, of 15 whom you have heard me talk so often. The young gentleman has been bred a scholar, and is designed for an employment in the service of his country. I am told he's a man of an excellent understanding.

Miss Hard. Is he? 20

Hard. Very generous.

Miss Hard. I believe I shall like him.

Hard. Young and brave.

Miss Hard. I'm sure I shall like him.

Hard. And very handsome. 25

Miss Hard. My dear papa, say no more (*kissing his hand*), he's mine, I'll have him.

Hard. And, to crown all, Kate, he's one of the most bashful and reserved young fellows in all the world.

Miss Hard. Eh! you have frozen me to death again. 30 That word 'reserved' has undone all the rest of his accomplishments. A reserved lover it is said always makes a suspicious husband.

Hard. On the contrary, modesty seldom resides in a breast that is not enriched with nobler virtues. It was 5 the very feature in his character that first struck me.

Miss Hard. He must have more striking features to catch me, I promise you. However, if he be so young, and so everything as you mention, I believe he'll do still. I think I'll have him.

10 *Hard.* Ay, Kate, but there is still an obstacle. It's more than an even wager he may not have you.

Miss Hard. My dear papa, why will you mortify one so? Well, if he refuses, instead of breaking my heart at his indifference, I'll only break my glass for its flattery, 15 set my cap to some newer fashion, and look out for some less difficult admirer.

Hard. Bravely resolved! In the mean time I'll go prepare the servants for his reception: as we seldom see company, they want as much training as a company of 20 recruits the first day's muster.   [*Exit.*

Miss Hard. (*Alone.*) Lud, this news of papa's puts me all in a flutter. Young, handsome; these he put last; but I put them foremost. Sensible, good-natured; I like all that. But then reserved and sheepish, that's 25 much against him. Yet can't he be cured of his timidity, by being taught to be proud of his wife? Yes, and can't I —But I vow I'm disposing of the husband, before I have secured the lover.

Enter MISS NEVILLE.

Miss Hard. I'm glad you're come, Neville, my dear. 30 Tell me, Constance, how do I look this evening? Is

there any thing whimsical about me? Is it one of my
well-looking days, child? am I in face to-day?

Miss Nev. Perfectly, my dear. Yet now I look again
— bless me! — sure no accident has happened among the
canary birds or the gold fishes. Has your brother or the 5
cat been meddling? or has the last novel been too moving?

Miss Hard. No; nothing of all this. I have been
threatened — I can scarce get it out — I have been threatened with a lover!

Miss Nev. And his name —   10

Miss Hard. Is Marlow.

Miss Nev. Indeed!

Miss Hard. The son of Sir Charles Marlow.

Miss Nev. As I live, the most intimate friend of
Mr. Hastings, my admirer. They are never asunder. 15
I believe you must have seen him when we lived in town.

Miss Hard. Never.

Miss Nev. He's a very singular character, I assure
you. Among women of reputation and virtue he is the
modestest man alive; but his acquaintance give him 20
a very different character among creatures of another
stamp: you understand me.

Miss Hard. An odd character, indeed. I shall never
be able to manage him. What shall I do? Pshaw, think
no more of him, but trust to occurrences for success. But 25
how goes on your own affair, my dear? has my mother
been courting you for my brother Tony as usual?

Miss Nev. I have just come from one of our agreeable
tête-à-têtes. She has been saying a hundred tender
things, and setting off her pretty monster as the very 30
pink of perfection.

13

Miss Hard. And her partiality is such, that she actually thinks him so. A fortune like yours is no small temptation. Besides, as she has the sole management of it, I'm not surprised to see her unwilling to let it go out of the 5 family.

Miss Nev. A fortune like mine, which chiefly consists in jewels, is no such mighty temptation. But at any rate if my dear Hastings be but constant, I make no doubt to be too hard for her at last. However, I let 10 her suppose that I am in love with her son, and she never once dreams that my affections are fixed upon another.

Miss Hard. My good brother holds out stoutly. I could almost love him for hating you so.

Miss Nev. It's a good-natured creature at bottom, 15 and I'm sure would wish to see me married to any body but himself. But my aunt's bell rings for our afternoon's walk round the improvements. *Allons!* Courage is necessary, as our affairs are critical.

Miss Hard. Would it were bed-time and all were well.

[*Exeunt.*

SCENE II. AN ALEHOUSE ROOM.

Several shabby fellows with punch and tobacco. TONY *at the head of the table, a little higher than the rest: a mallet in his hand.*

20 *Omnes.* Hurrea! hurrea! hurrea! bravo!

First Fel. Now, gentlemen, silence for a song. The 'squire is going to knock himself down for a song.

Omnes. Ay, a song, a song!

Tony. Then I'll sing you, gentlemen, a song I made 25 upon this alehouse, the Three Pigeons.

Song.

Let school-masters puzzle their brain,
    With grammar, and nonsense, and learning,
Good liquor, I stoutly maintain,
    Gives *genus* a better discerning.
Let them brag of their heathenish gods,   5
    Their Lethes, their Styxes, and Stygians,
Their qui's, and their quae's, and their quod's,
    They're all but a parcel of pigeons.
                    Toroddle, toroddle, toroll.

When Methodist preachers come down,   10
    A-preaching that drinking is sinful,
I'll wager the rascals a crown,
    They always preach best with a skinful.
For when you come down with your pence,
    For a slice of their scurvy religion,   15
I'll leave it to all men of sense,
    But you, my good friend, are the pigeon.
                    Toroddle, toroddle, toroll.

Then come put the jorum about,
    And let us be merry and clever,   20
Our hearts and our liquors are stout,
    Here's the Three Jolly Pigeons for ever.
Let some cry up woodcock or hare,
    Your bustards, your ducks, and your widgeons;
But of all the gay birds in the air,   25
    Here's a health to the Three Jolly Pigeons.
                    Toroddle, toroddle, toroll.

Omnes.   Bravo, bravo !

First Fel.   The 'squire has got spunk in him.

Second Fel.   I loves to hear him sing, bekeays he never gives us nothing that's low.

5   *Third Fel.*   O damn any thing that's low, I cannot bear it.

Fourth Fel.   The genteel thing is the genteel thing at any time.   If so be that a gentleman bees in a concatenation accordingly.

10   *Third Fel.*   I like the maxum of it, Master Muggins. What, though I am obligated to dance a bear, a man may be a gentleman for all that.   May this be my poison, if my bear ever dances but to the very genteelest of tunes; ' Water Parted,' or the minuet in ' Ariadne.'

15

Second Fel.   What a pity it is the 'squire is not come to his own.   It would be well for all the publicans within ten miles round of him.

Tony.   Ecod, and so it would, Master Slang.   I'd then
20 show what it was to keep choice of company.

Second Fel.   O he takes after his own father for that. To be sure old 'squire Lumpkin was the finest gentleman I ever set my eyes on.   For winding the straight horn, or beating a thicket for a hare, he never had his fellow.
25 It was a saying in the place that he kept the best horses and dogs in the whole county.

Tony.   Ecod, and when I'm of age, I'll be no bastard, I promise you.   I have been thinking of Bet Bouncer and the miller's grey mare to begin with.   But come my
30 boys, drink about and be merry, for you pay no reckoning.

Well, Stingo, what's the matter?

Enter LANDLORD.

Land.   There be two gentlemen in a post-chaise at the door.   They have lost their way upo' the forest; and they are talking something about Mr. Hardcastle.

Tony.   As sure as can be, one of them must be the gentleman that's coming down to court my sister.   Do 5 they seem to be Londoners?

Land.   I believe they may.   They look woundily like Frenchmen.

Tony.   Then desire them to step this way, and I'll set them right in a twinkling. (*Exit Landlord.*)   Gentlemen, as 10 they mayn't be good enough company for you, step down for a moment, and I'll be with you in the squeezing of a lemon.   [*Exeunt mob.*

Tony.   (*Alone.*)   Father-in-law has been calling me whelp and hound this half year.   Now if I pleased, I could 15 be so revenged on the old grumbletonian.   But then I'm afraid — afraid of what!   I shall soon be worth fifteen hundred a year, and let him frighten me out of that if he can.

Enter LANDLORD, *conducting* MARLOW *and* HASTINGS.

Marl.   What a tedious uncomfortable day have we had 20 of it!   We were told it was but forty miles across the country, and we have come above threescore.

Hast.   And all, Marlow, from that unaccountable reserve of yours, that would not let us inquire more frequently on the way.   25

Marl.   I own, Hastings, I am unwilling to lay myself under an obligation to every one I meet: and often stand the chance of an unmannerly answer.

Hast. At present, however, we are not likely to receive any answer.

Tony. No offence, gentlemen. But I'm told you have been inquiring for one Mr. Hardcastle in these parts. 5 Do you know what part of the country you are in?

Hast. Not in the least, Sir, but should thank you for information.

Tony. Nor the way you came?

Hast. No, Sir, but if you can inform us —

10   *Tony.* Why, gentlemen, if you know neither the road you are going, nor where you are, nor the road you came, the first thing I have to inform you is, that — you have lost your way.

Marl. We wanted no ghost to tell us that.

15   *Tony.* Pray, gentlemen, may I be so bold as to ask the place from whence you came.

Marl. That's not necessary toward directing us where we are to go.

Tony. No offence; but question for question is all 20 fair, you know. Pray, gentlemen, is not this same Hardcastle a cross-grain'd old-fashion'd, whimsical fellow, with an ugly face; a daughter, and a pretty son?

Hast. We have not seen the gentleman, but he has the family you mention.

25   *Tony.* The daughter, a tall, trapesing, trolloping, talkative maypole — the son, a pretty, well-bred, agreeable youth, that everybody is fond of.

Marl. Our information differs in this. The daughter is said to be well-bred and beautiful; the son, an awk- 30 ward booby, reared up and spoiled at his mother's apron-string.

Tony. He-he-hem!—Then gentlemen, all I have to tell you is, that you won't reach Mr. Hardcastle's house this night, I believe.

Hast. Unfortunate!

Tony. It's a damn'd long, dark, boggy, dirty, dangerous 5 way. Stingo, tell the gentlemen the way to Mr. Hardcastle's! (*Winking upon the Landlord.*) Mr. Hardcastle's, of Quagmire Marsh, you understand me?

Land. Master Hardcastle's! Lock-a-daisy, my masters, you're come a deadly deal wrong! When you came 10 to the bottom of the hill, you should have cross'd down Squash-Lane.

Marl. Cross down Squash-Lane!

Land. Then you were to keep straight forward, till you came to four roads. 15

Marl. Come to where four roads meet!

Tony. Ay; but you must be sure to take only one of them.

Marl. O Sir, you're facetious.

Tony. Then keeping to the right, you are to go side- 20 ways till you come upon Crack-skull common: there you must look sharp for the track of the wheel, and go forward till you come to farmer Murrain's barn. Coming to the farmer's barn you are to turn to the right, and then to the left, and then to the right about again, till you find 25 out the old mill.

Marl. Zounds, man! we could as soon find out the longitude!

Hast. What's to be done, Marlow?

Marl. This house promises but a poor reception; 30 though perhaps the landlord can accommodate us.

Land. Alack, master, we have but one spare bed in the whole house.

Tony. And to my knowledge, that's taken up by three lodgers already. (*After a pause, in which the rest seem disconcerted.*) I have hit it. Don't you think, Stingo, our landlady could accommodate the gentlemen by the fire-side, with — three chairs and a bolster?

Hast. I hate sleeping by the fire-side.

Marl. And I detest your three chairs and a bolster.

Tony. You do, do you! — then let me see — what if you go on a mile further, to the Buck's Head; the old Buck's Head on the hill, one of the best inns in the whole county?

Hast. O ho! so we have escaped an adventure for this night, however.

Land. (*Apart to Tony.*) Sure, you ben't sending them to your father's as an inn, be you?

Tony. Mum, you fool you. Let them find that out. (*To them.*) You have only to keep on straight forward, till you come to a large old house by the road side. You'll see a pair of large horns over the door. That's the sign. Drive up the yard, and call stoutly about you.

Hast. Sir, we are obliged to you. The servants can't miss the way?

Tony. No, no; but I tell you though, the landlord is rich, and going to leave off business; so he wants to be thought a gentleman, saving your presence, he! he! he! He'll be for giving you his company, and ecod, if you mind him, he'll persuade you that his mother was an alderman, and his aunt a justice of peace.

Land. A troublesome old blade to be sure; but a' keeps as good wines and beds as any in the whole country.

Marl. Well, if he supplies us with these, we shall want no farther connexion. We are to turn to the right, did you say?

Tony. No, no : straight forward. I'll just step myself and show you a piece of the way. (*To the Landlord.*) 5 Mum.

Land. Ah, bless your heart, for a sweet, pleasant — damn'd mischievous son.   [*Exeunt.*

ACT II.

Scene I. An old-fashioned house.

Enter Hardcastle, *followed by three or four awkward Servants.*

Hard. Well, I hope you are perfect in the table exercise I have been teaching you these three days. You all know your posts and your places, and can show that you have been used to good company, without ever stirring
5 from home.

Omnes. Ay, ay.

Hard. When company comes, you are not to pop out and stare, and then run in again, like frighted rabbits in a warren.

10 *Omnes.* No, no.

Hard. You, Diggory, whom I have taken from the barn, are to make a show at the side-table; and you, Roger, whom I have advanced from the plough, are to place yourself behind my chair. But you're not to stand
15 so, with your hands in your pockets. Take your hands from your pockets, Roger; and from your head, you blockhead you. See how Diggory carries his hands. They're a little too stiff, indeed, but that's no great matter.

20 *Dig.* Ay, mind how I hold them. I learned to hold my hands this way, when I was upon drill for the militia. And so being upon drill —

22

DIGGORY

"See how Diggory carries his hands."

Hard.　You must not be so talkative, Diggory.　You must be all attention to the guests.　You must hear us talk, and not think of talking; you must see us drink, and not think of drinking — you must see us eat, and not think of eating.　　　　　　　　　　　　　　　5

Dig.　By the laws, your worship, that's parfectly unpossible.　Whenever Diggory sees yeating going forward, ecod, he's always wishing for a mouthful himself.

Hard.　Blockhead!　Is not a belly-full in the kitchen as good as a belly-full in the parlour?　Stay your stomach 10 with that reflection.

Dig.　Ecod, I thank your worship, I'll make a shift to stay my stomach with a slice of cold beef in the pantry.

Hard.　Diggory, you are too talkative.　Then if I happen to say a good thing, or tell a good story at table, you 15 must not all burst out a-laughing, as if you made part of the company.

Dig.　Then ecod, your worship must not tell the story of ould grouse in the gun-room: I can't help laughing at that — he! he! he! — for the soul of me.　We have 20 laughed at that these twenty years — ha! ha! ha!

Hard.　Ha! ha! ha!　The story is a good one.　Well, honest Diggory, you may laugh at that — but still remember to be attentive.　Suppose one of the company should call for a glass of wine, how will you behave?　A glass of 25 wine, Sir, if you please (*To Diggory.*) — Eh, why don't you move?

Dig.　Ecod, your worship, I never have courage till I see the eatables and drinkables brought upo' the table, and then I'm as bauld as a lion.　　　　　　　　　　30

Hard.　What, will nobody move?

First Serv. I'm not to leave this place.

Second Serv. I'm sure it's no place of mine.

Third Serv. Nor mine, for sartain.

Dig. Wauns, and I'm sure it canna be mine.

5 *Hard.* You numbskulls! and so while, like your betters, you are quarrelling for places, the guests must be starved. O you dunces! I find I must begin all over again — But don't I hear a coach drive into the yard? To your posts, you blockheads. I'll go in the mean time, 10 and give my old friend's son a hearty reception at the gate.   [*Exit* HARDCASTLE.

Dig. By the elevens, my place is gone quite out of my head.

Roger. I know that my place is to be every where.

15 *First Serv.* Where the devil is mine?

Second Serv. My place is to be no where at all; and so ize go about my business.   [*Exeunt servants, running about as if frighted, different ways.*

Enter SERVANT *with candles, showing in* MARLOW *and* HASTINGS.

Serv. Welcome, gentlemen, very welcome! This way.

Hast. After the disappointments of the day, welcome 20 once more, Charles, to the comforts of a clean room, and a good fire. Upon my word, a very well-looking house, antique but creditable.

Marl. The usual fate of a large mansion. Having first ruined the master by good house-keeping, it at last 25 comes to levy contributions as an inn.

Hast. As you say, we passengers are to be taxed to pay all these fineries. I have often seen a good side-board, or a marble chimney-piece, though not actually put in the bill, inflame a reckoning confoundedly.

Marl. Travellers, George, must pay in all places: the only difference is, that in good inns you pay dearly for luxuries; in bad inns you are fleeced and starved.   5

Hast. You have lived pretty much among them. In truth, I have been often surprised, that you who have seen so much of the world, with your natural good sense, and your many opportunities, could never yet acquire a requisite share of assurance.   10

Marl. The Englishman's malady. But tell me, George, where could I have learned that assurance you talk of? My life has been chiefly spent in a college or an inn, in seclusion from that lovely part of the creation that chiefly teach men confidence. I don't know that I was ever famil- 15
iarly acquainted with a single modest woman, except my mother — But among females of another class, you know —

Hast. Ay, among them you are impudent enough of all conscience.

Marl. They are of *us*, you know.   20

Hast. But in the company of women of reputation I never saw such an idiot, such a trembler; you look for all the world as if you wanted an opportunity of stealing out of the room.

Marl. Why, man, that's because I do want to steal out 25
of the room. Faith, I have often formed a resolution to break the ice, and rattle away at any rate. But I don't know how, a single glance from a pair of fine eyes has totally overset my resolution. An impudent fellow may counterfeit modesty: but I'll be hanged if a modest man 30
can ever counterfeit impudence.

Hast. If you could but say half the fine things to them, that I have heard you lavish upon the bar-maid of an inn, or even a college bed-maker —

Marl. Why, George, I can't say fine things to them;
5 they freeze, they petrify me. They may talk of a comet, or a burning mountain, or some such bagatelle. But to me, a modest woman, drest out in all her finery, is the most tremendous object of the whole creation.

Hast. Ha! ha! ha! At this rate, man, how can you
10 ever expect to marry?

Marl. Never, unless, as among kings and princes, my bride were to be courted by proxy. If, indeed, like an eastern bridegroom, one were to be introduced to a wife he never saw before, it might be endured. But to go
15 through all the terrors of a formal courtship, together with the episode of aunts, grandmothers, and cousins, and at last to blurt out the broad staring question of, ' Madam, will you marry me? ' No, no, that's a strain much above me, I assure you.

20 *Hast.* I pity you. But how do you intend behaving to the lady you are come down to visit at the request of your father?

Marl. As I behave to all other ladies. Bow very low. Answer yes or no to all her demands — But for the rest, I
25 don't think I shall venture to look in her face till I see my father's again.

Hast. I'm surprised that one who is so warm a friend can be so cool a lover.

Marl. To be explicit, my dear Hastings, my chief
30 inducement down was to be instrumental in forwarding your happiness, not my own. Miss Neville loves you,

26

the family don't know you; as my friend you are sure of a reception, and let honour do the rest.

Hast. My dear Marlow! But I'll suppress the emotion. Were I a wretch, meanly seeking to carry off a fortune, you should be the last man in the world I would apply 5 to for assistance. But Miss Neville's person is all I ask, and that is mine, both from her deceased father's consent, and her own inclination.

Marl. Happy man! You have talents and art to captivate any woman. I'm doom'd to adore the sex, and yet 10 to converse with the only part of it I despise. This stammer in my address, and this awkward prepossessing visage of mine, can never permit me to soar above the reach of a milliner's 'prentice, or one of the duchesses of Drury-lane. Pshaw! this fellow here to interrupt us! 15

Enter HARDCASTLE.

Hard. Gentlemen, once more you are heartily welcome. Which is Mr. Marlow? Sir, you are heartily welcome. It's not my way, you see, to receive my friends with my back to the fire. I like to give them a hearty reception in the old style, at my gate. I like to see their horses 20 and trunks taken care of.

Marl. (*Aside.*) He has got our names from the servants already. (*To him.*) We approve your caution and hospitality, Sir. (*To Hastings.*) I have been thinking, George, of changing our travelling dresses in the morning. 25 I am grown confoundedly ashamed of mine.

Hard. I beg, Mr. Marlow, you'll use no ceremony in this house.

Hast. I fancy, Charles, you're right: the first blow is

half the battle.   I intend opening the campaign with the
white and gold.

Hard.   Mr. Marlow — Mr. Hastings — gentlemen —
pray be under no restraint in this house.   This is Liberty-
5 hall, gentlemen.   You may do just as you please here.

Marl.   Yet, George, if we open the campaign too fiercely
at first, we may want ammunition before it is over.   I
think to reserve the embroidery to secure a retreat.

Hard.   Your talking of a retreat, Mr. Marlow, puts me
10 in mind of the Duke of Marlborough, when we went to
besiege Denain.   He first summoned the garrison —

Marl.   Don't you think the *ventre d'or* waistcoat will
do with the plain brown?

Hard.   He first summoned the garrison, which might
15 consist of about five thousand men —

Hast.   I think not: brown and yellow mix but very
poorly.

Hard.   I say, gentlemen, as I was telling you, he summoned the garrison, which might consist of about five
20 thousand men —

Marl.   The girls like finery.

Hard.   Which might consist of about five thousand
men, well appointed with stores, ammunition, and other
implements of war.   ' Now,' says the Duke of Marl-
25 borough to George Brooks, that stood next to him — You
must have heard of George Brooks — ' I'll pawn my
dukedom,' says he, ' but I take that garrison without
spilling a drop of blood.'   So —

Marl.   What, my good friend, if you gave us a glass of
30 punch in the mean time, it would help us to carry on the
siege with vigour.

Hard. Punch, Sir! (*Aside.*) This is the most unaccountable kind of modesty I ever met with.

Marl. Yes, Sir, punch. A glass of warm punch, after our journey, will be comfortable. This is Liberty-hall, you know.   5

Hard. Here's cup, Sir.

Marl. (*Aside.*) So this fellow, in his Liberty-hall, will only let us have just what he pleases.

Hard. (*Taking the cup.*) I hope you'll find it to your mind. I have prepared it with my own hands, and I 10 believe you'll own the ingredients are tolerable. Will you be so good as to pledge me, Sir? Here, Mr. Marlow, here is to our better acquaintance.   (*Drinks.*)

Marl. (*Aside.*) A very impudent fellow this! but he's a character, and I'll humour him a little. Sir, my service 15 to you.   (*Drinks.*)

Hast. (*Aside.*) I see this fellow wants to give us his company, and forgets that he's an innkeeper, before he has learned to be a gentleman.

Marl. From the excellence of your cup, my old friend, 20 I suppose you have a good deal of business in this part of the country. Warm work, now and then at elections, I suppose?

Hard. No, Sir, I have long given that work over. Since our betters have hit upon the expedient of electing 25 each other, there is no business ' for us that sell ale.'

Hast. So, then you have no turn for politics, I find.

Hard. Not in the least. There was a time, indeed, I fretted myself about the mistakes of government, like other people; but finding myself every day grow more 30 angry, and the government growing no better, I left it to mend itself. Since that, I no more trouble my head about Heyder Ally or Ally Cawn, than about Ally Croaker. Sir, my service to you.

Hast. So that with eating above stairs, and drinking below, with receiving your friends within, and amusing them without, you lead a good pleasant bustling life of it.

Hard. I do stir about a great deal, that's certain. Half the differences of the parish are adjusted in this very parlour.

Marl. (*After drinking.*) And you have an argument in your cup, old gentleman, better than any in Westminster-hall.

Hard. Ay, young gentleman, that, and a little philosophy.

Marl. (*Aside.*) Well, this is the first time I ever heard of an inn-keeper's philosophy.

Hast. So then, like an experienced general, you attack them on every quarter. If you find their reason manageable, you attack it with your philosophy; if you find they have no reason, you attack them with this. Here's your health, my philosopher. (*Drinks.*)

Hard. Good, very good, thank you; ha! ha! ha! Your generalship puts me in mind of Prince Eugene, when he fought the Turks at the battle of Belgrade. You shall hear.

Marl. Instead of the battle of Belgrade, I believe it's almost time to talk about supper. What has your philosophy got in the house for supper?

Hard. For supper, Sir! (*Aside.*) Was ever such a request to a man in his own house!

Marl. Yes, Sir, supper, Sir; I begin to feel an appetite.

I shall make dev'lish work to-night in the larder, I promise you.

Hard. (*Aside.*) Such a brazen dog, sure, never my eyes beheld. (*To him.*) Why, really, Sir, as for supper I can't well tell. My Dorothy, and the cook-maid settle 5 these things between them. I leave these kind of things entirely to them.

Marl. You do, do you?

Hard. Entirely. By the by, I believe they are in actual consultation upon what's for supper this moment 10 in the kitchen.

Marl. Then I beg they'll admit me as one of their privy council. It's a way I have got. When I travel I always chuse to regulate my own supper. Let the cook be called. No offence, I hope, Sir.   15

Hard. O no, Sir, none in the least; yet I don't know how: our Bridget, the cook-maid, is not very communicative upon these occasions. Should we send for her, she might scold us all out of the house.

Hast. Let's see your list of the larder then. I ask it 20 as a favour. I always matched my appetite to my bill of fare.

Marl. (*To Hardcastle, who looks at them with surprise.*) Sir, he's very right, and it's my way too.

Hard. Sir, you have a right to command here. Here, 25 Roger, bring us the bill of fare for to-night's supper. I believe it's drawn out. Your manner, Mr. Hastings, puts me in mind of my uncle, colonel Wallop. It was a saying of his, that no man was sure of his supper till he had eaten it.   30

Hast. (*Aside.*) All upon the high rope! His uncle a

31

colonel! we shall soon hear of his mother being a justice of the peace. But let's hear the bill of fare.

Marl. (*Perusing.*) What's here? For the first course; for the second course; for the dessert. The devil, Sir, do you think we have brought down the whole Joiners' Company, or the corporation of Bedford, to eat up such a supper? Two or three little things, clean and comfortable, will do.

Hast. But let's hear it.

Marl. (*Reading.*) For the first course: at the top, a pig, and pruin sauce.

Hast. Damn your pig, I say.

Marl. And damn your pruin sauce, say I.

Hard. And yet, gentlemen, to men that are hungry, pig with pruin sauce is very good eating.

Marl. At the bottom a calf's tongue and brains.

Hast. Let your brains be knock'd out, my good Sir, I don't like them.

Marl. Or you may clap them on a plate by themselves. I do.

Hard. (*Aside.*) Their impudence confounds me. (*To them.*) Gentlemen, you are my guests, make what alterations you please. Is there any thing else you wish to retrench or alter, gentlemen?

Marl. Item: A pork pie, a boiled rabbit and sausages, a Florentine, a shaking pudding, and a dish of tiff — taff — taffety cream.

Hast. Confound your made dishes! I shall be as much at a loss in this house as at a green and yellow dinner at the French ambassador's table. I'm for plain eating.

Hard. I'm sorry, gentlemen, that I have nothing you

32

like, but if there be any thing you have a particular fancy
to —

Marl. Why, really, Sir, your bill of fare is so exquisite, that any one part of it is full as good as another.
Send us what you please. So much for supper. And
now to see that our beds are air'd, and properly taken
care of.

Hard. I entreat you'll leave all that to me. You shall
not stir a step.

Marl. Leave that to you! I protest, Sir, you must
excuse me ; I always look to these things myself.

Hard. I must insist, Sir, you'll make yourself easy on
that head.

Marl. You see I'm resolved on it. (*Aside.*) A very
troublesome fellow this, as ever I met with.

Hard. Well, Sir, I'm resolved at least to attend you.
(*Aside.*) This may be modern modesty, but I never saw
any thing look so like old-fashion'd impudence.

[*Exeunt* MARLOW *and* HARDCASTLE.

Hast. (*Alone.*) So I find this fellow's civilities begin
to grow troublesome. But who can be angry at those
assiduities which are meant to please him? Ha! what
do I see? Miss Neville, by all that's happy!

Enter MISS NEVILLE.

Miss Nev. My dear Hastings! To what unexpected
good fortune, to what accident, am I to ascribe this
happy meeting?

Hast. Rather let me ask the same question, as I could
never have hoped to meet my dearest Constance at an
inn.

Miss Nev. An inn! sure, you mistake! my aunt, my guardian, lives here. What could induce you to think this house an inn?

Hast. My friend, Mr. Marlow, with whom I came
5 down, and I have been sent here as to an inn, I assure you. A young fellow whom we accidentally met at a house hard by directed us hither.

Miss Nev. Certainly it must be one of my hopeful cousin's tricks, of whom you have heard me talk so often;
10 ha! ha! ha!

Hast. He whom your aunt intends for you? he of whom I have such just apprehensions?

Miss Nev. You have nothing to fear from him, I assure you. You'd adore him if you knew how heartily he
15 despises me. My aunt knows it too, and has undertaken to court me for him, and actually begins to think she has made a conquest.

Hast. Thou dear dissembler! You must know, my Constance, I have just seized this happy opportunity of
20 my friend's visit here to get admittance into the family. The horses that carried us down are now fatigued with their journey, but they'll soon be refreshed; and then, if my dearest girl will trust in her faithful Hastings, we shall soon be landed in France, where even among slaves the
25 laws of marriage are respected.

Miss Nev. I have often told you, that though ready to obey you, I yet should leave my little fortune behind with reluctance. The greatest part of it was left me by my uncle, the India director, and chiefly consists in jewels.
30 I have been for some time persuading my aunt to let me wear them. I fancy I'm very near succeeding. The

34

instant they are put into my possession you shall find me ready to make them and myself yours.

Hast. Perish the baubles! Your person is all I desire. In the mean time my friend Marlow must not be let into his mistake. I know the strange reserve of his temper is 5 such, that if abruptly informed of it, he would instantly quit the house before our plan was ripe for execution.

Miss Nev. But how shall we keep him in the deception? Miss Hardcastle is just returned from walking; what if we still continue to deceive him? — This, this way — 10

[*They confer.*

Enter MARLOW.

Marl. The assiduities of these good people tease me beyond bearing. My host seems to think it ill manners to leave me alone, and so he claps not only himself but his old-fashioned wife on my back. They talk of coming to sup with us too; and then, I suppose, we are to run the 15 gauntlet through all the rest of the family. — What have we got here!

Hast. My dear Charles! Let me congratulate you! — The most fortunate accident! — Who do you think is just alighted? 20

Marl. Cannot guess.

Hast. Our mistresses, boy, Miss Hardcastle and Miss Neville. Give me leave to introduce Miss Constance Neville to your acquaintance. Happening to dine in the neighbourhood, they called on their return to take fresh 25 horses here. Miss Hardcastle has just stept into the next room, and will be back in an instant. Wasn't it lucky? eh!

Marl. (*Aside.*) I have been mortified enough of all

conscience, and here comes something to complete my embarrassment.

Hast. Well, but wasn't it the most fortunate thing in the world?

5 *Marl.* Oh! yes. Very fortunate — a most joyful encounter — But our dresses, George, you know are in disorder — What if we should postpone the happiness till to-morrow? — To-morrow at her own house — It will be every bit as convenient — and rather more respectful — 10 To-morrow let it be.   [*Offering to go.*

Miss Nev. By no means, Sir. Your ceremony will displease her. The disorder of your dress will show the ardour of your impatience. Besides, she knows you are in the house, and will permit you to see her.

15 *Marl.* Oh, the devil! how shall I support it? hem! hem! Hastings, you must not go. You are to assist me, you know. I shall be confoundedly ridiculous. Yet, hang it! I'll take courage. Hem!

Hast. Pshaw, man! it's but the first plunge, and all's 20 over. She's but a woman, you know.

Marl. And of all women, she that I dread most to encounter.

Enter Miss Hardcastle, *as returned from walking.*

Hast. (*Introducing   them.*) Miss Hardcastle, Mr. Marlow. I'm proud of bringing two persons of such 25 merit together, that only want to know to esteem each other.

Miss Hard. (*Aside.*) Now, for meeting my modest gentleman with a demure face, and quite in his own manner. (*After a pause, in which he appears very uneasy and*

36

disconcerted.) I'm glad of your safe arrival, Sir. — I'm told you had some accidents by the way.

Marl. Only a few, madam. Yes, we had some. Yes, madam, a good many accidents, but should be sorry — madam — or rather glad of any accidents — that are so ₅ agreeably concluded. Hem!

Hast. (*To him*.) You never spoke better in your whole life. Keep it up, and I'll insure you the victory.

Miss Hard. I'm afraid you flatter, Sir. You that have seen so much of the finest company can find little enter- ₁₀ tainment in an obscure corner of the country.

Marl. (*Gathering courage*.) I have lived, indeed, in the world, madam : but I have kept very little company. I have been but an observer upon life, madam, while others were enjoying it. ₁₅

Miss Nev. But that, I am told, is the way to enjoy it at last.

Hast. (*To him*.) Cicero never spoke better. Once more, and you are confirmed in assurance for ever.

Marl. (*To him*.) Hem! stand by me then, and when ₂₀ I'm down, throw in a word or two to set me up again.

Miss Hard. An observer, like you, upon life were, I fear, disagreeably employed, since you must have had much more to censure than to approve.

Marl. Pardon me, madam. I was always willing to be ₂₅ amused. The folly of most people is rather an object of mirth than uneasiness.

Hast. (*To him*.) Bravo, bravo. Never spoke so well in your whole life. Well! Miss Hardcastle, I see that you and Mr. Marlow are going to be very good company. ₃₀ I believe our being here will but embarrass the interview.

Marl. Not in the least, Mr. Hastings. We like your company of all things. (*To him.*) Zounds! George, sure you won't go? how can you leave us?

Hast. Our presence will but spoil conversation, so we'll
5 retire to the next room. (*To him.*) You don't consider, man, that we are to manage a little *tête-à-tête* of our own.   [*Exeunt.*

Miss Hard. (*After a pause.*) But you have not been wholly an observer, I presume, Sir: the ladies, I should
10 hope, have employed some part of your addresses.

Marl. (*Relapsing into timidity.*) Pardon me, madam, I — I — I — as yet have studied — only — to — deserve them.

Miss Hard. And that, some say, is the very worst way
15 to obtain them.

Marl. Perhaps so, madam. But I love to converse only with the more grave and sensible part of the sex. — But I'm afraid I grow tiresome.

Miss Hard. Not at all, Sir; there is nothing I like so
20 much as grave conversation myself; I could hear it for ever. Indeed I have often been surprised how a man of sentiment could ever admire those light airy pleasures, where nothing reaches the heart.

Marl. It's — a disease — of the mind, madam. In
25 the variety of tastes there must be some who wanting a relish — for — um — a — um.

Miss Hard. I understand you, Sir. There must be some, who, wanting a relish for refined pleasures, pretend to despise what they are incapable of tasting.

30 *Marl.* My meaning, madam, but infinitely better expressed. And I can't help observing — a —

Miss Hard. (*Aside.*) Who could ever suppose this fellow impudent upon some occasions! (*To him.*) You were going to observe, Sir —

Marl. I was observing, madam — I protest, madam, I forget what I was going to observe. 5

Miss Hard. (*Aside.*) I vow and so do I. (*To him.*) You were observing, Sir, that in this age of hypocrisy — something about hypocrisy, Sir.

Marl. Yes, madam. In this age of hypocrisy there are few who upon strict enquiry do not — a — a — a — 10

Miss Hard. I understand you perfectly, Sir.

Marl. (*Aside.*) Egad! and that's more than I do myself.

Miss Hard. You mean that in this hypocritical age there are few that do not condemn in public what they 15 practice in private, and think they pay every debt to virtue when they praise it.

Marl. True, madam; those who have most virtue in their mouths, have least of it in their bosoms. But I'm sure I tire you, madam. 20

Miss Hard. Not in the least, Sir; there's something so agreeable and spirited in your manner, such life and force — pray, Sir, go on.

Marl. Yes, madam, I was saying — that there are some occasions — when a total want of courage, madam, 25 destroys all the — and puts us — upon a — a — a —

Miss Hard. I agree with you entirely, a want of courage upon some occasions assumes the appearance of ignorance, and betrays us when we most want to excel. I beg you'll proceed. 30

Marl. Yes, madam. Morally speaking, madam —

But I see Miss Neville expecting us in the next room.   I would not intrude for the world.

Miss Hard.   I protest, Sir, I never was more agreeably entertained in all my life.   Pray go on.

5 *Marl.*   Yes, madam, I was — But she beckons us to join her.   Madam, shall I do myself the honour to attend you

Miss Hard.   Well then, I'll follow.

Marl.   (*Aside.*)   This pretty smooth dialogue has done for me.   [*Exit.*

10 *Miss Hard.*   (*Alone.*)   Ha! ha! ha!   Was there ever such a sober sentimental interview?   I'm certain he scarce look'd in my face the whole time.   Yet the fellow, but for his unaccountable bashfulness, is pretty well too. He has good sense, but then so buried in his fears, that 15 it fatigues one more than ignorance.   If I could teach him a little confidence, it would be doing somebody that I know of a piece of service.   But who is that somebody? — That, faith, is a question I can scarce answer.   [*Exit.*

Enter TONY *and* MISS NEVILLE, *followed by* MRS. HARD-
CASTLE *and* HASTINGS.

Tony.   What do you follow me for, Cousin Con?   I 20 wonder you're not ashamed to be so very engaging.

Miss Nev.   I hope, cousin, one may speak to one's own relations, and not be to blame.

Tony.   Ay, but I know what sort of a relation you want to make me, though; but it won't do.   I tell you, Cousin 25 Con, it won't do; so I beg you'll keep your distance, I want no nearer relationship.

[*She follows, coquetting him, to the back scene.*

Mrs. Hard.   Well! I vow, Mr. Hastings, you are very

entertaining. There is nothing in the world I love to talk of so much as London, and the fashions, though I was never there myself.

Hast. Never there! You amaze me! From your air and manner, I concluded you had been bred all your life 5 either at Ranelagh, St. James's, or Tower Wharf.

Mrs. Hard. O! Sir, you're only pleased to say so. We country persons can have no manner at all. I'm in love with the town, and that serves to raise me above some of our neighbouring rustics; but who can have a manner, 10 that has never seen the Pantheon, the Grotto Gardens, the Borough, and such places where the nobility chiefly resort? All I can do is to enjoy London at second-hand. I take care to know every *tête-à-tête* from the Scandalous Magazine, and have all the fashions, as they come out in 15 a letter from the two Miss Rickets of Crooked-Lane. Pray how do you like this head, Mr. Hastings?

Hast. Extremely elegant and *dégagée*, upon my word, madam. Your *friseur* is a Frenchman, I suppose?

Mrs. Hard. I protest, I dressed it myself from a print 20 in the Ladies' Memorandum-book for the last year.

Hast. Indeed! Such a head in a side-box at the play-house would draw as many gazers as my Lady May'ress at a City Ball.

Mrs. Hard. I vow, since inoculation began, there is no 25 such thing to be seen as a plain woman; so one must dress a little particular, or one may escape in the crowd.

Hast. But that can never be your case, madam, in any dress. (*Bowing.*)

Mrs. Hard. Yet, what signifies my dressing when I 30 have such a piece of antiquity by my side as Mr. Hardcastle: all I can say will never argue down a single button from his clothes. I have often wanted him to throw off his great flaxen wig, and where he was bald, to plaster it over, like my Lord Pately, with powder.

5   *Hast.* You are right, madam; for, as among the ladies there are none ugly, so among the men there are none old.

Mrs. Hard. But what do you think his answer was? Why, with his usual Gothic vivacity, he said I only wanted
10 him to throw off his wig to convert it into a tête for my own wearing.

Hast. Intolerable! At your age you may wear what you please, and it must become you.

Mrs. Hard. Pray, Mr. Hastings, what do you take to
15 be the most fashionable age about town?

Hast. Some time ago, forty was all the mode; but I'm told the ladies intend to bring up fifty for the ensuing winter.

Mrs. Hard. Seriously? Then I shall be too young for
20 the fashion.

Hast. No lady begins now to put on jewels till she's past forty. For instance, Miss there, in a polite circle, would be considered as a child, as a mere maker of samplers.

25   *Mrs. Hard.* And yet Mrs. Niece thinks herself as much a woman, and is as fond of jewels as the oldest of us all.

Hast. Your niece, is she? And that young gentleman, a brother of yours, I should presume?

Mrs. Hard. My son, Sir. They are contracted to each
30 other. Observe their little sports. They fall in and out ten times a day, as they were man and wife already. (*To*

them.)   Well, Tony, child, what soft things are you saying
to your Cousin Constance this evening?

Tony.   I have been saying no soft things; but that it's
very hard to be followed about so.   Ecod! I've not a
place in the house now that's left to myself, but the
stable.

Mrs. Hard.   Never mind him, Con, my dear, he's in
another story behind your back.

Miss Nev.   There's something generous in my cousin's
manner.   He falls out before faces to be forgiven in private.

Tony.   That's a damned confounded — crack.

Mrs. Hard.   Ah! he's a sly one.   Don't you think
they're like each other about the mouth, Mr. Hastings?
The Blenkinsop mouth to a T.   They're of a size too.
Back to back, my pretties, that Mr. Hastings may see you.
Come, Tony.

Tony.   You had as good not make me, I tell you.

(Measuring.)

Miss Nev.   O lud! he has almost cracked my
head.

Mrs. Hard.   O, the monster! For shame, Tony.   You
a man, and behave so!

Tony.   If I'm a man, let me have my fortin.   Ecod!
I'll not be made a fool of no longer.

Mrs. Hard.   Is this, ungrateful boy, all that I'm to get
for the pains I have taken in your education?   I that
have rock'd you in your cradle, and fed that pretty mouth
with a spoon!   Did not I work that waistcoat to make
you genteel?   Did not I prescribe for you every day, and
weep while the receipt was operating?

43

Tony. Ecod! you had reason to weep, for you have been dosing me ever since I was born. I have gone through every receipt in the 'Complete Housewife' ten times over; and you have thoughts of coursing me through Quincy
5 next spring. But, ecod! I tell you, I'll not be made a fool of no longer.

Mrs. Hard. Wasn't it all for your good, viper? Wasn't it all for your good?

Tony. I wish you'd let me and my good alone then.
10 Snubbing this way when I'm in spirits. If I'm to have any good, let it come of itself; not to keep dinging it, dinging it into one so.

Mrs. Hard. That's false; I never see you when you're in spirits. No, Tony, you then go to the alehouse or
15 kennel. I'm never to be delighted with your agreeable wild notes, unfeeling monster!

Tony. Ecod! mamma, your own notes are the wildest of the two.

Mrs. Hard. Was ever the like? But I see he wants to
20 break my heart, I see he does.

Hast. Dear madam, permit me to lecture the young gentleman a little. I'm certain I can persuade him to his duty.

Mrs. Hard. Well! I must retire. Come, Constance, my love. You see, Mr. Hastings, the wretchedness of
25 my situation; was ever poor woman so plagued with a dear, sweet, pretty, provoking, undutiful boy!

[*Exeunt* Mrs. Hardcastle *and* Miss Neville.

Hastings, Tony

Tony. (*Singing.*) 'There was a young man riding by, and fain would have his will. Rang do didlo dee.' —

44

Don't mind her. Let her cry. It's the comfort of her heart. I have seen her and sister cry over a book for an hour together, and they said, they liked the book the better the more it made them cry.

Hast. Then you're no friend to the ladies, I find, my pretty young gentleman?

Tony. That's as I find 'um.

Hast. Not to her of your mother's choosing, I dare answer? And yet she appears to me a pretty, well-tempered girl.

Tony. That's because you don't know her as well as I. Ecod! I know every inch about her; and there's not a more bitter cantankerous toad in all Christendom.

Hast. (*Aside.*) Pretty encouragement this for a lover!

Tony. I have seen her since the height of *that.* She has as many tricks as a hare in a thicket, or a colt the first day's breaking.

Hast. To me she appears sensible and silent.

Tony. Ay, before company. But when she's with her playmates she's as loud as a hog in a gate.

Hast. But there is a meek modesty about her that charms me.

Tony. Yes, but curb her never so little, she kicks up, and you're flung in a ditch.

Hast. Well, but you must allow her a little beauty. — Yes, you must allow her some beauty.

Tony. Bandbox! She's all a made-up thing, mun. Ah! could you but see Bet Bouncer of these parts, you might then talk of beauty. Ecod, she has two eyes as black as sloes, and cheeks as broad and red as a pulpit cushion. She'd make two of she.

Hast.   Well, what say you to a friend that would take this bitter bargain off your hands?

Tony.   Anon!

Hast.   Would you thank him that would take Miss
5 Neville, and leave you to happiness and your dear Betsy?

Tony.   Ay; but where is there such a friend, for who would take her?

Hast.   I am he. If you but assist me, I'll engage to whip her off to France, and you shall never hear more of
10 her.

Tony.   Assist you! Ecod, I will, to the last drop of my blood. I'll clap a pair of horses to your chaise that shall trundle you off in a twinkling, and may be get you a part of her fortin beside in jewels, that you little dream of.

15   *Hast.*   My dear 'squire, this looks like a lad of spirit.

Tony.   Come along, then, and you shall see more of my spirit before you have done with me.   (*Singing.*)

> We are the boys
> That fears no noise
20   Where the thundering cannons roar.

                                        [*Exeunt.*

ACT III.

Scene I. The house.

Enter Hardcastle, *alone.*

Hard. What could my old friend Sir Charles mean by recommending his son as the modestest young man in town? To me he appears the most impudent piece of brass that ever spoke with a tongue. He has taken possession of the easy chair by the fire-side already. He took off his boots in the parlour and desired me to see them taken care of. I'm desirous to know how his impudence affects my daughter. — She will certainly be shocked at it.

Enter Miss Hardcastle, *plainly dressed.*

Hard. Well, my Kate, I see you have changed your dress, as I bid you; and yet, I believe, there was no great occasion.

Miss Hard. I find such a pleasure, Sir, in obeying your commands, that I take care to observe them without ever debating their propriety.

Hard. And yet, Kate, I sometimes give you some cause, particularly when I recommended my modest gentleman to you as a lover to-day.

Miss Hard. You taught me to expect something extraordinary, and I find the original exceeds the description.

Hard. I was never so surprised in my life! He has quite confounded all my faculties!

Miss Hard. I never saw any thing like it : and a man of the world too !

Hard. Ay, he learned it all abroad — what a fool was I, to think a young man could learn modesty by travelling. 5 He might as soon learn wit at a masquerade.

Miss Hard. It seems all natural to him.

Hard. A good deal assisted by bad company and a French dancing-master.

Miss Hard. Sure you mistake, papa ! A French 10 dancing-master could never have taught him that timid look — that awkward address — that bashful manner —

Hard. Whose look ? whose manner, child ?

Miss Hard. Mr. Marlow's : his *mauvaise honte*, his timidity, struck me at the first sight.

15 *Hard.* Then your first sight deceived you ; for I think him one of the most brazen first sights that ever astonished my senses.

Miss Hard. Sure, Sir, you rally ! I never saw any one so modest.

20 *Hard.* And can you be serious ! I never saw such a bouncing, swaggering puppy since I was born. Bully Dawson was but a fool to him.

Miss Hard. Surprising ! He met me with a respectful bow, a stammering voice, and a look fixed on the ground.

25 *Hard.* He met me with a loud voice, a lordly air, and a familiarity that made my blood freeze again.

Miss Hard. He treated me with diffidence and respect ; censured the manners of the age ; admired the prudence of girls that never laughed ; tired me with apologies for 30 being tiresome ; then left the room with a bow, and " Madam, I would not for the world detain you."

Hard. He spoke to me as if he knew me all his life before; asked twenty questions, and never waited for an answer; interrupted my best remarks with some silly pun; and when I was in my best story of the Duke of Marlborough and Prince Eugene, he asked if I had not 5 a good hand at making punch. Yes, Kate, he asked your father if he was a maker of punch.

Miss Hard. One of us must certainly be mistaken.

Hard. If he be what he has shown himself, I'm determined he shall never have my consent.   10

Miss Hard. And if he be the sullen thing I take him, he shall never have mine.

Hard. In one thing then we are agreed — to reject him.

Miss Hard. Yes. But upon conditions. For if you should find him less impudent, and I more presuming; if 15 you find him more respectful, and I more importunate — I don't know — the fellow is well enough for a man — Certainly we don't meet many such at a horse-race in the country.

Hard. If we should find him so — But that's impos- 20 sible. The first appearance has done my business. I'm seldom deceived in that.

Miss Hard. And yet there may be many good qualities under that first appearance.

Hard. Ay, when a girl finds a fellow's outside to her 25 taste, she then sets about guessing the rest of his furniture. With her a smooth face stands for good sense, and a genteel figure for every virtue.

Miss Hard. I hope, Sir, a conversation begun with a compliment to my good sense, won't end with a sneer at 30 my understanding?

Hard. Pardon me, Kate. But if young Mr. Brazen can find the art of reconciling contradictions, he may please us both, perhaps.

Miss Hard. And as one of us must be mistaken, what if we go to make farther discoveries?

Hard. Agreed. But depend on 't I'm in the right.

Miss Hard. And depend on 't I'm not much in the wrong.   [*Exeunt.*

Enter TONY, *running in with a casket.*

Tony. Ecod! I have got them. Here they are. My cousin Con's necklaces, bobs and all. My mother shan't cheat the poor souls out of their fortin neither. O! my genus, is that you?

Enter HASTINGS.

Hast. My dear friend, how have you managed with your mother? I hope you have amused her with pretending love for your cousin, and that you are willing to be reconciled at last? Our horses will be refreshed in a short time, and we shall soon be ready to set off.

Tony. And here's something to bear your charges by the way (*giving the casket*), your sweetheart's jewels. Keep them, and hang those, I say, that would rob you of one of them.

Hast. But how have you procured them from your mother?

Tony. Ask me no questions, and I'll tell you no fibs. I procured them by the rule of thumb. If I had not a key to every drawer in mother's bureau, how could I go to the alehouse as often as I do? An honest man may rob himself of his own at any time.

Hast. Thousands do it every day. But to be plain with you, Miss Neville is endeavouring to procure them from her aunt this very instant. If she succeeds, it will be the most delicate way at least of obtaining them.

Tony. Well, keep them, till you know how it will be. 5 But I know how it will be well enough, she'd as soon part with the only sound tooth in her head.

Hast. But I dread the effects of her resentment, when she finds she has lost them.

Tony. Never you mind her resentment, leave me to 10 manage that. I don't value her resentment the bounce of a cracker. Zounds! here they are. Morrice! Prance!

[*Exit* HASTINGS.

TONY, MRS. HARDCASTLE, *and* MISS NEVILLE.

Mrs. Hard. Indeed, Constance, you amaze me. Such a girl as you want jewels! It will be time enough for jewels, my dear, twenty years hence, when your beauty 15 begins to want repairs.

Miss Nev. But what will repair beauty at forty, will certainly improve it at twenty, madam.

Mrs. Hard. Yours, my dear, can admit of none. That natural blush is beyond a thousand ornaments. Besides, 20 child, jewels are quite out at present. Don't you see half the ladies of our acquaintance, my lady Kill-day-light, and Mrs. Crump, and the rest of them carry their jewels to town, and bring nothing but paste and marcasites back? 25

Miss Nev. But who knows, madam, but somebody that shall be nameless would like me best with all my little finery about me?

Mrs. Hard. Consult your glass, my dear, and then see if, with such a pair of eyes, you want any better sparklers. What do you think, Tony, my dear? does your cousin Con want any jewels in your eyes to set off her beauty?

5   *Tony.* That's as thereafter may be.

Miss Nev. My dear aunt, if you knew how it would oblige me!

Mrs. Hard. A parcel of old-fashioned rose and table cut things. They would make you look like the court of 10 King Solomon at a puppet-show. Besides, I believe, I can't readily come at them. They may be missing, for aught I know to the contrary.

Tony. (*Apart to Mrs. Hardcastle.*) Then why don't you tell her so at once, as she's so longing for them? Tell 15 her they're lost. It's the only way to quiet her. Say they're lost, and call me to bear witness.

Mrs. Hard. (*Apart to Tony.*) You know, my dear, I'm only keeping them for you. So if I say they're gone, you'll bear me witness, will you? He! he! he!

20   *Tony.* Never fear me. Ecod! I'll say I saw them taken out with my own eyes.

Miss Nev. I desire them but for a day, madam. Just to be permitted to show them as relics, and then they may be locked up again.

25   *Mrs. Hard.* To be plain with you, my dear Constance, if I could find them you should have them. They're missing, I assure you. Lost, for aught I know; but we must have patience, wherever they are.

Miss Nev. I'll not believe it; this is but a shallow pre- 30 tence to deny me. I know they are too valuable to be so slightly kept, and as you are to answer for the loss —

Mrs. Hard. Don't be alarmed, Constance. If they be lost I must restore an equivalent. But my son knows they are missing, and not to be found.

Tony. That I can bear witness to. They are missing, and not to be found, I'll take my oath on 't.   5

Mrs. Hard. You must learn resignation, my dear; for though we lose our fortune, yet we should not lose our patience. See me, how calm I am.

Miss Nev. Ay, people are generally calm at the misfortunes of others.   10

Mrs. Hard. Now I wonder a girl of your good sense should waste a thought upon such trumpery. We shall soon find them; and in the mean time you shall make use of my garnets till your jewels be found.

Miss Nev. I detest garnets!   15

Mrs. Hard. The most becoming things in the world to set off a clear complexion. You have often seen how well they look upon me. You shall have them.

                                       [Exit.

Miss Nev. I dislike them of all things. You shan't stir. — Was ever any thing so provoking — to mislay my 20 own jewels, and force me to wear her trumpery.

Tony. Don't be a fool. If she gives you the garnets, take what you can get. The jewels are your own already. I have stolen them out of her bureau, and she does not know it. Fly to your spark, he'll tell you more of the 25 matter. Leave me to manage her.

Miss Nev. My dear cousin!

Tony. Vanish. She's here and has missed them already. [*Exit* Miss Neville.] Zounds! how she fidgets and spits about like a catherine-wheel.   30

Enter MRS. HARDCASTLE.

Mrs. Hard. Confusion! thieves! robbers! we are cheated, plundered, broke open, undone.

Tony. What's the matter, what's the matter, mamma? I hope nothing has happened to any of the good family!

5 *Mrs. Hard.* We are robbed. My bureau has been broken open, the jewels taken out, and I'm undone.

Tony. Oh! is that all? Ha! ha! ha! By the laws, I never saw it better acted in my life. Ecod, I thought you was ruined in earnest, ha! ha! ha!

10 *Mrs. Hard.* Why, boy, I'm ruined in earnest. My bureau has been broken open, and all taken away.

Tony. Stick to that; ha! ha! ha! stick to that. I'll bear witness, you know, call me to bear witness.

Mrs. Hard. I tell you, Tony, by all that's precious, the 15 jewels are gone, and I shall be ruined for ever.

Tony. Sure I know they are gone, and I'm to say so.

Mrs. Hard. My dearest Tony, but hear me. They're gone, I say.

Tony. By the laws, mamma, you make me for to 20 laugh, ha! ha! I know who took them well enough, ha! ha! ha!

Mrs. Hard. Was there ever such a blockhead, that can't tell the difference between jest and earnest? I tell you I'm not in jest, booby!

25 *Tony.* That's right, that's right: you must be in a bitter passion, and then nobody will suspect either of us. I'll bear witness that they are gone.

Mrs. Hard. Was there ever such a cross-grain'd brute, that won't hear me! Can you bear witness that you're

no better than a fool? Was ever poor woman so beset
with fools on one hand, and thieves on the other?

Tony. I can bear witness to that.

Mrs. Hard. Bear witness again, you blockhead you,
and I'll turn you out of the room directly. My poor 5
niece, what will become of her! Do you laugh, you unfeeling brute, as if you enjoyed my distress?

Tony. I can bear witness to that.

Mrs. Hard. Do you insult me, monster? I'll teach
you to vex your mother, I will!   10

Tony. I can bear witness to that.

[*He runs off, she follows him.*

Enter Miss Hardcastle *and* Maid.

Miss Hard. What an unaccountable creature is that
brother of mine, to send them to the house as an inn, ha!
ha! I don't wonder at his impudence.

Maid. But what is more, madam, the young gentle- 15
man, as you passed by in your present dress, ask'd me if
you were the bar-maid. He mistook you for the bar-
maid, madam.

Miss Hard. Did he? Then as I live I'm resolved to
keep up the delusion. Tell me, Pimple, how do you like 20
my present dress? Don't you think I look something like
Cherry in the *Beaux' Stratagem?*

Maid. It's the dress, madam, that every lady wears
in the country, but when she visits or receives company.

Miss Hard. And are you sure he does not remember 25
my face or person?

Maid. Certain of it.

Miss Hard. I vow, I thought so; for though we spoke

for some time together, yet his fears were such that he never once looked up during the interview. Indeed, if he had, my bonnet would have kept him from seeing me.

Maid. But what do you hope from keeping him in his
5 mistake?

Miss Hard. In the first place I shall be seen, and that is no small advantage to a girl who brings her face to market. Then I shall perhaps make an acquaintance, and that's no small victory gained over one who never
10 addresses any but the wildest of her sex. But my chief aim is to take my gentleman off his guard, and like an invisible champion of romance, examine the giant's force before I offer to combat.

Maid. But are you sure you can act your part, and
15 disguise your voice so that he may mistake that, as he has already mistaken your person?

Miss Hard. Never fear me. I think I have got the true bar cant — Did your honour call? — Attend the Lion there. — Pipes and tobacco for the Angel. — The Lamb
20 has been outrageous this half hour.

Maid. It will do, madam. But he's here. [*Exit* MAID.

Enter MARLOW.

Marl. What a bawling in every part of the house. I have scarce a moment's repose. If I go to the best room, there I find my host and his story. If I fly to the
25 gallery, there we have my hostess with her curtesy down to the ground. I have at last got a moment to myself, and now for recollection.   [*Walks and muses.*

Miss Hard. Did you call, Sir? Did your honour call?

56

Marl. (*Musing.*)   As for Miss Hardcastle, she's too grave and sentimental for me.

Miss Hard.   Did your honour call?

[*She still places herself before him, he turning away.*

Marl.   No, child. (*Musing.*)   Besides, from the glimpse I had of her, I think she squints.   5

Miss Hard.   I'm sure, Sir, I heard the bell ring.

Marl.   No, no. (*Musing.*)   I have pleased my father, however, by coming down, and I'll to-morrow please myself by returning.   [*Taking out his tablets, and perusing.*

Miss Hard.   Perhaps the other gentleman called, Sir?   10

Marl.   I tell you, no.

Miss Hard.   I should be glad to know, Sir.   We have such a parcel of servants.

Marl.   No, no, I tell you.   (*Looks full in her face.*) Yes, child, I think I did call.   I wanted — I wanted — I   15 vow, child, you are vastly handsome.

Miss Hard.   O la, Sir, you'll make one asham'd.

Marl.   Never saw a more sprightly malicious eye.   Yes, yes, my dear, I did call.   Have you got any of your — a — what d'ye call it, in the house?   20

Miss Hard.   No, Sir, we have been out of that these ten days.

Marl.   One may call in this house, I find, to very little purpose.   Suppose I should call for a taste, just by way of trial, of the nectar of your lips; perhaps, I might be   25 disappointed in that too.

Miss Hard.   Nectar! nectar!   That's a liquor there's no call for in these parts.   French, I suppose.   We keep no French wines here, Sir.

Marl.   Of true English growth, I assure you.   30

57

Miss Hard. Then it's odd I should not know it. We brew all sorts of wines in this house, and I have lived here these eighteen years.

Marl. Eighteen years! Why one would think, child, 5 you kept the bar before you was born. How old are you?

Miss Hard. O! Sir, I must not tell my age. They say women and music should never be dated.

Marl. To guess at this distance you can't be much above forty. (*Approaching.*) Yet nearer I don't think so 10 much. (*Approaching.*) By coming close to some women, they look younger still; but when we come very close indeed — (*Attempting to kiss her.*)

Miss Hard. Pray, Sir, keep your distance. One would think you wanted to know one's age as they do horses, by 15 mark of mouth.

Marl. I protest, child, you use me extremely ill. If you keep me at this distance, how is it possible you and I can ever be acquainted?

Miss Hard. And who wants to be acquainted with you? 20 I want no such acquaintance, not I. I'm sure you did not treat Miss Hardcastle that was here awhile ago in this obstropalous manner. I'll warrant me, before her you look'd dash'd and kept bowing to the ground, and talk'd, for all the world, as if you was before a Justice of 25 Peace.

Marl. (*Aside.*) Egad! She has hit it, sure enough. (*To her.*) In awe of her, child? Ha! ha! ha! A mere awkward squinting thing, no, no. I find you don't know me. I laughed and rallied her a little; but I was unwill-30 ing to be too severe. No, I could not be too severe, curse me!

Miss Hard.   O! then, Sir, you are a favourite, I find, among the ladies?

Marl.   Yes, my dear, a great favourite.   And yet, hang me, I don't see what they find in me to follow.   At the Ladies' Club in town I'm called their agreeable Rattle. 5 Rattle, child, is not my real name, but one I'm known by. My name is Solomons, Mr. Solomons, my dear, at your service.   [*Offering to salute her.*

Miss Hard.   Hold, Sir, you are introducing me to your Club, not to yourself.   And you're so great a favourite 10 there, you say?

Marl.   Yes, my dear.   There's Mrs. Mantrap, Lady Betty Blackleg, the Countess of Sligo, Mrs. Longhorns, old Miss Biddy Buckskin, and your humble servant, keep up the spirit of the place.   15

Miss Hard.   Then it is a very merry place, I suppose?

Marl.   Yes, as merry as cards, supper, wine, and old women can make us.

Miss Hard.   And their agreeable Rattle, ha! ha! ha!

Marl.   (*Aside.*)   Egad! I don't quite like this chit. 20 She seems knowing, methinks.   You laugh, child?

Miss Hard.   I can't but laugh to think what time they all have for minding their work or their family.

Marl.   (*Aside.*)   All's well; she don't laugh at me.   (*To her.*)   Do you ever work, child?   25

Miss Hard.   Ay, sure.   There's not a screen or a quilt in the whole house but what can bear witness to that.

Marl.   Odso! then you must show me your embroidery. I embroider and draw patterns myself a little.   If you want a judge of your work you must apply to me.   30
                              [*Seizing her hand.*

Enter HARDCASTLE, *who stands in surprise.*

Miss Hard. Ay, but the colours do not look well by candle-light. You shall see all in the morning.

[*Struggling.*

Marl. And why not now, my angel? Such beauty fires beyond the power of resistance. — Pshaw! the father 5 here! My old luck: I never nick'd seven that I did not throw ames ace three times following. [*Exit* MARLOW.

Hard. So, madam! So I find this is your modest lover. This is your humble admirer that kept his eyes fixed on the ground, and only ador'd at humble distance. 10 Kate, Kate, art thou not ashamed to deceive your father so?

Miss Hard. Never trust me, dear papa, but he's still the modest man I first took him for, you'll be convinced of it as well as I.

15 *Hard.* By the hand of my body, I believe his impudence is infectious! Didn't I see him seize your hand? Didn't I see him haul you about like a milk-maid? and now you talk of his respect and his modesty, forsooth!

Miss Hard. But if I shortly convince you of his mod-20 esty, that he has only the faults that will pass off with time, and the virtues that will improve with age, I hope you'll forgive him.

Hard. The girl would actually make one run mad! I tell you I'll not be convinced. I am convinced. He 25 has scarce been three hours in the house, and he has already encroached on all my prerogatives. You may like his impudence, and call it modesty. But my son-in-law, madam, must have very different qualifications.

Miss Hard. Sir, I ask but this night to convince you.

Hard. You shall not have half the time, for I have thoughts of turning him out this very hour.

Miss Hard. Give me that hour then, and I hope to satisfy you. 5

Hard. Well, an hour let it be, then. But I'll have no trifling with your father. All fair and open, do you mind me.

Miss Hard. I hope, Sir, you have ever found that I considered your commands as my pride; for your kind- 10 ness is such, that my duty as yet has been inclination.

[*Exeunt.*

ACT IV.

Scene I. The house.

Enter Hastings *and* Miss Neville.

Hast. You surprise me! Sir Charles Marlow expected here this night! Where have you had your information?

Miss Nev. You may depend upon it. I just saw his letter to Mr. Hardcastle, in which he tells him he intends
5 setting out a few hours after his son.

Hast. Then, my Constance, all must be completed before he arrives. He knows me; and should he find me here, would discover my name, and perhaps my designs, to the rest of the family.

10 *Miss Nev.* The jewels, I hope, are safe.

Hast. Yes, yes. I have sent them to Marlow, who keeps the keys of our baggage. In the mean time I'll go to prepare matters for our elopement. I have had the 'squire's promise of a fresh pair of horses; and if I should
15 not see him again, will write him farther directions.

[*Exit.*

Miss Nev. Well! success attend you. In the mean time I'll go amuse my aunt with the old pretence of a violent passion for my cousin. [*Exit.*

Enter Marlow, *followed by a* Servant.

Marl. I wonder what Hastings could mean by sending
20 me so valuable a thing as a casket to keep for him, when

62

he knows the only place I have is the seat of a post-coach at an inn-door. Have you deposited the casket with the landlady, as I ordered you? Have you put it into her own hands?

Serv. Yes, your honour.   5

Marl. She said she'd keep it safe, did she?

Serv. Yes, she said she'd keep it safe enough; she ask'd me how I came by it, and she said she had a great mind to make me give an account of myself. [*Exit* SERVANT.

Marl. Ha! ha! ha! They're safe, however. What 10 an unaccountable set of beings have we got amongst! This little bar-maid though runs in my head most strangely, and drives out the absurdities of all the rest of the family. She's mine, she must be mine, or I'm greatly mistaken.

15

Enter HASTINGS.

Hast. Bless me! I quite forgot to tell her that I intended to prepare at the bottom of the garden. Marlow here, and in spirits too.

Marl. Give me joy, George! Crown me, shadow me with laurels! Well, George, after all, we modest fellows 20 don't want for success among the women.

Hast. Some women, you mean. But what success has your honour's modesty been crowned with now that it grows so insolent upon us?

Marl. Didn't you see the tempting, brisk, lovely, little 25 thing, that runs about the house with a bunch of keys to its girdle?

Hast. Well, and what then?

Marl. She's mine, you rogue you. Such fire, such

motion, such eyes, such lips — but, egad! she would not let me kiss them though.

Hast. But are you sure, so very sure of her?

Marl. Why, man, she talk'd of showing me her work above stairs, and I am to approve the pattern.

Hast. But how can you, Charles, go about to rob a woman of her honour?

Marl. Pshaw! pshaw! We all know the honour of the bar-maid of an inn. I don't intend to rob her, take my word for it.

Hast. I believe the girl has virtue.

Marl. And if she has, I should be the last man in the world that would attempt to corrupt it.

Hast. You have taken care, I hope, of the casket I sent you to lock up? It's in safety?

Marl. Yes, yes. It's safe enough. I have taken care of it. But how could you think the seat of a post-coach at an inn door a place of safety? Ah! numbskull! I have taken better precautions for you than you did for yourself — I have —

Hast. What!

Marl. I have sent it to the landlady to keep for you.

Hast. To the landlady!

Marl. The landlady!

Hast. You did?

Marl. I did. She's to be answerable for its forthcoming, you know.

Hast. Yes, she'll bring it forth, with a witness.

Marl. Wasn't I right? I believe you'll allow that I acted prudently upon this occasion?

Hast. (*Aside.*) He must not see my uneasiness.

64

Marl. You seem a little disconcerted though, me-thinks. Sure nothing has happened?

Hast. No, nothing. Never was in better spirits in all my life. And so you left it with the landlady, who, no doubt, very readily undertook the charge.   5

Marl. Rather too readily. For she not only kept the casket but, through her great precaution, was going to keep the messenger too. Ha! ha! ha!

Hast. He! he! he! They're safe, however.

Marl. As a guinea in a miser's purse.   10

Hast. (*Aside.*) So now all hopes of fortune are at an end, and we must set off without it. (*To him.*) Well, Charles, I'll leave you to your meditations on the pretty bar-maid, and, he! he! he! may you be as successful for yourself, as you have been for me!   [*Exit.* 15

Marl. Thank ye, George! I ask no more. Ha! ha! ha!

Enter HARDCASTLE.

Hard. I no longer know my own house. It's turned all topsey-turvey. His servants have got drunk already. I'll bear it no longer, and yet from my respect for his father, I'll be calm. (*To him.*) Mr. Marlow, your ser- 20 vant. I'm your very humble servant.   [*Bowing low.*

Marl. Sir, your humble servant. (*Aside.*) What's to be the wonder now?

Hard. I believe, Sir, you must be sensible, Sir, that no man alive ought to be more welcome than your father's 25 son, Sir. I hope you think so?

Marl. I do from my soul, Sir. I don't want much entreaty. I generally make my father's son welcome wherever he goes.

Hard. I believe you do, from my soul, Sir. But though I say nothing to your own conduct, that of your servants is insufferable. Their manner of drinking is setting a very bad example in this house, I assure you.

5 *Marl.* I protest, my very good Sir, that is no fault of mine. If they don't drink as they ought, *they* are to blame. I ordered them not to spare the cellar. I did, I assure you. (*To the side scene.*) Here, let one of my servants come up. (*To him.*) My positive directions were, 10 that as I did not drink myself, they should make up for my deficiencies below.

Hard. Then they had your orders for what they do! I'm satisfied!

Marl. They had, I assure you. You shall hear from 15 one of themselves.

Enter SERVANT, *drunk.*

Marl. You, Jeremy! Come forward, sirrah! What were you orders? Were you not told to drink freely, and call for what you thought fit, for the good of the house?

Hard. (*Aside.*) I begin to lose my patience.

20 *Jer.* Please your honour, Liberty and Fleet-street for ever! Though I'm but a servant, I'm as good as another man. I'll drink for no man before supper, Sir, dammy! Good liquour will sit upon a good supper, but a good supper will not sit upon — *hiccup* — upon my conscience, Sir.

25 *Marl.* You see, my old friend, the fellow is as drunk as he can possibly be. I don't know what you'd have more, unless you'd have the poor devil soused in a beer-barrel.

Hard. Zounds! he'll drive me distracted, if I contain myself any longer. Mr. Marlow. Sir; I have submitted

66

to your insolence for more than four hours, and I see no likelihood of its coming to an end. I'm now resolved to be master here, Sir, and I desire that you and your drunken pack may leave my house directly.

Marl. Leave your house! — Sure you jest, my good friend? What, when I'm doing what I can to please you?

Hard. I tell you, Sir, you don't please me; so I desire you'll leave my house.

Marl. Sure you cannot be serious? at this time o' night, and such a night. You only mean to banter me?

Hard. I tell you, Sir, I'm serious! and now that my passions are rouzed, I say this house is mine, Sir; this house is mine, and I command you to leave it directly.

Marl. Ha! ha! ha! A puddle in a storm. I shan't stir a step, I assure you. (*In a serious tone.*) This your house, fellow! It's my house. This is my house. Mine, while I choose to stay. What right have you to bid me leave this house, Sir? I never met with such impudence, curse me, never in my whole life before.

Hard. Nor I, confound me if ever I did. To come to my house, to call for what he likes, to turn me out of my own chair, to insult the family, to order his servants to get drunk, and then to tell me, "This house is mine, Sir." By all that's impudent, it makes me laugh. Ha! ha! ha! Pray, Sir (*bantering*), as you take the house, what think you of taking the rest of the furniture? There's a pair of silver candlesticks, and there's a fire-screen, and here's a pair of brazen-nosed bellows, perhaps you may take a fancy to them.

Marl. Bring me your bill, Sir; bring me your bill, and let's make no more words about it.

67

Hard. There are a set of prints too. What think you of the *Rake's Progress* for your own apartment?

Marl. Bring me your bill, I say; and I'll leave you and your infernal house directly.

5 *Hard.* Then there's a mahogany table that you may see your own face in.

Marl. My bill, I say.

Hard. I had forgot the great chair for your own particular slumbers, after a hearty meal.

10 *Marl.* Zounds! bring me my bill, I say, and let's hear no more on't.

Hard. Young man, young man, from your father's letter to me, I was taught to expect a well-bred modest man, as a visitor here, but now I find him no better than 15 a coxcomb and a bully; but he will be down here presently, and shall hear more of it. [*Exit.*

Marl. How's this! Sure I have not mistaken the house. Every thing looks like an inn. The servants cry "Coming!" The attendance is awkward; the bar-maid, 20 too, to attend us. But she's here, and will farther inform me. Whither so fast, child? A word with you.

Enter MISS HARDCASTLE.

Miss Hard. Let it be short then. I'm in a hurry. (*Aside.*) I believe he begins to find out his mistake. But it's too soon quite to undeceive him.

25 *Marl.* Pray, child, answer me one question. What are you, and what may your business in this house be?

Miss Hard. A relation of the family, Sir.

Marl. What, a poor relation?

Miss Hard. Yes, Sir, a poor relation appointed to keep

the keys, and to see that the guests want nothing in my power to give them.

Marl. That is, you act as the bar-maid of this inn.

Miss Hard. Inn! O law — what brought that in your head? One of the best families in the county keep an 5 inn! Ha! ha! ha! old Mr. Hardcastle's house an inn!

Marl. Mr. Hardcastle's house. Is this Mr. Hard-castle's house, child?

Miss Hard. Ay, sure. Whose else should it be?

Marl. So then all's out, and I have been damnably 10 imposed on. O, confound my stupid head, I shall be laugh'd at over the whole town. I shall be stuck up in caricature in all the print-shops — The *Dullissimo-Maccaroni.* To mistake this house of all others for an inn, and my father's old friend for an inn-keeper! What 15 a swaggering puppy must he take me for! What a silly puppy do I find myself! There again, may I be hanged, my dear, but I mistook you for the bar-maid.

Miss Hard. Dear me! dear me! I'm sure there's nothing in my behaviour to put me upon a level with one 20 of that stamp.

Marl. Nothing, my dear, nothing. But I was in for a list of blunders, and could not help making you a sub-scriber. My stupidity saw everything the wrong way. I mistook your assiduity for assurance, and your sim- 25 plicity for allurement. But it's over — This house I no more show my face in.

Miss Hard. I hope, Sir, I have done nothing to dis-oblige you. I'm sure I should be sorry to affront any gentleman who has been so polite, and said so many civil 30 things to me. I'm sure I should be sorry (*pretending to cry*) if he left the family upon my account. I'm sure I should be sorry, people said any thing amiss, since I have no fortune but my character.

Marl. (*Aside.*) By heaven, she weeps. This is the first mark of tenderness I ever had from a modest woman, and it touches me. (*To her.*) Excuse me, my lovely girl, you are the only part of the family I leave with reluctance. But to be plain with you, the difference of our birth, fortune and education makes an honourable connexion impossible; and I can never harbour a thought of seducing simplicity that trusted in my honour, of bringing ruin upon one, whose only fault was being too lovely.

Miss Hard. (*Aside.*) Generous man! I now begin to admire him. (*To him.*) But I am sure my family is as good as Miss Hardcastle's, and though I'm poor, that's no great misfortune to a contented mind, and, until this moment, I never thought that it was bad to want fortune.

Marl. And why now, my pretty simplicity?

Miss Hard. Because it puts me at a distance from one, that if I had a thousand pounds, I would give it all to.

Marl. (*Aside.*) This simplicity bewitches me, so that if I stay I'm undone. I must make one bold effort and leave her. (*To her.*) Your partiality in my favour, my dear, touches me most sensibly, and were I to live for myself alone, I could easily fix my choice. But I owe too much to the opinion of the world, too much to the authority of a father, so that — I can scarcely speak it — it affects me. Farewell.   [*Exit.*

Miss Hard. I never knew half his merit till now. He shall not go, if I have power or art to detain him. I'll still preserve the character in which I *stooped to conquer,*

but will undeceive my papa, who, perhaps, may laugh him
out of his resolution. [*Exit.*

Enter TONY, MISS NEVILLE

Tony. Ay, you may steal for yourselves the next time.
I have done my duty. She has got the jewels again, that's
a sure thing; but she believes it was all a mistake of the 5
servants.

Miss Nev. But, my dear cousin, sure you won't forsake us in this distress. If she in the least suspects that
I am going off, I shall certainly be locked up, or sent to
my aunt Pedigree's, which is ten times worse. 10

Tony. To be sure, aunts of all kinds are damned bad
things. But what can I do? I have got you a pair of
horses that will fly like Whistle-jacket, and I'm sure you
can't say but I have courted you nicely before her face.
Here she comes, we must court a bit or two more, for 15
fear she should suspect us.

[*They retire and seem to fondle.*

Enter MRS. HARDCASTLE.

Mrs. Hard. Well, I was greatly fluttered to be sure.
But my son tells me it was all a mistake of the servants.
I shan't be easy, however, till they are fairly married, and
then let her keep her own fortune. But what do I see! 20
fondling together, as I'm alive. I never saw Tony so
sprightly before. Ah! have I caught you, my pretty
doves! What, billing, exchanging stolen glances and
broken murmurs. Ah!

Tony. As for murmurs, mother, we grumble a little now 25
and then, to be sure. But there's no love lost between us.

Mrs. Hard. A mere sprinkling, Tony, upon the flame, only to make it burn brighter.

Miss Nev. Cousin Tony promises to give us more of his company at home. Indeed, he shan't leave us any more.
5 It won't leave us, cousin Tony, will it?

Tony. O! it's a pretty creature. No, I'd sooner leave my horse in a pound, than leave you when you smile upon one so. Your laugh makes you so becoming.

Miss Nev. Agreeable cousin! Who can help admiring
10 that natural humour, that pleasant, broad, red, thoughtless (*patting his cheek*), ah! it's a bold face.

Mrs. Hard. Pretty innocence!

Tony. I'm sure I always loved cousin Con's hazel eyes, and her pretty long fingers, that she twists this way and
15 that over the haspicolls, like a parcel of bobbins.

Mrs. Hard. Ah, he would charm the bird from the tree. I never was so happy before. My boy takes after his father, poor Mr. Lumpkin, exactly. The jewels, my dear Con, shall be yours incontinently. You shall have
20 them. Isn't he a sweet boy, my dear? You shall be married to-morrow, and we'll put off the rest of his education, like Dr. Drowsy's sermons, to a fitter opportunity.

Enter DIGGORY.

Dig. Where's the 'squire? I have got a letter for your worship.
25 *Tony.* Give it to my mamma. She reads all my letters first.

Dig. I had orders to deliver it into your own hands.

Tony. Who does it come from?

Dig. Your worship mun ask that o' the letter itself.

TONY LUMPKIN

"I can read your print hand very well."

Tony.   I could wish to know, though (*turning the letter, and gazing on it*).

Miss Nev.   (*Aside.*)   Undone, undone!   A letter to him from Hastings.   I know the hand.   If my aunt sees it we are ruined for ever.   I'll keep her employed as little if I can.   (*To Mrs. Hardcastle.*)   But I have not told you, madam, of my cousin's smart answer just now to Mr. Marlow.   We so laugh'd — You must know, madam. — This way a little, for he must not hear us.

[*They confer.*

Tony.   (*Still gazing.*)   A damn'd cramp piece of penmanship, as ever I saw in my life.   I can read your print hand very well.   But here there are such handles, and shanks, and dashes, that one can scarce tell the head from the tail.   'To Anthony Lumpkin, Esquire.'   It's very odd, I can read the outside of my letters, where my own name is, well enough.   But when I come to open it, it's all — buzz.   That's hard, very hard; for the inside of the letter is always the cream of the correspondence.

Mrs. Hard.   Ha! ha! ha!   Very well, very well.   And so my son was too hard for the philosopher.

Miss Nev.   Yes, madam; but you must hear the rest, madam.   A little more this way, or he may hear us. You'll hear how he puzzled him again.

Mrs. Hard.   He seems strangely puzzled now himself, methinks.

Tony.   (*Still gazing.*)   A damn'd up and down hand, as if it was disguised in liquor.   (*Reading.*)   Dear Sir, Ay, that's that.   Then there's an M, and a T, and an S, but whether the next be an izzard, or an R, confound me, I cannot tell.

73

Mrs. Hard. What's that, my dear? Can I give you any assistance?

Miss Nev. Pray, aunt, let me read it. Nobody reads a cramp hand better than I. (*Twitching the letter from*
5 *him.*) Do you know who it is from?

Tony. Can't tell, except from Dick Ginger the feeder.

Miss Nev. Ay, so it is. (*Pretending to read.*) Dear 'squire, hoping that you're in health, as I am at this present. The
10 gentlemen of the Shake-bag club has cut the gentlemen of the Goose-green quite out of feather. The odds — um — odd battle — um — long fighting — um — here, here, it's all about cocks and fighting; it's of no consequence, here, put it up, put it up.

    [*Thrusting the crumpled letter upon him.*

15 *Tony.* But I tell you, miss, it's of all the consequence in the world. I would not lose the rest of it for a guinea. Here, mother, do you make it out. Of no consequence!

    [*Giving Mrs. Hardcastle the letter.*

Mrs. Hard. How's this! (*Reads.*) " Dear 'squire, I'm now waiting for Miss Neville, with a post-chaise and pair,
20 at the bottom of the garden, but I find my horses yet unable to perform the journey. I expect you'll assist us with a pair of fresh horses, as you promised. Dispatch is necessary, as the hag (ay, the hag) your mother, will otherwise suspect us. Yours, Hastings." Grant me
25 patience. I shall run distracted. My rage chokes me.

Miss Nev. I hope, madam, you'll suspend your resentment for a few moments, and not impute to me any impertinence, or sinister design, that belongs to another.

Mrs. Hard. (*Curtesying very low.*) Fine-spoken, madam; you are most miraculously polite and engaging, and quite the very pink of courtesy and circumspection, madam. (*Changing her tone.*) And you, you great ill-fashioned oaf, with scarce sense enough to keep your mouth shut. Were 5 you, too, joined against me? But I'll defeat all your plots in a moment. As for you, madam, since you have got a pair of fresh horses ready, it would be cruel to disappoint them. So, if you please, instead of running away with your spark, prepare, this very moment, to run off 10 with me. Your old Aunt Pedigree will keep you secure, I'll warrant me. You too, Sir, may mount your horse, and guard us upon the way. Here, Thomas, Roger, Diggory! I'll show you, that I wish you better than you do yourselves. [*Exit.* 15

Miss Nev. So now I'm completely ruined.

Tony. Ay, that's a sure thing.

Miss Nev. What better could be expected from being connected with such a stupid fool, and after all the nods and signs I made him! 20

Tony. By the laws, miss, it was your own cleverness, and not my stupidity, that did your business. You were so nice and so busy with your Shake-bags and Goosegreens, that I thought you could never be making believe.

Enter HASTINGS.

Hast. So, Sir, I find by my servant, that you have 25 shown my letter, and betrayed us. Was this well done, young gentleman?

Tony. Here's another. Ask miss there, who betray'd you? Ecod, it was her doing, not mine.

Enter MARLOW.

Marl. So I have been finely used here among you. Rendered contemptible, driven into ill manners, despised, insulted, laughed at.

Tony. Here's another. We shall have old Bedlam
5 broke loose presently.

Miss Nev. And there, Sir, is the gentleman to whom we all owe every obligation.

Marl. What can I say to him, a mere boy, an idiot, whose ignorance and age are a protection?

10 *Hast.* A poor contemptible booby, that would but disgrace correction.

Miss Nev. Yet with cunning and malice enough to make himself merry with all our embarrassments.

Hast. An insensible cub.

15 *Marl.* Replete with tricks and mischief.

Tony. Baw! dam'me, but I'll fight you both one after the other — with baskets.

Marl. As for him, he's below resentment. But your conduct, Mr. Hastings, requires an explanation. You
20 knew of my mistakes, yet would not undeceive me.

Hast. Tortured as I am with my own disappointments, is this a time for explanations? It is not friendly, Mr. Marlow.

Marl. But, Sir —

25 *Miss Nev.* Mr. Marlow, we never kept on your mistake, till it was too late to undeceive you.

Enter SERVANT.

Serv. My mistress desires you'll get ready immediately, madam. The horses are putting to. Your hat and things

76

are in the next room.   We are to go thirty miles before
morning.   [*Exit* SERVANT.

Miss Nev.   Well, well: I'll come presently.

Marl.   (*To Hastings.*)   Was it well done, Sir, to assist
in rendering me ridiculous?   To hang me out for the scorn 5
of all my acquaintance?   Depend upon it, Sir, I shall
expect an explanation.

Hast.   Was it well done, Sir, if you're upon that subject,
to deliver what I entrusted to yourself, to the care of
another, Sir?   10

Miss Nev.   Mr. Hastings!   Mr. Marlow!   Why will
you increase my distress by this groundless dispute?   I
implore, I entreat you —

Enter SERVANT.

Serv.   Your cloak, madam.   My mistress is impatient.
                                                [*Exit* SERVANT.

Miss Nev.   I come.   Pray be pacified.   If I leave you 15
thus, I shall die with apprehension!

Enter SERVANT.

Serv.   Your fan, muff, and gloves, madam.   The horses
are waiting.

Miss Nev.   O, Mr. Marlow! if you knew what a scene
of constraint and ill-nature lies before me, I'm sure it 20
would convert your resentment into pity.

Marl.   I'm so distracted with a variety of passions,
that I don't know what I do.   Forgive me, madam.
George, forgive me.   You know my hasty temper, and
should not exasperate it.   25

Hast.   The torture of my situation is my only excuse.

77

Miss Nev. Well, my dear Hastings, if you have that esteem for me that I think, that I am sure you have, your constancy for three years will but increase the happiness of our future connexion. If —

5 *Mrs. Hard.* (*Within.*) Miss Neville. Constance, why Constance, I say!

Miss Nev. I'm coming. Well, constancy, remember, constancy is the word.   [*Exit.*

Hast. My heart! how can I support this? To be so 10 near happiness, and such happiness!

Marl. (*To Tony.*) You see now, young gentleman, the effects of your folly. What might be amusement to you, is here disappointment, and even distress.

Tony. (*From a reverie.*) Ecod, I have hit it. It's 15 here. Your hands. Yours and yours, my poor Sulky. My boots there, ho! Meet me two hours hence at the bottom of the garden; and if you don't find Tony Lumpkin a more good-natur'd fellow than you thought for, I'll give you leave to take my best horse, and Bet Bouncer 20 into the bargain. Come along. My boots, ho! [*Exeunt.*

ACT V.

SCENE I. THE HOUSE.

Enter HASTINGS and SERVANT.

Hast. You saw the old lady and Miss Neville drive off, you say.

Serv. Yes, your honour. They went off in a post-coach, and the young 'squire went on horseback. They're thirty miles off by this time. 5

Hast. Then all my hopes are over.

Serv. Yes, Sir. Old Sir Charles is arrived. He and the old gentleman of the house have been laughing at Mr. Marlow's mistake this half hour. They are coming this way. 10

Hast. Then I must not be seen. So now to my fruitless appointment at the bottom of the garden. This is about the time. [*Exit.*

Enter SIR CHARLES and HARDCASTLE.

Hard. Ha! ha! ha! The peremptory tone in which he sent forth his sublime commands. 15

Sir Charl. And the reserve with which I suppose he treated all your advances.

Hard. And yet he might have seen something in me above a common inn-keeper, too.

Sir Charl. Yes, Dick, but he mistook you for an un- 20 common inn-keeper, ha! ha! ha!

79

Hard. Well, I'm in too good spirits to think of any thing but joy. Yes, my dear friend, this union of our families will make our personal friendships hereditary, and though my daughter's fortune is but small —

5 *Sir Charl.* Why, Dick, will you talk of fortune to me? My son is possessed of more than a competence already, and can want nothing but a good and virtuous girl to share his happiness and increase it. If they like each other, as you say they do —

10 *Hard.* If, man! I tell you they do like each other. My daughter as good as told me so.

Sir Charl. But girls are apt to flatter themselves, you know.

Hard. I saw him grasp her hand in the warmest manner
15 myself; and here he comes to put you out of your *ifs*, I warrant him.

Enter MARLOW.

Marl. I come, Sir, once more, to ask pardon for my strange conduct. I can scarce reflect on my insolence without confusion.

20 *Hard.* Tut, boy, a trifle. You take it too gravely. An hour or two's laughing with my daughter will set all to rights again. She'll never like you the worse for it.

Marl. Sir, I shall be always proud of her approbation.

Hard. Approbation is but a cold word, Mr. Marlow; if
25 I am not deceived, you have something more than approbation thereabouts. You take me?

Marl. Really, Sir, I have not that happiness.

Hard. Come, boy, I'm an old fellow, and know what's what as well as you that are younger. I know what has
30 past between you; but mum.

Marl. Sure, Sir, nothing has past between us but the most profound respect on my side, and the most distant reserve on hers. You don't think, Sir, that my impudence has been past upon all the rest of the family?

Hard. Impudence! No, I don't say that — not quite 5 impudence — though girls like to be play'd with, and rumpled a little too, sometimes. But she has told no tales, I assure you.

Marl. I never gave her the slightest cause.

Hard. Well, well, I like modesty in its place well 10 enough. But this is over-acting, young gentleman. You may be open. Your father and I will like you the better for it.

Marl. May I die, Sir, if I ever —

Hard. I tell you, she don't dislike you; and as I'm 15 sure you like her —

Marl. Dear, Sir — I protest, Sir —

Hard. I see no reason why you should not be joined as fast as the parson can tie you.

Marl. But hear me, Sir — 20

Hard. Your father approves the match, I admire it, every moment's delay will be doing mischief, so —

Marl. But why won't you hear me? By all that's just and true, I never gave Miss Hardcastle the slightest mark of my attachment, or even the most distant hint to sus- 25 pect me of affection. We had but one interview, and that was formal, modest, and uninteresting.

Hard. (*Aside.*) This fellow's formal modest impudence is beyond bearing.

Sir Charl. And you never grasp'd her hand, or made 30 any protestations?

81

Marl. As Heaven is my witness, I came down in obedience to your commands. I saw the lady without emotion, and parted without reluctance. I hope you'll exact no farther proofs of my duty, nor prevent me from leaving
5 a house in which I suffer so many mortifications. [*Exit.*

Sir Charl. I'm astonished at the air of sincerity with which he parted.

Hard. And I'm astonished at the deliberate intrepidity of his assurance.

10 *Sir Charl.* I dare pledge my life and honour upon his truth.

Hard. Here comes my daughter, and I would stake my happiness upon her veracity.

Enter MISS HARDCASTLE.

Hard. Kate, come hither, child. Answer us sincerely
15 and without reserve: has Mr. Marlow made you any professions of love and affection?

Miss Hard. The question is very abrupt, Sir! But since you require unreserved sincerity, I think he has.

Hard. (*To Sir Charles.*) You see.

20 *Sir Charl.* And pray, madam, have you and my son had more than one interview?

Miss Hard. Yes, Sir, several.

Hard. (*To Sir Charles.*) You see.

Sir Charl. But did he profess any attachment?

25 *Miss Hard.* A lasting one.

Sir Charl. Did he talk of love?

Miss Hard. Much, Sir.

Sir Charl. Amazing! And all this formally?

Miss Hard. Formally.

Hard.   Now, my friend, I hope you are satisfied.

Sir Charl.   And how did he behave, madam?

Miss Hard.   As most profest admirers do.   Said some civil things of my face, talked much of his want of merit, and the greatness of mine; mentioned his heart, gave a short tragedy speech, and ended with pretended rapture.

Sir Charl.   Now I'm perfectly convinced indeed.   I know his conversation among women to be modest and submissive.   This forward, canting, ranting manner by no means describes him, and, I am confident, he never sat for the picture.

Miss Hard.   Then, what, Sir, if I should convince you to your face of my sincerity?   if you and my papa, in about half an hour, will place yourselves behind that screen, you shall hear him declare his passion to me in person.

Sir Charl.   Agreed.   And if I find him what you describe, all my happiness in him must have an end.   [*Exit.*

Miss Hard.   And if you don't find him what I describe — I fear my happiness must never have a beginning.

[*Exeunt.*

SCENE II.   THE BACK OF THE GARDEN.

Enter HASTINGS.

Hast.   What an idiot am I, to wait here for a fellow, who probably takes a delight in mortifying me.   He never intended to be punctual, and I'll wait no longer.   What do I see!   It is he!   and perhaps with news of my Constance.

Enter TONY, *booted and spattered.*

Hast. My honest 'squire! I now find you a man of your word. This looks like friendship.

Tony. Ay, I'm your friend, and the best friend you have in the world, if you knew but all. This riding, by
5 night, by the by, is cursedly tiresome. It has shook me worse than the basket of a stage-coach.

Hast. But how? where did you leave your fellow travellers? Are they in safety? Are they housed?

Tony. Five and twenty miles in two hours and a half
10 is no such bad driving. The poor beasts have smoked for it: rabbit me, but I'd rather ride forty miles after a fox than ten with such varment.

Hast. Well, but where have you left the ladies? I die with impatience.

15 *Tony.* Left them! Why where should I leave them but where I found them?

Hast. This is a riddle.

Tony. Riddle me this then. What's that goes round the house, and round the house, and never touches the
20 house?

Hast. I'm still astray.

Tony. Why, that's it, mon. I have led them astray. By jingo, there's not a pond or a slough within five miles of the place but they can tell the taste of.

25 *Hast.* Ha! ha! ha! I understand; you took them in a round, while they supposed themselves going forward, and so you have at last brought them home again.

Tony. You shall hear. I first took them down Feather-bed-lane, where we stuck fast in the mud. I

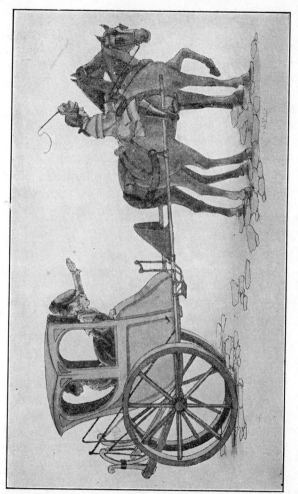

A POST CHAISE

then rattled them crack over the stones of Up-and-down Hill — I then introduced them to the gibbet on Heavy-tree Heath, and from that, with a circumbendibus, I fairly lodged them in the horse-pond at the bottom of the garden. 5

Hast. But no accident, I hope.

Tony. No, no. Only mother is confoundedly frightened. She thinks herself forty miles off. She's sick of the journey, and the cattle can scarce crawl. So if your own horses be ready, you may whip off with cousin, and I'll be 10 bound that no soul here can budge a foot to follow you.

Hast. My dear friend, how can I be grateful!

Tony. Ay, now it's dear friend, noble 'squire. Just now, it was all idiot, cub, and run me through the guts. Damn your way of fighting, I say. After we take a knock 15 in this part of the country, we kiss and be friends. But if you had run me through the guts, then I should be dead, and you might go kiss the hangman.

Hast. The rebuke is just. But I must hasten to relieve Miss Neville; if you keep the old lady employed, I 20 promise to take care of the young one. [*Exit* HASTINGS.

Tony. Never fear me. Here she comes. Vanish! She's got from the pond, and draggled up to the waist like a mermaid.

Enter MRS. HARDCASTLE.

Mrs. Hard. Oh, Tony, I'm killed. Shook! Battered 25 to death! I shall never survive it. That last jolt that laid us against the quickest hedge has done my business.

Tony. Alack, mamma, it was all your own fault. You would be for running away by night, without knowing one inch of the way. 30

85

Mrs. Hard. I wish we were at home again. I never met so many accidents in so short a journey. Drench'd in the mud, overturned in a ditch, stuck fast in a slough, jolted to a jelly, and at last to lose our way. Whereabouts
5 do you think we are, Tony?

Tony. By my guess we should come upon Crackskull common, about forty miles from home.

Mrs. Hard. O lud! O lud! The most notorious spot in all the country. We only want a robbery to make a
10 complete night on 't.

Tony. Don't be afraid, mamma, don't be afraid. Two of the five that kept here are hanged, and the other three may not find us. Don't be afraid. Is that a man that's galloping behind us? No; it's only a tree. Don't be
15 afraid.

Mrs. Hard. The fright will certainly kill me.

Tony. Do you see any thing like a black hat moving behind the thicket?

Mrs. Hard. O death!

20 *Tony.* No, it's only a cow. Don't be afraid, mamma; don't be afraid.

Mrs. Hard. As I'm alive, Tony, I see a man coming towards us. Ah! I'm sure on 't. If he perceives us we are undone.

25 *Tony.* (*Aside.*) Father-in-law, by all that's unlucky, come to take one of his night walks. (*To her.*) Ah, it's a highwayman with pistols as long as my arm. A damn'd ill-looking fellow.

Mrs. Hard. Good Heaven defend us! He approaches.

30 *Tony.* Do you hide yourself in that thicket, and leave me to manage him. If there be any danger I'll

86

cough and cry *hem*. When I cough be sure to keep close.

[*Mrs. Hardcastle hides behind a tree in the back scene.*

Enter HARDCASTLE.

Hard. I'm mistaken, or I heard voices of people in want of help. Oh, Tony, is that you? I did not expect you so soon back. Are your mother and her charge in 5 safety?

Tony. Very safe, Sir, at my Aunt Pedigree's. Hem.

Mrs. Hard. (*From behind.*) Ah, death! I find there's danger.

Hard. Forty miles in three hours; sure that's too 10 much, my youngster.

Tony. Stout horses and willing minds make short journeys, as they say. Hem.

Mrs. Hard. (*From behind.*) Sure he'll do the dear boy no harm. 15

Hard. But I heard a voice here; I should be glad to know from whence it came.

Tony. It was I, Sir, talking to myself, Sir. I was saying that forty miles in four hours was very good going. Hem. As to be sure it was. Hem. I have got a sort 20 of cold by being out in the air. We'll go in, if you please. Hem.

Hard. But if you talk'd to yourself, you did not answer yourself. I'm certain I heard two voices, and am resolved (*raising his voice*) to find the other out. 25

Mrs. Hard. (*From behind.*) Oh! he's coming to find me out. Oh!

Tony. What need you go, Sir, if I tell you? Hem.

87

I'll lay down my life for the truth — hem — I'll tell you all, Sir.   [*Detaining him.*

Hard.   I tell you, I will not be detained.   I insist on seeing.   It's in vain to expect I'll believe you.

5 *Mrs. Hard.* (*Running forward from behind.*) O lud! he'll murder my poor boy, my darling.   Here, good gentleman, whet your rage upon me.   Take my money, my life, but spare that young gentleman, spare my child, if you have any mercy.

10 *Hard.*   My wife! as I'm a Christian.   From whence can she come?   or what does she mean?

Mrs. Hard. (*Kneeling.*) Take compassion on us, good Mr. Highwayman.   Take our money, our watches, all we have, but spare our lives.   We will never bring you to 15 justice, indeed we won't, good Mr. Highwayman.

Hard.   I believe the woman's out of her sense.   What, Dorothy, don't you know me?

Mrs. Hard.   Mr. Hardcastle, as I'm alive!   My fears blinded me.   But who, my dear, could have expected to 20 meet you here, in this frightful place, so far from home? What has brought you to follow us?

Hard.   Sure, Dorothy, you have not lost your wits? So far from home, when you are within forty yards of your own door.   (*To him.*) This is one of your old tricks, you 25 graceless rogue, you.   (*To her.*) Don't you know the gate, and the mulberry-tree; and don't you remember the horse-pond, my dear?

Mrs. Hard.   Yes, I shall remember the horse-pond as long as I live; I have caught my death in it.   (*To Tony.*) 30 And is it to you, you graceless varlet, I owe all this?   I'll teach you to abuse your mother, I will!

Tony. Ecod, mother, all the parish says you have spoil'd me, and so you may take the fruits on 't.

Mrs. Hard. I'll spoil you, I will!

[*Follows him off the stage.*

Hard. There's morality, however, in his reply. [*Exit.*

Enter HASTINGS *and* MISS NEVILLE.

Hast. My dear Constance, why will you deliberate 5 thus? If we delay a moment, all is lost for ever. Pluck up a little resolution, and we shall soon be out of the reach of her malignity.

Miss Nev. I find it impossible. My spirits are so sunk with the agitations I have suffered, that I am unable to 10 face any new danger. Two or three years' patience will at last crown us with happiness.

Hast. Such a tedious delay is worse than inconstancy. Let us fly, my charmer. Let us date our happiness from this very moment. Perish fortune! Love and content 15 will increase what we possess beyond a monarch's revenue. Let me prevail!

Miss Nev. No, Mr. Hastings; no. Prudence once more comes to my relief, and I will obey its dictates. In the moment of passion fortune may be despised, but it 20 ever produces a lasting repentance. I'm resolved to apply to Mr. Hardcastle's compassion and justice for redress.

Hast. But though he had the will, he has not the power to relieve you.

Miss Nev. But he has influence, and upon that I am 25 resolved to rely.

Hast. I have no hopes. But since you persist, I must reluctantly obey you. [*Exeunt.*

89

SCENE III.   A ROOM AT MR. HARDCASTLE'S.

Enter SIR CHARLES *and* MISS HARDCASTLE.

Sir Charl.   What a situation am I in!   If what you say appears, I shall then find a guilty son.   If what he says be true, I shall then lose one, that, of all others, I most wish'd for a daughter.

5 *Miss Hard.*   I am proud of your approbation, and to show I merit it, if you place yourselves as I directed, you shall hear his explicit declaration.   But he comes.

Sir Charl.   I'll to your father, and keep him to the appointment.   [*Exit* SIR CHARLES.

Enter MARLOW.

10 *Marl.*   Though prepar'd for setting out, I come once more to take leave, nor did I, till this moment, know the pain I feel in the separation.

Miss Hard.   (*In her own natural manner.*)   I believe these sufferings cannot be very great, Sir, which you can
15 so easily remove.   A day or two longer, perhaps, might lessen your uneasiness, by showing the little value of what you now think proper to regret.

Marl.   (*Aside.*)   This girl every moment improves upon me.   (*To her.*)   It must not be, madam.   I have al-
20 ready trifled too long with my heart.   My very pride begins to submit to my passion.   The disparity of educa-tion and fortune, the anger of a parent, and the contempt of my equals, begin to lose their weight; and nothing can restore me to myself, but this painful effort of resolution.

25 *Miss Hard.*   Then go, Sir.   I'll urge nothing more to detain you.   Though my family be as good as hers you

came down to visit, and my education, I hope, not inferior, what are these advantages without equal affluence? I must remain contented with the slight approbation of imputed merit; I must have only the mockery of your addresses, while all your serious aims are fixed on fortune. 5

Enter HARDCASTLE *and* SIR CHARLES *from behind.*

Sir Charl. Here, behind this screen.

Hard. Ay, ay, make no noise. I'll engage my Kate covers him with confusion at last.

Marl. By heavens, madam, fortune was ever my 10 smallest consideration. Your beauty at first caught my eye; for who could see that without emotion. But every moment that I converse with you, steals in some new grace, heightens the picture, and gives it stronger expression. What at first seemed rustic plainness, now appears refined simplicity. What seem'd forward assurance, now strikes 15 me as the result of courageous innocence and conscious virtue.

Sir Charl. What can he mean? He amazes me!

Hard. I told you how it would be. Hush!

Marl. I am now determined to say, madam, and I 20 have too good an opinion of my father's discernment, when he sees you, to doubt his approbation.

Miss Hard. No, Mr. Marlow, I will not, cannot detain you. Do you think I could suffer a connexion, in which there is the smallest room for repentance? Do you think 25 I would take the mean advantage of a transient passion, to load you with confusion? Do you think I could ever relish that happiness, which was acquired by lessening yours?

Marl. By all that's good, I can have no happiness but what's in your power to grant me. Nor shall I ever feel repentance, but in not having seen your merits before. I will stay, even contrary to your wishes; and though
5 you should persist to shun me, I will make my respectful assiduities atone for the levity of my past conduct.

Miss Hard. Sir, I must entreat you'll desist. As our acquaintance began, so let it end, in indifference. I might have given an hour or two to levity; but seriously, Mr.
10 Marlow, do you think I could ever submit to a connexion, where I must appear mercenary and you imprudent? Do you think I could ever catch at the confident addresses of a secure admirer?

Marl. (*Kneeling.*) Does this look like security? Does
15 this look like confidence? No, madam, every moment that shows me your merit, only serves to increase my diffidence and confusion. Here let me continue —

Sir Charl. I can hold it no longer. Charles, Charles, how hast thou deceived me! Is this your indifference,
20 your uninteresting conversation?

Hard. Your cold contempt; your formal interview? What have you to say now?

Marl. That I'm all amazement? What can it mean?

Hard. It means that you can say and unsay things at
25 pleasure. That you can address a lady in private, and deny it in public; that you have one story for us, and another for my daughter!

Marl. Daughter! — This lady your daughter!

Hard. Yes, Sir, my only daughter. My Kate; whose
30 else should she be?

Marl. Oh, the devil!

Miss Hard. Yes, Sir, that very identical tall, squinting lady you were pleased to take me for (*curtesying*), she that you addressed as the mild, modest, sentimental man of gravity, and the bold, forward, agreeable Rattle of the Ladies' Club. Ha! ha! ha!   5

Marl. Zounds, there's no bearing this; its worse than death!

Miss Hard. In which of your characters, Sir, will you give us leave to address you? As the faltering gentleman, with looks on the ground, that speaks just to be heard, and 10 hates hypocrisy; or the loud confident creature, that keeps it up with Mrs. Mantrap, and old Miss Biddy Buckskin, till three in the morning? Ha! ha! ha!

Marl. O, curse on my noisy head. I never attempted to be impudent yet, that I was not taken down. I must 15 be gone.

Hard. By the hand of my body, but you shall not. I see it was all a mistake, and I am rejoiced to find it. You shall not. Sir, I tell you. I know she'll forgive you. Won't you forgive him, Kate? We'll all forgive you. 20 Take courage, man.   [*They retire, she tormenting him,
                                               to the back scene.*

Enter MRS. HARDCASTLE, TONY.

Mrs. Hard. So, so, they're gone off. Let them go, I care not.

Hard. Who gone?

Mrs. Hard. My dutiful niece and her gentleman, 25 Mr. Hastings, from town. He who came down with our modest visitor here.

Sir Charl. Who, my honest George Hastings? As

worthy a fellow as lives, and the girl could not have made a more prudent choice.

Hard. Then, by the hand of my body, I'm proud of the connexion.

5   *Mrs. Hard.* Well, if he has taken away the lady, he has not taken her fortune; that remains in this family to console us for her loss.

Hard. Sure, Dorothy, you would not be so mercenary?

Mrs. Hard. Ay, that's my affair, not yours.

10   *Hard.* But you know if your son, when of age, refuses to marry his cousin, her whole fortune is then at her own disposal.

Mrs. Hard. Ay, but he's not of age, and she has not thought proper to wait for his refusal.

Enter HASTINGS *and* MISS NEVILLE.

15   *Mrs. Hard.* (*Aside.*) What, returned so soon! I begin not to like it.

Hast. (*To Hardcastle.*) For my late attempt to fly off with your niece, let my present confusion be my punishment. We are now come back, to appeal from your justice
20 to your humanity. By her father's consent I first paid her my addresses, and our passions were first founded in duty.

Miss Nev. Since his death, I have been obliged to stoop to dissimulation to avoid oppression. In an hour of levity, I was ready even to give up my fortune to
25 secure my choice. But I'm now recover'd from the delusion, and hope from your tenderness what is denied me from a nearer connexion.

Mrs. Hard. Pshaw, pshaw, this is all but the whining end of a modern novel.

Hard. Be it what it will, I'm glad they're come back to reclaim their due. Come hither, Tony, boy. Do you refuse this lady's hand whom I now offer you?

Tony. What signifies my refusing? You know I can't refuse her till I'm of age, father.   5

Hard. While I thought concealing your age, boy, was likely to conduce to your improvement, I concurred with your mother's desire to keep it secret. But since I find she turns it to a wrong use, I must now declare you have been of age these three months.   10

Tony. Of age! Am I of age, father?

Hard. Above three months.

Tony. Then you'll see the first use I'll make of my liberty. (*Taking Miss Neville's hand.*) Witness all men by these presents, that I Anthony Lumpkin, esquire, of 15 BLANK place, refuse you, Constantia Neville, spinster, of no place at all, for my true and lawful wife. So Constance Neville may marry whom she pleases, and Tony Lumpkin is his own man again.

Sir Charl. O brave 'squire.   20

Hast. My worthy friend!

Mrs. Hard. My undutiful offspring!

Marl. Joy, my dear George, I give you joy sincerely. And could I prevail upon my little tyrant here to be less arbitrary, I should be the happiest man alive, if you 25 would return me the favour.

Hast. (*To Miss Hardcastle.*) Come, madam, you are now driven to the very last scene of all your contrivances. I know you like him, I'm sure he loves you, and you must and shall have him.   30

Hard. (*Joining their hands.*) And I say so too. And,

Mr. Marlow, if she makes as good a wife as she has a daughter, I don't believe you'll ever repent your bargain. So now to supper.   To-morrow we shall gather all the poor of the parish about us, and the Mistakes of the Night
5 shall be crown'd with a merry morning; so, boy, take her, and as you have been mistaken in the mistress, my wish is, that you may never be mistaken in the wife.

[*Exeunt omnes*

EPILOGUE

By Dr. GOLDSMITH

SPOKEN BY Mrs. BULKLEY

IN THE CHARACTER OF

MISS HARDCASTLE

WELL, having stoop'd to conquer with success,
And gain'd a husband without aid from dress,
Still, as a bar-maid, I could wish it too,
As I have conquer'd him, to conquer you:
And let me say, for all your resolution,   5
That pretty bar-maids have done execution.
Our life is all a play, compos'd to please,
' We have our exits and our entrances.'
The first act shows the simple country maid,
Harmless and young, of every thing afraid;   10
Blushes when hir'd, and with unmeaning action,
' I hopes as how to give you satisfaction.'
Her second act displays a livelier scene —
Th' unblushing bar-maid of a country inn,
Who whisks about the house, at market caters,   15
Talks loud, coquets the guests, and scolds the waiters.
Next the scene shifts to town, and there she soars,
The chop-house toast of ogling *connoisseurs*.
On 'squires and cits she there displays her arts,
And on the gridiron broils her lovers' hearts —   20

Epilogue.

And as she smiles, her triumphs to complete,
E'en Common Councilmen forget to eat.
The fourth act shows her wedded to the 'squire,
And madam now begins to hold it higher;
5   Pretends to taste, at Operas cries *caro*,
And quits her Nancy Dawson, for Che Faro:
Doats upon dancing, and in all her pride
Swims round the room, the Heinel of Cheapside:
Ogles and leers with artificial skill,
10   Till having lost in age the power to kill,
She sits all night at cards, and ogles at Spadille.
Such, through our lives the eventful history —
The fifth and last act still remains for me.
The bar-maid now for your protection prays,
15   Turns female Barrister, and pleads for Bayes.

EPILOGUE[1]

TO BE SPOKEN IN THE CHARACTER OF

TONY LUMPKIN

By J. CRADOCK, Esq.

WELL — now all's ended — and my comrades gone,
Pray what becomes of mother's nonly son?
A hopeful blade! — in town I'll fix my station,
And try to make a bluster in the nation;
As for my cousin Neville, I renounce her,   5
Off — in a crack — I'll carry big Bet Bouncer.

Why should not I in the great world appear?
I soon shall have a thousand pounds a year!
No matter what a man may here inherit,
In London — 'gad, they've some regard to spirit.   10
I see the horses prancing up the streets,
And big Bet Bouncer bobs to all she meets;
Then hoiks to jigs and pastimes ev'ry night —
Not to the play — they say it a'n't polite;
To Sadler's Wells perhaps, or operas go,   15
And once, by chance, to the *roratorio*.
Thus here and there, for ever up and down,
We'll set the fashions too to half the town;
And then at auctions — money ne'er regard,
Buy pictures like the great, ten pounds a yard: 20
Zounds, we shall make these London gentry say,
We know what's damn'd genteel as well as they.

[1] This came too late to be spoken.

THE RIVALS.

A COMEDY BY RICHARD BRINSLEY SHERIDAN

AS ACTED AT THE

THEATRE–ROYAL, COVENT–GARDEN

[First printed in 1775]

THE RIVALS

BY RICHARD BRINSLEY SHERIDAN

AUTHOR'S PREFACE

TO THE EDITION OF 1775.

A PREFACE to a play seems generally to be considered as a kind of closet-prologue, in which — if his piece had been successful — the author solicits that indulgence from the reader which he had before experienced from the audience : but as the scope and immediate object of a play is to please a mixed assembly in *representation* (whose judgment in the theatre at least is decisive), its degree of reputation is usually as determined as public, before it can be prepared for the cooler tribunal of the study. Thus any farther solicitude on the part of the writer becomes unnecessary at least, if not an intrusion : and if the piece has been condemned in the performance, I fear an address to the closet, like an appeal to posterity, is constantly regarded as the procrastination of a suit, from a consciousness of the weakness of the cause. From these considerations, the following comedy would certainly have been submitted to the reader, without any farther introduction than what it had in the representation, but that its success has probably been founded on a circumstance which the author is informed has not before attended a theatrical trial, and which consequently ought not to pass unnoticed.

I need scarcely add, that the circumstance alluded to was the withdrawing of the piece, to remove those imper-

fections in the first representation which were too obvious
to escape reprehension, and too numerous to admit of a
hasty correction. There are few writers, I believe, who,
even in the fullest consciousness of error, do not wish to
palliate the faults which they acknowledge; and, however
trifling the performance, to second their confession of its
deficiencies, by whatever plea seems least disgraceful to
their ability. In the present instance, it cannot be said
to amount either to candour or modesty in me, to acknowledge an extreme inexperience and want of judgment on
matters, in which, without guidance from practice, or spur
from success, a young man should scarcely boast of being
an adept. If it be said, that under such disadvantages
no one should attempt to write a play, I must beg leave to
dissent from the position, while the first point of experience
that I have gained on the subject is, a knowledge of the
candour and judgment with which an impartial public
distinguishes between the errors of inexperience and
incapacity, and the indulgence which it shows even to a
disposition to remedy the defects of either.

It were unnecessary to enter into any farther extenuation
of what was thought exceptionable in this play, but that
it has been said, that the managers should have prevented
some of the defects before its appearance to the public —
and in particular the uncommon length of the piece as
represented the first night. It were an ill return for the
most liberal and gentlemanly conduct on their side, to
suffer any censure to rest where none was deserved. Hurry
in writing has long been exploded as an excuse for an
author; — however, in the dramatic line, it may happen,
that both an author and a manager may wish to fill a chasm

in the entertainment of the public with a hastiness not altogether culpable. The season was advanced when I first put the play into Mr. Harris's hands: it was at that time at least double the length of any acting comedy. I profited by his judgment and experience in the curtailing of it — till, I believe, his feeling for the vanity of a young author got the better of his desire for correctness, and he left many excrescences remaining, because he had assisted in pruning so many more. Hence, though I was not uninformed that the acts were still too long, I flattered myself that, after the first trial, I might with safer judgment proceed to remove what should appear to have been most dissatisfactory. Many other errors there were, which might in part have arisen from my being by no means conversant with plays in general, either in reading or at the theatre. Yet I own that, in one respect, I did not regret my ignorance: for as my first wish in attempting a play was to avoid every appearance of plagiary, I thought I should stand a better chance of effecting this from being in a walk which I had not frequented, and where, consequently, the progress of invention was less likely to be interrupted by starts of recollection: for on subjects on which the mind has been much informed, invention is slow of exerting itself. Faded ideas float in the fancy like half-forgotten dreams; and the imagination in its fullest enjoyments becomes suspicious of its offspring, and doubts whether it has created or adopted.

With regard to some particular passages which on the first night's representation seemed generally disliked, I confess, that if I felt any emotion of surprise at the disapprobation, it was not that they were disapproved of,

but that I had not before perceived that they deserved it.
As some part of the attack on the piece was begun too
early to pass for the sentence of *judgment,* which is ever
tardy in condemning, it has been suggested to me, that
much of the disapprobation must have arisen from viru-
lence of malice, rather than severity of criticism: but as I
was more apprehensive of there being just grounds to
excite the latter than conscious of having deserved the
former, I continue not to believe that probable, which I
am sure must have been unprovoked. However, if it was
so, and I could even mark the quarter from whence it
came, it would be ungenerous to retort: for no passion
suffers more than malice from disappointment. For my
own part, I see no reason why the author of a play should
not regard a first night's audience as a candid and judicious
friend attending, in behalf of the public, at his last rehearsal. If he can dispense with flattery, he is sure at
least of sincerity, and even though the annotation be rude,
he may rely upon the justness of the comment. Considered in this light, that audience, whose *fiat* is essential
to the poet's claim, whether his object be fame or profit,
has surely a right to expect some deference to its opinion,
from principles of politeness at least, if not from gratitude.

As for the little puny critics, who scatter their peevish
strictures in private circles, and scribble at every author
who has the eminence of being unconnected with them, as
they are usually spleen-swoln from a vain idea of increasing
their consequence, there will always be found a petulance
and illiberality in their remarks, which should place them
as far beneath the notice of a gentleman, as their original

dulness had sunk them from the level of the most unsuccessful author.

It is not without pleasure that I catch at an opportunity of justifying myself from the charge of intending any national reflection in the character of Sir Lucius O'Trigger. If any gentleman opposed the piece from that idea, I thank them sincerely for their opposition; and if the condemnation of this comedy (however misconceived the provocation) could have added one spark to the decaying flame of national attachment to the country supposed to be reflected on, I should have been happy in its fate; and might with truth have boasted, that it had done more real service in its failure, than the successful morality of a thousand stage-novels will ever effect.

It is usual, I believe, to thank the performers in a new play, for the exertion of their several abilities. But where (as in this instance) their merit has been so striking and uncontroverted, as to call for the warmest and truest applause from a number of judicious audiences, the poet's after-praise comes like the feeble acclamation of a child to close the shouts of a multitude. The conduct, however, of the principals in a theatre cannot be so apparent to the public. I think it therefore but justice to declare, that from this theatre (the only one I can speak of from experience) those writers who wish to try the dramatic line will meet with that candour and liberal attention, which are generally allowed to be better calculated to lead genius into excellence, than either the precepts of judgment, or the guidance of experience.

THE AUTHOR.

PROLOGUE.

BY THE AUTHOR.

SPOKEN BY MR. WOODWARD AND MR. QUICK.

Enter SERJEANT-AT-LAW *and* ATTORNEY *following and
giving a paper.*

 Serj. What's here!—a vile cramp hand! I cannot
see
Without my spectacles.

 Att.   He means his fee.
Nay, Mr. Serjeant, good sir, try again. (*Gives money.*)

 Serj. The scrawl improves! (*more*) O come, 'tis
pretty plain.
5 Hey! how's this? Dibble!—sure it cannot be!
A poet's brief! a poet and a fee!

 Att. Yes, sir! though you without reward, I know,
Would gladly plead the Muse's cause.

 Serj.   So!—so!

 Att. And if the fee offends, your wrath should fall
10 On me.

 Serj. Dear Dibble, no offence at all.

 Att. Some sons of Phœbus in the courts we meet —

 Serj. And fifty sons of Phœbus in the Fleet!

 Att. Nor pleads he worse, who with a decent sprig
15 Of bays adorns his legal waste of wig.

 Serj. Full-bottomed heroes thus, on signs, unfurl

A leaf of laurel in a grove of curl!
Yet tell your client, that, in adverse days,
This wig is warmer than a bush of bays.

   Att. Do you, then, sir, my client's place supply,
Profuse of robe, and prodigal of tie —   5
Do you, with all those blushing powers of face,
And wonted bashful hesitating grace,
Rise in the court, and flourish on the case.   [*Exit.*

   Serj. For practice then suppose — this brief will
     show it, —
Me, Serjeant Woodward, — counsel for the poet.   10
Used to the ground, I know 'tis hard to deal
With this dread court, from whence there's no appeal;
No tricking here, to blunt the edge of law,
Or, damned in equity, escape by flaw:
But judgment given, your sentence must remain;   15
No writ of error lies — to Drury-lane:
Yet when so kind you seem, 'tis past dispute
We gain some favour, if not costs of suit.
No spleen is here! I see no hoarded fury; —
I think I never faced a milder jury!   20
Sad else our plight! where frowns are transportation,
A hiss the gallows, and a groan damnation!
But such the public candour, without fear
My client waives all right of challenge here.
No newsman from our session is dismissed,   25
Nor wit nor critic we scratch off the list;
His faults can never hurt another's ease,
His crime, at worst, a bad attempt to please:
Thus, all respecting, he appeals to all,
And by the general voice will stand or fall.   30

PROLOGUE.

BY THE AUTHOR.

SPOKEN ON THE TENTH NIGHT, BY MRS. BULKLEY.

Granted our cause, our suit and trial o'er,
The worthy serjeant need appear no more:
In pleasing I a different client choose,
He served the Poet — I would serve the Muse:
5 Like him, I'll try to merit your applause,
A female counsel in a female's cause.

   Look on this form,[1] — where humour, quaint and sly
Dimples the cheek, and points the beaming eye;
Where gay invention seems to boast its wiles
10 In amorous hint, and half-triumphant smiles;
While her light mask or covers satire's strokes,
Or hides the conscious blush her wit provokes.
Look on her well — does she seem formed to teach?
Should you expect to hear this lady preach?
15 Is grey experience suited to her youth?
Do solemn sentiments become that mouth?
Bid her be grave, those lips should rebel prove
To every theme that slanders mirth or love.

   Yet, thus adorned with every graceful art
20 To charm the fancy and yet reach the heart,
Must we displace her?   And instead advance

---

[1] Pointing to the figure of Comedy.

The goddess of the woful countenance —
The sentimental Muse! — Her emblems view,
The Pilgrim's Progress, and a sprig of rue!
View her — too chaste to look like flesh and blood —
Primly portrayed on emblematic wood!   5
There, fixed in usurpation, should she stand,
She'll snatch the dagger from her sister's hand:
And having made her votaries weep a flood,
Good heaven! she'll end her comedies in blood —
Bid Harry Woodward break poor Dunstal's crown!   10
Imprison Quick, and knock Ned Shuter down;
While sad Barsanti, weeping o'er the scene,
Shall stab herself — or poison Mrs. Green.

    Such dire encroachments to prevent in time,
Demands the critic's voice — the poet's rhyme.   15
Can our light scenes add strength to holy laws!
Such puny patronage but hurts the cause:
Fair virtue scorns our feeble aid to ask;
And moral truth disdains the trickster's mask.
For here their favourite stands,[1] whose brow severe   20
And sad, claims youth's respect, and pity's tear;
Who, when oppress'd by foes her worth creates,
Can point a poniard at the guilt she hates.

[1] Pointing to Tragedy.

DRAMATIS PERSONÆ.

AS ORIGINALLY ACTED AT COVENT-GARDEN THEATRE IN 1775.

SIR ANTHONY ABSOLUTE	*Mr. Shuter.*
CAPTAIN ABSOLUTE	*Mr. Woodward.*
FAULKLAND	*Mr. Lewis.*
ACRES	*Mr. Quick.*
SIR LUCIUS O'TRIGGER	*Mr. Lee.*
FAG	*Mr. Lee Lewes.*
DAVID	*Mr. Dunstal.*
THOMAS	*Mr. Fearon.*
MRS. MALAPROP	*Mrs. Green.*
LYDIA LANGUISH	*Miss Barsanti.*
JULIA	*Mrs. Bulkley.*
LUCY	*Mrs. Lessingham.*

Maid, Boy, Servants, &c.

SCENE : *Bath.*

Time of Action — Five Hours.

ACT I.

Scene I. A street.

Enter Thomas; *he crosses the stage;* Fag *follows, looking after him.*

Fag. What!   Thomas!   sure 'tis he? — What! Thomas! Thomas!

Thos. Hey! — Odd's life! Mr. Fag! — give us your hand, my old fellow-servant.

Fag. Excuse my glove, Thomas: — I'm devilish glad ₅ to see you, my lad. Why, my prince of charioteers, you look as hearty — but who the deuce thought of seeing you in Bath?

Thos. Sure, master, Madam Julia, Harry, Mrs. Kate, and the postillion, be all come.   ₁₀

Fag. Indeed!

Thos. Ay, master thought another fit of the gout was coming to make him a visit; — so he'd a mind to gi't the slip, and whip! we were all off at an hour's warning.

Fag. Ay, ay, hasty in every thing, or it would not be ₁₅ Sir Anthony Absolute!

Thos. But tell us, Mr. Fag, how does young master? Odd! Sir Anthony will stare to see the Captain here!

Fag. I do not serve Captain Absolute now.

Thos. Why sure!   ₂₀

Fag. At present I am employed by Ensign Beverley.

Thos. I doubt, Mr. Fag, you ha'n't changed for the better.

Fag. I have not changed, Thomas.

Thos. No! Why, didn't you say you had left young
5 master?

Fag. No. — Well, honest Thomas, I must puzzle you no farther: — briefly then — Captain Absolute and Ensign Beverley are one and the same person.

Thos. The devil they are!

10 *Fag.* So it is indeed, Thomas; and the ensign half of my master being on guard at present — the captain has nothing to do with me.

Thos. So, so! — What, this is some freak, I warrant! — Do tell us, Mr. Fag, the meaning o't — you know I ha'
15 trusted you.

Fag. You'll be secret, Thomas?

Thos. As a coach-horse.

Fag. Why then the cause of all this is — Love, — Love, Thomas, who, (as you may get read to you), has
20 been a masquerader ever since the days of Jupiter.

Thos. Ay, ay; — I guessed there was a lady in the case: — but pray, why does your master pass only for ensign? — Now if he had shammed general indeed —

Fag. Ah! Thomas, there lies the mystery o' the
25 matter. Hark'ee, Thomas, my master is in love with a lady of a very singular taste: a lady who likes him better as a half pay ensign than if she knew he was son and heir to Sir Anthony Absolute, a baronet of three thousand a year.

30 *Thos.* That is an odd taste indeed! — But has she got the stuff, Mr. Fag? Is she rich, hey?

Fag. Rich! — Why, I believe she owns half the stocks! Zounds! Thomas, she could pay the national debt as easily as I could my washer-woman! She has a lapdog that eats out of gold, — she feeds her parrot with small pearls, — and all her thread-papers are made of bank-notes.

Thos. Bravo, faith! — Odd! I warrant she has a set of thousands at least: — but does she draw kindly with the captain?

Fag. As fond as pigeons.

Thos. May one hear her name?

Fag. Miss Lydia Languish. — But there is an old tough aunt in the way; though, by the by, she has never seen my master — for we got acquainted with miss while on a visit in Gloucestershire.

Thos. Well — I wish they were once harnessed together in matrimony. — But pray, Mr. Fag, what kind of a place is this Bath? — I ha' heard a deal of it — here's a mort o' merry-making, hey?

Fag. Pretty well, Thomas, pretty well — 'tis a good lounge; in the morning we go to the pump-room (though neither my master nor I drink the waters); after breakfast we saunter on the parades, or play a game at billiards; at night we dance; but I'm tired of the place: their regular hours stupefy me — not a fiddle nor a card after eleven! — However, Mr. Faulkland's gentleman and I keep it up a little in private parties; — I'll introduce you there, Thomas — you'll like him much.

Thos. Sure I know Mr. Du-Peigne — you know his master is to marry Madam Julia.

Fag. I had forgot. — But, Thomas, you must polish

a little — indeed you must. — Here now — this wig! — What the devil do you do with a wig, Thomas? — None of the London whips of any degree of *ton* wear wigs now.

Thos. More's the pity! more's the pity, I say. — 5 Odd's life! when I heard how the lawyers and doctors had took to their own hair, I thought how 'twould go next: — odd rabbit it! when the fashion had got foot on the bar, I guessed 'twould mount to the box! — but 'tis all out of character, believe me, Mr. Fag: and look'ee, 10 I'll never gi' up mine — the lawyers and doctors may do as they will.

Fag. Well, Thomas, we'll not quarrel about that.

Thos. Why, bless you, the gentlemen of the professions ben't all of a mind — for in our village now, thoff Jack 15 Gauge, the exciseman, has ta'en to his carrots, there's little Dick the farrier swears he'll never forsake his bob, though all the college should appear with their own heads!

Fag. Indeed! well said, Dick! — But hold — mark! 20 mark! Thomas.

Thos. Zooks! 'tis the captain. — Is that the lady with him?

Fag. No, no, that is Madam Lucy, my master's mistress's maid. They lodge at that house — but I must 25 after him to tell him the news.

Thos. Odd! he's giving her money! — Well, Mr. Fag —

Fag. Good-bye, Thomas. I have an appointment in Gyde's Porch this evening at eight; meet me there, and 30 we'll make a little party.

[*Exeunt severally.*]

SCENE II. A DRESSING-ROOM IN MRS. MALAPROP'S LODG-
INGS.

LYDIA *sitting on a sofa, with a book in her hand.*
LUCY, *as just returned from a message.*

Lucy. Indeed, ma'am, I traversed half the town in
search of it: I don't believe there's a circulating library in
Bath I ha'n't been at.

Lyd. And could not you get *The Reward of Constancy?*

Lucy. No, indeed, ma'am.   5

Lyd. Nor *The Fatal Connection?*

Lucy. No, indeed, ma'am.

Lyd. Nor *The Mistakes of the Heart?*

Lucy. Ma'am, as ill luck would have it, Mr. Bull said
Miss Sukey Saunter had just fetched it away.   10

Lyd. Heigh-ho! — Did you inquire for *The Delicate
Distress?*

Lucy. Or, *The Memoirs of Lady Woodford?* Yes,
indeed, ma'am. I asked everywhere for it; and I might
have brought it from Mr. Frederick's but Lady Slattern   15
Lounger, who had just sent it home, had so soiled and
dog's-eared it, it wa'n't fit for a Christian to read.

Lyd. Heigh-ho! — Yes, I always know when Lady
Slattern has been before me. She has a most observing
thumb; and, I believe, cherishes her nails for the con-   20
venience of making marginal notes. — Well, child, what
have you brought me?

Lucy. Oh! here, ma'am. (*Taking books from under
her cloak, and from her pockets.*) This is *The Gordian Knot,*
— and this *Peregrine Pickle.* Here are *The Tears of* 25
Sensibility, and *Humphrey Clinker.* This is *The Memoirs*

117

of a Lady of Quality, written by herself, and here the second
volume of *The Sentimental Journey.*

Lyd. Heigh-ho! — What are those books by the glass?

Lucy. The great one is only *The Whole Duty of Man,*
5 where I press a few blonds, ma'am.

Lyd. Very well — give me the sal volatile.

Lucy. Is it in a blue cover, ma'am?

Lyd. My smelling-bottle, you simpleton!

Lucy. Oh, the drops! — here, ma'am.

10 *Lyd.* Hold! — here's some one coming — quick, see
who it is. (*Exit* LUCY.) Surely I heard my cousin
Julia's voice.

Reënter LUCY.

Lucy. Lud! ma'am, here is Miss Melville.

Lyd. Is it possible! —   [*Exit* LUCY.

Enter JULIA.

15 *Lyd.* My dearest Julia, how delighted am I! (*Embrace.*) How unexpected was this happiness!

Jul. True, Lydia — and our pleasure is the greater.
But what has been the matter? — you were denied to me
at first!

20 *Lyd.* Ah, Julia, I have a thousand things to tell you! —
But first inform me what has conjured you to Bath? —
Is Sir Anthony here?

Jul. He is — we are arrived within this hour! — and I
suppose he will be here to wait on Mrs. Malaprop as soon
25 as he is dressed.

Lyd. Then before we are interrupted, let me impart
to you some of my distress. — I know your gentle nature

will sympathize with me, though your prudence may condemn me. My letters have informed you of my whole connection with Beverley; but I have lost him, Julia! My aunt has discovered our intercourse by a note she intercepted, and has confined me ever since! Yet, would you 5 believe it? she has absolutely fallen in love with a tall Irish baronet she met one night since we have been here, at Lady Macshuffle's rout.

Jul. You jest, Lydia!

Lyd. No, upon my word. — She really carries on a kind 10 of correspondence with him, under a feigned name though, till she chooses to be known to him; — but it is a Delia or a Celia, I assure you.

Jul. Then, surely, she is now more indulgent to her niece.   15

Lyd. Quite the contrary. Since she has discovered her own frailty, she is become more suspicious of mine. Then I must inform you of another plague! — That odious Acres is to be in Bath to-day; so that I protest I shall be teased out of all spirits!   20

Jul. Come, come, Lydia, hope for the best — Sir Anthony shall use his interest with Mrs. Malaprop.

Lyd. But you have not heard the worst. Unfortunately I had quarrelled with my poor Beverley, just before my aunt made the discovery, and I have not seen 25 him since, to make it up.

Jul. What was his offence?

Lyd. Nothing at all! — But, I don't know how it was, as often as we had been together, we had never had a quarrel, and, somehow, I was afraid he would never give 30 me an opportunity. So, last Thursday, I wrote a letter to

myself, to inform myself that Beverley was at that time paying his addresses to another woman. I signed it *your friend unknown*, showed it to Beverley, charged him with his falsehood, put myself in a violent passion, and vowed
5 I'd never see him more.

Jul. And you let him depart so, and have not seen him since?

Lyd. 'Twas the next day my aunt found the matter out. I intended only to have teased him three days and a
10 half, and now I've lost him for ever.

Jul. If he is as deserving and sincere as you have represented him to me, he will never give you up so. Yet consider, Lydia, you tell me he is but an ensign, and you have thirty thousand pounds.

15 *Lyd.* But you know I lose most of my fortune if I marry without my aunt's consent, till of age; and that is what I have determined to do, ever since I knew the penalty. Nor could I love the man who would wish to wait a day for the alternative.

20 *Jul.* Nay, this is caprice!

Lyd. What, does Julia tax me with caprice? — I thought her lover Faulkland had inured her to it.

Jul. I do not love even his faults.

Lyd. But *apropos* — you have sent to him, I suppose?

25 *Jul.* Not yet, upon my word — nor has he the least idea of my being in Bath. Sir Anthony's resolution was so sudden, I could not inform him of it.

Lyd. Well, Julia, you are your own mistress (though under the protection of Sir Anthony), yet have you, for
30 this long year, been a slave to the caprice, the whim, the jealousy of this ungrateful Faulkland, who will ever delay

assuming the right of a husband, while you suffer him to be equally imperious as a lover.

Jul. Nay, you are wrong entirely. We were contracted before my father's death. That, and some consequent embarrassments, have delayed what I know 5 to be my Faulkland's most ardent wish. He is too generous to trifle on such a point : — and for his character, you wrong him there too. No, Lydia, he is too proud, too noble to be jealous; if he is captious, 'tis without dissembling; if fretful, without rudeness. Unused to the 10 fopperies of love, he is negligent of the little duties expected from a lover — but being unhackneyed in the passion, his affection is ardent and sincere; and as it engrosses his whole soul, he expects every thought and emotion of his mistress to move in unison with his. Yet, though his 15 pride calls for this full return, his humility makes him undervalue those qualities in him which would entitle him to it; and not feeling why he should be loved to the degree he wishes, he still suspects that he is not loved enough. This temper, I must own, has cost me many unhappy 20 hours; but I have learned to think myself his debtor, for those imperfections which arise from the ardour of his attachment.

Lyd. Well, I cannot blame you for defending him. But tell me candidly, Julia, had he never saved your life, 25 do you think you should have been attached to him as you are? — Believe me, the rude blast that overset your boat was a prosperous gale of love to him.

Jul. Gratitude may have strengthened my attachment to Mr. Faulkland, but I loved him before he had preserved 30 me; yet surely that alone were an obligation sufficient.

Lyd. Obligation! why a water spaniel would have done as much! — Well, I should never think of giving my heart to a man because he could swim.

Jul. Come, Lydia, you are too inconsiderate.

5 *Lyd.* Nay, I do but jest. — What's here?

Reënter LUCY *in a hurry.*

Lucy. O ma'am, here is Sir Anthony Absolute just come home with your aunt.

Lyd. They'll not come here. — Lucy, do you watch.
                                              [*Exit* LUCY.

Jul. Yet I must go. Sir Anthony does not know I am
10 here, and if we meet, he'll detain me, to show me the town. I'll take another opportunity of paying my respects to Mrs. Malaprop, when she shall treat me, as long as she chooses, with her select words so ingeniously misapplied, without being mispronounced.

Reënter LUCY.

15 *Lucy.* O Lud! ma'am, they are both coming upstairs.

Lyd. Well, I'll not detain you, coz. — Adieu, my dear Julia, I'm sure you are in haste to send to Faulkland. — There — through my room you'll find another staircase.

Jul. Adieu!   [*Embraces* LYDIA *and exit.*

20 *Lyd.* Here, my dear Lucy, hide these books. Quick, quick. — Fling *Peregrine Pickle* under the toilet — throw *Roderick Random* into the closet — put *The Innocent Adultery* into *The Whole Duty of Man* — thrust *Lord Aimworth* under the sofa — cram *Ovid* behind the bolster —
25 there — put *The Man of Feeling* into your pocket, — so, so — now lay *Mrs. Chapone* in sight, and leave *Fordyce's Sermons* open on the table.

Lucy. O burn it, ma'am! the hairdresser has torn away as far as *Proper Pride.*

Lyd. Never mind — open at *Sobriety.* — Fling me *Lord Chesterfield's Letters.* — Now for 'em.   [*Exit* LUCY.

Enter MRS. MALAPROP, *and* SIR ANTHONY ABSOLUTE.

Mrs. Mal. There, Sir Anthony, there sits the deliberate 5 simpleton who wants to disgrace her family, and lavish herself on a fellow not worth a shilling.

Lyd. Madam, I thought you once —

Mrs. Mal. You thought, miss! I don't know any business you have to think at all — thought does not 10 become a young woman. But the point we would request of you is, that you will promise to forget this fellow — to illiterate him, I say, quite from your memory.

Lyd. Ah, madam! our memories are independent of our wills. It is not so easy to forget.   15

Mrs. Mal. But I say it is, miss; there is nothing on earth so easy as to forget, if a person chooses to set about it. I'm sure I have as much forgot your poor dear uncle as if he had never existed — and I thought it my duty so to do; and let me tell you, Lydia, these violent memories don't 20 become a young woman.

Sir Anth. Why sure she won't pretend to remember what she's ordered not! — ay, this comes of her reading!

Lyd. What crime, madam, have I committed, to be treated thus?   25

Mrs. Mal. Now don't attempt to extirpate yourself from the matter; you know I have proof controvertible of it. — But tell me, will you promise to do as you're bid? Will you take a husband of your friends' choosing?

Lyd. Madam, I must tell you plainly, that had I no preference for any one else, the choice you have made would be my aversion.

Mrs. Mal. What business have you, miss, with pref-
5 erence and aversion? They don't become a young woman; and you ought to know, that as both always wear off, 'tis safest in matrimony to begin with a little aversion. I am sure I hated your poor dear uncle before marriage as if he had been a blackamoor — and yet, miss, you are
10 sensible what a wife I made! — and when it pleased Heaven to release me from him, 'tis unknown what tears I shed! — But suppose we were going to give you another choice, will you promise us to give up this Beverley?

Lyd. Could I belie my thoughts so far as to give that
15 promise, my actions would certainly as far belie my words.

Mrs. Mal. Take yourself to your room. — You are fit company for nothing but your own ill-humours.

Lyd. Willingly, ma'am — I cannot change for the worse.   [*Exit.*

20 *Mrs. Mal.* There's a little intricate hussy for you!

Sir Anth. It is not to be wondered at, ma'am, — all this is the natural consequence of teaching girls to read. Had I a thousand daughters, by Heaven! I'd as soon have them taught the black art as their alphabet!

25 *Mrs. Mal.* Nay, nay, Sir Anthony, you are an absolute misanthropy.

Sir Anth. In my way hither, Mrs. Malaprop, I observed your niece's maid coming forth from a circulating library! — She had a book in each hand — They were half-bound
30 volumes, with marble covers! — From that moment I guessed how full of duty I should see her mistress!

MRS. MALAPROP AND SIR ANTHONY ABSOLUTE
"Nay, nay, Sir Anthony, you are an absolute misanthropy."

Mrs. Mal. Those are vile places, indeed!

Sir Anth. Madam, a circulating library in a town is as
an evergreen tree of diabolical knowledge! It blossoms
through the year! — And depend on it, Mrs. Malaprop,
that they who are so fond of handling the leaves, will long 5
for the fruit at last.

Mrs. Mal. Fy, fy, Sir Anthony! you surely speak
laconically.

Sir Anth. Why, Mrs. Malaprop, in moderation now,
what would you have a woman know?   10

Mrs. Mal. Observe me, Sir Anthony. I would by no
means wish a daughter of mine to be a progeny of learning;
I don't think so much learning becomes a young woman:
for instance, I would never let her meddle with Greek, or
Hebrew, or algebra, or simony, or fluxions, or paradoxes, or 15
such inflammatory branches of learning — neither would
it be necessary for her to handle any of your mathematical,
astronomical, diabolical instruments. — But, Sir Anthony,
I would send her, at nine years old, to a boarding-school,
in order to learn a little ingenuity and artifice. Then, sir, 20
she should have a supercilious knowledge in accounts; —
and as she grew up, I would have her instructed in geometry, that she might know something of the contagious
countries; — but above all, Sir Anthony, she should be
mistress of orthodoxy, that she might not mis-spell, and 25
mis-pronounce words so shamefully as girls usually do;
and likewise that she might reprehend the true meaning of
what she is saying. This, Sir Anthony, is what I would
have a woman know; — and I don't think there is a superstitious article in it.   30

Sir Anth. Well, well, Mrs. Malaprop, I will dispute

the point no further with you; though I must confess, that you are a truly moderate and polite arguer, for almost every third word you say is on my side of the question. But, Mrs. Malaprop, to the more important point in
5 debate — you say you have no objection to my proposal?

Mrs. Mal.   None, I assure you.   I am under no positive engagement with Mr. Acres, and as Lydia is so obstinate against him, perhaps your son may have better success.

Sir Anth.   Well, madam, I will write for the boy directly.
10 He knows not a syllable of this yet, though I have for some time had the proposal in my head.   He is at present with his regiment.

Mrs. Mal.   We have never seen your son, Sir Anthony; but I hope no objection on his side.

15 *Sir Anth.*   Objection! — let him object if he dare! — No, no, Mrs. Malaprop, Jack knows that the least demur puts me in a frenzy directly.   My process was always very simple — in their younger days, 'twas "Jack, do this"; — if he demurred, I knocked him down — and if he grumbled
20 at that, I always sent him out of the room.

Mrs. Mal.   Ay, and the properest way, o' my conscience! — nothing is so conciliating to young people as severity. — Well, Sir Anthony, I shall give Mr. Acres his discharge, and prepare Lydia to receive your son's in-
25 vocations; — and I hope you will represent her to the captain as an object not altogether illegible.

Sir Anth.   Madam, I will handle the subject prudently. — Well, I must leave you; and let me beg you, Mrs. Malaprop, to enforce this matter roundly to the girl. —
30 Take my advice — keep a tight hand: if she rejects this proposal, clap her under lock and key; and if you were just

to let the servants forget to bring her dinner for three or four days, you can't conceive how she'd come about.

Mrs. Mal. Well, at any rate I shall be glad to get her from under my intuition. She has somehow discovered my partiality for Sir Lucius O'Trigger — sure, Lucy can't have betrayed me! — No, the girl is such a simpleton, I should have made her confess it. — Lucy! — Lucy! — (*Calls.*) Had she been one of your artificial ones, I should never have trusted her.

Reënter LUCY.

Lucy. Did you call, ma'am?

Mrs. Mal. Yes, girl. — Did you see Sir Lucius while you was out?

Lucy. No, indeed, ma'am, not a glimpse of him.

Mrs. Mal. You are sure, Lucy, that you never mentioned —

Lucy. Oh gemini! I'd sooner cut my tongue out.

Mrs. Mal. Well, don't let your simplicity be imposed on.

Lucy. No, ma'am.

Mrs. Mal. So, come to me presently, and I'll give you another letter to Sir Lucius; but mind, Lucy — if ever you betray what you are entrusted with (unless it be other people's secrets to me), you forfeit my malevolence for ever; and your being a simpleton shall be no excuse for your locality. [*Exit.*

Lucy. Ha! ha! ha! — So, my dear Simplicity, let me give you a little respite. (*Altering her manner.*) Let girls in my station be as fond as they please of appearing expert and knowing in their trusts; commend me to a mask of silliness, and a pair of sharp eyes for my own interest under it! — Let me see to what account have I turned my simplicity lately. (*Looks at a paper.*) For *abetting Miss Lydia Languish in a design of running away* *with an ensign! — in money, sundry times, twelve pound twelve; gowns, five; hats, ruffles, caps, etc., numberless! — From the said ensign, within this last month, six guineas and a half.* — About a quarter's pay! — Item, *from Mrs. Malaprop, for betraying the young people to her* — when I found matters were likely to be discovered — *two guineas, and a black paduasoy.* — Item, *from Mr. Acres, for carrying divers letters* — which I never delivered — *two guineas, and a pair of buckles.* — Item, *from Sir Lucius O'Trigger, three crowns, two gold pocket-pieces, and a silver snuff-box!* — Well done, Simplicity! — Yet I was forced to make my Hibernian believe, that he was corresponding, not with the aunt, but with the niece: for though not over rich, I found he had too much pride and delicacy to sacrifice the feelings of a gentleman to the necessities of his fortune. [*Exit.*

ACT II.

SCENE I. CAPTAIN ABSOLUTE'S LODGINGS.

CAPTAIN ABSOLUTE *and* FAG.

Fag. Sir, while I was there Sir Anthony came in: I told him, you had sent me to inquire after his health, and to know if he was at leisure to see you.

Abs. And what did he say, on hearing I was at Bath?

Fag. Sir, in my life I never saw an elderly gentleman 5 more astonished! He started back two or three paces, rapped out a dozen interjectural oaths, and asked, what the devil had brought you here.

Abs. Well, sir, and what did you say?

Fag. Oh, I lied, sir — I forget the precise lie; but you 10 may depend on't, he got no truth from me. Yet, with submission, for fear of blunders in future, I should be glad to fix what has brought us to Bath; in order that we may lie a little consistently. Sir Anthony's servants were curious, sir, very curious indeed. 15

Abs. You have said nothing to them?

Fag. Oh, not a word, sir, — not a word! Mr. Thomas, indeed, the coachman (whom I take to be the discreetest of whips) —

Abs. 'Sdeath! — you rascal! you have not trusted 20 him!

Fag. Oh, no, sir — no — no — not a syllable, upon my veracity! — He was, indeed, a little inquisitive; but

129

I was sly, sir — devilish sly! My master (said I), honest
Thomas (you know, sir, one says honest to one's inferiors),
is come to Bath to recruit — Yes, sir, I said to recruit —
and whether for men, money, or constitution, you know,
5 sir, is nothing to him, nor any one else.

Abs. Well, recruit will do — let it be so.

Fag. Oh, sir, recruit will do surprisingly — indeed,
to give the thing an air, I told Thomas, that your honour
had already enlisted five disbanded chairmen, seven
10 minority waiters, and thirteen billiard-makers.

Abs. You blockhead, never say more than is necessary.

Fag. I beg pardon, sir — I beg pardon — but, with
submission, a lie is nothing unless one supports it. Sir,
whenever I draw on my invention for a good current lie,
15 I always forge indorsements as well as the bill.

Abs. Well, take care you don't hurt your credit, by
offering too much security. — Is Mr. Faulkland returned?

Fag. He is above, sir, changing his dress.

Abs. Can you tell whether he has been informed of
20 Sir Anthony and Miss Melville's arrival?

Fag. I fancy not, sir; he has seen no one since he came
in but his gentleman, who was with him at Bristol. — I
think, sir, I hear Mr. Faulkland coming down —

Abs. Go, tell him I am here.

25 *Fag.* Yes, sir. (*Going.*) I beg pardon, sir, but
should Sir Anthony call, you will do me the favour to
remember that we are recruiting, if you please.

Abs. Well, well.

Fag. And, in tenderness to my character, if your
30 honour could bring in the chairmen and waiters, I should
esteem it as an obligation; for though I never scruple a

lie to serve my master, yet it hurts one's conscience to be
found out.   [*Exit.*

Abs. Now for my whimsical friend — if he does not
know that his mistress is here, I'll tease him a little before
I tell him —   5

Enter FAULKLAND.

Faulkland, you're welcome to Bath again; you are
punctual in your return.

Faulk. Yes; I had nothing to detain me, when I had
finished the business I went on. Well, what news since I
left you? how stand matters between you and Lydia?   10

Abs. Faith, much as they were; I have not seen her
since our quarrel; however, I expect to be recalled every
hour.

Faulk. Why don't you persuade her to go off with you
at once?   15

Abs. What, and lose two-thirds of her fortune? you
forget that, my friend. — No, no, I could have brought her
to that long ago.

Faulk. Nay then, you trifle too long — if you are sure
of her, propose to the aunt in your own character, and 20
write to Sir Anthony for his consent.

Abs. Softly, softly; for though I am convinced my
little Lydia would elope with me as Ensign Beverley, yet
am I by no means certain that she would take me with the
impediment of our friends' consent, a regular humdrum 25
wedding, and the reversion of a good fortune on my side:
no, no; I must prepare her gradually for the discovery, and
make myself necessary to her before I risk it. — Well, but,
Faulkland, you'll dine with us to-day at the hotel?

Faulk. Indeed I cannot; I am not in spirits to be of such a party.

Abs. By Heavens! I shall forswear your company. You are the most teasing, captious, incorrigible lover! — 5 Do love like a man.

Faulk. I own I am unfit for company.

Abs. Am not I a lover; ay, and a romantic one too? Yet do I carry every where with me such a confounded farrago of doubts, fears, hopes, wishes, and all the flimsy 10 furniture of a country miss's brain?

Faulk. Ah! Jack, your heart and soul are not, like mine, fixed immutably on one only object. You throw for a large stake, but losing, you could stake and throw again: — but I have set my sum of happiness on this cast, 15 and not to succeed, were to be stripped of all.

Abs. But, for Heaven's sake! what grounds for apprehension can your whimsical brain conjure up at present?

Faulk. What grounds for apprehension, did you say? Heavens! are there not a thousand! I fear for her spirits 20 — her health — her life. — My absence may fret her; her anxiety for my return, her fears for me may oppress her gentle temper: and for her health, does not every hour bring me cause to be alarmed? If it rains, some shower may even then have chilled her delicate frame! If the 25 wind be keen, some rude blast may have affected her! The heat of noon, the dews of the evening, may endanger the life of her, for whom only I value mine. O Jack! when delicate and feeling souls are separated, there is not a feature in the sky, not a movement of the elements, 30 not an aspiration of the breeze, but hints some cause for a lover's apprehension!

Abs. Ay, but we may choose whether we will take the hint or not. — So, then, Faulkland, if you were convinced that Julia were well and in spirits, you would be entirely content?

Faulk. I should be happy beyond measure — I am anxious only for that.

Abs. Then to cure your anxiety at once — Miss Melville is in perfect health, and is at this moment in Bath.

Faulk. Nay, Jack — don't trifle with me.

Abs. She is arrived here with my father within this hour.

Faulk. Can you be serious?

Abs. I thought you knew Sir Anthony better than to be surprised at a sudden whim of this kind. — Seriously, then, it is as I tell you — upon my honour.

Faulk. My dear friend! — Hollo, Du-Peigne! my hat. — My dear Jack — now nothing on earth can give me a moment's uneasiness.

Reënter FAG.

Fag. Sir, Mr. Acres, just arrived, is below.

Abs. Stay, Faulkland, this Acres lives within a mile of Sir Anthony, and he shall tell you how your mistress has been ever since you left her. — Fag, show the gentleman up. [*Exit* FAG.

Faulk. What, is he much acquainted in the family?

Abs. Oh, very intimate: I insist on your not going: besides, his character will divert you.

Faulk. Well, I should like to ask him a few questions.

Abs. He is likewise a rival of mine — that is, of my other self's, for he does not think his friend Captain

Absolute ever saw the lady in question; and it is ridiculous enough to hear him complain to me of one Beverley, a concealed skulking rival, who —

Faulk. Hush! — he's here.

Enter ACRES.

5   *Acres.* Ha! my dear friend, noble captain, and honest Jack, how do'st thou? just arrived, faith, as you see. — Sir, your humble servant. — Warm work on the roads. Jack! — Odds whips and wheels! I've travelled like a comet, with a tail of dust all the way as long as the Mall.

10   *Abs.* Ah! Bob, you are indeed an eccentric planet, but we know your attraction hither. — Give me leave to introduce Mr. Faulkland to you; Mr. Faulkland, Mr. Acres.

Acres. Sir, I am most heartily glad to see you: sir, 15 I solicit your connections. — Hey, Jack — what, this is Mr. Faulkland, who —

Abs. Ay, Bob, Miss Melville's Mr. Faulkland.

Acres. Odso! she and your father can be but just arrived before me: — I suppose you have seen them. Ah! 20 Mr. Faulkland, you are indeed a happy man.

Faulk. I have not seen Miss Melville yet, sir; — I hope she enjoyed full health and spirits in Devonshire?

Acres. Never knew her better in my life, sir, — never better. Odds blushes and blooms! she has been as healthy 25 as the German Spa.

Faulk. Indeed! — I did hear that she had been a little indisposed.

Acres. False, false, sir — only said to vex you: quite the reverse, I assure you.

Faulk. There, Jack, you see she has the advantage of me; I had almost fretted myself ill.

Abs. Now are you angry with your mistress for not having been sick?

Faulk. No, no, you misunderstand me: yet surely a ₅ little trifling indisposition is not an unnatural consequence of absence from those we love. — Now confess — isn't there something unkind in this violent, robust, unfeeling health?

Abs. Oh, it was very unkind of her to be well in your ₁₀ absence, to be sure!

Acres. Good apartments, Jack.

Faulk. Well, sir, but you was saying that Miss Melville has been so exceedingly well — what, then, she has been merry and gay, I suppose? — Always in spirits — hey? ₁₅

Acres. Merry, odds crickets! she has been the belle and spirit of the company wherever she has been — so lively and entertaining! so full of wit and humour!

Faulk. There, Jack, there. — Oh, by my soul! there is an innate levity in woman, that nothing can overcome. — ₂₀ What! happy, and I away!

Abs. Have done. — How foolish this is! just now you were only apprehensive for your mistress' spirits.

Faulk. Why, Jack, have I been the joy and spirit of the company? ₂₅

Abs. No indeed, you have not.

Faulk. Have I been lively and entertaining?

Abs. Oh, upon my word, I acquit you.

Faulk. Have I been full of wit and humour?

Abs. No, faith, to do you justice, you have been ₃₀ confoundedly stupid indeed.

Acres. What's the matter with the gentleman?

Abs. He is only expressing his great satisfaction at hearing that Julia has been so well and happy — that's all — hey, Faulkland?

5 *Faulk.* Oh! I am rejoiced to hear it — yes, yes, she has a happy disposition!

Acres. That she has indeed. — Then she is so accomplished — so sweet a voice — so expert at her harpsichord — such a mistress of flat and sharp, squallante, 10 rumblante, and quiverante! — There was this time month — odds minims and crochets! how she did chirrup at Mrs. Piano's concert!

Faulk. There again, what say you to this? You see she has been all mirth and song — not a thought 15 of me!

Abs. Pho! man, is not music the food of love?

Faulk. Well, well, it may be so. — Pray, Mr. — , what's his damned name? — Do you remember what songs Miss Melville sung?

20 *Acres.* Not I indeed.

Abs. Stay, now, they were some pretty melancholy purling-stream airs, I warrant; perhaps you may recollect; — did she sing, *When absent from my soul's delight?*

Acres. No, that wa'n't it.

25 *Abs.* Or, *Go, gentle gales!* [*Sings.*

Acres. Oh, no! nothing like it. Odds! now I recollect one of them — *My heart's my own, my will is free.* [*Sings.*

Faulk. Fool! fool that I am! to fix all my happiness on such a trifler! 'Sdeath! to make herself the pipe and 30 balladmonger of a circle! to soothe her light heart with catches and glees! — What can you say to this, sir?

Abs. Why, that I should be glad to hear my mistress had been so merry, sir.

Faulk. Nay, nay, nay — I'm not sorry that she has been happy — no, no, I am glad of that — I would not have her sad or sick — yet surely a sympathetic heart would have shown itself even in the choice of a song — she might have been temperately healthy, and somehow, plaintively gay; — but she has been dancing too, I doubt not!

Acres. What does the gentleman say about dancing?

Abs. He says the lady we speak of dances as well as she sings.

Acres. Ay, truly, does she — there was at our last race ball —

Faulk. There! — there — I told you so! I told you so! Oh! she thrives in my absence! — Dancing! but her whole feelings have been in opposition with mine; — I have been anxious, silent, pensive, sedentary — my days have been hours of care, my nights of watchfulness. — She has been all health! spirit! laugh! song! dance! —

Abs. For Heaven's sake, Faulkland, don't expose yourself so! — Suppose she has danced, what then? — does not the ceremony of society often oblige —

Faulk. Well, well, I'll contain myself — perhaps as you say — for form's sake. — What, Mr. Acres, you were praising Miss Melville's manner of dancing a minuet — hey?

Acres. Oh, I dare insure her for that — but what I was going to speak of was her country-dancing. Odds swimmings! she has such an air with her!

Faulk. Now disappointment on her! — Defend this,

Absolute; why don't you defend this? — Country-dances! jigs and reels! am I to blame now? A minuet I could have forgiven — I should not have minded that — I say I should not have regarded a minuet — but country-dances! — Zounds! had she made one in a cotillon — I believe I could have forgiven even that — but to be monkey-led for a night! — to run the gauntlet through a string of amorous palming puppies! — to show paces like a managed filly! — Oh, Jack, there never can be but one man in the world whom a truly modest and delicate woman ought to pair with in a country-dance; and, even then, the rest of the couples should be her great-uncles and aunts!

Abs. Ay, to be sure! — grandfathers and grand-mothers!

Faulk. If there be but one vicious mind in the set, 'twill spread like a contagion — the action of their pulse beats to the lascivious movement of the jig — their quivering, warm-breathed sighs impregnate the very air — the atmosphere becomes electrical to love, and each amor-ous spark darts through every link of the chain! — I must leave you — I own I am somewhat flurried — and that confounded looby has perceived it. [*Going.*

Abs. Nay, but stay, Faulkland, and thank Mr. Acres for his good news.

Faulk. Damn his news! [*Exit.*

Abs. Ha! ha! ha! poor Faulkland five minutes since — "nothing on earth could give him a moment's un-easiness!"

Acres. The gentleman wa'n't angry at my praising his mistress, was he?

Abs. A little jealous, I believe, Bob.

CAPTAIN JACK ABSOLUTE
"Ay, to be sure! — grandfathers and grandmothers!"

Acres. You don't say so? Ha! ha! jealous of me —
that's a good joke.

Abs. There's nothing strange in that, Bob; let me tell
you, that sprightly grace and insinuating manner of yours
will do some mischief among the girls here.   5

Acres. Ah! you joke — ha! ha! mischief — ha! ha!
but you know I am not my own property, my dear Lydia
has forestalled me. She could never abide me in the
country, because I used to dress so badly — but odds
frogs and tambours! I shan't take matters so here, now 10
ancient madam has no voice in it, I'll make my old clothes
know who's master. I shall straightway cashier the
hunting-frock, and render my leather breeches incapable.
My hair has been in training some time.

Abs. Indeed!   15

Acres. Ay — and thoff the side curls are a little restive,
my hind-part takes it very kindly.

Abs. Oh, you'll polish, I doubt not.

Acres. Absolutely I propose so — then if I can find
out this Ensign Beverley, odds triggers and flints! I'll 20
make him know the difference o't.

Abs. Spoke like a man! But pray, Bob, I observe
you have got an odd kind of a new method of swearing —

Acres. Ha! ha! you've taken notice of it — 'tis
genteel, isn't it! — I didn't invent it myself though; but 25
a commander in our militia, a great scholar, I assure you,
says that there is no meaning in the common oaths, and
that nothing but their antiquity makes them respectable;
— because, he says, the ancients would never stick to an
oath or two, but would say, by Jove! or by Bacchus! or 30
by Mars! or by Venus! or by Pallas, according to the

sentiment: so that to swear with propriety, says my little
major, the oath should be an echo to the sense; and this
we call the *oath referential* or *sentimental swearing* — ha!
ha! 'tis genteel, isn't it?

5   *Abs.*   Very genteel, and very new, indeed! — and I
dare say will supplant all other figures of imprecation.

Acres.   Ay, ay, the best terms will grow obsolete —-
Damns have had their day.

Reënter FAG.

Fag.   Sir, there is a gentleman below desires to see
10 you. — Shall I show him into the parlour?

Abs.   Ay, you may.

Acres.   Well, I must be gone —

Abs.   Stay; who is it, Fag?

Fag.   Your father, sir.

15 *Abs.*   You puppy, why didn't you show him up directly?
[*Exit* FAG.

Acres.   You have business with Sir Anthony. — I
expect a message from Mrs. Malaprop at my lodgings.
I have sent also to my dear friend Sir Lucius O'Trigger.
Adieu, Jack! we must meet at night, when you shall give
20 me a dozen bumpers to little Lydia.

Abs.   That I will with all my heart. — [*Exit* ACRES.
Now for a parental lecture — I hope he has heard nothing
of the business that has brought me here — I wish the
gout had held him fast in Devonshire, with all my soul!

Enter SIR ANTHONY ABSOLUTE.

25 Sir, I am delighted to see you here, looking so well! your
sudden arrival at Bath made me apprehensive for your
health.

Sir Anth. Very apprehensive, I dare say, Jack. — What, you are recruiting here, hey?

Abs. Yes, sir, I am on duty.

Sir Anth. Well, Jack, I am glad to see you, though I did not expect it, for I was going to write to you on a little 5 matter of business. — Jack, I have been considering that I grow old and infirm, and shall probably not trouble you long.

Abs. Pardon me, sir, I never saw you look more strong and hearty; and I pray frequently that you may continue 10 so.

Sir Anth. I hope your prayers may be heard, with all my heart. Well, then, Jack, I have been considering that I am so strong and hearty I may continue to plague you a long time. Now, Jack, I am sensible that the income of 15 your commission, and what I have hitherto allowed you, is but a small pittance for a lad of your spirit.

Abs. Sir, you are very good.

Sir Anth. And it is my wish, while yet I live, to have my boy make some figure in the world. I have resolved, 20 therefore, to fix you at once in a noble independence.

Abs. Sir, your kindness overpowers me — such generosity makes the gratitude of reason more lively than the sensations even of filial affection.

Sir Anth. I am glad you are so sensible of my attention 25 — and you shall be master of a large estate in a few weeks.

Abs. Let my future life, sir, speak my gratitude; I cannot express the sense I have of your munificence. — — Yet, sir, I presume you would not wish me to quit the army? 30

Sir Anth. Oh, that shall be as your wife chooses.

Abs. My wife, sir!

Sir Anth. Ay, ay, settle that between you — settle that between you.

Abs. A wife, sir, did you say?

5 *Sir Anth.* Ay, a wife — why, did not I mention her before?

Abs. Not a word of her, sir.

Sir Anth. Odd so! — I mustn't forget her though. — Yes, Jack, the independence I was talking of is by a
10 marriage — the fortune is saddled with a wife — but I suppose that makes no difference.

Abs. Sir! sir! — you amaze me!

Sir Anth. Why, what's the matter with the fool? Just now you were all gratitude and duty.

15 *Abs.* I was, sir, — you talked to me of independence and a fortune, but not a word of a wife.

Sir Anth. Why — what difference does that make? Odds life, sir! if you have the estate you must take it with the live stock on it, as it stands.

20 *Abs.* If my happiness is to be the price, I must beg leave to decline the purchase. — Pray, sir, who is the lady?

Sir Anth. What's that to you, sir? — Come, give me your promise to love, and to marry her directly.

25 *Abs.* Sure, sir, this is not very reasonable, to summon my affections for a lady I know nothing of!

Sir Anth. I am sure, sir, 'tis more unreasonable in you to object to a lady you know nothing of.

Abs. Then, sir, I must tell you plainly that my in-
30 clinations are fixed on another — my heart is engaged to an angel.

Sir Anth. Then pray let it send an excuse. It is very sorry — but business prevents its waiting on her.

Abs. But my vows are pledged to her.

Sir Anth. Let her foreclose, Jack; let her foreclose; they are not worth redeeming; besides, you have the 5 angel's vows in exchange, I suppose; so there can be no loss there.

Abs. You must excuse me, sir, if I tell you, once for all, that in this point I cannot obey you.

Sir Anth. Hark'ee, Jack; I have heard you for some 10 time with patience — I have been cool — quite cool; but take care — you know I am compliance itself — when I am not thwarted; — no one more easily led — when I have my own way; — but don't put me in a frenzy.

Abs. Sir, I must repeat it — in this I cannot obey you. 15

Sir Anth. Now damn me! if ever I call you Jack again while I live!

Abs. Nay, sir, but hear me.

Sir Anth. Sir, I won't hear a word — not a word! not one word! so give me your promise by a nod — and 20 I'll tell you what, Jack — I mean, you dog — if you don't, by —

Abs. What, sir, promise to link myself to some mass of ugliness! to —

Sir Anth. Zounds! sirrah! the lady shall be as ugly 25 as I choose: she shall have a lump on each shoulder; she shall be as crooked as the Crescent; her one eye shall roll like the bull's in Cox's Museum; she shall have a skin like a mummy, and the beard of a Jew — she shall be all this, sirrah! — yet I will make you ogle her all day, and sit 30 up all night to write sonnets on her beauty.

Abs. This is reason and moderation indeed!

Sir Anth. None of your sneering, puppy! no grinning, jackanapes!

Abs. Indeed, sir, I never was in a worse humour for
5 mirth in my life.

Sir Anth. 'Tis false, sir, I know you are laughing in your sleeve; I know you'll grin when I am gone, sirrah!

Abs. Sir, I hope I know my duty better.

Sir Anth. None of your passion, sir! none of your
10 violence, if you please! — It won't do with me, I promise you.

Abs. Indeed, sir, I never was cooler in my life.

Sir Anth. 'Tis a confounded lie! — I know you are in a passion in your heart; I know you are, you hypocritical
15 young dog! but it won't do.

Abs. Nay, sir, upon my word —

Sir Anth. So you will fly out! can't you be cool like me? What the devil good can passion do? — Passion is of no service, you impudent, insolent, overbearing rep-
20 robate! — There, you sneer again! don't provoke me! — but you rely upon the mildness of my temper — you do, you dog! you play upon the meekness of my disposition! — Yet take care — the patience of a saint may be overcome at last! — but mark! I give you six hours and a half to
25 consider of this: if you then agree, without any condition, to do everything on earth that I choose, why — confound you! I may in time forgive you. — If not, zounds! don't enter the same hemisphere with me! don't dare to breathe the same air, or use the same light with me;
30 but get an atmosphere and a sun of your own! I'll strip you of your commission; I'll lodge a five-and-threepence

in the hands of trustees, and you shall live on the interest.
— I'll disown you, I'll disinherit you, I'll unget you! and
damn me! if ever I call you Jack again!   [*Exit.*

Abs. Mild, gentle, considerate father — I kiss your
hands! What a tender method of giving his opinion in 5
these matters Sir Anthony has! I dare not trust him with
the truth. — I wonder what old wealthy hag it is that he
wants to bestow on me! — Yet he married himself for love!
and was in his youth a bold intriguer, and a gay companion!   10

Reënter FAG.

Fag. Assuredly, sir, your father is wroth to a degree;
he comes down stairs eight or ten steps at a time —
muttering, growling, and thumping the banisters all the
way: I and the cook's dog stand bowing at the door —
rap! he gives me a stroke on the head with his cane; bids 15
me carry that to my master; then kicking the poor turnspit into the area, damns us all, for a puppy triumvirate! —
Upon my credit, sir, were I in your place, and found my
father such very bad company, I should certainly drop his
acquaintance.   20

Abs. Cease your impertinence, sir, at present. —
Did you come in for nothing more? — Stand out of the
way!   [*Pushes him aside and exit.*

Fag. So! Sir Anthony trims my master: he is afraid
to reply to his father — then vents his spleen on poor Fag! 25
When one is vexed by one person, to revenge one's self
on another, who happens to come in the way, is the
vilest injustice! Ah! it shows the worst temper — the
basest —

Enter BOY.

Boy. Mr. Fag; Mr. Fag! your master calls you.

Fag. Well, you little dirty puppy, you need not bawl so! — The meanest disposition! the —

Boy. Quick, quick, Mr. Fag!

5 *Fag.* Quick! quick! you impudent jackanapes! am I to be commanded by you too? you little impertinent, insolent, kitchen-bred —

[*Exit kicking and beating him.*

SCENE II. THE NORTH PARADE.

Enter LUCY.

Lucy. So — I shall have another rival to add to my mistress' list — Captain Absolute. However, I shall not 10 enter his name till my purse has received notice in form. Poor Acres is dismissed! — Well, I have done him a last friendly office, in letting him know that Beverley was here before him. — Sir Lucius is generally more punctual, when he expects to hear from his *dear Dalia*, as he calls her: I 15 wonder he's not here! — I have a little scruple of conscience from this deceit; though I should not be paid so well, if my hero knew that Delia was near fifty, and her own mistress.

Enter SIR LUCIUS O'TRIGGER.

Sir Luc. Ha! my little ambassadress — upon my 20 conscience, I have been looking for you; I have been on the South Parade this half hour.

Lucy. (*Speaking simply.*) O gemini! and I have been waiting for your worship here on the North.

Sir Luc. Faith! — may be that was the reason we did not meet; and it is very comical too, how you could go out and I not see you — for I was only taking a nap at the Parade Coffee-house, and I chose the window on purpose that I might not miss you.

Lucy. My stars! Now I'd wager a sixpence I went by while you were asleep.

Sir Luc. Sure enough it must have been so — and I never dreamt it was so late, till I waked. Well, but my little girl, have you got nothing for me?

Lucy. Yes, but I have — I've got a letter for you in my pocket.

Sir Luc. O faith! I guessed you weren't come empty-handed. — Well — let me see what the dear creature says.

Lucy. There, Sir Lucius. (*Gives him a letter.*)

Sir Luc. (*Reads.*) *Sir — there is often a sudden incentive impulse in love, that has a greater induction than years of domestic combination: such was the commotion I felt at the first superfluous view of Sir Lucius O'Trigger.* — Very pretty, upon my word. — *Female punctuation forbids me to say more, yet let me add, that it will give me joy infallible to find Sir Lucius worthy the last criterion of my affections.*

DELIA. Upon my conscience! Lucy, your lady is a great mistress of language. Faith, she's quite the queen of the dictionary! — for the devil a word dare refuse coming at her call — though one would think it was quite out of hearing.

Lucy. Ay, sir, a lady of her experience —

Sir Luc. Experience! what, at seventeen?

Lucy. O true, sir — but then she reads so — my stars! how she will read off hand!

Sir Luc. Faith, she must be very deep read to write

this way — though she is rather an arbitrary writer too — for here are a great many poor words pressed into the service of this note, that would get their *habeas corpus* from any court in Christendom.

5 *Lucy*. Ah! Sir Lucius, if you were to hear how she talks of you!

Sir Luc. Oh, tell her I'll make her the best husband in the world, and Lady O'Trigger into the bargain. — But we must get the old gentlewoman's consent — and 10 do everything fairly.

Lucy. Nay, Sir Lucius, I thought you wa'n't rich enough to be so nice!

Sir Luc. Upon my word, young woman, you have hit it: — I am so poor, that I can't afford to do a dirty action. 15 — If I did not want money, I'd steal your mistress and her fortune with a great deal of pleasure. — However, my pretty girl (*gives her money*), here's a little something to buy you a ribbon; and meet me in the evening, and I'll give you an answer to this. So, hussy, take a kiss before- 20 hand to put you in mind. [*Kisses her.*

Lucy. O Lud! Sir Lucius — I never seed such a gemman! My lady won't like you if you're so impudent!

Sir Luc. Faith she will, Lucy! — That same — pho! what's the name of it? — modesty — is a quality in a 25 lover more praised by the women than liked; so, if your mistress asks you whether Sir Lucius ever gave you a kiss, tell her fifty — my dear.

Lucy. What, would you have me tell her a lie?

Sir Luc. Ah, then, you baggage! I'll make it a truth 30 presently.

Lucy. For shame now! here is some one coming.

SIR LUCIUS O'TRIGGER AND LUCY
"Very pretty, upon my word."

Sir Luc. Oh, faith, I'll quiet your conscience!

[*Exit, humming a tune.*

Enter FAG.

Fag. So, so, ma'am! I humbly beg pardon.

Lucy. O Lud! now, Mr. Fag — you flurry one so.

Fag. Come, come, Lucy, here's no one by — so a little less simplicity, with a grain or two more sincerity, if you please. — You play false with us, madam — I saw you give the baronet a letter. My master shall know this — and if he don't call him out, I will.

Lucy. Ha! ha! ha! you gentlemen's gentlemen are so hasty. — That letter was from Mrs. Malaprop, simpleton. — She is taken with Sir Lucius's address.

Fag. How! what tastes some people have! — Why, I suppose I have walked by her window a hundred times. — But what says our young lady? any message to my master?

Lucy. Sad news, Mr. Fag. — A worse rival than Acres! Sir Anthony Absolute has proposed his son.

Fag. What, Captain Absolute?

Lucy. Even so — I overheard it all.

Fag. Ha! ha! ha! very good, faith. Good bye, Lucy, I must away with this news.

Lucy. Well, you may laugh — but it is true, I assure you. (*Going.*) But, Mr. Fag, tell your master not to be cast down by this.

Fag. Oh, he'll be so disconsolate!

Lucy. And charge him not to think of quarrelling with young Absolute.

Fag. Never fear! never fear!

Lucy. Be sure — bid him keep up his spirits.

Fag. We will — we will.   [*Exeunt severally.*

ACT III.

Scene I. The north parade.

Enter Captain Absolute.

Abs. 'Tis just as Fag told me, indeed. Whimsical
enough, faith! My father wants to force me to marry
the very girl I am plotting to run away with! He must
not know of my connection with her yet awhile. He has
5 too summary a method of proceeding in these matters.
However, I'll read my recantation instantly. My con-
version is something sudden, indeed — but I can assure
him it is very sincere. So, so — here he comes. He looks
plaguy gruff.   [*Steps aside.*

Enter Sir Anthony Absolute.

10 *Sir Anth.* No. — I'll die sooner than forgive him. Die,
did I say? I'll live these fifty years to plague him. At
our last meeting, his impudence had almost put me out of
temper. An obstinate, passionate, self-willed boy! Who
can he take after? This is my return for getting him
15 before all his brothers and sisters! — for putting him, at
twelve years old, into a marching regiment, and allowing
him fifty pounds a year, besides his pay, ever since! But I
have done with him; he's anybody's son for me. I never
will see him more, never — never — never.

Abs. (*Aside, coming forward.*) Now for a penitential face.

Sir Anth. Fellow, get out of my way!

Abs. Sir, you see a penitent before you.

Sir Anth. I see an impudent scoundrel before me. 5

Abs. A sincere penitent. I am come, sir, to acknowledge my error, and to submit entirely to your will.

Sir Anth. What's that?

Abs. I have been revolving, and reflecting, and considering on your past goodness, and kindness, and condescension to me. 10

Sir Anth. Well, sir?

Abs. I have been likewise weighing and balancing what you were pleased to mention concerning duty, and obedience, and authority. 15

Sir Anth. Well, puppy?

Abs. Why then, sir, the result of my reflections is — a resolution to sacrifice every inclination of my own to your satisfaction.

Sir Anth. Why now you talk sense — absolute sense — 20 I never heard anything more sensible in my life. Confound you! you shall be Jack again.

Abs. I am happy in the appellation.

Sir Anth. Why then, Jack, my dear Jack, I will now inform you who the lady really is. Nothing but your 25 passion and violence, you silly fellow, prevented my telling you at first. Prepare, Jack, for wonder and rapture — prepare. What think you of Miss Lydia Languish?

Abs. Languish! What, the Languishes of Worcestershire? 30

Sir Anth. Worcestershire! no. Did you never meet

Mrs. Malaprop and her niece, Miss Languish, who came into our country just before you were last ordered to your regiment?

Abs. Malaprop! Languish! I don't remember ever
5 to have heard the names before. Yet, stay — I think I do recollect something. Languish! Languish! She squints, don't she? A little red-haired girl?

Sir Anth. Squints! A red-haired girl! Zounds! no.

Abs. Then I must have forgot; it can't be the same
10 person.

Sir Anth. Jack! Jack! what think you of blooming, love-breathing seventeen?

Abs. As to that, sir, I am quite indifferent. If I can please you in the matter, 'tis all I desire.

15 *Sir Anth.* Nay, but Jack, such eyes! such eyes! so innocently wild! so bashfully irresolute! not a glance but speaks and kindles some thought of love! Then, Jack, her cheeks! her cheeks, Jack! so deeply blushing at the insinuations of her tell-tale eyes! Then, Jack, her lips!
20 O Jack, lips smiling at their own discretion; and if not smiling, more sweetly pouting; more lovely in sullenness!

Abs. That's she indeed. Well done, old gentleman.
[Aside.

Sir Anth. Then, Jack, her neck! O Jack! Jack!

Abs. And which is to be mine, sir, the niece, or the aunt?

25 *Sir Anth.* Why, you unfeeling, insensible puppy, I despise you! When I was of your age, such a description would have made me fly like a rocket! The aunt indeed! Odds life! when I ran away with your mother, I would not have touched anything old or ugly to gain an empire

30 *Abs.* Not to please your father, sir?

Sir Anth. To please my father! zounds! not to please
— Oh, my father — odd so! — yes — yes; if my father
indeed had desired — that's quite another matter. Though
he wa'n't the indulgent father that I am, Jack.

Abs. I dare say not, sir.   5

Sir Anth. But, Jack, you are not sorry to find your
mistress is so beautiful?

Abs. Sir, I repeat it — if I please you in this affair, 'tis
all I desire. Not that I think a woman the worse for being
handsome; but, sir, if you please to recollect, you before 10
hinted something about a hump or two, one eye, and a few
more graces of that kind — now, without being very nice,
I own I should rather choose a wife of mine to have the
usual number of limbs, and a limited quantity of back:
and though one eye may be very agreeable, yet as the 15
prejudice has always run in favour of two, I would not wish
to affect a singularity in that article.

Sir Anth. What a phlegmatic sot it is! Why, sirrah,
you're an anchorite! — a vile, insensible stock. You a
soldier! — you're a walking block, fit only to dust the 20
company's regimentals on! Odds life! I have a great
mind to marry the girl myself.

Abs. I am entirely at your disposal, sir: if you should
think of addressing Miss Languish yourself, I suppose you
would have me marry the aunt; or if you should change 25
your mind, and take the old lady — 'tis the same to me —
I'll marry the niece.

Sir Anth. Upon my word, Jack, thou'rt either a very
great hypocrite, or — but, come, I know your indifference
on such a subject must be all a lie — I'm sure it must — 30
come, now — come, confess Jack — you have been lying —

ha'n't you? You have been playing the hypocrite, hey! —
I'll never forgive you, if you ha'n't been lying and playing
the hypocrite.

Abs. I'm sorry, sir, that the respect and duty which I
bear to you should be so mistaken.

Sir Anth. Hang your respect and duty! But come
along with me, I'll write a note to Mrs. Malaprop, and
you shall visit the lady directly. Her eyes shall be the
Promethean torch to you — come along, I'll never forgive
you, if you don't come back stark mad with rapture and
impatience — if you don't, egad, I will marry the girl
myself! [*Exeunt.*

SCENE II. JULIA'S DRESSING-ROOM.

FAULKLAND *discovered alone.*

Faulk. They told me Julia would return directly;
I wonder she is not yet come! How mean does this
captious, unsatisfied temper of mine appear to my cooler
judgment! Yet I know not that I indulge it in any other
point: but on this one subject, and to this one subject,
whom I think I love beyond my life, I am ever ungenerously fretful and madly capricious! I am conscious of it —
yet I cannot correct myself! What tender honest joy
sparkled in her eyes when we met! how delicate was the
warmth of her expressions! I was ashamed to appear less
happy — though I had come resolved to wear a face of
coolness and upbraiding. Sir Anthony's presence prevented my proposed expostulations: Yet I must be
satisfied that she has not been so very happy in my absence.
She is coming! Yes! — I know the nimbleness of her

tread, when she thinks her impatient Faulkland counts the moments of her stay.

Enter JULIA.

Jul. I had not hoped to see you again so soon.

Faulk. Could I, Julia, be contented with my first welcome — restrained as we were by the presence of a third person?

Jul. O Faulkland, when your kindness can make me thus happy, let me not think that I discovered something of coldness in your first salutation.

Faulk. 'Twas but your fancy, Julia. I was rejoiced to see you — to see you in such health. Sure I had no cause for coldness?

Jul. Nay then, I see you have taken something ill. You must not conceal from me what it is.

Faulk. Well, then — shall I own to you that my joy at hearing of your health and arrival here, by your neighbour Acres, was somewhat damped by his dwelling much on the high spirits you had enjoyed in Devonshire — on your mirth — your singing — dancing — and I know not what! For such is my temper, Julia, that I should regard every mirthful moment in your absence as a treason to constancy. The mutual tear that steals down the cheek of parting lovers is a compact, that no smile shall live there till they meet again.

Jul. Must I never cease to tax my Faulkland with this teasing minute caprice? Can the idle reports of a silly boor weigh in your breast against my tried affection?

Faulk. They have no weight with me, Julia: No, no — I am happy if you have been so — yet only say, that you

did not sing with mirth — say that you thought of Faulkland in the dance.

Jul. I never can be happy in your absence. If I wear
a countenance of content, it is to show that my mind
5 holds no doubt of my Faulkland's truth. If I seemed sad,
it were to make malice triumph; and say, that I had fixed
my heart on one, who left me to lament his roving, and
my own credulity. Believe me, Faulkland, I mean not
to upbraid you, when I say, that I have often dressed
10 sorrow in smiles, lest my friends should guess whose
unkindness had caused my tears.

Faulk. You were ever all goodness to me. Oh, I
am a brute, when I but admit a doubt of your true constancy!

15 *Jul.* If ever without such cause from you, as I will not
suppose possible, you find my affections veering but a
point, may I become a proverbial scoff for levity and base
ingratitude.

Faulk. Ah! Julia, that last word is grating to me. I
20 would I had no title to your gratitude! Search your heart,
Julia; perhaps what you have mistaken for love, is but
the warm effusion of a too thankful heart.

Jul. For what quality must I love you?

Faulk. For no quality! To regard me for any quality
25 of mind or understanding, were only to esteem me. And
for person — I have often wished myself deformed, to be
convinced that I owed no obligation there for any part of
your affection.

Jul. Where nature has bestowed a show of nice atten-
30 tion in the features of a man, he should laugh at it as mis-
placed. I have seen men, who in this vain article, perhaps,

might rank above you; but my heart has never asked my eyes if it were so or not.

Faulk. Now this is not well from you, Julia — I despise person in a man — yet if you loved me as I wish, though I were an Æthiop, you'd think none so fair.   5

Jul. I see you are determined to be unkind! The contract which my poor father bound us in gives you more than a lover's privilege.

Faulk. Again, Julia, you raise ideas that feed and justify my doubts. I would not have been more free — 10 no — I am proud of my restraint. Yet — yet — perhaps your high respect alone for this solemn compact has fettered your inclinations, which else had made a worthier choice. How shall I be sure, had you remained unbound in thought and promise, that I should still have been the 15 object of your persevering love?

Jul. Then try me now. Let us be free as strangers as to what is past: my heart will not feel more liberty!

Faulk. There now! so hasty, Julia! so anxious to be free! If your love for me were fixed and ardent, you 20 would not lose your hold, even though I wished it!

Jul. Oh! you torture me to the heart! I cannot bear it.

Faulk. I do not mean to distress you. If I loved you less I should never give you an uneasy moment. But 25 hear me. All my fretful doubts arise from this. Women are not used to weigh and separate the motives of their affections: the cold dictates of prudence, gratitude, or filial duty, may sometimes be mistaken for the pleadings of the heart. I would not boast — yet let me say, that I 30 have neither age, person, nor character, to found dislike on; my fortune such as few ladies could be charged with indiscretion in the match. O Julia! when love receives such countenance from prudence, nice minds will be suspicious of its birth.

5   *Jul.* I know not whither your insinuations would tend: — but as they seem pressing to insult me, I will spare you the regret of having done so. — I have given you no cause for this!   [*Exit in tears.*

  Faulk. In tears! Stay, Julia: stay but for a moment.
10 — The door is fastened! — Julia! — my soul — but for one moment! — I hear her sobbing! — 'Sdeath! what a brute am I to use her thus! Yet stay. — Ay — she is coming now: — how little resolution there is in woman! — how a few soft words can turn them! — No, faith! — she
15 is not coming either. — Why, Julia — my love — say but that you forgive me — come but to tell me that — now this is being too resentful. Stay! she is coming too — I thought she would — no steadiness in any thing: her going away must have been a mere trick then — she
20 *shan't* see that I was hurt by it. — I'll affect indifference — (*Hums a tune: then listens.*) No — zounds! she's not coming! — nor don't intend it, I suppose. — This is not steadiness, but obstinacy! Yet I deserve it. — What, after so long an absence to quarrel with her tenderness! —
25 'twas barbarous and unmanly! — I should be ashamed to see her now. — I'll wait till her just resentment is abated — and when I distress her so again, may I lose her forever, and be linked instead to some antique virago, whose gnawing passions, and long hoarded spleen, shall
30 make me curse my folly half the day and all the night!   [*Exit.*

SCENE III. MRS. MALAPROP'S LODGINGS.

MRS. MALAPROP, *with a letter in her hand,*
and CAPTAIN ABSOLUTE.

Mrs. Mal. Your being Sir Anthony's son, captain,
would itself be a sufficient accommodation; but from the
ingenuity of your appearance, I am convinced you deserve
the character here given of you.

Abs. Permit me to say, madam, that as I never yet
have had the pleasure of seeing Miss Languish, my principal inducement in this affair at present is the honour of
being allied to Mrs. Malaprop; of whose intellectual
accomplishments, elegant manners, and unaffected learning, no tongue is silent.

Mrs. Mal. Sir, you do me infinite honour! I beg,
captain, you'll be seated. (*They sit.*) Ah! few gentlemen, now-a-days, know how to value the ineffectual
qualities in a woman! few think how a little knowledge
becomes a gentlewoman! — Men have no sense now but
for the worthless flower of beauty!

Abs. It is but too true, indeed, ma'am; — yet I fear
our ladies should share the blame — they think our
admiration of beauty so great, that knowledge in them
would be superfluous. Thus, like garden-trees, they
seldom show fruit, till time has robbed them of the more
specious blossom. — Few, like Mrs. Malaprop and the
orange-tree, are rich in both at once.

Mrs. Mal. Sir, you overpower me with good-breeding.
— He is the very pine-apple of politeness! — You are not
ignorant, captain, that this giddy girl has somehow con-

trived to fix her affections on a beggarly, strolling, eaves-
dropping ensign, whom none of us have seen, and nobody
knows anything of.

Abs. Oh, I have heard the silly affair before. — I'm
5 not at all prejudiced against her on that account.

Mrs. Mal. You are very good and very considerate,
captain. I am sure I have done everything in my power
since I exploded the affair; long ago I laid my positive
conjunctions on her, never to think on the fellow again; —
10 I have since laid Sir Anthony's preposition before her;
but, I am sorry to say, she seems resolved to decline every
particle that I enjoin her.

Abs. It must be very distressing, indeed, ma'am.

Mrs. Mal. Oh! it gives me the hydrostatics to such a
15 degree! — I thought she had persisted from corresponding
with him; but, behold, this very day, I have interceded
another letter from the fellow; I believe I have it in my
pocket.

Abs. Oh, the devil! my last note. [*Aside.*

20 *Mrs. Mal.* Ay, here it is.

Abs. Ay, my note indeed! O the little traitress Lucy.
[*Aside.*

Mrs. Mal. There, perhaps you may know the writing.
[*Gives him the letter.*

Abs. I think I have seen the hand before — yes, I
certainly must have seen this hand before —

25 *Mrs. Mal.* Nay, but read it, captain.

Abs. (*Reads.*) *My soul's idol, my adored Lydia!* —
Very tender indeed!

Mrs. Mal. Tender! ay, and profane too, o' my conscience.

Abs. (*Reads.*)   *I am excessively alarmed at the intelligence you send me, the more so as my new rival —*

Mrs. Mal.   That's you, sir.

Abs. (*Reads.*)   *Has universally the character of being an accomplished gentleman and a man of honour.*   Well, that's handsome enough.

Mrs. Mal.   Oh, the fellow has some design in writing so.

Abs.   That he had, I'll answer for him, ma'am.

Mrs. Mal.   But go on, sir — you'll see presently.

Abs. (*Reads.*)   *As for the old weather-beaten she-dragon who guards you* — Who can he mean by that?

Mrs. Mal.   Me, sir! — me! — he means me! — There — what do you think now? — but go on a little further.

Abs.   Impudent   scoundrel! — (*Reads.*)   *it shall go hard but I will elude her vigilance, as I am told that the same ridiculous vanity, which makes her dress up her coarse features, and deck her dull chat with hard words which she don't understand —*

Mrs. Mal.   There, sir, an attack upon my language! what do you think of that? — an aspersion upon my parts of speech! was ever such a brute! Sure, if I reprehend any thing in this world, it is the use of my oracular tongue, and a nice derangement of epitaphs!

Abs.   He deserves to be hanged and quartered! let me see — (*Reads.*)   *same ridiculous vanity* —

Mrs. Mal.   You need not read it again, sir.

Abs.   I beg pardon, ma'am. — (*Reads.*)   *does also lay her open to the grossest deceptions from flattery and pretended admiration* — an impudent coxcomb! — *so that I have a scheme to see you shortly with the old harridan's consent, and even to make her a go-between in our interview.* — Was ever such assurance?

Mrs. Mal. Did you ever hear anything like it? — he'll elude my vigilance, will he — yes, yes! ha! ha! he's very likely to enter these doors; we'll try who can plot best!

Abs. So we will, ma'am — so we will! Ha! ha! ha! a conceited puppy, ha! ha! ha! — Well, but, Mrs. Malaprop, as the girl seems so infatuated by this fellow, suppose you were to wink at her corresponding with him for a little time — let her even plot an elopement with him — then do you connive at her escape — while I, just in the nick, will have the fellow laid by the heels, and fairly contrive to carry her off in his stead.

Mrs. Mal. I am delighted with the scheme; never was anything better perpetrated!

Abs. But, pray, could not I see the lady for a few minutes now? — I should like to try her temper a little.

Mrs. Mal. Why, I don't know — I doubt she is not prepared for a visit of this kind. There is a decorum in these matters.

Abs. O Lord! she won't mind me — only tell her Beverley —

Mrs. Mal. Sir!

Abs. Gently, good tongue.   [*Aside.*

Mrs. Mal. What did you say of Beverley?

Abs. Oh, I was going to propose that you should tell her, by way of jest, that it was Beverley who was below; she'd come down fast enough then — ha! ha! ha!

Mrs. Mal. 'Twould be a trick she well deserves; besides, you know the fellow tells her he'll get my consent to see her — ha! ha! Let him if he can, I say again.

Lydia, come down here! (*Calling.*) He'll make me a
go-between in their interviews! — ha! ha! ha! Come
down, I say, Lydia! I don't wonder at your laughing, ha!
ha! ha! his impudence is truly ridiculous.

Abs. 'Tis very ridiculous, upon my soul, ma'am, 5
ha! ha! ha!

Mrs. Mal. The little hussy won't hear. Well, I'll
go and tell her at once who it is — she shall know that
Captain Absolute is come to wait on her. And I'll make
her behave as becomes a young woman.   10

Abs. As you please, ma'am.

Mrs. Mal. For the present, captain, your servant.
Ah! you've not done laughing yet, I see — elude my
vigilance; yes, yes; ha! ha! ha!   [*Exit.*

Abs. Ha! ha! ha! one would think now that I might 15
throw off all disguise at once, and seize my prize with
security; but such is Lydia's caprice, that to undeceive
were probably to lose her. I'll see whether she knows me.

[*Walks aside, and seems engaged in looking at the pictures.*

Enter LYDIA.

Lyd. What a scene am I now to go through! surely 20
nothing can be more dreadful than to be obliged to listen
to the loathsome addresses of a stranger to one's heart.
I have heard of girls persecuted as I am, who have appealed
in behalf of their favoured lover to the generosity of his
rival; suppose I were to try it — there stands the hated 25
rival — an officer too! — but oh, how unlike my Beverley!
I wonder he don't begin — truly he seems a very negligent
wooer! — quite at his ease, upon my word! — I'll speak
first — Mr. Absolute.

Abs. Ma'am. [*Turns round.*

Lyd. O heavens! Beverley!

Abs. Hush! — hush, my life! softly! be not surprised!

Lyd. I am so astonished! and so terrified! and so
5 overjoyed! — for Heaven's sake! how came you here?

Abs. Briefly, I have deceived your aunt — I was
informed that my new rival was to visit here this evening,
and contriving to have him kept away, have passed myself
on her for Captain Absolute.

10 *Lyd.* O charming! And she really takes you for young
Absolute!

Abs. Oh, she's convinced of it.

Lyd. Ha! ha! ha! I can't forbear laughing to think
how her sagacity is overreached!

15 *Abs.* But we trifle with our precious moments — such
another opportunity may not occur; then let me now
conjure my kind, my condescending angel, to fix the time
when I may rescue her from undeserving persecution, and
with a licensed warmth plead for my reward.

20 *Lyd.* Will you then, Beverley, consent to forfeit that
portion of my paltry wealth? — that burden on the wings
of love?

Abs. Oh, come to me — rich only thus — in loveliness!
Bring no portion to me but thy love — 'twill be generous
25 in you, Lydia — for well you know, it is the only dower
your poor Beverley can repay.

Lyd. How persuasive are his words! — how charming
will poverty be with him! [*Aside.*

Abs. Ah! my soul, what a life will we then live!
30 Love shall be our idol and support! we will worship
him with a monastic strictness; abjuring all worldly toys,

to centre every thought and action there. Proud of calamity, we will enjoy the wreck of wealth; while the surrounding gloom of adversity shall make the flame of our pure love show doubly bright. By Heavens! I would fling all goods of fortune from me with a prodigal hand, 5 to enjoy the scene where I might clasp my Lydia to my bosom and say, the world affords no smile to me but here. (*Embracing her.*) If she holds out now, the devil is in it!
                                                                                   [*Aside.*

Lyd. Now could I fly with him to the antipodes! but my persecution is not yet come to a crisis.   [*Aside.* 10

> Reënter MRS. MALAPROP, *listening.*

Mrs. Mal. I am impatient to know how the little hussy deports herself.   [*Aside.*
Abs. So pensive, Lydia! — is then your warmth abated?
Mrs. Mal. Warmth abated! — so! — she has been in 15 a passion, I suppose.   [*Aside.*
Lyd. No — nor ever can while I have life.
Mrs. Mal. An ill-tempered little devil! She'll be in a passion all her life — will she?   [*Aside.*
Lyd. Think not the idle threats of my ridiculous aunt 20 can ever have any weight with me.
Mrs. Mal. Very dutiful, upon my word!   [*Aside.*
Lyd. Let her choice be Captain Absolute, but Beverley is mine.
Mrs. Mal. I am astonished at her assurance! — to his 25 face — this is to his face!   [*Aside.*
Abs. Thus then let me enforce my suit.   [*Kneeling.*
Mrs. Mal. (*Aside.*) Ay, poor young man! — down

on his knees entreating for pity! — I can contain no longer. (*Coming forward.*) Why, thou vixen! — I have overheard you.

    Abs. Oh, confound her vigilance!   [*Aside.*

5 *Mrs. Mal.* Captain Absolute, I know not how to apologize for her shocking rudeness.

    Abs. (*Aside.*) So all's safe, I find. (*Aloud.*) I have hopes, madam, that time will bring the young lady —

    Mrs. Mal. Oh, there's nothing to be hoped for from
10 her! she's as headstrong as an allegory on the banks of Nile.

    Lyd. Nay, madam, what do you charge me with now?

    Mrs. Mal. Why, thou unblushing rebel — didn't you tell this gentleman to his face that you loved another better? — didn't you say you never would be his?

15 *Lyd.* No, madam — I did not.

    Mrs. Mal. Good Heavens! what assurance! — Lydia, Lydia, you ought to know that lying don't become a young woman! — Didn't you boast that Beverley, that stroller Beverley, possessed your heart? — Tell me that, I say.

20 *Lyd.* 'Tis true, ma'am, and none but Beverley —

    Mrs. Mal. Hold! — hold, Assurance! — you shall not be so rude.

    Abs. Nay, pray, Mrs. Malaprop, don't stop the young lady's speech: she's very welcome to talk thus — it does
25 not hurt me in the least, I assure you.

    Mrs. Mal. You are too good, captain — too amiably patient — but come with me, miss. — Let us see you again soon, captain — remember what we have fixed.

    Abs. I shall, ma'am.

30 *Mrs. Mal.* Come, take a graceful leave of the gentleman.

MRS. MALAPROP

"She's as headstrong as an allegory on the banks of Nile!"

Lyd. May every blessing wait on my Beverley, my beloved Bev —

Mrs. Mal. Hussy! I'll choke the word in your throat! — come along — come along.

[*Exeunt severally;* CAPTAIN ABSOLUTE *kissing his hand to* LYDIA — MRS. MALAPROP *stopping her from speaking.*

SCENE IV. ACRES' LODGINGS.

ACRES, *as just dressed, and* DAVID.

Acres. Indeed, David — do you think I become it so? 5

Dav. You are quite another creature, believe me, master, by the mass! an we've any luck we shall see the Devon monkerony in all the print-shops in Bath!

Acres. Dress does make a difference, David.

Dav. 'Tis all in all, I think. — Difference! why, an 10 you were to go now to Clod-Hall, I am certain the old lady wouldn't know you: master Butler wouldn't believe his own eyes, and Mrs. Pickle would cry, Lard presarve me! Our dairy-maid would come giggling to the door, and I warrant Dolly Tester, your honour's favourite, would blush 15 like my waistcoat. — Oons! I'll hold a gallon, there an't a dog in the house but would bark, and I question whether Phillis would wag a hair of her tail!

Acres. Ay, David, there's nothing like polishing.

Dav. So I says of your honour's boots; but the boy 20 never heeds me!

Acres. But, David, has Mr. De-la-grace been here? I must rub up my balancing, and chasing, and boring.

Dav. I'll call again, sir.

167

Acres. Do — and see if there are any letters for me at the post-office.

Dav. I will. — By the mass, I can't help looking at your head! — if I hadn't been at the cooking, I wish I may die if I should have known the dish again myself! [*Exit.*

Acres. (*Practising a dancing-step.*) Sink, slide — coupée. — Confound the first inventors of cotillons! say I — they are as bad as algebra to us country gentlemen — I can walk a minuet easy enough when I am forced! — and I have been accounted a good stick in a country-dance. — Odds jigs and tabours! I never valued your cross-over to couple — figure in — right and left — and I'd foot it with e'er a captain in the country! — but these outlandish heathen allemandes and cotillons are quite beyond me! — I shall never prosper at 'em, that's sure — mine are true-born English legs — they don't understand their curst French lingo! — their *pas* this, and *pas* that, and *pas* t'other! — my feet don't like to be called paws! no, 'tis certain I have most Antigallican toes!

Enter SERVANT.

Serv. Here is Sir Lucius O'Trigger to wait on you, sir.

Acres. Show him in. [*Exit* SERVANT.

Enter SIR LUCIUS O'TRIGGER.

Sir Luc. Mr. Acres, I am delighted to embrace you.

Acres. My dear Sir Lucius, I kiss your hands.

Sir Luc. Pray, my friend, what has brought you so suddenly to Bath?

Acres. Faith! I have followed Cupid's Jack-a-lantern, and find myself in a quagmire at last. — In short, I have been very ill-used, Sir Lucius. — I don't choose to mention names, but look on me as on a very ill-used gentleman.

Sir Luc.   Pray what is the case? — I ask no names.

Acres.   Mark me, Sir Lucius, I fall as deep as need be in love with a young lady — her friends take my part — I 5 follow her to Bath — send word of my arrival; and receive answer, that the lady is to be otherwise disposed of. — This, Sir Lucius, I call being ill-used.

Sir Luc.   Very ill, upon my conscience. — Pray, can you divine the cause of it?   10

Acres.   Why, there's the matter; she has another lover, one Beverley, who, I am told, is now in Bath. — Odds slanders and lies! he must be at the bottom of it.

Sir Luc.   A rival in the case, is there? — and you think he has supplanted you unfairly?   15

Acres.   Unfairly! to be sure he has.   He never could have done it fairly.

Sir Luc.   Then sure you know what is to be done!

Acres.   Not I, upon my soul!

Sir Luc.   We wear no swords here, but you understand 20 me.

Acres.   What! fight him!

Sir Luc.   Ay, to be sure: what can I mean else?

Acres.   But he has given me no provocation.

Sir Luc.   Now, I think he has given you the greatest 25 provocation in the world.   Can a man commit a more heinous offence against another than to fall in love with the same woman?   Oh, by my soul! it is the most unpardonable breach of friendship.

Acres.   Breach of friendship! ay, ay; but I have no 30 acquaintance with this man.   I never saw him in my life.

Sir Luc. That's no argument at all — he has the less right then to take such a liberty.

Acres. Gad, that's true — I grow full of anger, Sir Lucius! — I fire apace! Odds hilts and blades! I find
5 a man may have a deal of valour in him, and not know it! But couldn't I contrive to have a little right of my side?

Sir Luc. What the devil signifies right, when your honour is concerned? Do you think Achilles, or my little Alexander the Great, ever inquired where the right lay?
10 No, by my soul, they drew their broadswords, and left the lazy sons of peace to settle the justice of it.

Acres. Your words are a grenadier's march to my heart! I believe courage must be catching! I certainly do feel a kind of valour rising as it were — a kind of courage,
15 as I may say. — Odds flints, pans, and triggers! I'll challenge him directly.

Sir Luc. Ah, my little friend, if I had Blunderbuss Hall here, I could show you a range of ancestry, in the O'Trigger line, that would furnish the new room; every
20 one of whom had killed his man! — For though the mansion-house and dirty acres have slipped through my fingers, I thank heaven our honour and the family-pictures are as fresh as ever.

Acres. O, Sir Lucius! I have had ancestors too! —
25 every man of 'em colonel or captain in the militia! — Odds balls and barrels! say no more — I'm braced for it. The thunder of your words has soured the milk of human kindness in my breast; — Zounds! as the man in the play says, *I could do such deeds!*

30 *Sir Luc.* Come, come, there must be no passion at all in the case — these things should always be done civilly.

Acres. I must be in a passion, Sir Lucius — I must be in a rage. — Dear Sir Lucius, let me be in a rage, if you love me. Come, here's pen and paper. (*Sits down to write.*) I would the ink were red! — Indite, I say indite! — How shall I begin? Odds bullets and blades! I'll write a good ₅ bold hand, however.

Sir Luc. Pray compose yourself.

Acres. Come — now, shall I begin with an oath? Do, Sir Lucius, let me begin with a damme.

Sir Luc. Pho! pho! do the thing decently, and like ₁₀ a Christian. Begin now — *Sir* —

Acres. That's too civil by half.

Sir Luc. *To prevent the confusion that might arise* —

Acres. Well —

Sir Luc. *From our both addressing the same lady* —   ₁₅

Acres. Ay, there's the reason — *same lady* — well —

Sir Luc. *I shall expect the honour of your company* —

Acres. Zounds! I'm not asking him to dinner.

Sir Luc. Pray be easy.

Acres. Well then, *honour of your company* —   ₂₀

Sir Luc. *To settle our pretensions* —

Acres. Well.

Sir Luc. Let me see, ay, King's-Mead-Fields will do — *in King's-Mead-Fields.*

Acres. So, that's done — Well, I'll fold it up presently; ₂₅ my own crest — a hand and dagger shall be the seal.

Sir Luc. You see now this little explanation will put a stop at once to all confusion or misunderstanding that might arise between you.

Acres. Ay, we fight to prevent any misunderstanding. ₃₀

Sir Luc. Now, I'll leave you to fix your own time.

Take my advice, and you'll decide it this evening if you can; then let the worst come of it, 'twill be off your mind to-morrow.

Acres. Very true.

5 *Sir Luc.* So I shall see nothing more of you, unless it be by letter, till the evening. — I would do myself the honour to carry your message; but, to tell you a secret, I believe I shall have just such another affair on my own hands. There is a gay captain here, who put a jest on me 10 lately, at the expense of my country, and I only want to fall in with the gentleman, to call him out.

Acres. By my valour, I should like to see you fight first! Odds life! I should like to see you kill him if it was only to get a little lesson.

15 *Sir Luc.* I shall be very proud of instructing you. — Well, for the present — but remember now, when you meet your antagonist, do everything in a mild and agreeable manner. — Let your courage be as keen, but at the same time as polished, as your sword. [*Exeunt severally.*

ACT IV.

Scene I.   Acres' lodgings.

Acres and David.

Dav. Then, by the mass, sir! I would do no such thing — ne'er a Sir Lucius O'Trigger in the kingdom should make me fight, when I wa'n't so minded. Oons! what will the old lady say when she hears o't?

Acres. Ah! David, if you had heard Sir Lucius! — Odds sparks and flames! he would have roused your valour.

Dav. Not he, indeed. I hate such bloodthirsty cormorants. Look'ee, master, if you'd wanted a bout at boxing, quarter-staff, or short-staff, I should never be the man to bid you cry off: but for your curst sharps and snaps, I never knew any good come of 'em.

Acres. But my honour, David, my honour! I must be very careful of my honour.

Dav. Ay, by the mass! and I would be very careful of it; and I think in return my honour couldn't do less than to be very careful of me.

Acres. Odds blades! David, no gentleman will ever risk the loss of his honour.

Dav. I say then, it would be but civil in honour never to risk the loss of a gentleman. — Look'ee, master, this honour seems to me to be a marvellous false friend: ay,

truly, a very courtier-like servant. — Put the case, I was
a gentleman (which, thank God, no one can say of me);
well — my honour makes me quarrel with another gentleman of my acquaintance. — So — we fight. (Pleasant
5 enough that!) Boh! I kill him — (the more's my luck!)
now, pray who gets the profit of it? — Why, my honour.
But put the case that he kills me! — by the mass! I go
to the worms, and my honour whips over to my enemy.

Acres. No, David — in that case — Odds crowns and
10 laurels! — your honour follows you to the grave.

Dav. Now, that's just the place where I could make a
shift to do without it.

Acres. Zounds! David, you are a coward! — It
doesn't become my valour to listen to you. — What, shall
15 I disgrace my ancestors? — Think of that, David — think
what it would be to disgrace my ancestors!

Dav. Under favour, the surest way of not disgracing
them, is to keep as long as you can out of their company.
Look'ee now, master, to go to them in such haste — with
20 an ounce of lead in your brains — I should think might
as well be let alone. Our ancestors are very good kind of
folks; but they are the last people I should choose to have
a visiting acquaintance with.

Acres. But, David, now, you don't think there is such
25 very, very, very great danger, hey? — Odds life! people
often fight without any mischief done!

Dav. By the mass, I think 'tis ten to one against you!
— Oons! here to meet some lion-headed fellow, I warrant,
with his double-barrelled swords, and cut-and-thrust
30 pistols! — Lord bless us! it makes me tremble to think
o't — Those be such desperate bloody-minded weapons!

Well, I never could abide 'em — from a child I never could fancy 'em! — I suppose there an't been so merciless a beast in the world as your loaded pistol!

Acres. Zounds! I won't be afraid! — Odds fire and fury! you shan't make me afraid. — Here is the challenge, and I have sent for my dear friend Jack Absolute to carry it for me.

Dav. Ay, i' the name of mischief, let him be the messenger. — For my part, I wouldn't lend a hand to it for the best horse in your stable. By the mass! it don't look like another letter. It is, as I may say, a designing and malicious-looking letter; and I warrant smells of gunpowder like a soldier's pouch! — Oons! I wouldn't swear it mayn't go off!

Acres. Out, you poltroon! you ha'n't the valour of a grasshopper.

Dav. Well, I say no more — 'twill be sad news, to be sure, at Clod-Hall! but I ha' done. — How Phillis will howl when she hears of it! — Ay, poor bitch, she little thinks what shooting her master's going after! And I warrant old Crop, who has carried your honour, field and road, these ten years, will curse the hour he was born.

[*Whimpering.*

Acres. It won't do, David — I am determined to fight — so get along, you coward, while I'm in the mind.

Enter SERVANT.

Ser. Captain Absolute, sir.

Acres. Oh! show him up.   [*Exit* SERVANT.

Dav. Well, Heaven send we be all alive this time to-morrow.

Acres. What's that? — Don't provoke me, David!

Dav. Good-bye, master. [*Whimpering.*

Acres. Get along, you cowardly, dastardly, croaking raven! [*Exit* DAVID.

Enter CAPTAIN ABSOLUTE.

5 *Abs.* What's the matter, Bob?

Acres. A vile, sheep-hearted blockhead! If I hadn't the valour of St. George and the dragon to boot —

Abs. But what did you want with me, Bob?

Acres. Oh! — There (*Gives him the challenge.*)

10 *Abs.* (*Aside.*) *To Ensign Beverley.* — So, what's going on now! — (*Aloud.*) Well, what's this?

Acres. A challenge!

Abs. Indeed! Why, you won't fight him; will you, Bob?

15 *Acres.* Egad, but I will, Jack. Sir Lucius has wrought me to it. He has left me full of rage — and I'll fight this evening, that so much good passion mayn't be wasted.

Abs. But what have I to do with this?

Acres. Why, as I think you know something of this 20 fellow, I want you to find him out for me, and give him this mortal defiance.

Abs. Well, give it to me, and trust me he gets it.

Acres. Thank you, my dear friend, my dear Jack; but it is giving you a great deal of trouble.

25 *Abs.* Not in the least — I beg you won't mention it. — No trouble in the world, I assure you.

Acres. You are very kind. — What it is to have a friend! — You couldn't be my second, could you, Jack?

Abs. Why no, Bob — not in this affair — it would not 30 be quite so proper.

176

Acres. Well, then, I must get my friend Sir Lucius. I shall have your good wishes, however, Jack?

Abs. Whenever he meets you, believe me.

Reënter SERVANT.

Ser. Sir Anthony Absolute is below, inquiring for the captain.   5

Abs. I'll come instantly. (*Exit* SERVANT.) Well, my little hero, success attend you.   [*Going.*

Acres. Stay — stay, Jack. — If Beverley should ask you what kind of a man your friend Acres is, do tell him I am a devil of a fellow — will you, Jack?   10

Abs. To be sure I shall. I'll say you are a determined dog — hey, Bob?

Acres. Ay, do, do — and if that frightens him, egad, perhaps he mayn't come. So tell him I generally kill a man a week; will you, Jack?   15

Abs. I will, I will; I'll say you are called in the country Fighting Bob.

Acres. Right — right — 'tis all to prevent mischief; for I don't want to take his life if I clear my honour.

Abs. No! — that's very kind of you.   20

Acres. Why, you don't wish me to kill him — do you, Jack?

Abs. No, upon my soul, I do not. But a devil of a fellow, hey?   [*Going.*

Acres. True, true — but stay — stay, Jack — you may add, that you never saw me in such a rage before — a 25 most devouring rage!

Abs. I will, I will.

Acres. Remember, Jack — a determined dog.

Abs. Ay, ay, Fighting Bob!   [*Exeunt severally.*

SCENE II.   MRS. MALAPROP'S LODGINGS.

MRS. MALAPROP *and* LYDIA.

Mrs. Mal.   Why, thou perverse one! — tell me what
you can object to him? Isn't he a handsome man? —
tell me that. A genteel man? a pretty figure of a man?

Lyd.   (*Aside.*)   She little thinks whom she is praising!
5 — (*Aloud.*)   So is Beverley, ma'am.

Mrs. Mal.   No caparisons, miss, if you please. Caparisons don't become a young woman. No! Captain
Absolute is indeed a fine gentleman!

Lyd.   Ay, the Captain Absolute you have seen.   [*Aside.*

10 *Mrs. Mal.*   Then he's so well bred; — so full of alacrity,
and adulation! — and has so much to say for himself: —
in such good language too! His physiognomy so grammatical! Then his presence is so noble! I protest, when
I saw him, I thought of what Hamlet says in the play: —

15 " Hesperian curls — the front of Job himself! —
       An eye, like March, to threaten at command! —
       A station, like Harry Mercury, new — "
Something about kissing — on a hill — however, the
similitude struck me directly.

20 *Lyd.*   How enraged she'll be presently, when she dis-
covers her mistake!   [*Aside.*

Enter SERVANT.

Ser.   Sir Anthony and Captain Absolute are below,
ma'am.

Mrs. Mal.   Show them up here.   (*Exit* SERVANT.)
25 Now, Lydia, I insist on your behaving as becomes a young

woman. Show your good breeding, at least, though you have forgot your duty.

Lyd. Madam, I have told you my resolution! — I shall not only give him no encouragement, but I won't even speak to, or look at him.   5

[*Flings herself into a chair, with her face from the door.*

Enter SIR ANTHONY ABSOLUTE *and* CAPTAIN ABSOLUTE.

Sir Anth. Here we are, Mrs. Malaprop; come to mitigate the frowns of unrelenting beauty, — and difficulty enough I had to bring this fellow. — I don't know what's the matter; but if I had not held him by force, he'd have given me the slip.   10

Mrs. Mal. You have infinite trouble, Sir Anthony, in the affair. I am ashamed for the cause! (*Aside to* LYDIA.) Lydia, Lydia, rise, I beseech you! — pay your respects!

Sir Anth. I hope, madam, that Miss Languish has 15 reflected on the worth of this gentleman, and the regard due to her aunt's choice, and my alliance. (*Aside to* CAPTAIN ABSOLUTE.) Now, Jack, speak to her.

Abs. (*Aside.*) What the devil shall I do! (*Aside to* SIR ANTHONY.) You see, sir, she won't even look at me 20 whilst you are here. I knew she wouldn't! I told you so. Let me entreat you, sir, to leave us together!

[*Seems to expostulate with his father.*

Lyd. (*Aside.*) I wonder I ha'n't heard my aunt exclaim yet! sure she can't have looked at him! — perhaps their regimentals are alike, and she is something 25 blind.

Sir Anth. I say, sir, I won't stir a foot yet!

Mrs. Mal. I am sorry to say, Sir Anthony, that my affluence over my niece is very small. (*Aside to* LYDIA.) Turn round, Lydia: I blush for you!

Sir Anth. May I not flatter myself, that Miss Languish
5 will assign what cause of dislike she can have to my son! (*Aside to* CAPTAIN ABSOLUTE). Why don't you begin, Jack? — Speak, you puppy — speak!

Mrs. Mal. It is impossible, Sir Anthony, she can have any. She will not say she has. (*Aside to* LYDIA.)
10 Answer, hussy! why don't you answer?

Sir Anth. Then, madam, I trust that a childish and hasty predilection will be no bar to Jack's happiness. (*Aside to* CAPTAIN ABSOLUTE.) Zounds! sirrah! why don't you speak!

15 *Lyd.* (*Aside.*) I think my lover seems as little inclined to conversation as myself. — How strangely blind my aunt must be!

Abs. Hem! hem! madam — hem! (*Attempts to speak, then returns to* SIR ANTHONY.) Faith! sir, I am so
20 confounded! — and — so — so — confused! — I told you I should be so, sir — I knew it. — The — the — tremor of my passion entirely takes away my presence of mind.

Sir Anth. But it don't take away your voice, fool, does it? — Go up, and speak to her directly!

[CAPTAIN ABSOLUTE *makes signs to* MRS. MALAPROP *to leave them together.*

25 *Mrs. Mal.* Sir Anthony, shall we leave them together? (*Aside to* LYDIA.) Ah! you stubborn little vixen!

Sir Anth. Not yet, ma'am, not yet! (*Aside to* CAPTAIN ABSOLUTE.) What the devil are you at? unlock your jaws, sirrah, or —

Abs. (*Aside.*) Now Heaven send she may be too sullen to look round! — I must disguise my voice. (*Draws near* LYDIA, *and speaks in a low hoarse tone.*) Will not Miss Languish lend an ear to the mild accents of true love? Will not — ⁵

Sir Anth. What the devil ails the fellow? Why don't you speak out? — not stand croaking like a frog in a quinsy!

Abs. The — the — excess of my awe, and my — my — modesty, quite choke me! ¹⁰

Sir Anth. Ah! your modesty again! — I'll tell you what, Jack; if you don't speak out directly, and glibly too, I shall be in such a rage! — Mrs. Malaprop, I wish the lady would favour us with something more than a side-front.   [MRS. MALAPROP *seems to chide* LYDIA. ¹⁵

Abs. (*Aside.*) So all will out, I see! (*Goes up to* LYDIA, *speaks softly.*) Be not surprised, my Lydia, suppress all surprise at present.

Lyd. (*Aside.*) Heavens! 'tis Beverley's voice! Sure he can't have imposed on Sir Anthony too! (*Looks* ²⁰ *round by degrees, then starts up.*) Is this possible! — my Beverley! — how can this be? — my Beverley?

Abs. Ah! 'tis all over.   [*Aside.*

Sir Anth. Beverley! — the devil — Beverley! — What can the girl mean? — This is my son, Jack Absolute. ²⁵

Mrs. Mal. For shame, hussy! for shame! your head runs so on that fellow, that you have him always in your eyes! — beg Captain Absolute's pardon directly.

Lyd. I see no Captain Absolute, but my loved Beverley!

Sir Anth. Zounds! the girl's mad! — her brain's ³⁰ turned by reading.

Mrs. Mal. O' my conscience, I believe so! — What do you mean by Beverley, hussy? — You saw Captain Absolute before to-day; there he is — your husband that shall be.

5   *Lyd.* With all my soul, ma'am — when I refuse my Beverley ——

Sir Anth. Oh! she's as mad as Bedlam! — or has this fellow been playing us a rogue's trick! — Come here, sirrah, who the devil are you?

10   *Abs.* Faith, sir, I am not quite clear myself; but I'll endeavour to recollect.

Sir Anth. Are you my son or not? — answer for your mother, you dog, if you won't for me.

Mrs. Mal. Ay, sir, who are you? O mercy! I begin
15 to suspect! —

Abs. (*Aside.*) Ye powers of impudence, befriend me! (*Aloud.*) Sir Anthony, most assuredly I am your wife's son and that I sincerely believe myself to be yours also, I hope my duty has always shown. — Mrs. Malaprop, I am
20 your most respectful admirer, and shall be proud to add affectionate nephew. — I need not tell my Lydia, that she sees her faithful Beverley, who, knowing the singular generosity of her temper, assumed that name and station, which has proved a test of the most disinterested love,
25 which he now hopes to enjoy in a more elevated character.

Lyd. So! — there will be no elopement after all!

                              [*Sullenly.*

Sir Anth. Upon my soul, Jack, thou art a very impudent fellow! to do you justice, I think I never saw a piece of more consummate assurance!

30   *Abs.* Oh, you flatter me, sir — you compliment —

'tis my modesty, you know, sir, — my modesty that has stood in my way.

Sir Anth. Well, I am glad you are not the dull, insensible varlet you pretended to be, however! — I'm glad you have made a fool of your father, you dog — I am. So this was your *penitence,* your *duty* and *obedience!* — I thought it was sudden! — *You never heard their names before,* not you! — *what, the Languishes of Worcestershire* hey? — *if you could please me in the affair it was all you desired!* — Ah! — you   dissembling   villain! — What! (*pointing to* LYDIA) *she squints, don't she? — a little red-haired girl!* — hey? — Why, you hypocritical young rascal! — I wonder you a'n't ashamed to hold up your head!

Abs. 'Tis with difficulty, sir. — I am confused — very much confused, as you must perceive.

Mrs. Mal. O Lud! Sir Anthony! — a new light breaks in upon me! — hey! — how! what! captain, did you write the letters then? — What — am I to thank you for the elegant compilation of *an old weather-beaten she-dragon* — hey! — O mercy! — was it you that reflected on my parts of speech?

Abs. Dear sir! my modesty will be overpowered at last, if you don't assist me — I shall certainly not be able to stand it!

Sir Anth. Come, come, Mrs. Malaprop, we must forget and forgive; — odds life! matters have taken so clever a turn all of a sudden, that I could find in my heart to be so good-humoured! and so gallant! hey! Mrs. Malaprop!

Mrs. Mal. Well, Sir Anthony, since you desire it, we will not anticipate the past! — so mind, young people — our retrospection will be all to the future.

Sir Anth. Come, we must leave them together; Mrs. Malaprop, they long to fly into each other's arms, I warrant! — Jack — isn't the cheek as I said, hey? — and the eye, you rogue! — and the lip — hey? Come, Mrs.
5 Malaprop, we'll not disturb their tenderness — theirs is the time of life for happiness! — *Youth's the season made for joy* (*Sings.*) Hey! — Odds life! I'm in such spirits, — I don't know what I could not do! — Permit me, ma'am (*Gives his hand to* Mrs. Malaprop.) Tol-de-rol —
10 'gad, I should like to have a little fooling myself — Tol-de-rol! de-rol.

> [*Exit, singing and handing* Mrs. Malaprop. —
> Lydia *sits sullenly in her chair.*

Abs. (*Aside.*) So much thought bodes me no good. — (*Aloud.*) So grave, Lydia!

Lyd. Sir!

15 *Abs.* (*Aside.*) So! — egad! I thought as much! — that monosyllable has froze me! (*Aloud.*) What, Lydia, now that we are as happy in our friends' consent, as in our mutual vows —

Lyd. Friends' consent indeed!   [*Peevishly.*

20 *Abs.* Come, come, we must lay aside some of our romance — a little wealth and comfort may be endured after all. And for your fortune, the lawyers shall make such settlements as —

Lyd. Lawyers! I hate lawyers!

25 *Abs.* Nay, then, we will not wait for their lingering forms, but instantly procure the licence, and —

Lyd. The licence! — I hate licence!

Abs. Oh my love! be not so unkind! — thus let me entreat —

Lyd. Psha! — what signifies kneeling, when you know I must have you?

Abs. (*Rising.*) Nay, madam, there shall be no constraint upon your inclinations, I promise you. — If I have lost your heart, I resign the rest   (*Aside.*) 'Gad, I must 5 try what a little spirit will do.

Lyd. (*Rising.*) Then, sir, let me tell you, the interest you had there was acquired by a mean, unmanly imposition, and deserves the punishment of fraud. What, you have been treating me like a child! — humouring my romance! 10 and laughing, I suppose, at your success!

Abs. You wrong me, Lydia, you wrong me — only hear —

Lyd. So, while I fondly imagined we were deceiving my relations, and flattered myself that I should outwit 15 and incense them all — behold my hopes are to be crushed at once, by my aunt's consent and approbation — and I am myself the only dupe at last! (*Walking about in a heat.*) But here, sir, here is the picture — Beverley's picture! (*taking a miniature from her bosom*) which I have 20 worn, night and day, in spite of threats and entreaties! — There, sir; (*flings it to him*) and be assured I throw the original from my heart as easily.

Abs. Nay, nay, ma'am, we will not differ as to that. — Here (*taking out a picture*), here is Miss Lydia Languish. — 25 What a difference! — ay, there is the heavenly assenting smile that first gave soul and spirit to my hopes! — those are the lips which sealed a vow, as yet scarce dry in Cupid's calendar! and there the half-resentful blush, that would have checked the ardour of my thanks! — Well, all that's 30 past! — all over indeed! — There, madam — in beauty, that copy is not equal to you, but in my mind its merit over the original, in being still the same, is such — that — I cannot find in my heart to part with it. [*Puts it up again.*

    Lyd. (*Softening.*) 'Tis your own doing, sir — I — I
5 — I suppose you are perfectly satisfied.

    Abs. O, most certainly — sure, now, this is much better than being in love! — ha! ha! ha! — there's some spirit in this! — What signifies breaking some scores of solemn promises: — all that's of no consequence, you know. —
10 To be sure people will say, that miss don't know her own mind — but never mind that! Or, perhaps, they may be ill-natured enough to hint, that the gentleman grew tired of the lady and forsook her — but don't let that fret you.

    Lyd. There is no bearing his insolence.

                              [*Bursts into tears.*

Reënter MRS. MALAPROP *and* SIR ANTHONY ABSOLUTE.

15   *Mrs. Mal.* Come, we must interrupt your billing and cooing awhile.

    Lyd. This is worse than your treachery and deceit, you base ingrate!   [*Sobbing.*

    Sir Anth. What the devil's the matter now! — Zounds!
20 Mrs. Malaprop, this is the oddest billing and cooing I ever heard! — but what the deuce is the meaning of it? — I am quite astonished!

    Abs. Ask the lady, sir.

    Mrs. Mal. Oh mercy! — I'm quite analysed, for my
25 part! — Why, Lydia, what is the reason of this?

    Lyd. Ask the gentleman, ma'am.

    Sir Anth. Zounds! I shall be in a frenzy! — Why, Jack, you are not come out to be any one else, are you?

Mrs. Mal. Ay, sir, there's no more trick, is there? — you are not like Cerberus, three gentlemen at once, are you?

Abs. You'll not let me speak — I say the lady can account for this much better than I can.   5

Lyd. Ma'am, you once commanded me never to think of Beverley again — there is the man — I now obey you: for, from this moment, I renounce him for ever.   [*Exit.*

Mrs. Mal. O mercy! and miracles! what a turn here is — why sure, captain, you haven't behaved disrespect- 10 fully to my niece.

Sir Anth. Ha! ha! ha! — ha! ha! ha! — now I see it. Ha! ha! ha! — now I see it — you have been too lively, Jack.

Abs. Nay, sir, upon my word —   15

Sir Anth. Come, no lying, Jack — I'm sure 'twas so.

Mrs. Mal. O Lud! Sir Anthony! — O fy, captain!

Abs. Upon my soul, ma'am —

Sir Anth. Come, no excuses, Jack; why, your father, you rogue, was so before you: — the blood of the Absolutes 20 was always impatient. — Ha! ha! ha! poor little Lydia! why, you've frightened her, you dog, you have.

Abs. By all that's good, sir —

Sir Anth. Zounds! say no more, I tell you — Mrs. Malaprop shall make your peace. — You must make his 25 peace, Mrs. Malaprop: — you must tell her 'tis Jack's way — tell her 'tis all our ways — it runs in the blood of our family! — Come away, Jack — Ha! ha! ha! Mrs. Malaprop — a young villain!   [*Pushing him out.*

Mrs. Mal. O! Sir Anthony! — O fy, captain!   30
          [*Exeunt severally.*

SCENE III. THE NORTH PARADE.

Enter SIR LUCIUS O'TRIGGER.

Sir Luc. I wonder where this Captain Absolute hides himself! Upon my conscience! these officers are always in one's way in love affairs: — I remember I might have married lady Dorothy Carmine, if it had not been for a
5 little rogue of a major, who ran away with her before she could get a sight of me! And I wonder too what it is the ladies can see in them to be so fond of them — unless it be a touch of the old serpent in 'em, that makes the little creatures be caught, like vipers, with a bit of red cloth.
10 Ha! isn't this the captain coming? — faith it is! — There is a probability of succeeding about that fellow, that is mighty provoking! Who is he talking to?   [*Steps aside.*

Enter CAPTAIN ABSOLUTE.

Abs. (*Aside.*) To what fine purpose I have been plotting! a noble reward for all my schemes, upon my
15 soul! — a little gipsy! — I did not think her romance could have made her so absurd either. 'Sdeath, I never was in a worse humour in my life! — I could cut my own throat, or any other person's, with the greatest pleasure in the world!

20 *Sir Luc.* Oh, faith! I'm in the luck of it. I never could have found him in a sweeter temper for my purpose — to be sure I'm just come in the nick! Now to enter into conversation with him, and so quarrel genteelly. (*Goes up to* CAPTAIN ABSOLUTE.) With regard to that
25 matter, captain, I must beg leave to differ in opinion with you.

188

Abs. Upon my word, then, you must be a very subtle
disputant: — because, sir, I happened just then to be
giving no opinion at all.

Sir Luc. That's no reason. For give me leave to tell
you, a man may think an untruth as well as speak one.   5

Abs. Very true, sir; but if a man never utters his
thoughts, I should think they might stand a chance of
escaping controversy.

Sir Luc. Then, sir, you differ in opinion with me, which
amounts to the same thing.   10

Abs. Hark'ee, Sir Lucius; if I had not before known
you to be a gentleman, upon my soul, I should not have
discovered it at this interview : for what you can drive at,
unless you mean to quarrel with me, I cannot conceive !

Sir Luc. I humbly thank you, sir, for the quickness   15
of your apprehension. (*Bowing.*) You have named the
very thing I would be at.

Abs. Very well, sir; I shall certainly not balk your
inclinations. — But I should be glad if you would please
to explain your motives.   20

Sir Luc. Pray sir, be easy; the quarrel is a very pretty
quarrel as it stands ; we should only spoil it by trying to
explain it. However, your memory is very short, or you
could not have forgot an affront you passed on me within
this week. So, no more, but name your time and place.   25

Abs. Well, sir, since you are so bent on it, the sooner
the better; let it be this evening — here, by the Spring
Gardens. We shall scarcely be interrupted.

Sir Luc. Faith ! that same interruption in affairs of
this nature shows very great ill-breeding. I don't know   30
what's the reason, but in England, if a thing of this kind

gets wind, people make such a pother, that a gentleman can never fight in peace and quietness. However, if it's the same to you, captain, I should take it as a particular kindness if you'd let us meet in King's-Mead-Fields, as a 5 little business will call me there about six o'clock, and I may despatch both matters at once.

Abs. 'Tis the same to me exactly. A little after six, then, we will discuss this matter more seriously.

Sir Luc. If you please, sir; there will be very pretty 10 small-sword light, though it won't do for a long shot. So that matter's settled, and my mind's at ease!   [*Exit.*

Enter FAULKLAND.

Abs. Well met! I was going to look for you. O Faulkland! all the demons of spite and disappointment have conspired against me! I'm so vexed, that if I had 15 not the prospect of a resource in being knocked o' the head by-and-by, I should scarce have spirits to tell you the cause.

Faulk. What can you mean? — Has Lydia changed her mind? — I should have thought her duty and inclination would now have pointed to the same object.

20 *Abs.* Ay, just as the eyes do of a person who squints: when her love-eye was fixed on me, t'other, her eye of duty, was finely obliqued: but when duty bid her point that the same way, off t'other turned on a swivel, and secured its retreat with a frown!

25 *Faulk.* But what's the resource you —

Abs. Oh, to wind up the whole, a good-natured Irishman here has (*mimicking* SIR LUCIUS) begged leave to have the pleasure of cutting my throat; and I mean to indulge him — that's all.

Faulk. Prithee, be serious!

Abs. 'Tis fact, upon my soul! Sir Lucius O'Trigger — you know him by sight — for some affront, which I am sure I never intended, has obliged me to meet him this evening at six o'clock: 'tis on that account I wished to see you; you must go with me.

Faulk. Nay, there must be some mistake, sure. Sir Lucius shall explain himself, and I dare say matters may be accommodated. But this evening, did you say? I wish it had been any other time.

Abs. Why? there will be light enough: there will (as Sir Lucius says) be very pretty small-sword light, though it will not do for a long shot. Confound his long shots!

Faulk. But I am myself a good deal ruffled by a difference I have had with Julia. My vile tormenting temper has made me treat her so cruelly, that I shall not be myself till we are reconciled.

Abs. By Heavens! Faulkland, you don't deserve her!

Enter SERVANT *gives* FAULKLAND *a letter, and exit.*

Faulk. Oh, Jack! this is from Julia. I dread to open it! I fear it may be to take a last leave! — perhaps to bid me return her letters, and restore — Oh, how I suffer for my folly!

Abs. Here, let me see. (*Takes the letter and opens it.*) Ay, a final sentence, indeed! — 'tis all over with you, faith!

Faulk. Nay, Jack, don't keep me in suspense!

Abs. Hear then. — (*Reads.*) *As I am convinced that my dear Faulkland's own reflections have already upbraided him for his last unkindness to me, I will not add a word on the subject. I wish to speak with you as soon as possible. Yours ever and truly,* JULIA. There's stubbornness and resentment for you! (*Gives him the letter.*) Why, man, you don't seem one whit the happier at this!

5   *Faulk.* O yes, I am; but — but —

   Abs. Confound your buts! you never hear anything that would make another man bless himself, but you immediately damn it with a but!

   Faulk. Now, Jack, as you are my friend, own honestly 10 — don't you think there is something forward, something indelicate, in this haste to forgive? Women should never sue for reconciliation: that should always come from us. They should retain their coldness till wooed to kindness; and their pardon, like their love, should " not unsought 15 be won."

   Abs. I have not patience to listen to you! thou'rt incorrigible! so say no more on the subject. I must go to settle a few matters. Let me see you before six, remember, at my lodgings. A poor industrious devil like 20 me, who have toiled, and drudged, and plotted to gain my ends, and am at last disappointed by other people's folly, may in pity be allowed to swear and grumble a little; but a captious sceptic in love, a slave to fretfulness and whim, who has no difficulties but of his own creating, is a subject 25 more fit for ridicule than compassion!   [*Exit.*

   Faulk. I feel his reproaches; yet I would not change this too exquisite nicety for the gross content with which he tramples on the thorns of love! His engaging me in this duel has started an idea in my head, which I will instantly 30 pursue. I'll use it as the touchstone of Julia's sincerity and disinterestedness. If her love prove pure and sterling ore, my name will rest on it with honour; and once I've stamped it there, I lay aside my doubts for ever! But if the dross of selfishness, the alloy of pride, predominate, 'twill be best to leave her as a toy for some less cautious fool to sigh for!   [*Exit.* 5

ACT V.

Scene I. Julia's dressing-room.

Julia discovered alone.

Jul. How this message has alarmed me! what dreadful accident can he mean? why such charge to be alone? — O Faulkland! — how many unhappy moments — how many tears have you cost me.

Enter Faulkland.

5 *Jul.* What means this? — why this caution, Faulkland?

Faulk. Alas! Julia, I am come to take a long farewell.

Jul. Heavens! what do you mean?

Faulk. You see before you a wretch, whose life is 10 forfeited. Nay, start not! — the infirmity of my temper has drawn all this misery on me. I left you fretful and passionate — an untoward accident drew me into a quarrel — the event is, that I must fly this kingdom instantly. O Julia, had I been so fortunate as to have 15 called you mine entirely, before this mischance had fallen on me, I should not so deeply dread my banishment!

Jul. My soul is oppressed with sorrow at the nature of your misfortune: had these adverse circumstances arisen from a less fatal cause, I should have felt strong 20 comfort in the thought that I could now chase from your

bosom every doubt of the warm sincerity of my love. My
heart has long known no other guardian — I now entrust
my person to your honour — we will fly together. When
safe from pursuit, my father's will may be fulfilled — and
I receive a legal claim to be the partner of your sorrows, 5
and tenderest comforter. Then on the bosom of your
wedded Julia, you may lull your keen regret to slumbering;
while virtuous love, with a cherub's hand, shall smooth
the brow of upbraiding thought, and pluck the thorn from
compunction. 10

Faulk. O Julia! I am bankrupt in gratitude! but the
time is so pressing, it calls on you for so hasty a resolution!
— Would you not wish some hours to weigh the advantages
you forego, and what little compensation poor Faulkland
can make you beside his solitary love? 15

Jul. I ask not a moment. No, Faulkland, I have loved
you for yourself: and if I now, more than ever, prize the
solemn engagement which so long has pledged us to each
other, it is because it leaves no room for hard aspersions
on my fame, and puts the seal of duty to an act of love. 20
But let us not linger. Perhaps this delay —

Faulk. 'Twill be better I should not venture out again
till dark. Yet am I grieved to think what numberless
distresses will press heavy on your gentle disposition!

Jul. Perhaps your fortune may be forfeited by this 25
unhappy act. I know not whether 'tis so; but sure that
alone can never make us unhappy. The little I have will
be sufficient to support us; and exile never should be
splendid.

Faulk. Ay, but in such an abject state of life, my 30
wounded pride perhaps may increase the natural fretfulness

of my temper, till I become a rude, morose companion, beyond your patience to endure. Perhaps the recollection of a deed my conscience cannot justify may haunt me in such gloomy and unsocial fits, that I shall hate the tender-
5 ness that would relieve me, break from your arms, and quarrel with your fondness!

Jul. If your thoughts should assume so unhappy a bent, you will the more want some mild and affectionate spirit to watch over and console you: one who, by bearing
10 your infirmities with gentleness and resignation, may teach you so to bear the evils of your fortune.

Faulk. Julia, I have proved you to the quick! and with this useless device I throw away all my doubts. How shall I plead to be forgiven this last unworthy effect
15 of my restless, unsatisfied disposition?

Jul. Has no such disaster happened as you related?

Faulk. I am ashamed to own that it was pretended; yet in pity, Julia, do not kill me with resenting a fault which never can be repeated: but sealing, this once, my
20 pardon, let me to-morrow, in the face of Heaven, receive my future guide and monitress, and expiate my past folly by years of tender adoration.

Jul. Hold, Faulkland! — that you are free from a crime, which I before feared to name, Heaven knows how
25 sincerely I rejoice! These are tears of thankfulness for that! But that your cruel doubts should have urged you to an imposition that has wrung my heart, gives me now a pang more keen than I can express!

Faulk. By Heavens! Julia —

30   *Jul.* Yet hear me. — My father loved you, Faulkland! and you preserved the life that tender parent gave me;

in his presence I pledged my hand — joyfully pledged it — where before I had given my heart. When, soon after, I lost that parent, it seemed to me that Providence had, in Faulkland, shown me whither to transfer without a pause, my grateful duty, as well as my affection : hence I have been content to bear from you what pride and delicacy would have forbid me from another. I will not upbraid you, by repeating how you have trifled with my sincerity —

Faulk. I confess it all! yet hear —

Jul. After such a year of trial, I might have flattered myself that I should not have been insulted with a new probation of my sincerity, as cruel as unnecessary! I now see it is not in your nature to be content or confident in love. With this conviction — I never will be yours. While I had hopes that my persevering attention, and unreproaching kindness, might in time reform your temper, I should have been happy to have gained a dearer influence over you; but I will not furnish you with a licensed power to keep alive an incorrigible fault, at the expense of one who never would contend with you.

Faulk. Nay, but, Julia, by my soul and honour, if after this —

Jul. But one word more. — As my faith has once been given to you, I never will barter it with another. I shall pray for your happiness with the truest sincerity; and the dearest blessing I can ask of Heaven to send you will be to charm you from that unhappy temper, which alone has prevented the performance of our solemn engagement. All I request of you is, that you will yourself reflect upon this infirmity, and when you number up the many true delights it has deprived you of, let it not be your least regret, that it lost you the love of one who would have followed you in beggary through the world! [*Exit.*

Faulk. She's gone — for ever! — There was an awful resolution in her manner, that riveted me to my place. —
5 O fool! — dolt! — barbarian! Cursed as I am, with more imperfections than my fellow-wretches, kind Fortune sent a heaven-gifted cherub to my aid, and, like a ruffian, I have driven her from my side! — I must now haste to my appointment. Well, my mind is tuned for such a scene.
10 I shall wish only to become a principal in it, and reverse the tale my cursed folly put me upon forging here. — O Love! — tormentor! — fiend! — whose influence, like the moon's, acting on men of dull souls, makes idiots of them, but meeting subtler spirits, betrays their course, and urges
15 sensibility to madness! [*Exit.*

Enter LYDIA *and* MAID.

Maid. My mistress, ma'am, I know, was here just now — perhaps she is only in the next room. [*Exit.*

Lyd. Heigh-ho! Though he has used me so, this fellow runs strangely in my head. I believe one lecture
20 from my grave cousin will make me recall him. (*Reënter* JULIA.) O Julia, I am come to you with such an appetite for consolation. — Lud! child, what's the matter with you? You have been crying! — I'll be hanged if that Faulkland has not been tormenting you!
25 *Jul.* You mistake the cause of my uneasiness! — Something has flurried me a little. Nothing that you can guess at. (*Aside.*) I would not accuse Faulkland to a sister!

Lyd. Ah! whatever vexations you may have, I can

198

assure you mine surpass them.   You know who Beverley
proves to be?

Jul.   I will now own to you, Lydia, that Mr. Faulkland
had before informed me of the whole affair.   Had young
Absolute been the person you took him for, I should not 5
have accepted your confidence on the subject, without a
serious endeavour to counteract your caprice.

Lyd.   So, then, I see I have been deceived by every one!
But I don't care — I'll never have him.

Jul.   Nay, Lydia —   10

Lyd.   Why, is it not provoking? when I thought we
were coming to the prettiest distress imaginable, to find
myself made a mere Smithfield bargain of at last!   There
had I projected one of the most sentimental elopements! —
so becoming a disguise! — so amiable a ladder of ropes! — 15
conscious moon — four horses — Scotch parson — with
such surprise to Mrs. Malaprop — and such paragraphs
in the newspapers! — Oh, I shall die with disappointment!

Jul.   I don't wonder at it!

Lyd.   Now — sad reverse! — what have I to expect, 20
but, after a deal of flimsy preparation with a bishop's
licence, and my aunt's blessing, to go simpering up to the
altar; or perhaps be cried three times in a country church,
and have an unmannerly fat clerk ask the consent of every
butcher in the parish to join John Absolute and Lydia 25
Languish, spinster!   Oh, that I should live to hear myself
called spinster!

Jul.   Melancholy indeed!

Lyd.   How mortifying, to remember the dear delicious
shifts I used to be put to, to gain half a minute's conversa- 30
tion with this fellow!   How often have I stole forth, in

the coldest night in January, and found him in the garden,
stuck like a dripping statue! There would he kneel to me
in the snow, and sneeze and cough so pathetically! he
shivering with cold and I with apprehension! and while
5 the freezing blast numbed our joints, how warmly would
he press me to pity his flame, and glow with mutual ardour!
— Ah, Julia, that was something like being in love.

Jul. If I were in spirits, Lydia, I should chide you
only by laughing heartily at you; but it suits more the
10 situation of my mind, at present, earnestly to entreat you
not to let a man, who loves you with sincerity, suffer that
unhappiness from your caprice, which I know too well
caprice can inflict.

Lyd. O Lud! what has brought my aunt here?

Enter MRS. MALAPROP, FAG, *and* DAVID.

15 *Mrs. Mal.* So! so! here's fine work! — here's fine
suicide, parricide, and simulation, going on in the fields!
and Sir Anthony not to be found to prevent the antistrophe!

Jul. For Heaven's sake, madam, what's the meaning
20 of this?

Mrs. Mal. That gentleman can tell you — 'twas he
enveloped the affair to me.

Lyd. Do, sir, will you, inform us? [*To* FAG.

Fag. Ma'am, I should hold myself very deficient in
25 every requisite that forms the man of breeding, if I delayed
a moment to give all the information in my power to a lady
so deeply interested in the affair as you are.

Lyd. But quick! quick, sir!

Fag. True, ma'am, as you say, one should be quick in

divulging matters of this nature; for should we be tedious, perhaps while we are flourishing on the subject, two or three lives may be lost!

Lyd. O patience! — Do, ma'am, for Heaven's sake! tell us what is the matter? 5

Mrs. Mal. Why, murder's the matter! slaughter's the matter! killing's the matter! — but he can tell you the perpendiculars.

Lyd. Then, prithee, sir, be brief.

Fag. Why then, ma'am, as to murder — I cannot take 10 upon me to say — and as to slaughter, or manslaughter, that will be as the jury finds it.

Lyd. But who, sir — who are engaged in this?

Fag. Faith, ma'am, one is a young gentleman whom I should be very sorry any thing was to happen to — a very 15 pretty behaved gentleman! We have lived much together, and always on terms.

Lyd. But who is this? who! who! who?

Fag. My master, ma'am — my master — I speak of my master. 20

Lyd. Heavens! What, Captain Absolute!

Mrs. Mal. Oh, to be sure, you are frightened now!

Jul. But who are with him, sir?

Fag. As to the rest, ma'am, this gentleman can inform you better than I. 25

Jul. Do speak, friend. [*To* DAVID.

Dav. Look'ee, my lady — by the mass! there's mischief going on. Folks don't use to meet for amusement with firearms, firelocks, fire-engines, fire-screens, fire-office, and the devil knows what other crackers beside! — This, 30 my lady, I say, has an angry savour.

Jul. But who is there beside Captain Absolute, friend?

Dav. My poor master — under favour for mentioning him first. You know me, my lady — I am David — and my master of course is, or was, Squire Acres. Then comes
5 Squire Faulkland.

Jul. Do, ma'am, let us instantly endeavour to prevent mischief.

Mrs. Mal. O fy! — it would be very inelegant in us: — we should only participate things.

10 *Dav.* Ah! do, Mrs. Aunt, save a few lives — they are desperately given, believe me. — Above all, there is that bloodthirsty Philistine, Sir Lucius O'Trigger.

Mrs. Mal. Sir Lucius O'Trigger? O mercy! have they drawn poor little dear Sir Lucius into the scrape? —
15 Why, how you stand, girl! you have no more feeling than one of the Derbyshire putrifactions!

Lyd. What are we to do, madam?

Mrs. Mal. Why fly with the utmost felicity, to be sure, to prevent mischief! — Here, friend, you can show us
20 the place?

Fag. If you please, ma'am, I will conduct you. — David, do you look for Sir Anthony.   [*Exit* DAVID.

Mrs. Mal. Come, girls! this gentleman will exhort us. — Come, sir, you're our envoy — lead the way, and we'll
25 precede.

Fag. Not a step before the ladies for the world!

Mrs. Mal. You're sure you know the spot?

Fag. I think I can find it, ma'am; and one good thing is, we shall hear the report of the pistols as we draw near,
30 so we can't well miss them; — never fear, ma'am, never fear.   [*Exeunt, he talking.*

SCENE II. THE SOUTH PARADE.

Enter CAPTAIN ABSOLUTE, *putting his sword under his great coat.*

Abs. A sword seen in the streets of Bath would raise as great an alarm as a mad dog. — How provoking this is in Faulkland ! — never punctual ! I shall be obliged to go without him at last. — Oh, here's Sir Anthony ! how shall I escape him ? 5

[*Muffles up his face, and takes a circle to go off.*

Enter SIR ANTHONY ABSOLUTE.

Sir Anth. How one may be deceived at a little distance ! only that I see he don't know me, I could have sworn that was Jack ! — Hey ! Gad's life ! it is. — Why, Jack, what are you afraid of ? hey ! — sure I'm right. — Why Jack, Jack Absolute ! [*Goes up to him.* 10

Abs. Really, sir, you have the advantage of me : — I don't remember ever to have had the honour — my name is Saunderson, at your service.

Sir Anth. Sir, I beg your pardon — I took you — hey ? — why, zounds ! it is — Stay (*Looks up to his face.*) 15 So, so — your humble servant, Mr. Saunderson ! Why, you scoundrel, what tricks are you after now ?

Abs. Oh, a joke, sir, a joke ! I came here on purpose to look for you, sir.

Sir Anth. You did ! well, I am glad you were so lucky : 20 — but what are you muffled up so for ? — what's this for ? — hey !

Abs. 'Tis cool, sir ; isn't ? — rather chilly somehow ; — but I shall be late — I have a particular engagement.

Sir Anth. Stay! — Why, I thought you were looking for me? — Pray, Jack, where is't you are going?

Abs. Going, sir!

Sir Anth. Ay, where are you going?

5 *Abs.* Where am I going?

Sir Anth. You unmannerly puppy!

Abs. I was going, sir, to — to — to — to Lydia — sir, to Lydia — to make matters up if I could ; — and I was looking for you, sir, to — to —

10 *Sir Anth.* To go with you, I suppose. — Well, come along.

Abs. Oh! zounds! no, sir, not for the world! — I wished to meet with you, sir, — to — to — to — You find it cool, I'm sure, sir — you'd better not stay out.

15 *Sir Anth.* Cool! — not at all. — Well, Jack — and what will you say to Lydia?

Abs. Oh, sir, beg her pardon, humour her — promise and vow : but I detain you, sir — consider the cold air on your gout.

20 *Sir Anth.* Oh, not at all! — not at all! I'm in no hurry. — Ah! Jack, you youngsters, when once you are wounded here (*Putting his hand to* CAPTAIN ABSOLUTE'S *breast.*) Hey! what the deuce have you got here?

Abs. Nothing, sir — nothing.

25 *Sir Anth.* What's this? — here's something hard.

Abs. Oh, trinkets, sir! trinkets! — a bauble for Lydia!

Sir Anth. Nay, let me see your taste. (*Pulls his coat open, the sword falls.*) Trinkets! — a bauble for Lydia! —

30 Zounds! sirrah, you are not going to cut her throat, are you?

Abs. Ha! ha! ha! — I thought it would divert you, sir, though I didn't mean to tell you till afterwards.

Sir Anth. You didn't? — Yes, this is a very diverting trinket, truly!

Abs. Sir, I'll explain to you. — You know, sir, Lydia is 5 romantic, devilish romantic, and very absurd of course: now, sir, I intend, if she refuses to forgive me, to unsheath this sword, and swear I'll fall upon its point, and expire at her feet!

Sir Anth. Fall upon a fiddlestick's end! — why, I 10 suppose it is the very thing that would please her. — Get along, you fool!

Abs. Well, sir, you shall hear of my success — you shall hear. — *O Lydia! — forgive me, or this pointed steel —* says I.   15

Sir Anth. O, booby! *stab away and welcome* — says she. — Get along!   [*Exit* CAPTAIN ABSOLUTE.

Enter DAVID, *running.*

Dav. Stop him! stop him! Murder! Thief! Fire! — Stop fire! Stop fire! — O Sir Anthony — call! call! bid'm stop! Murder! Fire!   20

Sir Anth. Fire! Murder! — Where?

Dav. Oons! he's out of sight! and I'm out of breath, for my part! O Sir Anthony, why didn't you stop him? why didn't you stop him?

Sir Anth. Zounds! the fellow's mad! — Stop whom? 25 stop Jack?

Dav. Ay, the captain, sir! — there's murder and slaughter —

Sir Anth. Murder!

Dav. Ay, please you, Sir Anthony, there's all kinds of murder, all sorts of slaughter to be seen in the fields: there's fighting going on, sir — bloody sword-and-gun fighting!

5   *Sir Anth.* Who are going to fight, dunce?

Dav. Every body that I know of, Sir Anthony: — every body is going to fight, my poor master, Sir Lucius O'Trigger, your son, the captain —

Sir Anth. Oh, the dog! I see his tricks. — Do you 10 know the place?

Dav. King's-Mead-Fields.

Sir Anth. You know the way?

Dav. Not an inch; but I'll call the mayor — aldermen — constables — churchwardens — and beadles — we can't 15 be too many to part them.

Sir Anth. Come along — give me your shoulder! we'll get assistance as we go — the lying villain! — Well! I shall be in such a frenzy! — So — this was the history of his trinkets! I'll bauble him!   [*Exeunt.*

SCENE III.   KING'S-MEAD-FIELDS.

Enter SIR LUCIUS O'TRIGGER *and* ACRES, *with pistols.*

20   *Acres.* By my valour! then, Sir Lucius, forty yards is a good distance. Odds levels and aims! — I say it is a good distance.

Sir Luc. Is it for muskets or small field-pieces? Upon my conscience, Mr. Acres, you must leave those things to 25 me. — Stay now — I'll show you. (*Measures paces along the stage.*) There now, that is a very pretty distance — a pretty gentleman's distance.

Acres. Zounds! we might as well fight in a sentry-box! I tell you, Sir Lucius, the farther he is off, the cooler I shall take my aim.

Sir Luc. Faith! then I suppose you would aim at him best of all if he was out of sight! 5

Acres. No, Sir Lucius; but I should think forty or eight-and-thirty yards —

Sir Luc. Pho! pho! nonsense! three or four feet between the mouths of your pistols is as good as a mile.

Acres. Odds bullets, no! — by my valour! there is no 10 merit in killing him so near: do, my dear Sir Lucius, let me bring him down at a long shot: — a long shot, Sir Lucius, if you love me!

Sir Luc. Well, the gentleman's friend and I must settle that. — But tell me now, Mr. Acres, in case of an accident, 15 is there any little will or commission I could execute for you?

Acres. I am much obliged to you, Sir Lucius — but I don't understand —

Sir Luc. Why, you may think there's no being shot at without a little risk — and if an unlucky bullet should 20 carry a quietus with it — I say it will be no time then to be bothering you about family matters.

Acres. A quietus!

Sir Luc. For instance, now — if that should be the case — would you choose to be pickled and sent home? — 25 or would it be the same to you to lie here in the Abbey? — I'm told there is very snug lying in the Abbey.

Acres. Pickled! — Snug lying in the Abbey! — Odds tremors! Sir Lucius, don't talk so!

Sir Luc. I suppose, Mr. Acres, you never were engaged 30 in an affair of this kind before?

Acres. No, Sir Lucius, never before.

Sir Luc. Ah! that's a pity! — there's nothing like being used to a thing. — Pray now, how would you receive the gentleman's shot?

5 *Acres.* Odds files! — I've practised that — there, Sir Lucius — there. (*Puts himself in an attitude.*) A side-front, hey? Odd! I'll make myself small enough: I'll stand edgeways.

Sir Luc. Now — you're quite out — for if you stand 10 so when I take my aim —   [*Levelling at him.*

Acres. Zounds! Sir Lucius — are you sure it is not cocked?

Sir Luc. Never fear.

Acres. But — but — you don't know — it may go off 15 of its own head!

Sir Luc. Pho! be easy. — Well, now if I hit you in the body, my bullet has a double chance — for if it misses a vital part of your right side — 'twill be very hard if it don't succeed on the left!

20 *Acres.* A vital part?

Sir Luc. But, there — fix yourself so (*Placing him.*) let him see the broad-side of your full front — there — now a ball or two may pass clean through your body, and never do any harm at all.

25 *Acres.* Clean through me! — a ball or two clean through me!

Sir Luc. Ay, may they — and it is much the genteelest attitude into the bargain.

Acres. Look'ee! Sir Lucius — I'd just as lieve be 30 shot in an awkward posture as a genteel one; so, by my valour! I will stand edgeways.

SIR LUCIUS O'TRIGGER AND BOB ACRES

"I feel it oozing out as it were at the palms of my hands!"

Sir Luc.   (*Looking at his watch.*)   Sure they don't mean to disappoint us — Hah! — no, faith — I think I see them coming.

Acres.   Hey — what! — coming! —

Sir Luc.   Ay. — Who are those yonder getting over the stile?

Acres.   There are two of them indeed! — well — let them come — hey, Sir Lucius! — we — we — we — we — won't run.

Sir Luc.   Run!

Acres.   No — I say — we won't run, by my valour!

Sir Luc.   What the devil's the matter with you?

Acres.   Nothing — nothing — my dear friend — my dear Sir Lucius — but I — I — I don't feel quite so bold, somehow, as I did.

Sir Luc.   O fy — consider your honour.

Acres.   Ay — true — my honour.   Do, Sir Lucius, edge in a word or two every now and then about my honour.

Sir Luc.   Well, here they're coming.   [*Looking.*

Acres.   Sir Lucius — if I wa'n't with you, I should almost think I was afraid. — If my valour should leave me! — Valour will come and go.

Sir Luc.   Then pray keep it fast, while you have it.

Acres.   Sir Lucius — I doubt it is going — yes — my valour is certainly going! — it is sneaking off! — I feel it oozing out as it were at the palms of my hands!

Sir Luc.   Your honour — your honour! — Here they are.

Acres.   O mercy! — now — that I was safe at Clod-Hall! or could be shot before I was aware!

Enter FAULKLAND *and* CAPTAIN ABSOLUTE.

Sir Luc. Gentlemen, your most obedient. — Hah! — what, Captain Absolute! — So, I suppose, sir, you are come here, just like myself — to do a kind office, first for your friend — then to proceed to business on your own 5 account.

Acres. What, Jack! — my dear Jack! — my dear friend!

Abs. Hark'ee, Bob, Beverley's at hand.

Sir Luc. Well, Mr. Acres — I don't blame your saluting 10 the gentleman civilly. (*To* FAULKLAND.) So, Mr. Beverley, if you'll choose your weapons, the captain and I will measure the ground.

Faulk. My weapons, sir!

Acres. Odds life! Sir Lucius, I'm not going to fight 15 Mr. Faulkland; these are my particular friends.

Sir Luc. What, sir, did you not come here to fight Mr. Acres?

Faulk. Not I, upon my word, sir.

Sir Luc. Well, now, that's mighty provoking! But I 20 hope, Mr. Faulkland, as there are three of us come on purpose for the game, you won't be so cantankerous as to spoil the party by sitting out.

Abs. O pray, Faulkland, fight to oblige Sir Lucius.

Faulk. Nay, if Mr. Acres is so bent on the matter —

25 *Acres.* No, no, Mr. Faulkland; — I'll bear my disappointment like a Christian. — Look'ee, Sir Lucius, there's no occasion at all for me to fight; and if it is the same to you, I'd as lieve let it alone.

Sir Luc. Observe me, Mr. Acres — I must not be

trifled with. You have certainly challenged somebody —
and you came here to fight him. Now, if that gentleman
is willing to represent him, I can't see, for my soul, why
it isn't just the same thing.

Acres. Why no — Sir Lucius — I tell you, 'tis one 5
Beverley I've challenged — a fellow, you see, that dare
not show his face! — If he were here, I'd make him give up
his pretensions directly.

Abs. Hold, Bob — let me set you right — there is
no such man as Beverley in the case. — The person who 10
assumed that name is before you; and as his pretensions
are the same in both characters, he is ready to support
them in whatever way you please.

Sir Luc. Well, this is lucky. — Now you have an
opportunity — 15

Acres. What, quarrel with my dear friend Jack
Absolute? — not if he were fifty Beverleys! Zounds!
Sir Lucius, you would not have me so unnatural.

Sir Luc. Upon my conscience, Mr. Acres, your valour
has oozed away with a vengeance! 20

Acres. Not in the least! Odds backs and abettors!
I'll be your second with all my heart — and if you should
get a quietus, you may command me entirely. I'll get
you snug lying in the Abbey here; or pickle you, and send
you over to Blunderbuss-hall, or any thing of the kind, 25
with the greatest pleasure.

Sir Luc. Pho! pho! you are little better than a coward.

Acres. Mind, gentlemen, he calls me a coward; coward
was the word, by my valour!

Sir Luc. Well, sir?
30

Acres. Look'ee, Sir Lucius, 'tisn't that I mind the word

coward — coward may be said in joke — but if you had called me a poltroon, odds daggers and balls —

Sir Luc. Well, sir?

Acres. I should have thought you a very ill-bred man.

5 *Sir Luc.* Pho! you are beneath my notice.

Abs. Nay, Sir Lucius, you can't have a better second than my friend Acres. — He is a most determined dog — called in the country, Fighting Bob. — He generally kills a man a week — don't you, Bob?

10 *Acres.* Ay — at home!

Sir Luc. Well, then, captain, 'tis we must begin — so come out, my little counsellor (*draws his sword*) — and ask the gentleman, whether he will resign the lady, without forcing you to proceed against him.

15 *Abs.* Come on then, sir (*draws*); since you won't let it be an amicable suit, here's my reply.

Enter SIR ANTHONY ABSOLUTE, DAVID, MRS. MALAPROP, LYDIA, *and* JULIA.

Dav. Knock 'em all down, sweet Sir Anthony; knock down my master in particular; and bind his hands over to their good behaviour!

20 *Sir Anth.* Put up, Jack, put up, or I shall be in a frenzy — how came you in a duel, sir?

Abs. Faith, sir, that gentleman can tell you better than I; 'twas he called on me, and you know, sir, I serve his majesty.

25 *Sir Anth.* Here's a pretty fellow; I catch him going to cut a man's throat, and he tells me, he serves his majesty — Zounds! sirrah, then how durst you draw the king's sword against one of his subjects?

Abs.　Sir, I tell you! that gentleman called me out, without explaining his reasons.

Sir Anth.　Gad! sir, how came you to call my son out, without explaining your reasons?

Sir Luc.　Your son, sir, insulted me in a manner which 5 my honour could not brook.

Sir Anth.　Zounds! Jack, how durst you insult the gentleman in a manner which his honour could not brook?

Mrs. Mal.　Come, come, let's have no honour before ladies. — Captain Absolute, come here — How could you 10 intimidate us so? — Here's Lydia has been terrified to death for you.

Abs.　For fear I should be killed, or escape, ma'am?

Mrs. Mal.　Nay, no delusions to the past — Lydia is convinced; speak, child.　　　　　　　　　　　　15

Sir Luc.　With your leave, ma'am, I must put in a word here: I believe I could interpret the young lady's silence. Now mark —

Lyd.　What is it you mean, sir?

Sir Luc.　Come, come, Delia, we must be serious now — 20 this is no time for trifling.

Lyd.　'Tis true, sir; and your reproof bids me offer this gentleman my hand, and solicit the return of his affections.

Abs.　O! my little angel, say you so! — Sir Lucius — I 25 perceive there must be some mistake here, with regard to the affront which you affirm I have given you. I can only say, that it could not have been intentional. And as you must be convinced, that I should not fear to support a real injury, you shall now see that I am not ashamed to 30 atone for an inadvertency — I ask your pardon. — But

for this lady, while honoured with her approbation, I will
support my claim against any man whatever.

Sir Anth.   Well said, Jack, and I'll stand by you, my
boy.

5   *Acres.*   Mind, I give up all my claim — I make no
pretensions to any thing in the world; and if I can't get
a wife without fighting for her, by my valour! I'll live a
bachelor.

Sir Luc.   Captain, give me your hand: an affront
10 handsomely acknowledged becomes an obligation; and
as for the lady, if she chooses to deny her own hand-
writing, here —   [*Takes out letters.*

Mrs. Mal.   O, he will dissolve my mystery! — Sir
Lucius, perhaps there's some mistake — perhaps I can
15 illuminate —

Sir Luc.   Pray, old gentlewoman, don't interfere where
you have no business. — Miss Languish, are you my Delia,
or not?

Lyd.   Indeed, Sir Lucius, I am not.

                    [*Walks aside with* Captain Absolute.

20   *Mrs. Mal.*   Sir Lucius O'Trigger — ungrateful as you
are — I own the soft impeachment — pardon my blushes
I am Delia.

Sir Luc.   You Delia — pho! pho! be easy.

Mrs. Mal.   Why, thou barbarous Vandyke — those
25 letters are mine — When you are more sensible of my
benignity — perhaps I may be brought to encourage your
addresses.

Sir Luc.   Mrs. Malaprop, I am extremely sensible of
your condescension; and whether you or Lucy have put
30 this trick on me, I am equally beholden to you. — And,

to show you I am not ungrateful, Captain Absolute, since
you have taken that lady from me, I'll give you my Delia
into the bargain.

Abs.   I am much obliged to you, Sir Lucius; but here's
my friend, Fighting Bob, unprovided for.   5

Sir Luc.   Hah! little Valour — here, will you make
your fortune?

Acres.   Odds wrinkles!   No. — But give me your hand,
Sir Lucius, forget and forgive; but if ever I give you a
chance of pickling me again, say Bob Acres is a dunce, 10
that's all.

Sir Anth.   Come, Mrs. Malaprop, don't be cast down —
you are in your bloom yet.

Mrs. Mal.   O Sir Anthony — men are all barbarians.
                              [*All retire but* JULIA *and* FAULKLAND.

Jul.   (*Aside.*) He seems dejected and unhappy — 15
not sullen; there was some foundation, however, for the
tale he told me — O woman! how true should be your
judgment, when your resolution is so weak!

Faulk.   Julia! — how can I sue for what I so little
deserve?   I dare not presume — yet Hope is the child of 20
Penitence.

Jul.   O! Faulkland, you have not been more faulty in
your unkind treatment of me, than I am now in wanting
inclination to resent it.   As my heart honestly bids me
place my weakness to the account of love, I should be 25
ungenerous not to admit the same plea for yours.

Faulk.   Now I shall be blest indeed!

Sir Anth.   (*Coming forward.*)   What's going on here?
— So you have been quarrelling too, I warrant!   Come,
Julia, I never interfered before; but let me have a hand in 30

the matter at last. — All the faults I have ever seen in my
friend Faulkland seemed to proceed from what he calls the
delicacy and warmth of his affection for you.— There,
marry him directly, Julia; you'll find he'll mend sur-
5 prisingly!   [*The rest come forward.*

Sir Luc.   Come, now, I hope there is no dissatisfied
person, but what is content; for as I have been disappointed myself, it will be very hard if I have not the
satisfaction of seeing other people succeed better.

10 *Acres.*   You are right, Sir Lucius. — So Jack, I wish
you joy — Mr. Faulkland the same. — Ladies, — come
now, to show you I'm neither vexed nor angry, odds
tabors and pipes!   I'll order the fiddles in half an hour to
the New Rooms — and I insist on your all meeting me there.

15 *Sir Anth.*   'Gad! sir, I like your spirit; and at night
we single lads will drink a health to the young couples, and
a husband to Mrs. Malaprop.

Faulk.   Our partners are stolen from us, Jack — I hope
to be congratulated by each other — yours for having
20 checked in time the errors of an ill-directed imagination,
which might have betrayed an innocent heart; and mine,
for having, by her gentleness and candour, reformed the
unhappy temper of one, who by it made wretched whom
he loved most, and tortured the heart he ought to have
25 adored.

Abs.   Well, Jack, we have both tasted the bitters, as
well as the sweets of love; with this difference only, that
you always prepared the bitter cup for yourself, while I —

Lyd.   Was always obliged to me for it, hey! Mr.
30 Modesty? — But, come, no more of that — our happiness
is now as unalloyed as general.

Jul.   Then let us study to preserve it so: and while
Hope pictures to us a flattering scene of future bliss, let
us deny its pencil those colours which are too bright to be
lasting. — When hearts deserving happiness would unite
their fortunes, Virtue would crown them with an unfading 5
garland of modest hurtless flowers; but ill-judging Passion
will force the gaudier rose into the wreath, whose thorn
offends them when its leaves are dropped !

[*Exeunt omnes.*

EPILOGUE

BY THE AUTHOR.

SPOKEN BY MRS. BULKLEY.

Ladies, for you — I heard our poet say —
He'd try to coax some moral from his play:
" One moral's plain," cried I, " without more fuss;
Man's social happiness all rests on us:
5 Through all the drama — whether damned or not —
Love gilds the scene, and women guide the plot.
From every rank obedience is our due —
D'ye doubt? — The world's great stage shall prove it true."

The cit, well skilled to shun domestic strife,
10 Will sup abroad; but first he'll ask his wife:
John Trot, his friend, for once will do the same,
But then — he'll just step home to tell his dame.

The surly squire at noon resolves to rule,
And half the day — Zounds! madam is a fool!
15 Convinced at night, the vanquished victor says,
Ah, Kate! you women have such coaxing ways.

The jolly toper chides each tardy blade,
Till reeling Bacchus calls on Love for aid:
Then with each toast he sees fair bumpers swim,
20 And kisses Chloe on the sparkling brim!

Nay, I have heard that statesmen — great and wise —
Will sometimes counsel with a lady's eyes!
The servile suitors watch her various face,
She smiles preferment, or she frowns disgrace,
Curtsies a pension here — there nods a place.   5

Nor with less awe, in scenes of humbler life,
Is viewed the mistress, or is heard the wife.
The poorest peasant of the poorest soil,
The child of poverty, and heir to toil,
Early from radiant Love's impartial light   10
Steals one small spark to cheer this world of night:
Dear spark! that oft through winter's chilling woes
Is all the warmth his little cottage knows!

The wandering tar, who not for years has pressed
The widowed partner of his day of rest,   15
On the cold deck, far from her arms removed,
Still hums the ditty which his Susan loved;
And while around the cadence rude is blown,
The boatswain whistles in a softer tone.

The soldier, fairly proud of wounds and toil,   20
Pants for the triumph of his Nancy's smile;
But ere the battle should he list her cries,
The lover trembles — and the hero dies!
That heart, by war and honour steeled to fear,
Droops on a sigh, and sickens at a tear!   25

But ye more cautious, ye nice-judging few,
Who give to beauty only beauty's due,

Epilogue.

Though friends to love — ye view with deep regret
Our conquests marred, our triumphs incomplete,
Till polished with more lasting charms disclose,
And judgment fix the darts which beauty throws!
5   In female breasts did sense and merit rule,
The lover's mind would ask no other school;
Shamed into sense, the scholars of our eyes,
Our beaux from gallantry would soon be wise;
Would gladly light, their homage to improve,
10 The lamp of knowledge at the torch of love!

THE SCHOOL FOR SCANDAL.

A COMEDY BY RICHARD BRINSLEY SHERIDAN

AS ACTED AT

THEATRE–ROYAL, DRURY–LANE

[First printed in 1777]

A PORTRAIT.

ADDRESSED TO MRS. CREWE, WITH THE
COMEDY OF THE SCHOOL FOR SCANDAL.

BY R. B. SHERIDAN, ESQ.

Tell me, ye prim adepts in Scandal's school,
Who rail by precept, and detract by rule,
Lives there no character, so tried, so known,
So decked with grace, and so unlike your own,
That even you assist her fame to raise,   5
Approve by envy, and by silence praise!
Attend! — a model shall attract your view —
Daughters of calumny, I summon you!
You shall decide if this a portrait prove,
Or fond creation of the Muse and Love.   10
Attend, ye virgin critics, shrewd and sage,
Ye matron censors of this childish age,
Whose peering eye and wrinkled front declare
A fixed antipathy to young and fair;
By cunning, cautious; or by nature, cold,   15
In maiden madness, virulently bold! —
Attend, ye skilled to coin the precious tale,
Creating proof, where innuendos fail!
Whose practised memories, cruelly exact,
Omit no circumstance, except the fact! —   20

A Portrait.

Attend, all ye who boast, — or old   young, —
The living libel of a slanderous tongue!
So shall my theme as far contrasted be,
As saints by fiends, or hymns by calumny.
5 Come, gentle Amoret (for 'neath that name
In worthier verse is sung thy beauty's fame);
Come — for but thee who seeks the Muse? and while
Celestial blushes check thy conscious smile,
With timid grace, and hesitating eye,
10 The perfect model, which I boast, supply: —
Vain Muse! couldst thou the humblest sketch create
Of her, or slightest charm couldst imitate —
Could they blest strain in kindred colours trace
The faintest wonder of her form and face —
15 Poets would study the immortal line,
And Reynolds own his art subdued by thine;
That art, which well might added lustre give
To Nature's best, and Heaven's superlative:
On Granby's cheek might bid new glories rise,
20 Or point a purer beam from Devon's eyes!
Hard is the task to shape that beauty's praise,
Whose judgment scorns the homage flattery pays!
But praising Amoret we cannot err,
No tongue o'ervalues Heaven, or flatters her!
25 Yet she by Fate's perverseness — she alone
Would doubt our truth, nor deem such praise her own.
Adorning fashion, unadorned by dress,
Simple from taste, and not from carelessness;
Discreet in gesture, in deportment mild,
30 Not stiff with prudence, nor uncouthly wild:
No state has Amoret; no studied mien;

She frowns no goddess, and she moves no queen.
The softer charm that in her manner lies
Is framed to captivate, yet not surprise;
It justly suits the expression of her face, —
'Tis less than dignity, and more than grace!   5
On her pure cheek the native hue is such,
That, formed by Heaven to be admired so much,
The hand divine, with a less partial care,
Might well have fixed a fainter crimson there,
And bade the gentle inmate of her breast —   10
Inshrinèd Modesty — supply the rest.
But who the peril of her lips shall paint?
Strip them of smiles — still, still all words are faint.
But moving Love himself appears to teach
Their action, though denied to rule her speech;   15
And thou who seest her speak, and dost not hear,
Mourn not her distant accents 'scape thine ear;
Viewing those lips, thou still may'st make pretence
To judge of what she says, and swear 'tis sense:
Clothed with such grace, with such expression fraught,   20
They move in meaning, and they pause in thought!
But dost thou farther watch, with charmed surprise,
The mild irresolution of her eyes,
Curious to mark how frequent they repose,
In brief eclipse and momentary close —   25
Ah! seest thou not an ambushed Cupid there,
Too timorous of his charge, with jealous care
Veils and unveils those beams of heavenly light,
Too full, too fatal else, for mortal sight?
Nor yet, such pleasing vengeance fond to meet,   30
In pardoning dimples hope a safe retreat.

A Portrait.

What though her peaceful breast should ne'er allow
Subduing frowns to arm her altered brow,
By Love, I swear, and by his gentle wiles,
More fatal still the mercy of her smiles!
5 Thus lovely, thus adorned, possessing all
Of bright or fair that can to woman fall,
The height of vanity might well be thought
Prerogative in her, and Nature's fault.
Yet gentle Amoret, in mind supreme
10 As well as charms, rejects the vainer theme;
And, half mistrustful of her beauty's store,
She barbs with wit those darts too keen before: —
Read in all knowledge that her sex should reach,
Though Greville, or the Muse, should deign to teach,
15 Fond to improve, nor timorous to discern
How far it is a woman's grace to learn;
In Millar's dialect she would not prove
Apollo's priestess, but Apollo's love,
Graced by those signs which truth delights to own,
20 The timid blush, and mild submitted tone:
Whate'er she says, though sense appear throughout,
Displays the tender hue of female doubt;
Decked with that charm, how lovely wit appears,
How graceful science, when that robe she wears!
25 Such too her talents, and her bent of mind,
As speak a sprightly heart by thought refined:
A taste for mirth, by contemplation schooled,
A turn for ridicule, by candour ruled,
A scorn of folly, which she tries to hide;
30 An awe of talent, which she owns with pride!
 Peace, idle Muse! no more thy strain prolong,

But yield a theme, thy warmest praises wrong;
Just to her merit, though thou canst not raise
Thy feeble verse, behold th' acknowledged praise
Has spread conviction through the envious train,
And cast a fatal gloom o'er Scandal's reign!   5
And lo! each pallid hag, with blistered tongue,
Mutters assent to all thy zeal has sung —
Owns all the colours just — the outline true;
Thee my inspirer, and my model — CREWE!

PROLOGUE.

WRITTEN BY MR. GARRICK.

A School for Scandal! tell me, I beseech you,
Needs there a school this modish art to teach you?
No need of lessons now, the knowing think;
We might as well be taught to eat and drink.
5 Caused by a dearth of scandal, should the vapours
Distress our fair ones — let them read the papers;
Their powerful mixtures such disorders hit;
Crave what you will — there's *quantum sufficit.*
"Lord!" cries my Lady Wormwood (who loves tattle,
10 And puts much salt and pepper in her prattle),
Just risen at noon, all night at cards when threshing
Strong tea and scandal — "Bless me, how refreshing!
Give me the papers, Lisp — how bold and free! [*Sips.*
Last night Lord L. (Sips) was caught with Lady D.
15 For aching heads what charming sal volatile! [*Sips.*
If Mrs. B. will still continue flirting,
We hope she'll DRAW, *or we'll* UNDRAW *the curtain.*
Fine satire, poz — in public all abuse it,
But, by ourselves (*Sips*), our praise we can't refuse it.
20 Now, Lisp, read you — there, at that dash and star":
"Yes, ma'am — *A certain lord had best beware,*
Who lives not twenty miles from Grosvenor Square;
For, should he Lady W. find willing,

Wormwood is bitter " — " Oh! that's me! the villain!
Throw it behind the fire, and never more
Let that vile paper come within my door."
Thus at our friends we laugh, who feel the dart;
To reach our feelings, we ourselves must smart.　　　5
Is our young bard so young, to think that he
Can stop the full spring-tide of calumny?
Knows he the world so little, and its trade?
Alas! the devil's sooner raised than laid.
So strong, so swift, the monster there's no gagging:　　　10
Cut Scandal's head off, still the tongue is wagging.
Proud of your smiles once lavishly bestowed,
Again our young Don Quixote takes the road:
To show his gratitude he draws his pen,
And seeks this hydra, Scandal, in his den.　　　15
For your applause all perils he would through —
He'll fight — that's write — a cavalliero true,
Till every drop of blood — that's ink — is spilt for you.

DRAMATIS PERSONÆ.

AS ORIGINALLY ACTED AT DRURY-LANE THEATRE IN 1777.

SIR PETER TEAZLE	Mr. King.
SIR OLIVER SURFACE	Mr. Yates.
SIR HARRY BUMPER	Mr. Gawdry.
SIR BENJAMIN BACKBITE	Mr. Dodd.
JOSEPH SURFACE	Mr. Palmer.
CHARLES SURFACE	Mr. Smith.
CARELESS	Mr. Farren.
SNAKE	Mr. Packer.
CRABTREE	Mr. Parsons.
ROWLEY	Mr. Aikin.
MOSES	Mr. Baddeley.
TRIP	Mr. Lamask.
LADY TEAZLE	Mrs. Abington.
LADY SNEERWELL	Miss Sherry.
MRS. CANDOUR	Miss Pope.
MARIA	Miss P. Hopkins.

Gentlemen, Maid, and Servants

SCENE : *London*

ACT I.

Scene I. Lady sneerwell's dressing-room.

Lady Sneerwell discovered at her toilet; Snake drinking chocolate.

Lady Sneer. The paragraphs, you say, Mr. Snake, were all inserted?

Snake. They were, madam; and, as I copied them myself in a feigned hand, there can be no suspicion whence they came.

Lady Sneer. Did you circulate the report of Lady Brittle's intrigue with Captain Boastall?

Snake. That's in as fine a train as your ladyship could wish. In the common course of things, I think it must reach Mrs. Clackitt's ears within four-and-twenty hours; and then, you know, the business is as good as done.

Lady Sneer. Why, truly, Mrs. Clackitt has a very pretty talent, and a great deal of industry.

Snake. True, madam, and has been tolerably successful in her day. To my knowledge, she has been the cause of six matches being broken off, and three sons being disinherited; of four forced elopements, nine separate maintenances, and two divorces. Nay, I have more than once traced her causing a *tête-à-tête* in the " Town and Country Magazine," when the parties, perhaps, had never seen each other's face before in the course of their lives.

Lady Sneer.   She certainly has talents, but her manner is gross.

5 *Snake.*   'Tis very true.   She generally designs well, has a free tongue and a bold invention; but her colouring is too dark, and her outlines often extravagant.   She wants that delicacy of tint, and mellowness of sneer, which distinguish your ladyship's scandal.

10 *Lady Sneer.*   You are partial, Snake.

Snake.   Not in the least; everybody allows that Lady Sneerwell can do more with a word or look than many can with the most laboured detail, even when they happen to have a little truth on their side to support it.

15 *Lady Sneer.*   Yes, my dear Snake; and I am no hypocrite to deny the satisfaction I reap from the success of my efforts.   Wounded myself, in the early part of my life, by the envenomed tongue of slander, I confess I have since known no pleasure equal to the reducing others to 20 the level of my own reputation.

Snake.   Nothing can be more natural.   But, Lady Sneerwell, there is one affair in which you have lately employed me, wherein, I confess, I am at a loss to guess your motives.

25 *Lady Sneer.*   I conceive you mean with respect to my neighbour, Sir Peter Teazle, and his family?

Snake.   I do.   Here are two young men, to whom Sir Peter has acted as a kind of guardian since their father's death; the eldest possessing the most amiable 30 character, and universally well spoken of — the youngest, the most dissipated and extravagant young fellow in the kingdom, without friends or character: the former an avowed admirer of your ladyship, and apparently your favourite; the latter attached to Maria, Sir Peter's ward, and confessedly beloved by her. Now, on the face of these circumstances, it is utterly unaccountable to me, why 5 you, the widow of a city knight, with a good jointure, should not close with the passion of a man of such character and expectations as Mr. Surface; and more so why you should be so uncommonly earnest to destroy the mutual attachment subsisting between his brother Charles 10 and Maria.

Lady Sneer. Then, at once to unravel this mystery, I must inform you that love has no share whatever in the intercourse between Mr. Surface and me.

Snake. No!   15

Lady Sneer. His real attachment is to Maria, or her fortune; but, finding in his brother a favoured rival, he has been obliged to mask his pretensions, and profit by my assistance.

Snake. Yet still I am more puzzled why you should 20 interest yourself in his success.

Lady Sneer. Heavens! how dull you are! Cannot you surmise the weakness which I hitherto, through shame, have concealed even from you? Must I confess that Charles — that extravagant, that bankrupt in for- 25 tune and reputation — that he it is for whom I am thus anxious and malicious, and to gain whom I would sacrifice everything?

Snake. Now, indeed, your conduct appears consistent: but how came you and Mr. Surface so confidential? 30

Lady Sneer. For our mutual interest. I have found

him out a long time since. I know him to be artful, self-
ish, and malicious — in short, a sentimental knave;
while with Sir Peter, and indeed with all his acquaintance,
he passes for a youthful miracle of prudence, good sense,
5 and benevolence.

Snake. Yes; yet Sir Peter vows he has not his equal
in England; and, above all, he praises him as a man of
sentiment.

Lady Sneer. True; and with the assistance of his
10 sentiment and hypocrisy he has brought Sir Peter entirely
into his interest with regard to Maria; while poor Charles
has no friend in the house — though, I fear, he has a powerful one in Maria's heart, against whom we must direct
our schemes.

Enter SERVANT.

15 *Ser.* Mr. Surface.

Lady Sneer. Show him up.   [*Exit* SERVANT.
He generally calls about this time. I don't wonder at
people giving him to me for a lover.

Enter JOSEPH SURFACE.

Jos. Surf. My dear Lady Sneerwell, how do you do to-
20 day? Mr. Snake, your most obedient.

Lady Sneer. Snake has just been rallying me on our
mutual attachment, but I have informed him of our real
views. You know how useful he has been to us; and,
believe me, the confidence is not ill-placed.

25 *Jos. Surf.* Madam, it is impossible for me to suspect a
man of Mr. Snake's sensibility and discernment.

Lady Sneer. Well, well, no compliments now; but

tell me when you saw your mistress, Maria — or, what is more material to me, your brother.

Jos. Surf. I have not seen either since I left you; but I can inform you that they never meet. Some of your stories have taken a good effect on Maria. 5

Lady Sneer. Ah, my dear Snake! the merit of this belongs to you. But do your brother's distresses increase?

Jos. Surf. Every hour. I am told he has had another execution in the house yesterday. In short, his dissipation and extravagance exceed any thing I have ever 10 heard of.

Lady Sneer. Poor Charles!

Jos. Surf. True, madam; notwithstanding his vices, one can't help feeling for him. Poor Charles! I'm sure I wish it were in my power to be of any essential service 15 to him; for the man who does not share in the distresses of a brother, even though merited by his own misconduct, deserves —

Lady Sneer. O Lud! you are going to be moral, and forget that you are among friends. 20

Jos. Surf. Egad, that's true! I'll keep that sentiment till I see Sir Peter. However, it is certainly a charity to rescue Maria from such a libertine, who if he is to be reclaimed, can be so only by a person of your ladyship's superior accomplishments and understanding. 25

Snake. I believe, Lady Sneerwell, here's company coming: I'll go and copy the letter I mentioned to you. Mr. Surface, your most obedient.

Jos. Surf. Sir, your very devoted. [*Exit* SNAKE. Lady Sneerwell, I am very sorry you have put any farther 30 confidence in that fellow.

235

Lady Sneer. Why so?

Jos. Surf. I have lately detected him in frequent conference with old Rowley, who was formerly my father's steward, and has never, you know, been a friend of
5 mine.

Lady Sneer. And do you think he would betray us?

Jos. Surf. Nothing more likely: take my word for't, Lady Sneerwell, that fellow hasn't virtue enough to be faithful even to his own villany. Ah, Maria!

Enter MARIA.

10 *Lady Sneer.* Maria, my dear, how do you do? What's the matter?

Mar. Oh! there's that disagreeable lover of mine, Sir Benjamin Backbite, has just called at my guardian's, with his odious uncle, Crabtree; so I slipped out, and ran
15 hither to avoid them.

Lady Sneer. Is that all?

Jos. Surf. If my brother Charles had been of the party, madam, perhaps you would not have been so much alarmed.

20 *Lady Sneer.* Nay, now you are severe; for I dare swear the truth of the matter is, Maria heard you were here. But, my dear, what has Sir Benjamin done, that you should avoid him so?

Mar. Oh, he has done nothing — but 'tis for what he
25 has said: his conversation is a perpetual libel on all his acquaintance.

Jos. Surf. Ay, and the worst of it is, there is no advantage in not knowing him; for he'll abuse a stranger just as soon as his best friend: and his uncle's as bad.

236

Lady Sneer. Nay, but we should make allowance; Sir Benjamin is a wit and a poet.

Mar. For my part, I own, madam, wit loses its respect with me, when I see it in company with malice. What do you think, Mr. Surface? 5

Jos. Surf. Certainly, madam; to smile at the jest which plants a thorn in another's breast is to become a principal in the mischief.

Lady Sneer. Pshaw! there's no possibility of being witty without a little ill nature: the malice of a good 10 thing is the barb that makes it stick. What's your opinion, Mr. Surface?

Jos. Surf. To be sure, madam; that conversation, where the spirit of raillery is suppressed, will ever appear tedious and insipid. 15

Mar. Well, I'll not debate how far scandal may be allowable; but in a man, I am sure, it is always contemptible. We have pride, envy, rivalship, and a thousand motives to depreciate each other; but the male slanderer must have the cowardice of a woman before he can traduce 20 one.

Reënter SERVANT.

Ser. Madam, Mrs. Candour is below, and, if your ladyship's at leisure, will leave her carriage.

Lady Sneer. Beg her to walk in. [*Exit* SERVANT. Now, Maria, here is a character to your taste; for, though 25 Mrs. Candour is a little talkative, everybody allows her to be the best natured and best sort of woman.

Mar. Yes, with a very gross affectation of good nature and benevolence, she does more mischief than the direct malice of old Crabtree. 30

Jos. Surf. I' faith that's true, Lady Sneerwell: whenever I hear the current running against the characters of my friends, I never think them in such danger as when Candour undertakes their defence.

5 *Lady Sneer.* Hush! — here she is!

Enter MRS. CANDOUR.

Mrs. Can. My dear Lady Sneerwell, how have you been this century? — Mr. Surface, what news do you hear? — though indeed it is no matter, for I think one hears nothing else but scandal.

10 *Jos. Surf.* Just so, indeed, ma'am.

Mrs. Can. Oh, Maria! child, — what, is the whole affair off between you and Charles? His extravagance, I presume — the town talks of nothing else.

Mar. I am very sorry, ma'am, the town has so little 15 to do.

Mrs. Can. True, true, child: but there's no stopping people's tongues. I own I was hurt to hear it, as I indeed was to learn, from the same quarter, that your guardian, Sir Peter, and Lady Teazle have not agreed lately as well 20 as could be wished.

Mar. 'Tis strangely impertinent for people to busy themselves so.

Mrs. Can. Very true, child: but what's to be done? People will talk — there's no preventing it. Why, it was 25 but yesterday I was told that Miss Gadabout had eloped with Sir Filigree Flirt. But, Lord! there's no minding what one hears; though, to be sure, I had this from very good authority.

Mar. Such reports are highly scandalous.

JOSEPH SURFACE

Mrs. Can. So they are, child — shameful, shameful! But the world is so censorious, no character escapes. Lord, now who would have suspected your friend, Miss Prim, of an indiscretion? Yet such is the ill nature of people, that they say her uncle stopped her last week, just as she was stepping into the York Mail with her dancing-master.

Mar. I'll answer for't there are no grounds for that report.

Mrs. Can. Ah, no foundation in the world, I dare swear; no more, probably, than for the story circulated last month, of Mrs. Festino's affair with Colonel Cassino — though, to be sure, that matter was never rightly cleared up.

Jos. Surf. The licence of invention some people take is monstrous indeed.

Mar. 'Tis so; but, in my opinion, those who report such things are equally culpable.

Mrs. Can. To be sure they are; tale-bearers are as bad as the tale-makers — 'tis an old observation, and a very true one: but what's to be done, as I said before? how will you prevent people from talking? To-day, Mrs. Clackitt assured me, Mr. and Mrs. Honeymoon were at last become mere man and wife, like the rest of their acquaintance. And at the same time Miss Tattle, who was by, affirmed, that Lord Buffalo had discovered his lady at a house of no extraordinary fame; and that Sir Harry Bouquet and Tom Saunter were to measure swords on a similar provocation. But, Lord, do you think I would report these things! No, no! tale-bearers, as I said before, are just as bad as the tale-makers.

Jos. Surf. Ah! Mrs. Candour, if everybody had your forbearance and good nature!

Mrs. Can. I confess, Mr. Surface, I cannot bear to hear people attacked behind their backs; and when ugly
5 circumstances come out against our acquaintance, I own I always love to think the best. By the by, I hope 'tis not true that your brother is absolutely ruined?

Jos. Surf. I am afraid his circumstances are very bad indeed, ma'am.

10 *Mrs. Can.* Ah! I heard so — but you must tell him to keep up his spirits; everybody almost is in the same way: Lord Spindle, Sir Thomas Splint, Captain Quinze, and Mr. Nickit — all up, I hear, within this week; so, if Charles is undone, he'll find half his acquaintance ruined
15 too, and that, you know, is a consolation.

Jos. Surf. Doubtless, ma'am — a very great one.

Reënter SERVANT.

Ser. Mr. Crabtree and Sir Benjamin Backbite. [*Exit.*
Lady Sneer. So, Maria, you see your lover pursues you; positively you shan't escape.

Enter CRABTREE *and* SIR BENJAMIN BACKBITE.

20 *Crab.* Lady Sneerwell, I kiss your hand. Mrs. Candour, I don't believe you are acquainted with my nephew, Sir Benjamin Backbite. Egad, ma'am, he has a pretty wit, and is a pretty poet too. Isn't he, Lady Sneerwell?

Sir Ben. Oh, fie, uncle!

25 *Crab.* Nay, egad it's true; I back him at a rebus or a charade against the best rhymer in the kingdom. Has your ladyship heard the epigram he wrote last week on

Lady Frizzle's feather catching fire? — Do, Benjamin, repeat it, or the charade you made last night extempore at Mrs. Drowzie's conversazione. Come now; your first is the name of a fish, your second a great naval commander, and — 5

Sir Ben. Uncle, now — pr'ythee —

Crab. I' faith, ma'am, 'twould surprise you to hear how ready he is at all these sort of things.

Lady Sneer. I wonder, Sir Benjamin, you never publish any thing. 10

Sir Ben. To say truth, ma'am, 'tis very vulgar to print; and as my little productions are mostly satires and lampoons on particular people, I find they circulate more by giving copies in confidence to the friends of the parties. However, I have some love elegies, which, when favoured 15 with this lady's smiles, I mean to give the public.

[*Pointing to* MARIA.

Crab. (*To* MARIA.) 'Fore heaven, ma'am, they'll immortalize you! — you will be handed down to posterity, like Petrarch's Laura, or Waller's Saccharissa.

Sir Ben. (*To* MARIA.) Yes, madam, I think you will 20 like them, when you shall see them on a beautiful quarto page, where a neat rivulet of text shall meander through a meadow of margin. 'Fore Gad they will be the most elegant things of their kind!

Crab. But, ladies, that's true — have you heard the 25 news?

Mrs. Can. What, sir, do you mean the report of —

Crab. No, ma'am, that's not it. — Miss Nicely is going to be married to her own footman.

Mrs. Can. Impossible! 30

241

Crab. Ask Sir Benjamin.

Sir Ben. 'Tis very true, ma'am: every thing is fixed, and the wedding liveries bespoke.

Crab. Yes — and they do say there were pressing
5 reasons for it.

Lady Sneer. Why, I have heard something of this before.

Mrs. Can. It can't be — and I wonder any one should believe such a story of so prudent a lady as Miss Nicely.

Sir Ben. O Lud! ma'am, that's the very reason 'twas
10 believed at once. She has always been so cautious and so reserved, that everybody was sure there was some reason for it at bottom.

Mrs. Can. Why, to be sure, a tale of scandal is as fatal to the credit of a prudent lady of her stamp as a fever
15 is generally to those of the strongest constitutions. But there is a sort of puny sickly reputation, that is always ailing, yet will outlive the robuster characters of a hundred prudes.

Sir Ben. True, madam, there are valetudinarians in
20 reputation as well as constitution, who, being conscious of their weak part, avoid the least breath of air, and supply their want of stamina by care and circumspection.

Mrs. Can. Well, but this may be all a mistake. You know, Sir Benjamin, very trifling circumstances
25 often give rise to the most injurious tales.

Crab. That they do, I'll be sworn, ma'am. O Lud! Mr. Surface, pray is it true that your uncle, Sir Oliver, is coming home?

Jos. Surf. Not that I know of, indeed, sir.

30 *Crab.* He has been in the East Indies a long time. You can scarcely remember him, I believe? Sad comfort,

whenever he returns, to hear how your brother has gone on!

Jos. Surf.   Charles has been imprudent, sir, to be sure; but I hope no busy people have already prejudiced Sir Oliver against him.   He may reform.   5

Sir Ben.   To be sure he may: for my part, I never believed him to be so utterly void of principle as people say; and, though he has lost all his friends, I am told nobody is better spoken of by the Jews.

Crab.   That's true, egad, nephew.   If the Old Jewry 10 was a ward, I believe Charles would be an alderman: no man more popular there, 'fore Gad!   I hear he pays as many annuities as the Irish tontine; and that, whenever he is sick, they have prayers for the recovery of his health in all the synagogues.   15

Sir Ben.   Yet no man lives in greater splendour.   They tell me, when he entertains his friends he will sit down to dinner with a dozen of his own securities; have a score of tradesmen waiting in the antechamber, and an officer behind every guest's chair.   20

Jos. Surf.   This may be entertainment to you, gentlemen, but you pay very little regard to the feelings of a brother.

Mar.   (*Aside.*)   Their malice is intolerable!— (*Aloud.*) Lady Sneerwell, I must wish you a good morning: I'm 25 not very well.   [*Exit.*

Mrs. Can.   O dear! she changes colour very much.

Lady Sneer.   Do, Mrs. Candour, follow her: she may want your assistance.

Mrs. Can.   That I will, with all my soul, ma'am.— Poor 30 dear girl, who knows what her situation may be!   [*Exit.*

Lady Sneer. 'Twas nothing but that she could not bear to hear Charles reflected on, notwithstanding their difference.

Sir Ben. The young lady's *penchant* is obvious.

5 *Crab.* But, Benjamin, you must not give up the pursuit for that: follow her, and put her into good humour. Repeat her some of your own verses. Come, I'll assist you.

Sir Ben. Mr. Surface, I did not mean to hurt you; but depend on't, your brother is utterly undone.

10 *Crab.* O Lud, ay! undone as ever man was — can't raise a guinea!

Sir Ben. And every thing sold, I'm told, that was movable.

Crab. I have seen one that was at his house. Not 15 a thing left but some empty bottles that were overlooked, and the family pictures, which I believe are framed in the wainscots.

Sir Ben. And I'm very sorry also to hear some bad stories against him. [*Going.*

20 *Crab.* Oh, he has done many mean things, that's certain.

Sir Ben. But, however, as he's your brother —

[*Going.*

Crab. We'll tell you all at another opportunity.

[*Exeunt* CRABTREE *and* SIR BENJAMIN.

Lady Sneer. Ha! ha! 'tis very hard for them to leave 25 a subject they have not quite run down.

Jos. Surf. And I believe the abuse was no more acceptable to your ladyship than Maria.

Lady Sneer. I doubt her affections are farther engaged than we imagine. But the family are to be here this even-

ing, so you may as well dine where you are, and we shall
have an opportunity of observing farther; in the meantime, I'll go and plot mischief, and you shall study sentiment.   [*Exeunt.*

SCENE II.   A ROOM IN SIR PETER TEAZLE'S HOUSE.

Enter SIR PETER TEAZLE.

Sir Pet.   When an old bachelor marries a young wife, 5
what is he to expect?   'Tis now six months since Lady
Teazle made me the happiest of men — and I have been
the most miserable dog ever since!   We tiffed a little going
to church, and fairly quarrelled before the bells had done
ringing.   I was more than once nearly choked with gall 10
during the honeymoon, and had lost all comfort in life
before my friends had done wishing me joy.   Yet I chose
with caution — a girl bred wholly in the country, who
never knew luxury beyond one silk gown, nor dissipation
above the annual gala of a race ball.   Yet she now plays 15
her part in all the extravagant fopperies of fashion and
the town, with as ready a grace as if she never had seen
a bush or a grass-plot out of Grosvenor Square!   I am
sneered at by all my acquaintance, and paragraphed in
the newspapers.   She dissipates my fortune, and contra- 20
dicts all my humours; yet the worst of it is, I doubt I
love her, or I should never bear all this.   However, I'll
never be weak enough to own it.

Enter ROWLEY.

Row.   Oh! Sir Peter, your servant: how is it with you,
sir?   25

Sir Pet. Very bad, Master Rowley, very bad. I meet with nothing but crosses and vexations.

Row. What can have happened since yesterday?

Sir Pet. A good question to a married man!

5 *Row.* Nay, I'm sure, Sir Peter, your lady can't be the cause of your uneasiness.

Sir Pet. Why, has any body told you she was dead?

Row. Come, come, Sir Peter, you love her, notwithstanding your tempers don't exactly agree.

10 *Sir Pet.* But the fault is entirely hers, Master Rowley. I am, myself, the sweetest-tempered man alive, and hate a teasing temper; and so I tell her a hundred times a day.

Row. Indeed!

15 *Sir Pet.* Ay; and what is very extraordinary, in all our disputes she is always in the wrong! But Lady Sneerwell, and the set she meets at her house, encourage the perverseness of her disposition. Then, to complete my vexation, Maria, my ward, whom I ought to have the 20 power of a father over, is determined to turn rebel too, and absolutely refuses the man whom I have long resolved on for her husband; meaning, I suppose, to bestow herself on his profligate brother.

Row. You know, Sir Peter, I have always taken the 25 liberty to differ with you on the subject of these two young gentlemen. I only wish you may not be deceived in your opinion of the elder. For Charles, my life on't! he will retrieve his errors yet. Their worthy father, once my honoured master, was, at his years, nearly as wild a 30 spark; yet, when he died, he did not leave a more benevolent heart to lament his loss.

246

Sir Pet. You are wrong, Master Rowley. On their father's death, you know, I acted as a kind of guardian to them both, till their uncle Sir Oliver's liberality gave them an early independence: of course, no person could have more opportunities of judging of their hearts, and 5 I was never mistaken in my life. Joseph is indeed a model for the young men of the age. He is a man of sentiment, and acts up to the sentiments he professes; but, for the other, take my word for't, if he had any grain of virtue by descent, he has dissipated it with the rest of his inherit- 10 ance. Ah! my old friend, Sir Oliver, will be deeply mortified when he finds how part of his bounty has been misapplied.

Row. I am sorry to find you so violent against the young man, because this may be the most critical period 15 of his fortune. I came hither with news that will surprise you.

Sir Pet. What! let me hear.

Row. Sir Oliver is arrived, and at this moment in town. 20

Sir Pet. How! you astonish me! I thought you did not expect him this month.

Row. I did not: but his passage has been remarkably quick.

Sir Pet. Egad, I shall rejoice to see my old friend. 25 'Tis sixteen years since we met. We have had many a day together: — but does he still enjoin us not to inform his nephews of his arrival?

Row. Most strictly. He means, before it is known, to make some trial of their dispositions. 30

Sir Pet. Ah! there needs no art to discover their merits

— however, he shall have his way; but, pray, does he know I am married?

Row. Yes, and will soon wish you joy.

Sir Pet. What, as we drink health to a friend in a consumption! Ah! Oliver will laugh at me. We used to rail at matrimony together, but he has been steady to his text. Well, he must be soon at my house, though — I'll instantly give orders for his reception. But, Master Rowley, don't drop a word that Lady Teazle and I ever disagree.

Row. By no means.

Sir Pet. For I should never be able to stand Noll's jokes; so I'll have him think, Lord forgive me! that we are a very happy couple.

Row. I understand you : — but then you must be very careful not to differ while he is in the house with you.

Sir Pet. Egad, and so we must — and that's impossible. Ah! Master Rowley, when an old bachelor marries a young wife, he deserves — no — the crime carries its punishment along with it.   [*Exeunt.*

ACT II.

SCENE I. A ROOM IN SIR PETER TEAZLE'S HOUSE.

Enter SIR PETER *and* LADY TEAZLE.

Sir Pet. Lady Teazle, Lady Teazle, I'll not bear it!

Lady Teaz. Sir Peter, Sir Peter, you may bear it or not, as you please; but I ought to have my own way in every thing, and, what's more, I will too. What! though I was educated in the country, I know very well that women of fashion in London are accountable to nobody after they are married. 5

Sir Pet. Very well, ma'am, very well; so a husband is to have no influence, no authority?

Lady Teaz. Authority! No, to be sure: if you wanted authority over me, you should have adopted me, and not married me: I am sure you were old enough. 10

Sir Pet. Old enough!—ay, there it is. Well, well, Lady Teazle, though my life may be made unhappy by your temper, I'll not be ruined by your extravagance! 15

Lady Teaz. My extravagance! I'm sure I'm not more extravagant than a woman of fashion ought to be.

Sir Pet. No, no, madam, you shall throw away no more sums on such unmeaning luxury. 'Slife! to spend as much to furnish your dressing-room with flowers in 20 winter as would suffice to turn the Pantheon into a green-house, and give a *fête champêtre* at Christmas.

Lady Teaz. And am I to blame, Sir Peter, because flowers are dear in cold weather? You should find fault with the climate, and not with me. For my part, I'm sure I wish it was spring all the year round, and that roses
5 grew under our feet!

Sir Pet. Oons! madam — if you had been born to this, I shouldn't wonder at you talking thus; but you forget what your situation was when I married you.

Lady Teaz. No, no, I don't; 'twas a very disagreeable
10 one or I should never have married you.

Sir Pet. Yes, yes, madam, you were then in somewhat a humbler style — the daughter of a plain country squire. Recollect, Lady Teazle, when I saw you first sitting at your tambour, in a pretty figured linen gown, with a bunch
15 of keys at your side, your hair combed smooth over a roll, and your apartment hung round with fruits in worsted, of your own working.

Lady Teaz. Oh, yes! I remember it very well, and a curious life I led. My daily occupation to inspect the
20 dairy, superintend the poultry, make extracts from the family receipt-book, and comb my aunt Deborah's lap-dog.

Sir Pet. Yes, yes, ma'am, 'twas so indeed.

Lady Teaz. And then you know, my evening amuse-
25 ments! To draw patterns for ruffles, which I had not materials to make up; to play Pope Joan with the curate; to read a sermon to my aunt; or to be stuck down to an old spinet to strum my father to sleep after a fox-chase.

Sir Pet. I am glad you have so good a memory. Yes,
30 madam, these were the recreations I took you from; but now you must have your coach — *vis-à-vis* — and three

SIR PETER AND LADY TEAZLE

"And am I to blame, Sir Peter, because flowers are dear in cold weather?"

powdered footmen before your chair; and, in the summer, a pair of white cats to draw you to Kensington Gardens. No recollection, I suppose, when you were content to ride double, behind the butler, on a docked coach-horse.

Lady Teaz. No — I swear I never did that: I deny 5 the butler and the coach-horse.

Sir Pet. This, madam, was your situation; and what have I done for you? I have made you a woman of fashion, of fortune, of rank — in short, I have made you my wife.   10

Lady Teaz. Well then, and there is but one thing more you can make me to add to the obligation, that is —

Sir Pet. My widow, I suppose?

Lady Teaz. Hem! hem!

Sir Pet. I thank you, madam — but don't flatter 15 yourself, for, though your ill conduct may disturb my peace of mind, it shall never break my heart, I promise you: however, I am equally obliged to you for the hint.

Lady Teaz. Then why will you endeavour to make yourself so disagreeable to me, and thwart me in every 20 little elegant expense?

Sir Pet. 'Slife, madam, I say, had you any of these little elegant expenses when you married me?

Lady Teaz. Lud, Sir Peter! would you have me be out of the fashion?   25

Sir Pet. The fashion, indeed! what had you to do with the fashion before you married me?

Lady Teaz. For my part, I should think you would like to have your wife thought a woman of taste.

Sir Pet. Ay — there again — taste! Zounds! madam, 30 you had no taste when you married me!

Lady Teaz. That's very true, indeed, Sir Peter! and, after having married you, I should never pretend to taste again, I allow. But now, Sir Peter, since we have finished our daily jangle, I presume I may go to my engage-
5 ment at Lady Sneerwell's.

Sir Pet. Ay, there's another precious circumstance — a charming set of acquaintance you have made there!

Lady Teaz. Nay, Sir Peter, they are all people of rank and fortune, and remarkably tenacious of reputation.

10 *Sir Pet.* Yes, egad, they are tenacious of reputation with a vengeance; for they don't choose any body should have a character but themselves! Such a crew! Ah! many a wretch has rid on a hurdle who has done less mischief than these utterers of forged tales, coiners of scandal,
15 and clippers of reputation.

Lady Teaz. What, would you restrain the freedom of speech?

Sir Pet. Ah! they have made you just as bad as any one of the society.

20 *Lady Teaz.* Why, I believe I do bear a part with a tolerable grace.

Sir Pet. Grace indeed!

Lady Teaz. But I vow I bear no malice against the people I abuse: when I say an ill-natured thing, 'tis out
25 of pure good humour; and I take it for granted they deal exactly in the same manner with me. But, Sir Peter, you know you promised to come to Lady Sneerwell's too.

Sir Pet. Well, well, I'll call in, just to look after my own character.

30 *Lady Teaz.* Then, indeed, you must make haste after me, or you'll be too late. So good-bye to ye. [*Exit.*

Sir Pet. So — I have gained much by my intended expostulation! Yet with what a charming air she contradicts every thing I say, and how pleasantly she shows her contempt for my authority! Well, though I can't make her love me, there is great satisfaction in quarrelling 5 with her; and I think she never appears to such advantage as when she is doing every thing in her power to plague me. [*Exit.*

SCENE II.　A ROOM IN LADY SNEERWELL'S HOUSE.

LADY SNEERWELL, MRS. CANDOUR, CRABTREE, SIR BEN-
　JAMIN BACKBITE, *and* JOSEPH SURFACE, *discovered.*

Lady Sneer. Nay, positively, we will hear it.
Jos. Surf. Yes, yes, the epigram, by all means. 10
Sir Ben. O plague on't, uncle! 'tis mere nonsense.
Crab. No, no; 'fore Gad, very clever for an extempore!
Sir Ben. But, ladies, you should be acquainted with the circumstance. You must know, that one day last week, as Lady Betty Curricle was taking the dust in 15 Hyde Park, in a sort of duodecimo phaeton, she desired me to write some verses on her ponies; upon which, I took out my pocket-book, and in one moment produced the following: —

　　Sure never were seen two such beautiful ponies; 20
　　Other horses are clowns, but these macaronies:
　　To give them this title I'm sure can't be wrong,
　　Their legs are so slim, and their tails are so long.

Crab. There, ladies, done in the smack of a whip, and on horseback too. 25

Jos. Surf. A very Phœbus, mounted — indeed, Sir Benjamin!

Sir Ben. Oh dear, sir! trifles — trifles.

Enter LADY TEAZLE *and* MARIA.

Mrs. Can. I must have a copy.

5 *Lady Sneer.* Lady Teazle, I hope we shall see Sir Peter?

Lady Teaz. I believe he'll wait on your ladyship presently.

Lady Sneer. Maria, my love, you look grave. Come, you shall sit down to piquet with Mr. Surface.

10 *Mar.* I take very little pleasure in cards — however, I'll do as your ladyship pleases.

Lady Teaz. I am surprised Mr. Surface should sit down with her; I thought he would have embraced this opportunity of speaking to me before Sir Peter came.

[*Aside.*

15 *Mrs. Can.* Now, I'll die, but you are so scandalous, I'll forswear your society.

Lady Teaz. What's the matter, Mrs. Candour?

Mrs. Can. They'll not allow our friend Miss Vermilion to be handsome.

20 *Lady Sneer.* Oh, surely she is a pretty woman.

Crab. I am very glad you think so, ma'am.

Mrs. Can. She has a charming fresh colour.

Lady Teaz. Yes, when it is fresh put on.

Mrs. Can. Oh, fie! I'll swear her colour is natural:
25 I have seen it come and go!

Lady Teaz. I dare swear you have, ma'am: it goes off at night, and comes again in the morning.

Sir Ben. True, ma'am, it not only comes and goes;

but, what's more, egad, her maid can fetch and carry it!

Mrs. Can. Ha! ha! ha! how I hate to hear you talk so! But surely, now, her sister is, or was, very handsome.

Crab. Who? Mrs. Evergreen? O Lord! she's six-5 and-fifty if she's an hour!

Mrs. Can. Now positively you wrong her; fifty-two or fifty-three is the utmost — and I don't think she looks more.

Sir Ben. Ah! there's no judging by her looks, unless 10 one could see her face.

Lady Sneer. Well well, if Mrs. Evergreen does take some pains to repair the ravages of time, you must allow she effects it with great ingenuity; and surely that's better than the careless manner in which the widow Ochre 15 caulks her wrinkles.

Sir Ben. Nay, now, Lady Sneerwell, you are severe upon the widow. Come, come, 'tis not that she paints so ill — but, when she has finished her face, she joins it on so badly to her neck, that she looks like a mended statue, 20 in which the connoisseur may see at once that the head is modern, though the trunk's antique.

Crab. Ha! ha! ha! Well said, nephew!

Mrs. Can. Ha! ha! ha! Well, you make me laugh; but I vow I hate you for it. What do you think of Miss 25 Simper?

Sir Ben. Why, she has very pretty teeth.

Lady Teaz. Yes; and on that account, when she is neither speaking nor laughing (which very seldom happens), she never absolutely shuts her mouth, but leaves 30 it always a-jar, as it were — thus. [*Shows her teeth.*

Mrs. Can. How can you be so ill-natured?

Lady Teaz. Nay, I allow even that's better than the pains Mrs. Prim takes to conceal her losses in front She draws her mouth till it positively resembles the
5 aperture of a poor's-box, and all her words appear to slide out edgewise, as it were — thus: *How do you do, madam? Yes, madam.*   [*Mimics.*

Lady Sneer. Very well, Lady Teazle; I see you can be a little severe.

10 *Lady Teaz.* In defence of a friend it is but justice. But here comes Sir Peter to spoil our pleasantry.

Enter SIR PETER TEAZLE.

Sir Pet. Ladies, your most obedient. — (*Aside.*) Mercy on me, here is the whole set! a character dead at every word, I suppose.

15 *Mrs. Can.* I am rejoiced you are come, Sir Peter. They have been so censorious — and Lady Teazle as bad as any one.

Sir Pet. That must be very distressing to you, indeed, Mrs. Candour.

20 *Mrs. Can.* Oh, they will allow good qualities to nobody; not even good nature to our friend Mrs. Pursy.

Lady Teaz. What, the fat dowager who was at Mrs. Quadrille's last night?

Mrs. Can. Nay, her bulk is her misfortune; and, 25 when she takes so much pains to get rid of it, you ought not to reflect on her.

Lady Sneer. That's very true, indeed.

Lady Teaz. Yes, I know she almost lives on acids and small whey; laces herself by pulleys; and often, in the

hottest noon in summer, you may see her on a little squat
pony, with her hair plaited up behind like a drummer's
and puffing round the Ring on a full trot.

Mrs. Can. I thank you, Lady Teazle, for defending
her. 5

Sir Pet. Yes, a good defence, truly.

Mrs. Can. Truly, Lady Teazle is as censorious as
Miss Sallow.

Crab. Yes, and she is a curious being to pretend to be
censorious — an awkward gawky, without any one good 1c
point under heaven.

Mrs. Can. Positively you shall not be so very severe.
Miss Sallow is a near relation of mine by marriage, and,
as for her person, great allowance is to be made; for, let
me tell you, a woman labours under many disadvantages 15
who tries to pass for a girl of six-and-thirty.

Lady Sneer. Though, surely, she is handsome still —
and for the weakness in her eyes, considering how much
she reads by candlelight, it is not to be wondered at.

Mrs. Can. True, and then as to her manner; upon my 20
word I think it is particularly graceful, considering she
never had the least education: for you know her mother
was a Welsh milliner, and her father a sugar-baker at
Bristol.

Sir Ben. Ah! you are both of you too good-natured! 25

Sir Pet. Yes, damned good-natured! This their own
relation! mercy on me! [*Aside.*

Mrs. Can. For my part, I own I cannot bear to hear
a friend ill-spoken of.

Sir Pet. No, to be sure! 30

Sir Ben. Oh! you are of a moral turn. Mrs. Candour

and I can sit for an hour and hear Lady Stucco talk sentiment.

Lady Teaz.   Nay, I vow Lady Stucco is very well with the dessert after dinner; for she's just like the French fruit one cracks for mottoes — made up of paint and proverb.

Mrs. Can.   Well, I will never join in ridiculing a friend; and so I constantly tell my cousin Ogle, and you all know what pretensions she has to be critical on beauty.

Crab.   Oh, to be sure! she has herself the oddest countenance that ever was seen; 'tis a collection of features from all the different countries of the globe.

Sir Ben.   So she has, indeed — an Irish front —

Crab.   Caledonian locks —

Sir Ben.   Dutch nose —

Crab.   Austrian lips —

Sir Ben.   Complexion of a Spaniard —

Crab.   And teeth *à la Chinoise* —

Sir Ben.   In short, her face resembles a *table d'hôte* at Spa — where no two guests are of a nation —

Crab.   Or a congress at the close of a general war — wherein all the members, even to her eyes, appear to have a different interest, and her nose and chin are the only parties likely to join issue.

Mrs. Can.   Ha! ha! ha!

Sir Pet.   Mercy on my life! — a person they dine with twice a week!   [*Aside.*

Mrs. Can.   Nay, but I vow you shall not carry the laugh off so — for give me leave to say, that Mrs. Ogle —

Sir Pet.   Madam, madam, I beg your pardon — there's no stopping these good gentlemen's tongues.

But when I tell you, Mrs. Candour, that the lady they are abusing is a particular friend of mine, I hope you'll not take her part.

Lady Sneer. Ha! ha! ha! well said, Sir Peter! but you are a cruel creature — too phlegmatic yourself for 5 a jest, and too peevish to allow wit in others.

Sir Pet. Ah, madam, true wit is more nearly allied to good nature than your ladyship is aware of.

Lady Teaz. True, Sir Peter: I believe they are so near akin that they can never be united.   10

Sir Ben. Or rather, suppose them man and wife, because one seldom sees them together.

Lady Teaz. But Sir Peter is such an enemy to scandal, I believe he would have it put down by parliament.

Sir Pet. 'Fore heaven, madam, if they were to con- 15 sider the sporting with reputation of as much importance as poaching on manors, and pass an act for the preservation of fame, as well as game, I believe many would thank them for the bill.

Lady Sneer. O Lud! Sir Peter; would you deprive us 20 of our privileges?

Sir Pet. Ay, madam; and then no person should be permitted to kill characters and run down reputations, but qualified old maids and disappointed widows.

Lady Sneer. Go, you monster!   25

Mrs. Can. But, surely, you would not be quite so severe on those who only report what they hear?

Sir Pet. Yes, madam, I would have law merchant for them too; and in all cases of slander currency, whenever the drawer of the lie was not to be found, the injured 30 parties should have a right to come on any of the indorsers.

Crab. Well, for my part, I believe there never was a scandalous tale without some foundation.

Lady Sneer. Come, ladies, shall we sit down to cards in the next room?

Enter SERVANT, *who whispers* SIR PETER.

5 *Sir Pet.* I'll be with them directly. (*Exit* SERVANT. I'll get away unperceived.   [*Aside.*

Lady Sneer. Sir Peter, you are not going to leave us?

Sir Pet. Your ladyship must excuse me; I'm called away by particular business. But I leave my character

10 behind me.   [*Exit.*

Sir Ben. Well — certainly, Lady Teazle, that lord of yours is a strange being: I could tell you some stories of him would make you laugh heartily if he were not your husband.

15 *Lady Teaz.* Oh, pray don't mind that; come, do let's hear them.

[*Exeunt all but* JOSEPH SURFACE *and* MARIA.

Jos. Surf. Maria, I see you have no satisfaction in this society.

Mar. How is it possible I should? If to raise malicious

20 smiles at the infirmities or misfortunes of those who have never injured us be the province of wit or humour, Heaven grant me a double portion of dulness!

Jos. Surf. Yet they appear more ill-natured than they are; they have no malice at heart.

25 *Mar.* Then is their conduct still more contemptible; for, in my opinion, nothing could excuse the intemperance of their tongues but a natural and uncontrollable bitterness of mind.

Jos. Surf. Undoubtedly, madam; and it has always been a sentiment of mine, that to propagate a malicious truth wantonly is more despicable than to falsify from revenge. But can you, Maria, feel thus for others, and be unkind to me alone? Is hope to be denied the tender- 5 est passion?

Mar. Why will you distress me by renewing this subject?

Jos. Surf. Ah, Maria! you would not treat me thus, and oppose your guardian, Sir Peter's will, but that I see that profligate Charles is still a favoured rival. 10

Mar. Ungenerously urged! But, whatever my sentiments are for that unfortunate young man, be assured I shall not feel more bound to give him up, because his distresses have lost him the regard even of a brother.

Jos. Surf. Nay, but, Maria, do not leave me with a 15 frown: by all that's honest, I swear — [*Kneels.*

Reënter LADY TEAZLE *behind.*

(*Aside.*) Gad's life, here's Lady Teazle. (*Aloud to* MARIA.) You must not — no, you shall not — for, though I have the greatest regard for Lady Teazle —

Mar. Lady Teazle! 20

Jos. Surf. Yet were Sir Peter to suspect —

Lady Teaz. (*Coming forward.*) What is this, pray? Does he take her for me? — Child, you are wanted in the next room. (*Exit* MARIA.) What is all this, pray?

Jos. Surf. Oh, the most unlucky circumstance in 25 nature! Maria has somehow suspected the tender concern I have for your happiness, and threatened to acquaint Sir Peter with her suspicions, and I was just endeavouring to reason with her when you came in.

Lady Teaz. Indeed! but you seemed to adopt a very tender mode of reasoning — do you usually argue on your knees?

Jos. Surf. Oh, she's a child, and I thought a little
5 bombast — But, Lady Teazle, when are you to give me your judgment on my library, as you promised?

Lady Teaz. No, no; I begin to think it would be imprudent, and you know I admit you as a lover no farther than fashion requires.

10 *Jos. Surf.* True — a mere Platonic cicisbeo, what every wife is entitled to.

Lady Teaz. Certainly, one must not be out of the fashion. However, I have so many of my country prejudices left, that, though Sir Peter's ill humour may vex
15 me ever so, it never shall provoke me to —

Jos. Surf. The only revenge in your power. Well, I applaud your moderation.

Lady Teaz. Go — you are an insinuating wretch! But we shall be missed — let us join the company.

20 *Jos. Surf.* But we had best not return together.

Lady Teaz. Well, don't stay; for Maria sha'n't come to hear any more of your reasoning, I promise you. [*Exit.*

Jos. Surf. A curious dilemma, truly, my politics have run me into! I wanted, at first, only to ingratiate my-
25 self with Lady Teazle, that she might not be my enemy with Maria; and I have, I don't know how, become her serious lover. Sincerely I begin to wish I had never made such a point of gaining so very good a character, for it has led me into so many cursed rogueries that I doubt I shall
30 be exposed at last. [*Exit.*

SCENE III. A ROOM IN SIR PETER TEAZLE'S HOUSE.

Enter SIR OLIVER SURFACE *and* ROWLEY.

Sir Oliv. Ha! ha! ha! so my old friend is married, hey? — a young wife out of the country. Ha! ha! ha! that he should have stood bluff to old bachelor so long, and sink into a husband at last!

Row. But you must not rally him on the subject, Sir Oliver; 'tis a tender point, I assure you, though he has been married only seven months.

Sir Oliv. Then he has been just half a year on the stool of repentance! — Poor Peter! But you say he has entirely given up Charles — never sees him, hey?

Row. His prejudice against him is astonishing, and I am sure greatly increased by a jealousy of him with Lady Teazle, which he has industriously been led into by a scandalous society in the neighbourhood, who have contributed not a little to Charles's ill name. Whereas the truth is, I believe, if the lady is partial to either of them, his brother is the favourite.

Sir Oliv. Ay, I know there are a set of malicious, prating, prudent gossips, both male and female, who murder characters to kill time, and will rob a young fellow of his good name before he has years to know the value of it. But I am not to be prejudiced against my nephew by such, I promise you! No, no: if Charles has done nothing false or mean, I shall compound for his extravagance.

Row. Then, my life on't, you will reclaim him. Ah, sir, it gives me new life to find that your heart is not turned against him, and that the son of my good old master has one friend, however, left.

Sir Oliv. What! shall I forget, Master Rowley, when I was at his years myself? Egad, my brother and I were neither of us very prudent youths; and yet, I believe, you have not seen many better men than your old master was?

5　*Row.* Sir, 'tis this reflection gives me assurance that Charles may yet be a credit to his family. But here comes Sir Peter.

Sir Oliv. Egad, so he does! Mercy on me! he's greatly altered, and seems to have a settled married look! 10 One may read husband in his face at this distance!

Enter Sir Peter Teazle

Sir Pet. Ha! Sir Oliver — my old friend! Welcome to England a thousand times!

Sir Oliv. Thank you, thank you, Sir Peter! and i' faith I am glad to find you well, believe me!

15　*Sir Pet.* Oh! 'tis a long time since we met — fifteen years, I doubt, Sir Oliver, and many a cross accident in the time.

Sir Oliv. Ay, I have had my share. But, what! I find you are married, hey, my old boy? Well, well, it can't be helped; and so — I wish you joy with all my heart!

20　*Sir Pet.* Thank you, thank you, Sir Oliver. — Yes, I have entered into — the happy state; but we'll not talk of that now.

Sir Oliv. True, true, Sir Peter; old friends should not begin on grievances at first meeting. No, no, no.

25　*Row.* (*Aside to* Sir Oliver.) Take care, pray, sir.

Sir Oliv. Well, so one of my nephews is a wild rogue, hey?

Sir Pet. Wild! Ah! my old friend, I grieve for your disappointment there; he's a lost young man, indeed. However, his brother will make you amends; Joseph is, indeed, what a youth should be — everybody in the world speaks well of him.

Sir Oliv. I am sorry to hear it; he has too good a character to be an honest fellow. Everybody speaks well of him! Pshaw! then he has bowed as low to knaves 5 and fools as to the honest dignity of genius and virtue.

Sir Pet. What, Sir Oliver! do you blame him for not making enemies?

Sir Oliv. Yes, if he has merit enough to deserve them.

Sir Pet. Well, well — you'll be convinced when you 10 know him. 'Tis edification to hear him converse; he professes the noblest sentiments.

Sir Oliv. Oh, plague of his sentiments! If he salutes me with a scrap of morality in his mouth, I shall be sick directly. But, however, don't mistake me, Sir Peter; 15 I don't mean to defend Charles's errors: but, before I form my judgment of either of them, I intend to make a trial of their hearts; and my friend Rowley and I have planned something for the purpose.

Row. And Sir Peter shall own for once he has been 20 mistaken.

Sir Pet. Oh, my life on Joseph's honour!

Sir Oliv. Well — come, give us a bottle of good wine, and we'll drink the lads' health, and tell you our scheme.

Sir Pet. *Allons*, then! 25

Sir Oliv. And don't, Sir Peter, be so severe against your old friend's son. Odds my life! I am not sorry he has run out of the course a little: for my part, I hate to see prudence clinging to the green suckers of youth; 'tis like ivy round a sapling, and spoils the growth of the 30 tree. [*Exeunt.*

ACT III.

Scene I. A room in sir peter teazle's house.

Enter Sir Peter Teazle, Sir Oliver Surface, *and*
Rowley.

Sir Pet. Well, then, we will see this fellow first, and
have our wine afterwards. But how is this, Master
Rowley? I don't see the jet of your scheme.

Row. Why, sir, this Mr. Stanley, whom I was speaking
5 of, is nearly related to them by their mother. He was
once a merchant in Dublin, but has been ruined by a series
of undeserved misfortunes. He has applied, by letter,
since his confinement, both to Mr. Surface and Charles:
from the former he has received nothing but evasive prom-
10 ises of future service, while Charles has done all that his
extravagance has left him power to do; and he is, at this
time, endeavouring to raise a sum of money, part of which,
in the midst of his own distresses, I know he intends for
the service of poor Stanley.

15 *Sir Oliv.* Ah! he is my brother's son.

Sir Pet. Well, but how is Sir Oliver personally to —

Row. Why, sir, I will inform Charles and his brother
that Stanley has obtained permission to apply personally
to his friends; and, as they have neither of them ever
20 seen him, let Sir Oliver assume his character, and he will
have a fair opportunity of judging, at least, of the benev-

266

olence of their dispositions: and believe me, sir, you will find in the youngest brother one who, in the midst of folly and dissipation, has still, as our immortal bard expresses it, —

> " a heart to pity, and a hand,   5
> Open as day, for melting charity."

Sir Pet. Pshaw! What signifies his having an open hand or purse either, when he has nothing left to give? Well, well, make the trial, if you please. But where is the fellow whom you brought for Sir Oliver to examine, 10 relative to Charles's affairs.

Row. Below, waiting his commands, and no one can give him better intelligence. — This, Sir Oliver, is a friendly Jew, who, to do him justice, has done every thing in his power to bring your nephew to a proper sense 15 of his extravagance.

Sir Pet. Pray let us have him in.

Row. Desire Mr. Moses to walk upstairs.

[*Calls to* SERVANT.

Sir Pet. But, pray, why should you suppose he will speak the truth?   20

Row. Oh, I have convinced him that he has no chance of recovering certain sums advanced to Charles but through the bounty of Sir Oliver, who he knows is arrived; so that you may depend on his fidelity to his own interests. I have also another evidence in my power, one Snake, 25 whom I have detected in a matter little short of forgery, and shall shortly produce to remove some of your prejudices, Sir Peter, relative to Charles and Lady Teazle.

Sir Pet. I have heard too much on that subject.

Row. Here comes the honest Israelite.   30

Enter MOSES.

— This is Sir Oliver.

Sir Oliv.   Sir, I understand you have lately had great dealings with my nephew Charles.

Mos.   Yes, Sir Oliver, I have done all I could for him; but he was ruined before he came to me for assistance.

Sir Oliv.   That was unlucky, truly; for you have had no opportunity of showing your talents.

Mos.   None at all; I hadn't the pleasure of knowing his distresses till he was some thousands worse than nothing.

Sir Oliv.   Unfortunate, indeed! But I suppose you have done all in your power for him, honest Moses?

Mos.   Yes, he knows that. This very evening I was to have brought him a gentleman from the city, who does not know him, and will, I believe, advance him some money.

Sir Pet.   What, one Charles has never had money from before?

Mos.   Yes, Mr. Premium, of Crutched Friars, formerly a broker.

Sir Pet.   Egad, Sir Oliver, a thought strikes me! — Charles, you say, does not know Mr. Premium?

Mos.   Not at all.

Sir Pet.   Now then, Sir Oliver, you may have a better opportunity of satisfying yourself than by an old romancing tale of a poor relation: go with my friend Moses, and represent Premium, and then, I'll answer for it, you'll see your nephew in all his glory.

Sir Oliv.   Egad, I like this idea better than the other, and I may visit Joseph afterwards as old Stanley.

Sir Pet. True — so you may.

Row. Well, this is taking Charles rather at a disadvantage, to be sure. However, Moses, you understand Sir Peter, and will be faithful?

Mos. You may depend upon me. (*Looks at his* 5 *watch.*) This is near the time I was to have gone.

Sir Oliv. I'll accompany you as soon as you please, Moses — But hold! I have forgot one thing — how the plague shall I be able to pass for a Jew?

Mos. There's no need — the principal is Christian. 10

Sir Oliv. Is he? I'm very sorry to hear it. But, then again, an't I rather too smartly dressed to look like a money lender?

Sir Pet. Not at all; 'twould not be out of character, if you went in your own carriage — would it, Moses? 15

Mos. Not in the least.

Sir Oliv. Well, but how must I talk; there's certainly some cant of usury and mode of treating that I ought to know.

Sir Pet. Oh, there's not much to learn. The great 20 point, as I take it, is to be exorbitant enough in your demands. Hey, Moses?

Mos. Yes, that's a very great point.

Sir Oliv. I'll answer for't I'll not be wanting in that. I'll ask him eight or ten per cent. on the loan, at least. 25

Mos. If you ask him no more than that, you'll be discovered immediately.

Sir Oliv. Hey! what, the plague! how much then?

Mos. That depends upon the circumstances. If he appears not very anxious for the supply, you should re- 30 quire only forty or fifty per cent.; but if you find him in great distress, and want the moneys very bad, you may ask double.

Sir Pet. A good honest trade you're learning, Sir Oliver!

5   *Sir Oliv.* Truly, I think so — and not unprofitable.

Mos. Then, you know, you haven't the moneys yourself, but are forced to borrow them for him of a friend.

Sir Oliv. Oh! I borrow it of a friend, do I?

10   *Mos.* And your friend is an unconscionable dog: but you can't help that.

Sir Oliv. My friend an unconscionable dog, is he?

Mos. Yes, and he himself has not the moneys by him, but is forced to sell stock at a great loss.

15   *Sir Oliv.* He is forced to sell stock at a great loss, is he? Well, that's very kind of him.

Sir Pet. I' faith, Sir Oliver — Mr. Premium, I mean — you'll soon be master of the trade. But, Moses! would not you have him run out a little against the Annuity 20 Bill? That would be in character, I should think.

Mos. Very much.

Row. And lament that a young man now must be at years of discretion before he is suffered to ruin himself?

Mos. Ay, great pity!

25   *Sir Pet.* And abuse the public for allowing merit to an act whose only object is to snatch misfortune and imprudence from the rapacious gripe of usury, and give the minor a chance of inheriting his estate without being undone by coming into possession.

30   *Sir Oliv.* So, so — Moses shall give me farther instructions as we go together.

Sir Pet.   You will not have much time, for your nephew lives hard by.

Sir Oliv.   Oh, never fear! my tutor appears so able, that though Charles lived in the next street, it must be my own fault if I am not a complete rogue before I turn 5 the corner.   [*Exit with* MOSES.

Sir Pet.   So, now, I think Sir Oliver will be convinced: you are partial, Rowley, and would have prepared Charles for the other plot.

Row.   No, upon my word, Sir Peter.   10

Sir Pet.   Well, go bring me this Snake, and I'll hear what he has to say presently.   I see Maria, and want to speak with her.   (*Exit* ROWLEY.)   I should be glad to be convinced my suspicions of Lady Teazle and Charles were unjust.   I have never yet opened my mind on this 15 subject to my friend Joseph — I am determined I will do it — he will give me his opinion sincerely.

Enter MARIA.

So, child, has Mr. Surface returned with you?

Mar.   No, sir; he was engaged.

Sir Pet.   Well, Maria, do you not reflect, the more you 20 converse with that amiable young man, what return his partiality for you deserves?

Mar.   Indeed, Sir Peter, your frequent importunity on this subject distresses me extremely — you compel me to declare, that I know no man who has ever paid me a par- 25 ticular attention whom I would not prefer to Mr. Surface.

Sir Pet.   So — here's perverseness!   No, no, Maria, 'tis Charles only whom you would prefer.   'Tis evident his vices and follies have won your heart.

Mar. This is unkind, sir. You know I have obeyed you in neither seeing nor corresponding with him: I have heard enough to convince me that he is unworthy my regard. Yet I cannot think it culpable, if, while my
5 understanding severely condemns his vices, my heart suggests some pity for his distresses.

Sir Pet. Well, well, pity him as much as you please; but give your heart and hand to a worthier object.

Mar. Never to his brother!

10 *Sir Pet.* Go, perverse and obstinate! But take care, madam; you have never yet known what the authority of a guardian is: don't compel me to inform you of it.

Mar. I can only say, you shall not have just reason. 'Tis true, by my father's will, I am for a short period
15 bound to regard you as his substitute; but must cease to think you so, when you would compel me to be miserable.

[*Exit.*

Sir Pet. Was ever man so crossed as I am, every thing conspiring to fret me! I had not been involved in matrimony a fortnight, before her father, a hale and hearty
20 man, died, on purpose, I believe, for the pleasure of plaguing me with the care of his daughter. — (LADY TEAZLE *sings without.*) But here comes my helpmate! She appears in great good humour. How happy I should be if I could tease her into loving me, though but a
25 little!

Enter LADY TEAZLE.

Lady Teaz. Lud! Sir Peter, I hope you haven't been quarrelling with Maria? It is not using me well to be ill-humoured when I am not by.

272

Sir Pet. Ah, Lady Teazle, you might have the power to make me good-humoured at all times.

Lady Teaz. I am sure I wish I had; for I want you to be in a charming sweet temper at this moment. Do be good-humoured now, and let me have two hundred pounds, 5 will you?

Sir Pet. Two hundred pounds; what, an't I to be in a good humour without paying for it! But speak to me thus, and i' faith there's nothing I could refuse you. You shall have it; but seal me a bond for the repayment. 10

Lady Teaz. Oh, no — there — my note of hand will do as well. 　　　　　　　　　　*[Offering her hand.*

Sir Pet. And you shall no longer reproach me with not giving you an independent settlement. I mean shortly to surprise you: but shall we always live thus, hey? 15

Lady Teaz. If you please. I'm sure I don't care how soon we leave off quarrelling, provided you'll own you were tired first.

Sir Pet. Well — then let our future contest be, who shall be most obliging. 20

Lady Teaz. I assure you, Sir Peter, good nature becomes you. You look now as you did before we were married, when you used to walk with me under the elms, and tell me stories of what a gallant you were in your youth, and chuck me under the chin, you would; and 25 asked me if I thought I could love an old fellow, who would deny me nothing — didn't you?

Sir Pet. Yes, yes, and you were as kind and attentive —

Lady Teaz. Ay, so I was, and would always take your part, when my acquaintance used to abuse you, and turn 30 you into ridicule.

Sir Pet.   Indeed!

Lady Teaz.   Ay, and when my cousin Sophy has called you a stiff, peevish old bachelor, and laughed at me for thinking of marrying one who might be my father, I have 5 always defended you, and said, I didn't think you so ugly by any means.

Sir Pet.   Thank you.

Lady Teaz.   And I dared say you'd make a very good sort of a husband.

10   *Sir Pet.*   And you prophesied right; and we shall now be the happiest couple —

Lady Teaz.   And never differ again?

Sir Pet.   No, never! — though at the same time, indeed, my dear Lady Teazle, you must watch your 15 temper very seriously; for in all our little quarrels, my dear, if you recollect, my love, you always began first.

Lady Teaz.   I beg your pardon, my dear Sir Peter: indeed, you always gave the provocation.

20   *Sir Pet.*   Now see, my angel! take care -— contradicting isn't the way to keep friends.

Lady Teaz.   Then don't you begin it, my love!

Sir Pet.   There, now! you — you are going on. You don't perceive, my life, that you are just doing the very 25 thing which you know always makes me angry.

Lady Teaz.   Nay, you know, if you will be angry without any reason, my dear —

Sir Pet.   There! now you want to quarrel again.

Lady Teaz.   No, I'm sure I don't: but, if you will be so 30 peevish —

Sir Pet.   There now! who begins first?

Lady Teaz. Why, you, to be sure. I said nothing — but there's no bearing your temper.

Sir Pet. No, no, madam: the fault's in your own temper.

Lady Teaz. Ay, you are just what my cousin Sophy 5 said you would be.

Sir Pet. Your cousin Sophy is a forward, impertinent gipsy.

Lady Teaz. You are a great bear, I'm sure, to abuse my relations. 10

Sir Pet. Now may all the plagues of marriage be doubled on me, if ever I try to be friends with you any more!

Lady Teaz. So much the better.

Sir Pet. No, no, madam: 'tis evident you never cared 15 a pin for me, and I was a madman to marry you — a pert, rural coquette, that had refused half the honest squires in the neighborhood.

Lady Teaz. And I am sure I was a fool to marry you — an old dangling bachelor, who was single at fifty, only 20 because he never could meet with any one who would have him.

Sir Pet. Ay, ay, madam; but you were pleased enough to listen to me: you never had such an offer before.

Lady Teaz. No! didn't I refuse Sir Tivy Terrier, who 25 everybody said would have been a better match? for his estate is just as good as yours, and he has broke his neck since we have been married.

Sir Pet. I have done with you, madam! You are an unfeeling, ungrateful — but there's an end of everything. 30 I believe you capable of everything that is bad. Yes,

275

madam, I now believe the reports relative to you and Charles, madam. Yes, madam, you and Charles are, not without grounds —

Lady Teaz. Take care, Sir Peter! you had better not
5 insinuate any such thing! I'll not be suspected without cause, I promise you.

Sir Pet. Very well, madam! very well! A separate maintenance as soon as you please. Yes, madam, or a divorce! I'll make an example of myself for the benefit
10 of all old bachelors. Let us separate, madam.

Lady Teaz. Agreed! agreed! And now, my dear Sir Peter, we are of a mind once more, we may be the happiest couple, and never differ again, you know: ha! ha! ha! Well, you are going to be in a passion, I see, and I shall
15 only interrupt you — so, bye! bye!   [*Exit.*

Sir Pet. Plagues and tortures! can't I make her angry either! Oh, I am the most miserable fellow! But I'll not bear her presuming to keep her temper: no! she may break my heart, but she sha'n't keep her temper.   [*Exit.*

SCENE II. A ROOM IN CHARLES SURFACE'S HOUSE.

Enter TRIP, MOSES, *and* SIR OLIVER SURFACE.

20 *Trip.* Here, Master Moses! if you'll stay a moment I'll try whether — what's the gentleman's name?

Sir Oliv. Mr. Moses, what is my name?

[*Aside to* MOSES.

Mos. Mr. Premium.

Trip. Premium — very well.   [*Exit, taking snuff.*

25 *Sir Oliv.* To judge by the servants, one wouldn't be-

lieve the master was ruined.   But what! — sure, this was my brother's house?

Mos.   Yes, sir; Mr. Charles bought it of Mr. Joseph, with the furniture, pictures, &c., just as the old gentleman left it.   Sir Peter thought it a piece of extravagance in ₅ him.

Sir Oliv.   In my mind, the other's economy in selling it to him was more reprehensible by half.

Reënter Trip.

Trip.   My master says you must wait, gentlemen: he has company, and can't speak with you yet.   ₁₀

Sir Oliv.   If he knew who it was wanted to see him, perhaps he would not send such a message.

Trip.   Yes, yes, sir; he knows you are here — I did not forget little Premium: no, no, no.

Sir Oliv.   Very well; and I pray, sir, what may be ₁₅ your name?

Trip.   Trip, sir; my name is Trip, at your service.

Sir Oliv.   Well, then, Mr. Trip, you have a pleasant sort of place here, I guess?

Trip.   Why, yes — here are three or four of us pass ₂₀ our time agreeably enough: but then our wages are sometimes a little in arrear — and not very great either — but fifty pounds a year, and find our own bags and bouquets.

Sir Oliv.   Bags and bouquets! halters and bastinadoes! ₂₅
[*Aside.*

Trip.   And *à propos*, Moses, have you been able to get me that little bill discounted?

Sir Oliv.   Wants to raise money too! — mercy on me!

Has his distresses too, I warrant, like a lord, and affects
creditors and duns. [*Aside.*

Mos. 'Twas not to be done, indeed, Mr. Trip.

Trip. Good lack, you surprise me! My friend Brush
5 has indorsed it, and I thought when he put his name at
the back of a bill 'twas the same as cash.

Mos. No, 'twouldn't do.

Trip. A small sum — but twenty pounds. Hark'ee,
Moses, do you think you couldn't get it me by way of
10 annuity?

Sir Oliv. An annuity! ha! ha! a footman raise money
by way of annuity! Well done, luxury, egad. [*Aside.*

Mos. Well, but you must insure your place.

Trip. Oh, with all my heart! I'll insure my place,
15 and my life too, if you please.

Sir Oliv. It's more than I would your neck. [*Aside.*

Mos. But is there nothing you could deposit?

Trip. Why, nothing capital of my master's wardrobe
has dropped lately; but I could give you a mortgage on
20 some of his winter clothes, with equity of redemption
before November — or you shall have the reversion of the
French velvet, or a post-obit on the blue and silver; —
these, I should think, Moses, with a few pair of point
ruffles, as a collateral security — hey, my little fellow?

25 *Mos.* Well, well. [*Bell rings.*

Trip. Egad, I heard the bell! I believe, gentlemen,
I can now introduce you. Don't forget the annuity,
little Moses! This way, gentlemen, I'll insure my place,
you know.

30 *Sir Oliv.* (*Aside.*) If the man be a shadow of the
master, this is the temple of dissipation indeed! [*Exeunt.*

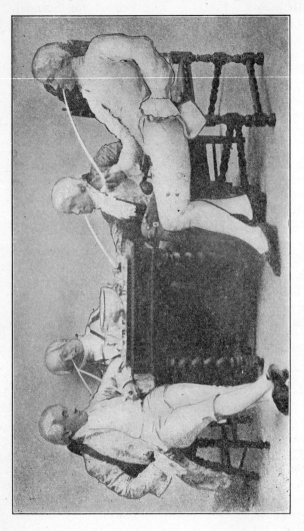

CHARLES SURFACE   GENTLEMAN   SIR HARRY BUMPER   CARELESS

"At least, I never feel my losses."

SCENE III.　ANOTHER ROOM IN THE SAME.

CHARLES SURFACE, SIR HARRY BUMPER, CARELESS, *and*
GENTLEMEN, *discovered drinking.*

Chas. Surf. 'Fore heaven, 'tis true!—there's the great
degeneracy of the age. Many of our acquaintance have
taste, spirit, and politeness; but, plague on't, they won't
drink.

Care. It is so, indeed, Charles! they give in to all the 5
substantial luxuries of the table, and abstain from nothing
but wine and wit. Oh, certainly society suffers by it in-
tolerably! for now, instead of the social spirit of raillery
that used to mantle over a glass of bright Burgundy,
their conversation is become just like the Spa-water they 10
drink, which has all the pertness and flatulency of champagne, without its spirit or flavour.

1 Gent. But what are they to do who love play better
than wine?

Care. True! there's Sir Harry diets himself for gaming, 15
and is now under a hazard regimen.

Chas. Surf. Then he'll have the worst of it. What!
you wouldn't train a horse for the course by keeping him
from corn? For my part, egad, I am never so successful
as when I am a little merry: let me throw on a bottle of 20
champagne, and I never lose.

All. Hey, what?

Care. At least I never feel my losses, which is exactly
the same thing.

2 Gent. Ay, that I believe. 25

Chas. Surf. And then, what man can pretend to be a
believer in love, who is an abjurer of wine? 'Tis the test

by which the lover knows his own heart. Fill a dozen bumpers to a dozen beauties, and she that floats at the top is the maid that has bewitched you.

Care. Now then, Charles, be honest, and give us your real favourite.

Chas. Surf. Why, I have withheld her only in compassion to you. If I toast her, you must give a round of her peers, which is impossible — on earth.

Care. Oh! then we'll find some canonised vestals or heathen goddesses that will do, I warrant!

Chas. Surf. Here then, bumpers, you rogues! bumpers! Maria! Maria! —

Sir Har. Maria who?

Chas. Surf. Oh, damn the surname! — 'tis too formal to be registered in Love's calendar — Maria!

All. Maria!

Chas. Surf. But, now, Sir Harry, beware, we must have beauty superlative.

Care. Nay, never study, Sir Harry: we'll stand to the toast, though your mistress should want an eye, and you know you have a song will excuse you.

Sir Har. Egad, so I have! and I'll give him the song instead of the lady.   [*Sings.*

Here's to the maiden of bashful fifteen;
Here's to the widow of fifty;
Here's to the flaunting extravagant quean,
And here's to the housewife that's thrifty.

Chorus. Let the toast pass, —
Drink to the lass,
I'll warrant she'll prove an excuse for the glass.

Here's to the charmer whose dimples we prize;
Now to the maid who has none, sir:
Here's to the girl with a pair of blue eyes,
And here's to the nymph with but one, sir.

Chorus.   Let the toast pass, &c.   5

Here's to the maid with a bosom of snow:
Now to her that's as brown as a berry:
Here's to the wife with a face full of woe,
And now to the damsel that's merry.

Chorus.   Let the toast pass, &c.   10

For let 'em be clumsy, or let 'em be slim,
Young or ancient, I care not a feather;
So fill a pint bumper quite up to the brim,
So fill up your glasses, nay, fill to the brim,
And let us e'en toast them together.   15

Chorus.   Let the toast pass, &c.

   All.   Bravo! bravo!

   Enter TRIP, *and whispers* CHARLES SURFACE.

Chas. Surf.   Gentlemen, you must excuse me a little. —
Careless, take the chair, will you?

   Care.   Nay, pr'ythee, Charles, what now? This is   20
one of your peerless beauties, I suppose, has dropped in
by chance!

Chas. Surf.   No, faith! To tell you the truth, 'tis a
Jew and a broker, who are come by appointment.

   Care.   Oh! let's have the Jew in.   25

1 *Gent.*   Ay, and the broker too, by all means.

2 *Gent.*   Yes, yes, the Jew and the broker.

Chas. Surf.   Egad, with all my heart! — Trip, bid the
gentlemen walk in. — (*Exit* TRIP.)   Though there's one
5 of them a stranger, I can tell you.

Care.   Charles, let us give them some generous Burgundy, and perhaps they'll grow conscientious.

Chas. Surf.   Oh, hang 'em no! wine does but draw
forth a man's natural qualities; and to make them drink
10 would only be to whet their knavery.

Reënter TRIP, *with* SIR OLIVER SURFACE *and* MOSES.

Chas. Surf.   So, honest Moses; walk in, pray, Mr.
Premium — that's the gentleman's name, isn't it, Moses?

Mos.   Yes, sir.

Chas. Surf.   Set chairs, Trip. — Sit down, Mr. Pre-
15 mium. — Glasses, Trip. — (TRIP *gives chairs and glasses,
and exit.*)   Sit down, Moses. — Come, Mr. Premium,
I'll give you a sentiment; here's *Success to usury!* —
Moses, fill the gentleman a bumper.

Mos.   Success to usury!   [*Drinks.*

20 *Care.*   Right, Moses — usury is prudence and industry,
and deserves to succeed.

Sir Oliv.   Then here's — All the success it deserves!
                                                   [*Drinks.*

Care.   No, no, that won't do! Mr. Premium, you
have demurred at the toast, and must drink it in a pint
25 bumper.

1 *Gent.*   A pint bumper, at least.

Mos.   Oh, pray, sir, consider — Mr. Premium's a
gentleman.

Care. And therefore loves good wine.

2 *Gent.* Give Moses a quart glass — this is mutiny, and a high contempt for the chair.

Care. Here, now for't! I'll see justice done to the last drop of my bottle. 5

Sir Oliv. Nay, pray, gentlemen — I did not expect this usage.

Chas. Surf. No, hang it, you shan't; Mr. Premium's a stranger.

Sir Oliv. Odd! I wish I was well out of their com- 10 pany. [*Aside.*

Care. Plague on 'em then! if they won't drink, we'll not sit down with them. Come, Harry, the dice are in the next room. — Charles, you'll join us when you have finished your business with the gentlemen? 15

Chas. Surf. I will! I will! [*Exeunt* SIR HARRY BUMPER *and* GENTLEMEN; CARELESS *following.*] Careless!

Care. (*Returning.*) Well!

Chas. Surf. Perhaps I may want you.

Care. Oh, you know I am always ready: word, note, 20 or bond, 'tis all the same to me. [*Exit.*

Mos. Sir, this is Mr. Premium, a gentleman of the strictest honour and secrecy; and always performs what he undertakes. Mr. Premium, this is —

Chas. Surf. Pshaw! have done. Sir, my friend Moses 25 is a very honest fellow, but a little slow at expression: he'll be an hour giving us our titles. Mr. Premium, the plain state of the matter is this: I am an extravagant young fellow who wants to borrow money; you I take to be a prudent old fellow, who have got money to lend. I 30 am blockhead enough to give fifty per cent. sooner than not have it; and you, I presume, are rogue enough to take a hundred if you can get it. Now, sir, you see we are acquainted at once, and may proceed to business without farther ceremony.

5 *Sir Oliv.* Exceeding frank, upon my word. I see, sir, you are not a man of many compliments.

Chas. Surf. Oh, no, sir! plain dealing in business I always think best.

Sir Oliv. Sir, I like you the better for it. However, 10 you are mistaken in one thing; I have no money to lend, but I believe I could procure some of a friend; but then he's an unconscionable dog. Isn't he, Moses? And must sell stock to accommodate you. Mustn't he, Moses?

Mos. Yes, indeed! You know I always speak the 15 truth, and scorn to tell a lie!

Chas. Surf. Right. People that speak truth generally do. But these are trifles, Mr. Premium. What! I know money isn't to be bought without paying for't!

Sir Oliv. Well, but what security could you give? 20 You have no land, I suppose?

Chas. Surf. Not a mole-hill, nor a twig, but what's in the bough-pots out of the window!

Sir Oliv. Nor any stock, I presume?

Chas. Surf. Nothing but live stock — and that's only 25 a few pointers and ponies. But pray, Mr. Premium, are you acquainted at all with any of my connections?

Sir Oliv. Why, to say truth, I am.

Chas. Surf. Then you must know that I have a devil- ish rich uncle in the East Indies, Sir Oliver Surface, from 30 whom I have the greatest expectations?

Sir Oliv. That you have a wealthy uncle, I have heard;

but how your expectations will turn out is more, I believe, than you can tell.

Chas. Surf. Oh, no! — there can be no doubt. They tell me I'm a prodigious favourite, and that he talks of leaving me every thing.

Sir Oliv. Indeed! this is the first I've heard of it.

Chas. Surf. Yes, yes, 'tis just so. Moses knows 'tis true; don't you, Moses?

Mos. Oh, yes! I'll swear to't.

Sir Oliv. Egad, they'll persuade me presently I'm at Bengal.　　　　　　　　　　　　　　　　　　　*[Aside.*

Chas. Surf. Now I propose, Mr. Premium, if it's agreeable to you, a post-obit on Sir Oliver's life: though at the same time the old fellow has been so liberal to me, that I give you my word, I should be very sorry to hear that anything had happened to him.

Sir Oliv. Not more than I should, I assure you. But the bond you mention happens to be just the worst security you could offer me — for I might live to a hundred and never see the principal.

Chas. Surf. Oh, yes, you would! the moment Sir Oliver dies, you know, you would come on me for the money.

Sir Oliv. Then I believe I should be the most unwelcome dun you ever had in your life.

Chas. Surf. What! I suppose you're afraid that Sir Oliver is too good a life?

Sir Oliv. No, indeed I am not; though I have heard he is as hale and healthy as any man of his years in Christendom.

Chas. Surf. There again, now, you are misinformed.

No, no, the climate has hurt him considerably, poor uncle Oliver. Yes, yes, he breaks apace, I'm told — and is so much altered lately that his nearest relations would not know him.

5 *Sir Oliv.* No! Ha! ha! ha! so much altered lately that his nearest relations would not know him! Ha! ha! ha! egad — ha! ha! ha!

Chas. Surf. Ha! ha! — you're glad to hear that, little Premium?

10 *Sir Oliv.* No, no, I'm not.

Chas. Surf. Yes, yes, you are — ha! ha! ha! — you know that mends your chance.

Sir Oliv. But I'm told Sir Oliver is coming over; nay, some say he is actually arrived.

15 *Chas. Surf.* Pshaw! sure I must know better than you whether he's come or not. No, no, rely on't he's at this moment at Calcutta. Isn't he, Moses?

Mos. Oh, yes, certainly.

Sir Oliv. Very true, as you say, you must know better 20 than I, though I have it from pretty good authority. Haven't I, Moses?

Mos. Yes, most undoubted!

Sir Oliv. But, sir, as I understand you want a few hundreds immediately, is there nothing you could dispose of?

25 *Chas. Surf.* How do you mean?

Sir Oiiv. For instance, now, I have heard that your father left behind him a great quantity of massy old plate.

Chas. Surf. O Lud! that's gone long ago. Moses can 30 tell you how better than I can.

Sir Oliv. (*Aside.*) Good lack! all the family race-

286

cups and corporation-bowls! (*Aloud.*) Then it was also supposed that his library was one of the most valuable and compact.

Chas. Surf. Yes, yes, so it was — vastly too much so for a private gentleman. For my part, I was always of a communicative disposition, so I thought it a shame to keep so much knowledge to myself.

Sir Oliv. (*Aside.*) Mercy upon me! learning that had run in the family like an heir-loom! — (*Aloud.*) Pray, what has become of the books?

Chas. Surf. You must inquire of the auctioneer, Master Premium, for I don't believe even Moses can direct you.

Mos. I know nothing of books.

Sir Oliv. So, so, nothing of the family property left, I suppose?

Chas. Surf. Not much, indeed; unless you have a mind to the family pictures. I have got a room full of ancestors above; and if you have a taste for old paintings, egad, you shall have 'em a bargain!

Sir Oliv. Hey! what the devil! sure, you wouldn't sell your forefathers, would you?

Chas. Surf. Every man of them, to the best bidder.

Sir Oliv. What! your great-uncles and aunts?

Chas. Surf. Ay, and my great-grandfathers and grandmothers too.

Sir Oliv. (*Aside.*) Now I give him up! (*Aloud.*) What the plague, have you no bowels for your own kindred? Odds life! do you take me for Shylock in the play, that you would raise money of me on your own flesh and blood?

Chas. Surf. Nay, my little broker, don't be angry: what need you care, if you have your money's worth?

Sir Oliv. Well, I'll be the purchaser: I think I can dispose of the family canvas. (*Aside.*) Oh, I'll never
5 forgive him this! never!

Reënter CARELESS.

Care. Come, Charles, what keeps you?

Chas. Surf. I can't come yet. I' faith, we are going to have a sale above stairs; here's little Premium will buy all my ancestors!

10 *Care.* Oh, burn your ancestors!

Chas. Surf. No, he may do that afterwards, if he pleases. Stay, Careless, we want you: egad, you shall be auctioneer — so come along with us.

Care. Oh, have with you, if that's the case. I can
15 handle a hammer as well as a dice-box! Going! going!

Sir Oliv. Oh, the profligates!   [*Aside.*

Chas. Surf. Come, Moses, you shall be appraiser, if we want one. Gad's life, little Premium, you don't seem to like the business?

20 *Sir Oliv.* Oh, yes, I do, vastly! Ha! ha! ha! yes, yes, I think it a rare joke to sell one's family by auction — ha! ha! (*Aside.*) Oh, the prodigal!

Chas. Surf. To be sure! when a man wants money, where the plague should he get assistance, if he can't
25 make free with his own relations!   [*Exeunt.*

Sir Oliv. I'll never forgive him; never! never!

ACT IV.

SCENE I. A PICTURE ROOM IN CHARLES SURFACE'S
HOUSE.

Enter CHARLES SURFACE, SIR OLIVER SURFACE, MOSES,
and CARELESS.

Chas. Surf. Walk in, gentlemen, pray walk in; — here they are, the family of the Surfaces, up to the Conquest.

Sir Oliv. And, in my opinion, a goodly collection.

Chas. Surf. Ay, ay, these are done in the true spirit of portrait-painting; no *volontière grace* or expression. 5 Not like the works of your modern Raphaels, who give you the strongest resemblance, yet contrive to make your portrait independent of you; so that you may sink the original and not hurt the picture. No, no; the merit of these is the inveterate likeness — all stiff and awkward as the 10 originals, and like nothing in human nature besides.

Sir Oliv. Ah! we shall never see such figures of men again.

Chas. Surf. I hope not. Well, you see, Master Premium, what a domestic character I am; here I sit of an 15 evening surrounded by my family. But come, get to your pulpit, Mr. Auctioneer; here's an old gouty chair of my grandfather's will answer the purpose.

Care. Ay, ay, this will do. But, Charles, I haven't a hammer; and what's an auctioneer without his hammer? 20

Chas. Surf. Egad, that's true. What parchment have we here? Oh, our genealogy in full. (*Taking pedigree down.*) Here, Careless, you shall have no common bit of mahogany, here's the family tree for you, you rogue!
5 This shall be your hammer, and now you may knock down my ancestors with their own pedigree.

Sir Oliv. What an unnatural rogue! — an *ex post facto* parricide!   [*Aside.*

Care. Yes, yes, here's a list of your generation indeed;
10 — faith, Charles, this is the most convenient thing you could have found for the business, for 'twill not only serve as a hammer, but a catalogue into the bargain. Come, begin — A-going, a-going, a-going!

Chas. Surf. Bravo, Charles! Well, here's my great-
15 uncle, Sir Richard Raveline, a marvellous good general in his day, I assure you. He served in all the Duke of Marlborough's wars, and got that cut over his eye at the battle of Malplaquet. What say you, Mr. Premium? look at him — there's a hero! not cut out of his feathers, as your
20 modern clipped captains are, but enveloped in wig and regimentals, as a general should be. What do you bid?

Sir Oliv. (*Aside to* MOSES.) Bid him speak.

Mos. Mr. Premium would have you speak.

Chas. Surf. Why, then, he shall have him for ten
25 pounds, and I'm sure that's not dear for a staff-officer.

Sir Oliv. (*Aside.*) Heaven deliver me! his famous uncle Richard for ten pounds! — (*Aloud.*) Very well, sir, I take him at that.

Chas. Surf. Careless, knock down my uncle Richard —
30 Here, now, is a maiden sister of his, my great-aunt Deborah, done by Kneller, in his best manner, and esteemed a

very formidable likeness. There she is, you see, a shepherdess feeding her flock. You shall have her for five pounds ten — the sheep are worth the money.

Sir Oliv. (*Aside.*) Ah! poor Deborah! a woman who set such a value on herself! — (*Aloud.*) Five pounds ten 5 — she's mine.

Chas. Surf. Knock down my aunt Deborah! Here, now, are two that were a sort of cousins of theirs. — You see, Moses, these pictures were done some time ago, when beaux wore wigs, and the ladies their own hair. 10

Sir Oliv. Yes, truly, head-dresses appear to have been a little lower in those days.

Chas. Surf. Well, take that couple for the same.

Mos. 'Tis a good bargain.

Chas. Surf. Careless! — This, now, is a grandfather of 15 my mother's, a learned judge, well known on the western circuit. — What do you rate him at, Moses?

Mos. Four guineas.

Chas. Surf. Four guineas! Gad's life, you don't bid me the price of his wig. — Mr. Premium, you have more 20 respect for the woolsack; do let us knock his lordship down at fifteen.

Sir Oliv. By all means.

Care. Gone!

Chas. Surf. And there are two brothers of his, William 25 and Walter Blunt, Esquires, both members of parliament, and noted speakers; and, what's very extraordinary, I believe, this is the first time they were ever bought or sold.

Sir Oliv. That is very extraordinary, indeed! I'll take them at your own price, for the honour of parlia- 30 ment.

Care. Well said, little Premium! I'll knock them down at forty.

Chas. Surf. Here's a jolly fellow — I don't know what relation, but he was mayor of Norwich: take him at 5 eight pounds.

Sir Oliv. No, no, six will do for the mayor.

Chas. Surf. Come, make it guineas, and I'll throw you the two aldermen there into the bargain.

Sir Oliv. They're mine.

10 *Chas. Surf.* Careless, knock down the mayor and aldermen. But, plague on't! we shall be all day retailing in this manner; do let us deal wholesale: what say you, little Premium? Give me three hundred pounds for the rest of the family in the lump.

15 *Care.* Ay, ay, that will be the best way.

Sir Oliv. Well, well, any thing to accommodate you; they are mine. But there is one portrait which you have always passed over.

Care. What, that ill-looking little fellow over the set-
20 tee?

Sir Oliv. Yes, sir, I mean that; though I don't think him so ill-looking a little fellow, by any means.

Chas. Surf. What, that? Oh; that's my uncle Oliver! 'twas done before he went to India.

25 *Care.* Your uncle Oliver! Gad, then you'll never be friends, Charles. That, now, to me, is as stern a looking rogue as ever I saw; an unforgiving eye, and a disinheriting countenance! an inveterate knave, depend on't. Don't you think so, little Premium?

30 *Sir Oliv.* Upon my soul, sir, I do not; I think it is as honest a looking face as any in the room, dead or alive.

CHARLES SURFACE

"What, that? Oh; that's my uncle Oliver!"

But I suppose uncle Oliver goes with the rest of the lumber?

Chas. Surf.   No, hang it! I'll not part with poor Noll. The old fellow has been very good to me, and, egad, I'll keep his picture while I've a room to put it in.   5

Sir Oliv.   (*Aside.*) The rogue's my nephew after all! — (*Aloud.*) But, sir, I have somehow taken a fancy to that picture.

Chas. Surf.   I'm sorry for't, for you certainly will not have it.   Oons, haven't you got enough of them?   10

Sir Oliv.   (*Aside.*) I forgive him every thing! — (*Aloud.*) But, sir, when I take a whim in my head, I don't value money.   I'll give you as much for that as for all the rest.

Chas. Surf.   Don't tease me, master broker; I tell you   15 I'll not part with it, and there's an end of it.

Sir Oliv.   (*Aside.*) How like his father the dog is! — (*Aloud.*) Well, well, I have done. — (*Aside.*) I did not perceive it before, but I think I never saw such a striking resemblance. — (*Aloud.*) Here is a draft for your sum.   20

Chas. Surf.   Why, 'tis for eight hundred pounds!

Sir Oliv.   You will not let Sir Oliver go?

Chas. Surf.   Zounds! no! I tell you, once more.

Sir Oliv.   Then never mind the difference, we'll balance that another time.   But give me your hand on the   25 bargain; you are an honest fellow, Charles — I beg pardon, sir, for being so free. — Come, Moses.

Chas. Surf.   Egad, this is a whimsical old fellow! — But hark'ee, Premium, you'll prepare lodgings for these gentlemen.   30

Sir Oliv.   Yes, yes, I'll send for them in a day or two.

Chas. Surf. But hold; do now send a genteel convey-ance for them, for, I assure you, they were most of them used to ride in their own carriages.

Sir Oliv. I will, I will — for all but Oliver.

5 *Chas. Surf.* Ay, all but the little nabob.

Sir Oliv. You're fixed on that?

Chas. Surf. Peremptorily.

Sir Oliv. (*Aside.*) A dear extravagant rogue! — (*Aloud.*) Good day! — Come, Moses. (*Aside.*) Let me 10 hear now who dares call him profligate.

[*Exit with* MOSES.

Care. Why, this is the oddest genius of the sort I ever met with.

Chas. Surf. Egad, he's the prince of brokers, I think. I wonder how the devil Moses got acquainted with so 15 honest a fellow. — Ha! here's Rowley. — Do, Careless, say I'll join the company in a few moments.

Care. I will — but don't let that old blockhead per-suade you to squander any of that money on old musty debts, or any such nonsense; for tradesmen, Charles, are 20 the most exorbitant fellows.

Chas. Surf. Very true, and paying them is only en-couraging them.

Care. Nothing else.

Chas. Surf. Ay, ay, never fear. — (*Exit* CARELESS.) 25 So! this was an odd old fellow, indeed. Let me see, two-thirds of these five hundred and thirty odd pounds are mine by right. 'Fore heaven! I find one's ancestors are more valuable relations than I took them for! — Ladies and gentlemen, your most obedient and very grate-30 ful servant. [*Bows ceremoniously to the pictures.*

Enter ROWLEY.

Ha! old Rowley! egad, you are just come in time to take leave of your old acquaintance.

Row. Yes, I heard they were a-going. But I wonder you can have such spirits under so many distresses.

Chas. Surf. Why, there's the point! my distresses are 5 so many, that I can't afford to part with my spirits; but I shall be rich and splenetic, all in good time. However, I suppose you are surprised that I am not more sorrowful at parting with so many near relations; to be sure, 'tis very affecting, but you see they never move a muscle, so 10 why should I?

Row. There's no making you serious a moment.

Chas. Surf. Yes, faith, I am so now. Here, my honest Rowley, here, get me this changed directly, and take a hundred pounds of it immediately to old Stanley. 15

Row. A hundred pounds! Consider only —

Chas. Surf. Gad's life, don't talk about it! poor Stanley's wants are pressing, and, if you don't make haste, we shall have some one call that has a better right to the money. 20

Row. Ah! there's the point! I never will cease dunning you with the old proverb —

Chas. Surf. *Be just before you're generous.* — Why, so I would if I could; but Justice is an old, hobbling beldame, and I can't get her to keep pace with Generosity, for the 25 soul of me.

Row. Yet, Charles, believe me, one hour's reflection —

Chas. Surf. Ay, ay, it's very true; but, hark'ee, Rowley, while I have, by Heaven I'll give; and now for hazard. [*Exeunt.* 30

Scene II. Another room in the same.

Enter Sir Oliver Surface *and* Moses.

Mos. Well, sir, I think, as Sir Peter said, you have seen Mr. Charles in high glory; 'tis great pity he's so extravagant.

Sir Oliv. True, but he would not sell my picture.

5   *Mos.* And loves wine and women so much.

Sir Oliv. But he would not sell my picture.

Mos. And games so deep.

Sir Oliv. But he would not sell my picture. Oh, here's Rowley.

Enter Rowley.

10   *Row.* So, Sir Oliver, I find you have made a purchase —

Sir Oliv. Yes, yes, our young rake has parted with his ancestors like old tapestry.

Row. And here has he commissioned me to re-deliver you part of the purchase money — I mean, though, in 15 your necessitous character of old Stanley.

Mos. Ah! there is the pity of all; he is so charitable.

Row. And I left a hosier and two tailors in the hall, who, I'm sure, won't be paid, and this hundred would satisfy them.

20   *Sir Oliv.* Well, well, I'll pay his debts, and his benevolence too. But now I am no more a broker and you shall introduce me to the elder brother as old Stanley.

Row. Not yet awhile; Sir Peter, I know, means to call there about this time.

Enter TRIP.

Trip. Oh, gentlemen, I beg pardon for not showing you out; this way — Moses, a word.   [*Exit with* MOSES.

Sir Oliv. There's a fellow for you! Would you believe it, that puppy intercepted the Jew on our coming, and wanted to raise money before he got to his master! 5

Row. Indeed!

Sir Oliv. Yes, they are now planning an annuity business. Ah, Master Rowley, in my days servants were content with the follies of their masters, when they were worn a little threadbare; but now they have their vices, like 10 their birthday clothes, with the gloss on.   [*Exeunt.*

SCENE III. A LIBRARY IN JOSEPH SURFACE'S HOUSE.

Enter JOSEPH SURFACE *and* SERVANT.

Jos. Surf. No letter from Lady Teazle?

Ser. No, sir.

Jos. Surf. (*Aside.*) I am surprised she has not sent, if she is prevented from coming. Sir Peter certainly does 15 not suspect me. Yet I wish I may not lose the heiress, through the scrape I have drawn myself into with the wife; however, Charles's imprudence and bad character are great points in my favour.   [*Knocking without.*

Ser. Sir, I believe that must be Lady Teazle. 20

Jos. Surf. Hold! See whether it is or not, before you go to the door: I have a particular message for you if it should be my brother.

Ser. 'Tis her ladyship, sir; she always leaves her chair at the milliner's in the next street. 25

Jos. Surf. Stay, stay; draw that screen before the window — that will do; — my opposite neighbour is a maiden lady of so curious a temper. — (*Servant draws the screen, and exits.*) I have a difficult hand to play in this 5 affair. Lady Teazle has lately suspected my views on Maria; but she must by no means be let into that secret, — at least, till I have her more in my power.

Enter LADY TEAZLE.

Lady Teaz. What, sentiment in soliloquy now? Have you been very impatient? O Lud! don't pretend to look 10 grave. I vow I couldn't come before.

Jos. Surf. O madam, punctuality is a species of constancy very unfashionable in a lady of quality.

[*Places chairs, and sits after* LADY TEAZLE *is seated.*

Lady Teaz. Upon my word, you ought to pity me. Do you know Sir Peter is grown so ill-natured to me of 15 late, and so jealous of Charles too — that's the best of the story, isn't it?

Jos. Surf. I am glad my scandalous friends keep that up. [*Aside.*

Lady Teaz. I am sure I wish he would let Maria marry 20 him, and then perhaps he would be convinced; don't you, Mr. Surface?

Jos. Surf. (*Aside.*) Indeed I do not. — (*Aloud.*) Oh, certainly I do! for then my dear Lady Teazle would also be convinced how wrong her suspicions were of my having 25 any design on the silly girl.

Lady Teaz. Well, well, I'm inclined to believe you. But isn't it provoking to have the most ill-natured things said of one? And there's my friend Lady Sneerwell has

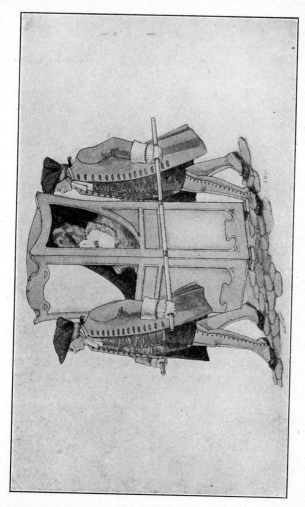

A Sedan Chair

circulated I don't know how many scandalous tales of me, and all without any foundation too; that's what vexes me.

Jos. Surf. Ay, madam, to be sure, that is the provoking circumstance — without foundation; yes, yes, there's the mortification, indeed; for when a scandalous story is believed against one, there certainly is no comfort like the consciousness of having deserved it.

Lady Teaz. No, to be sure, then I'd forgive their malice; but to attack me, who am really so innocent, and who never say an ill-natured thing of any body — that is, of any friend; and then Sir Peter, too, to have him so peevish, and so suspicious, when I know the integrity of my own heart — indeed 'tis monstrous!

Jos. Surf. But, my dear Lady Teazle, 'tis your own fault if you suffer it. When a husband entertains a groundless suspicion of his wife, and withdraws his confidence from her, the original compact is broken, and she owes it to the honour of her sex to endeavour to outwit him.

Lady Teaz. Indeed! So that, if he suspects me without cause, it follows, that the best way of curing his jealousy is to give him reason for't?

Jos. Surf. Undoubtedly — for your husband should never be deceived in you: and in that case it becomes you to be frail in compliment to his discernment.

Lady Teaz. To be sure, what you say is very reasonable, and when the consciousness of my innocence —

Jos. Surf. Ah, my dear madam, there is the great mistake! 'tis this very conscious innocence that is of the greatest prejudice to you. What is it makes you negligent of

forms, and careless of the world's opinion? why, the consciousness of your own innocence. What makes you
thoughtless in your conduct, and apt to run into a thousand
little imprudences? why, the consciousness of your own
5 innocence. What makes you impatient of Sir Peter's
temper, and outrageous at his suspicions? why, the consciousness of your innocence.

Lady Teaz.   'Tis very true!

Jos. Surf.   Now, my dear Lady Teazle, if you would
10 but once make a trifling *faux pas*, you can't conceive how
cautious you would grow, and how ready to humour and
agree with your husband.

Lady Teaz.   Do you think so?

Jos. Surf.   Oh, I am sure on't; and then you would find
15 all scandal would cease at once, for — in short, your character at present is like a person in a plethora, absolutely
dying from too much health.

Lady Teaz.   So, so; then I perceive your prescription
is, that I must sin in my own defence, and part with my
20 virtue to preserve my reputation?

Jos. Surf.   Exactly so, upon my credit, ma'am.

Lady Teaz.   Well, certainly this is the oddest doctrine,
and the newest receipt for avoiding calumny!

Jos. Surf.   An infallible one, believe me. Prudence,
25 like experience, must be paid for.

Lady Teaz.   Why, if my understanding were once convinced —

Jos. Surf.   Oh, certainly, madam, your understanding
should be convinced. Yes, yes — Heaven forbid I should
30 persuade you to do any thing you thought wrong. No, no,
I have too much honour to desire it.

Lady Teaz. Don't you think we may as well leave honour out of the argument?   [*Rises.*

Jos. Surf. Ah, the ill effects of your country education, I see, still remain with you.

Lady Teaz. I doubt they do indeed; and I will fairly 5 own to you, that if I could be persuaded to do wrong, it would be by Sir Peter's ill usage sooner than your honourable logic, after all.

Jos. Surf. Then, by this hand, which he is unworthy of —   [*Taking her hand.* 10

Reënter SERVANT.

'Sdeath, you blockhead — what do you want?

Ser. I beg your pardon, sir, but I thought you would not choose Sir Peter to come up without announcing him.

Jos. Surf. Sir Peter! — Oons — the devil!

Lady Teaz. Sir Peter! O Lud! I'm ruined! I'm 15 ruined!

Ser. Sir, 'twasn't I let him in.

Lady Teaz. Oh! I'm quite undone! What will become of me? Now, Mr. Logic — Oh! mercy, sir, he's on the stairs — I'll get behind here — and if ever I'm so im- 20 prudent again —   [*Goes behind the screen.*

Jos. Surf. Give me that book.

       [*Sits down.* SERVANT *pretends to adjust his chair.*

Enter SIR PETER TEAZLE.

Sir Pet. Ay, ever improving himself — Mr. Surface, Mr. Surface —   [*Pats* JOSEPH *on the shoulder.*

Jos. Surf. Oh, my dear Sir Peter, I beg your pardon. — 25 (*Gaping, throws away the book.*) I have been dozing over a stupid book. Well, I am much obliged to you for this call. You haven't been here, I believe, since I fitted up this room. Books, you know, are the only things I am a coxcomb in.

5   *Sir Pet.* 'Tis very neat indeed. Well, well, that's proper; and you can make even your screen a source of knowledge — hung, I perceive, with maps.

  Jos. Surf. Oh, yes, I find great use in that screen.

  Sir Pet. I dare say you must, certainly, when you want 10 to find any thing in a hurry.

  Jos. Surf. Ay, or to hide any thing in a hurry either.
                                     [*Aside.*

  Sir Pet. Well, I have a little private business —

  Jos. Surf. You need not stay.   [*To* SERVANT.

  Ser. No, sir.   [*Exit.*

15   *Jos. Surf.* Here's a chair, Sir Peter — I beg —

  Sir Pet. Well, now we are alone, there is a subject, my dear friend, on which I wish to unburden my mind to you — a point of the greatest moment to my peace; in short, my good friend, Lady Teazle's conduct of late has made 20 me very unhappy.

  Jos. Surf. Indeed! I am very sorry to hear it.

  Sir Pet. 'Tis but too plain she has not the least regard for me; but, what's worse, I have pretty good authority to suppose she has formed an attachment to another.

25   *Jos. Surf.* Indeed! you astonish me!

  Sir Pet. Yes! and, between ourselves, I think I've discovered the person.

  Jos. Surf. How! you alarm me exceedingly.

  Sir Pet. Ay, my dear friend, I knew you would sym-30 pathise with me!

Jos. Surf. Yes, believe me, Sir Peter, such a discovery would hurt me just as much as it would you.

Sir Pet. I am convinced of it. Ah! it is a happiness to have a friend whom we can trust even with one's family secrets. But have you no guess who I mean? 5

Jos. Surf. I haven't the most distant idea. It can't be Sir Benjamin Backbite!

Sir Pet. Oh, no! What say you to Charles?

— *Jos Surf.* My brother! impossible!

Sir Pet. Oh, my dear friend, the goodness of your own 10 heart misleads you. You judge of others by yourself.

Jos. Surf. Certainly, Sir Peter, the heart that is conscious of its own integrity is ever slow to credit another's treachery.

Sir Pet. True; but your brother has no sentiment — 15 you never hear him talk so.

Jos. Surf. Yet I can't but think Lady Teazle herself has too much principle.

Sir Pet. Ay; but what is principle against the flattery of a handsome, lively young fellow? 20

Jos. Surf. That's very true.

Sir Pet. And then, you know, the difference of our ages makes it very improbable that she should have any great affection for me; and if she were to be frail, and I were to make it public, why the town would only laugh at 25 me, the foolish old bachelor, who had married a girl.

Jos. Surf. That's true, to be sure — they would laugh.

Sir Pet. Laugh! ay, and make ballads, and paragraphs, and the devil knows what of me. 30

Jos. Surf. No, you must never make it public.

Sir Pet. But then again — that the nephew of my old friend, Sir Oliver, should be the person to attempt such a wrong, hurts me more nearly.

Jos. Surf. Ay, there's the point. When ingratitude barbs the dart of injury, the wound has double danger in it.

Sir Pet. Ay — I, that was, in a manner, left his guardian; in whose house he had been so often entertained; who never in my life denied him — my advice!

Jos. Surf. Oh, 'tis not to be credited! There may be a man capable of such baseness, to be sure; but, for my part, till you can give me positive proofs, I cannot but doubt it. However, if it should be proved on him, he is no longer a brother of mine — I disclaim kindred with him: for the man who can break the laws of hospitality, and tempt the wife of his friend, deserves to be branded as the pest of society.

Sir Pet. What a difference there is between you! What noble sentiments!

Jos. Surf. Yet I cannot suspect Lady Teazle's honour.

Sir Pet. I am sure I wish to think well of her, and to remove all ground of quarrel between us. She has lately reproached me more than once with having made no settlement on her; and, in our last quarrel, she almost hinted that she should not break her heart if I was dead. Now, as we seem to differ in our ideas of expense, I have resolved she shall have her own way, and be her own mistress in that respect for the future; and, if I were to die she will find I have not been inattentive to her interest while living. Here, my friend, are the drafts of two deeds, which I wish to have your opinion on. By one, she will enjoy eight hundred a year independent while I live; and, by the other, the bulk of my fortune at my death.

Jos. Surf. This conduct, Sir Peter, is indeed truly generous. — (*Aside.*) I wish it may not corrupt my pupil.

Sir Pet. Yes, I am determined she shall have no cause to complain, though I would not have her acquainted with the latter instance of my affection yet awhile.

Jos. Surf. Nor I, if I could help it.   [*Aside.*

Sir Pet. And now, my dear friend, if you please, we will talk over the situation of your hopes with Maria.

Jos. Surf. (*Softly.*) Oh, no, Sir Peter; another time, if you please.

Sir Pet. I am sensibly chagrined at the little progress you seem to make in her affections.

Jos. Surf. (*Softly.*) I beg you will not mention it. What are my disappointments when your happiness is in debate! — (*Aside.*) 'Sdeath, I shall be ruined every way!

Sir Pet. And though you are averse to my acquainting Lady Teazle with your passion, I'm sure she's not your enemy in the affair.

Jos. Surf. Pray, Sir Peter, now oblige me. I am really too much affected by the subject we have been speaking of to bestow a thought on my own concerns. The man who is entrusted with his friend's distresses can never —

Reënter SERVANT.

Well, sir?

Ser. Your brother, sir, is speaking to a gentleman in the street, and says he knows you are within.

Jos. Surf. 'Sdeath, blockhead, I'm not within — I'm out for the day.

Sir Pet. Stay — hold — a thought has struck me : — you shall be at home.

Jos. Surf. Well, well, let him come up. — (*Exit* SERV- ANT.) He'll interrupt Sir Peter, however. [*Aside.*

5 *Sir Pet.* Now, my good friend, oblige me, I entreat you. Before Charles comes, let me conceal myself somewhere, then do you tax him on the point we have been talking, and his answer may satisfy me at once.

Jos. Surf. Oh, fie, Sir Peter ! would you have me join 10 in so mean a trick ? — to trepan my brother too ?

Sir Pet. Nay, you tell me you are sure he is innocent ; if so, you do him the greatest service by giving him an opportunity to clear himself, and you will set my heart at rest. Come, you shall not refuse me : (*Going up.*) here, 15 behind the screen will be — Hey ! what the devil ! there seems to be one listener here already — I'll swear I saw a petticoat !

Jos. Surf. Ha ! ha ! ha ! Well, this is ridiculous enough. I'll tell you, Sir Peter, though I hold a man of 20 intrigue to be a most despicable character, yet, you know, it does not follow that one is to be an absolute Joseph either ! Hark'ee, 'tis a little French milliner, a silly rogue that plagues me ; and having some character to lose, on your coming, sir, she ran behind the screen.

25 *Sir Pet.* Ah, Joseph ! Joseph ! Did I ever think that you — But, egad, she has overheard all I have been say- ing of my wife.

Jos. Surf. Oh, 'twill never go any farther, you may depend upon it !

30 *Sir Pet.* No ! then, faith, let her hear it out. — Here's a closet will do as well.

Jos. Surf.   Well, go in there.

Sir Pet.   Sly rogue! sly rogue!   [*Goes into the closet.*

Jos. Surf.   A narrow escape, indeed! and a curious situation I'm in, to part man and wife in this manner.

Lady Teaz.   (*Peeping.*)   Couldn't I steal off?   5

Jos. Surf.   Keep close, my angel!

Sir Pet.   (*Peeping.*)   Joseph, tax him home.

Jos. Surf.   Back, my dear friend!

Lady Teaz.   (*Peeping.*)   Couldn't you lock Sir Peter in?

Jos. Surf.   Be still, my life!   10

Sir Pet.   (*Peeping.*)   You're sure the little milliner won't blab?

Jos. Surf.   In, in, my dear Sir Peter! — 'Fore Gad, I wish I had a key to the door.

Enter CHARLES SURFACE.

Chas. Surf.   Holla! brother, what has been the matter?   15 Your fellow would not let me up at first.   What! have you had a Jew with you?

Jos. Surf.   No, brother, I assure you.

Chas. Surf.   But what has made Sir Peter steal off? I though he had been with you.   20

Jos. Surf.   He was, brother; but, hearing you were coming, he did not choose to stay.

Chas. Surf.   What! was the old gentleman afraid I wanted to borrow money of him?

Jos. Surf.   No, sir: but I am sorry to find, Charles,   25 you have lately given that worthy man grounds for great uneasiness.

Chas. Surf.   Yes, they tell me I do that to a great many worthy men.   But how so, pray?

Jos. Surf. To be plain with you, brother, he thinks you are endeavouring to gain Lady Teazle's affections from him.

Chas. Surf. Who, I? O Lud! not I, upon my word. — Ha! ha! ha! so the old fellow has found out that he
5 has got a young wife, has he? — or, what is worse, Lady Teazle has found out she has an old husband?

Jos. Surf. This is no subject to jest on, brother. He who can laugh —

Chas. Surf. True, true, as you were going to say —
10 then, seriously, I never had the least idea of what you charge me with, upon my honour.

Jos. Surf. Well, it will give Sir Peter great satisfaction to hear this.   [*Raising his voice.*

Chas. Surf. To be sure, I once thought the lady seemed
15 to have taken a fancy to me; but, upon my soul, I never gave her the least encouragement. Besides, you know my attachment to Maria.

Jos. Surf. But sure, brother, even if Lady Teazle had betrayed the fondest partiality for you —

20 *Chas. Surf.* Why, look'ee, Joseph, I hope I shall never deliberately do a dishonourable action; but if a pretty woman was purposely to throw herself in my way — and that pretty woman married to a man old enough to be her father —

25 *Jos. Surf.* Well!

Chas. Surf. Why, I believe I should be obliged to —

Jos. Surf. What?

Chas. Surf. To borrow a little of your morality, that's all. But, brother, do you know now that you surprise me
30 exceedingly, by naming me with Lady Teazle; for, i' faith, I always understood you were her favourite.

308

Jos. Surf. Oh, for shame, Charles! This retort is foolish.

Chas. Surf. Nay, I swear I have seen you exchange such significant glances —

Jos. Surf. Nay, nay, sir, this is no jest.　　　　5

Chas. Surf. Egad, I'm serious! Don't you remember one day, when I called here —

Jos. Surf. Nay, pr'ythee, Charles —

Chas. Surf. And found you together —

Jos. Surf. Zounds, sir, I insist —　　　　10

Chas. Surf. And another time when your servant —

Jos. Surf. Brother, brother, a word with you! — (*Aside.*) Gad, I must stop him.

Chas Surf. Informed, I say, that —

Jos. Surf. Hush! I beg your pardon, but Sir Peter has 15 overheard all we have been saying. I knew you would clear yourself, or I should not have consented.

Chas. Surf. How, Sir Peter! Where is he?

Jos. Surf. Softly, there!　　　　[*Points to the closet.*

Chas. Surf. Oh, 'fore Heaven, I'll have him out. Sir 20 Peter, come forth!

Jos. Surf. No, no —

Chas. Surf. I say, Sir Peter, come into court. — (*Pulls in* Sir Peter.) What! my old guardian! — What! turn inquisitor, and take evidence incog.? Oh, fie! Oh, 25 fie!

Sir Pet. Give me your hand, Charles — I believe I have suspected you wrongfully; but you mustn't be **angry** with Joseph — 'twas my plan!

Chas. Surf. Indeed!　　　　30

Sir Pet. But I acquit you. I promise you I don't

think near so ill of you as I did: what I have heard has given me great satisfaction.

Chas. Surf. Egad, then, 'twas lucky you didn't hear any more. Wasn't it, Joseph?

5   *Sir Pet.* Ah! you would have retorted on him.

Chas. Surf. Ah, ay, that was a joke.

Sir Pet. Yes, yes, I know his honour too well.

Chas. Surf. But you might as well have suspected him as me in this matter, for all that. Mightn't he, Joseph?

10   *Sir Pet.* Well, well, I believe you.

Jos. Surf. Would they were both out of the room!

                                          [*Aside.*

Sir. Pet. And in future, perhaps, we may not be such strangers.

     Reënter SERVANT, *and whispers* JOSEPH SURFACE.

Ser. Lady Sneerwell is below, and says she will come 15 up.

Jos. Surf. Lady Sneerwell! Gad's life! she must not come here. (*Exit* SERVANT.) Gentlemen, I beg pardon — I must wait on you down stairs: here is a person come on particular business.

20   *Chas. Surf.* Well, you can see him in another room. Sir Peter and I have not met a long time, and I have something to say to him.

Jos. Surf. (*Aside.*) They must not be left together. — (*Aloud.*) I'll send Lady Sneerwell away, and return di-25 rectly. — (*Aside to* SIR PETER.) Sir Peter, not a word of the French milliner.

Sir Pet. (*Aside to* JOSEPH SURFACE.) I! not for the world! (*Exit* JOSEPH SURFACE.) Ah, Charles, if you associated more with your brother, one might indeed hope for your reformation. He is a man of sentiment. Well, there is nothing in the world so noble as a man of sentiment.

Chas. Surf. Pshaw! he is too moral by half; and so 5 apprehensive of his good name, as he calls it.

Sir Pet. No, no, — come, come, — you wrong him. No, no! Joseph is no rake, but he is no such saint either, in that respect. — (*Aside.*) I have a great mind to tell him — we should have such a laugh at Joseph. 10

Chas. Surf. Oh, hang him! he's a very anchorite, a young hermit!

Sir Pet. Hark'ee — you must not abuse him: he may chance to hear of it again, I promise you.

Chas. Surf. Why, you won't tell him? 15

Sir Pet. No — but — this way. — (*Aside.*) Egad, I'll tell him. — (*Aloud.*) Hark'ee — have you a mind to have a good laugh at Joseph?

Chas. Surf. I should like it of all things.

Sir Pet. Then, i' faith, we will! I'll be quit with him 20 for discovering me. He had a girl with him when I called. [*Whispers.*

Chas. Surf. What! Joseph? you jest.

Sir Pet. Hush! — a little French milliner — and the best of the jest is — she's in the room now. 25

Chas. Surf. The devil she is!

Sir Pet. Hush! I tell you. [*Points to the screen.*

Chas. Surf. Behind the screen! 'Slife, let's unveil her!

Sir Pet. No, no, he's coming: — you sha'n't, indeed!

Chas. Surf. Oh, egad, we'll have a peep at the little 30 milliner!

311

Sir Pet. Not for the world! — Joseph will never forgive me.

Chas. Surf. I'll stand by you —

Sir Pet. Odds, here he is!

[CHARLES SURFACE *throws down the screen.*

Reënter JOSEPH SURFACE.

5 —*Chas. Surf.* Lady Teazle, by all that's wonderful.

Sir Pet. Lady Teazle, by all that's damnable!

Chas. Surf. Sir Peter, this is one of the smartest French milliners I ever saw. Egad, you seem all to have been diverting yourselves here at hide and seek, and I don't see 10 who is out of the secret. Shall I beg your ladyship to inform me? Not a word! — Brother, will you be pleased to explain this matter? What! is Morality dumb too? — Sir Peter, though I found you in the dark, perhaps you are not so now! All mute! — Well — though I can make 15 nothing of the affair, I suppose you perfectly understand one another; so I'll leave you to yourselves. — (*Going.*) Brother, I'm so sorry to find you have given that worthy man grounds for so much uneasiness. — Sir Peter! there's nothing in the world so noble as a man of sentiment!

[*Exit.*

20 *Jos. Surf.* Sir Peter — notwithstanding — I confess — that appearances are against me — if you will afford me your patience — I make no doubt — but I shall explain every thing to your satisfaction.

Sir Pet. If you please, sir.

25 *Jos. Surf.* The fact is, sir, that Lady Teazle, knowing my pretensions to your ward Maria — I say, sir, Lady Teazle, being apprehensive of the jealousy of your temper

— and knowing my friendship to the family — she, sir, I say — called here — in order that — I might explain these pretensions — but on your coming — being apprehensive — as I said — of your jealousy — she withdrew — and this, you may depend on it, is the whole truth of the matter.

Sir Pet.   A very clear account, upon my word; and I dare swear the lady will vouch for every article of it.

Lady Teaz.   For not one word of it, Sir Peter!

Sir Pet.   How! don't you think it worth while to agree in the lie?

Lady Teaz.   There is not one syllable of truth in what that gentleman has told you.

Sir Pet.   I believe you, upon my soul, ma'am!

Jos. Surf.   (*Aside to* LADY TEAZLE.)   'Sdeath, madam, will you betray me?

Lady Teaz.   Good Mr. Hypocrite, by your leave, I'll speak for myself.

Sir Pet.   Ay, let her alone, sir; you'll find she'll make out a better story than you, without prompting.

Lady Teaz.   Hear me, Sir Peter! — I came here on no matter relating to your ward, and even ignorant of this gentleman's pretensions to her.   But I came, seduced by his insidious arguments, at least to listen to his pretended passion, if not to sacrifice your honour to his baseness.

Sir Pet.   Now, I believe, the truth is coming, indeed!

Jos. Surf.   The woman's mad!

Lady Teaz.   No, sir; she has recovered her senses, and your own arts have furnished her with the means. — Sir Peter, I do not expect you to credit me — but the tenderness you expressed for me, when I am sure you could not

think I was a witness to it, has so penetrated to my heart,
that had I left the place without the shame of this discovery, my future life should have spoken the sincerity of
my gratitude. As for that smooth-tongued hypocrite, who
would have seduced the wife of his too credulous friend,
while he affected honourable addresses to his ward — I
behold him now in a light so truly despicable, that I shall
never again respect myself for having listened to him.

[Exit.

Jos. Surf. Notwithstanding all this, Sir Peter, Heaven
knows —

Sir Pet. That you are a villain! and so I leave you to
your conscience.

Jos. Surf. You are too rash, Sir Peter; you shall hear
me. The man who shuts out conviction by refusing
to —

Sir Pet. Oh, damn your sentiments!

    [*Exeunt* Sir Peter *and* Joseph Surface, *talking.*

ACT V.

SCENE I. THE LIBRARY IN JOSEPH SURFACE'S HOUSE.

Enter JOSEPH SURFACE *and* SERVANT.

Jos. Surf. Mr. Stanley! and why should you think I would see him? you must know he comes to ask something.

Ser. Sir, I should not have let him in, but that Mr. Rowley came to the door with him.

Jos. Surf. Pshaw! blockhead! to suppose that I should now be in a temper to receive visits from poor relations! — Well, why don't you show the fellow up?

Ser. I will, sir. — Why, sir, it was not my fault that Sir Peter discovered my lady —

Jos. Surf. Go, fool! — (*Exit* SERVANT.) Sure Fortune never played a man of my policy such a trick before! My character with Sir Peter, my hopes with Maria, destroyed in a moment! I'm in a rare humour to listen to other people's distresses! I shan't be able to bestow even a benevolent sentiment on Stanley. — So! here he comes, and Rowley with him. I must try to recover myself, and put a little charity into my face, however.   [*Exit.*

Enter SIR OLIVER SURFACE *and* ROWLEY.

Sir Oliv. What! does he avoid us? That was he, was it not?

315

Row. It was, sir. But I doubt you are come a little too abruptly. His nerves are so weak, that the sight of a poor relation may be too much for him. I should have gone first to break it to him.

5　*Sir Oliv.* Oh, plague of his nerves! Yet this is he whom Sir Peter extols as a man of the most benevolent way of thinking.

Row. As to his way of thinking, I cannot pretend to decide; for, to do him justice, he appears to have as much 10 speculative benevolence as any private gentleman in the kingdom, though he is seldom so sensual as to indulge himself in the exercise of it.

Sir Oliv. Yet he has a string of charitable sentiments at his fingers' ends.

15　*Row.* Or, rather, at his tongue's end, Sir Oliver; for I believe there is no sentiment he has such faith in as that *Charity begins at home.*

Sir Oliv. And his, I presume, is of that domestic sort which never stirs abroad at all.

20　*Row.* I doubt you'll find it so; but he's coming. I mustn't seem to interrupt you; and you know, immediately as you leave him, I come in to announce your arrival in your real character.

Sir Oliv. True; and afterwards you'll meet me at Sir 25 Peter's.

Row. Without losing a moment.　　　　　[*Exit.*

Sir Oliv. I don't like the complaisance of his features.

Reënter JOSEPH SURFACE.

Jos. Surf. Sir, I beg you ten thousand pardons for keeping you a moment waiting. — Mr. Stanley, I presume.

Sir Oliv. At your service.

Jos. Surf. Sir, I beg you will do me the honour to sit down — I entreat you, sir.

Sir Oliv. Dear sir — there's no occasion. — (*Aside.*) Too civil by half! 5

Jos. Surf. I have not the pleasure of knowing you, Mr. Stanley; but I am extremely happy to see you look so well. You were nearly related to my mother, I think, Mr. Stanley?

Sir Oliv. I was, sir; so nearly that my present property, 10 I fear, may do discredit to her wealthy children, else I should not have presumed to trouble you.

Jos. Surf. Dear sir, there needs no apology; — he that is in distress, though a stranger, has a right to claim kindred with the wealthy. I am sure I wish I was one of 15 that class, and had it in my power to offer you even a small relief.

Sir Oliv. If your uncle, Sir Oliver, were here, I should have a friend.

Jos. Surf. I wish he was, sir, with all my heart: you 20 should not want an advocate with him, believe me, sir.

Sir Oliv. I should not need one — my distresses would recommend me. But I imagined his bounty would enable you to become the agent of his charity.

Jos. Surf. My dear sir, you were strangely misin- 25 formed. Sir Oliver is a worthy man, a very worthy man; but avarice, Mr. Stanley, is the vice of age. I will tell you, my good sir, in confidence, what he has done for me has been a mere nothing; though people, I know, have thought otherwise, and for my part, I never chose to contradict the 30 report.

Sir Oliv.   What! has he never transmitted you bullion — rupees — pagodas?

Jos. Surf.   Oh, dear sir, nothing of the kind.   No, no; a few presents now and then — china, shawls, congo tea, 5 avadavats and Indian crackers — little more, believe me.

Sir Oliv.   Here's gratitude for twelve thousand pounds! — Avadavats and Indian crackers!   [*Aside.*

Jos. Surf.   Then, my dear sir, you have heard, I doubt not, of the extravagance of my brother: there are very 10 few would credit what I have done for that unfortunate young man.

Sir Oliv.   Not I, for one!   [*Aside.*

Jos. Surf.   The sums I have lent him!   Indeed I have been exceedingly to blame; it was an amiable weakness; 15 however, I don't pretend to defend it — and now I feel it doubly culpable, since it has deprived me of the pleasure of serving you, Mr. Stanley, as my heart dictates.

Sir Oliv.   (*Aside.*)   Dissembler!   (*Aloud.*)   Then, sir, you can't assist me?

20 *Jos. Surf.*   At present, it grieves me to say, I cannot; but, whenever I have the ability, you may depend upon hearing from me.

Sir Oliv.   I am extremely sorry —

Jos. Surf.   Not more than I, believe me; to pity, with-25out the power to relieve, is still more painful than to ask and be denied.

Sir Oliv.   Kind sir, your most obedient humble servant.

Jos. Surf.   You leave me deeply affected, Mr. Stanley. 30 — William, be ready to open the door.   [*Calls to* SERVANT.

Sir Oliv.   Oh, dear sir, no ceremony.

Jos. Surf. Your very obedient.

Sir Oliv. Your most obsequious.

Jos. Surf. You may depend upon hearing from me, whenever I can be of service.

Sir Oliv. Sweet sir, you are too good! 5

Jos. Surf. In the meantime I wish you health and spirits.

Sir Oliv. Your ever grateful and perpetual humble servant.

Jos. Surf. Sir, yours as sincerely. 10

Sir Oliv. (*Aside.*) Now I am satisfied. [*Exit.*

Jos. Surf. This is one bad effect of a good character; it invites application from the unfortunate, and there needs no small degree of address to gain the reputation of benevolence without incurring the expense. The silver 15 ore of pure charity is an expensive article in the catalogue of a man's good qualities; whereas the sentimental French plate I use instead of it makes just as good a show, and pays no tax.

Reënter ROWLEY.

Row. Mr. Surface, your servant: I was apprehensive 20 of interrupting you, though my business demands immediate attention, as this note will inform you.

Jos. Surf. Always happy to see Mr. Rowley, — a rascal. — (*Aside. Reads the letter.*) Sir Oliver Surface! — My uncle arrived! 25

Row. He is, indeed: we have just parted — quite well, after a speedy voyage, and impatient to embrace his worthy nephew.

Jos. Surf. I am astonished! — William! stop Mr. Stanley, if he's not gone. [*Calls to* SERVANT. 30

Row. Oh! he's out of reach, I believe.

Jos. Surf. Why did you not let me know this when you came in together?

Row. I thought you had particular business. But I must be gone to inform your brother, and appoint him here to meet your uncle. He will be with you in a quarter of an hour.

Jos. Surf. So he says. Well, I am strangely overjoyed at his coming. (*Aside.*) Never, to be sure, was any thing so unlucky!

Row. You will be delighted to see how well he looks.

Jos. Surf. Oh! I'm overjoyed to hear it. (*Aside.*) Just at this time!

Row. I'll tell him how impatiently you expect him.

Jos. Surf. Do, do; pray give my best duty and affection. Indeed, I cannot express the sensations I feel at the thought of seeing him. (*Exit* ROWLEY.) Certainly his coming just at this time is the cruellest piece of ill fortune.

[*Exit.*

SCENE II. A ROOM IN SIR PETER TEAZLE'S HOUSE.

Enter MRS. CANDOUR *and* MAID.

Maid. Indeed, ma'am, my lady will see nobody at present.

Mrs. Can. Did you tell her it was her friend Mrs. Candour?

Maid. Yes, ma'am; but she begs you will excuse her.

Mrs. Can. Do go again; I shall be glad to see her, if it be only for a moment, for I am sure she must be in great distress. (*Exit* MAID.) Dear heart, how provoking!

I'm not mistress of half the circumstances! We shall have the whole affair in the newspapers, with the names of the parties at length, before I have dropped the story at a dozen houses.

Enter SIR BENJAMIN BACKBITE.

Oh, dear Sir Benjamin! you have heard, I suppose — 5

Sir Ben. Of Lady Teazle and Mr. Surface —

Mrs. Can. And Sir Peter's discovery —

Sir Ben. Oh, the strangest piece of business, to be sure!

Mrs. Can. Well, I never was so surprised in my life. I am so sorry for all parties, indeed. 10

Sir Ben. Now, I don't pity Sir Peter at all: he was so extravagantly partial to Mr. Surface.

Mrs. Can. Mr. Surface! Why, 'twas with Charles Lady Teazle was detected.

Sir Ben. No, no, I tell you: Mr. Surface is the gallant. 15

Mrs. Can. No such thing! Charles is the man. 'Twas Mr. Surface brought Sir Peter on purpose to discover them.

Sir Ben. I tell you I had it from one —

Mrs. Can. And I have it from one —

Sir Ben. Who had it from one, who had it — 20

Mrs. Can. From one immediately. But here comes Lady Sneerwell; perhaps she knows the whole affair.

Enter LADY SNEERWELL.

Lady Sneer. So, my dear Mrs. Candour, here's a sad affair of our friend Lady Teazle!

Mrs. Can. Ay, my dear friend, who would have thought — 25

Lady Sneer. Well, there is no trusting appearances; though, indeed, she was always too lively for me.

Mrs. Can. To be sure, her manners were a little too free; but then she was so young!

5 *Lady Sneer.* And had, indeed, some good qualities.

Mrs. Can. So she had, indeed. But have you heard the particulars?

Lady Sneer. No; but everybody says that Mr. Surface —

10 *Sir Ben.* Ay, there; I told you Mr. Surface was the man.

Mrs. Can. No, no: indeed it was Charles.

Lady Sneer. Charles! You alarm me, Mrs. Candour!

Mrs. Can. Yes, yes; he was the lover. Mr. Surface, 15 to do him justice, was only the informer.

Sir Ben. Well, I'll not dispute with you, Mrs. Candour; but, be it which it may, I hope that Sir Peter's wound will not —

Mrs. Can. Sir Peter's wound! Oh, mercy! I didn't 20 hear a word of their fighting.

Lady Sneer. Nor I, a syllable.

Sir Ben. No! what, no mention of the duel?

Mrs. Can. Not a word.

Sir Ben. Oh, yes: they fought before they left the 25 room.

Lady Sneer. Pray, let us hear.

Mrs. Can. Ay, do oblige us with the duel.

Sir Ben. Sir, says Sir Peter, immediately after the discovery, *you are a most ungrateful fellow.*

30 *Mrs. Can.* Ay, to Charles —

Sir Ben. No, no — to Mr. Surface — *a most ungrateful*

322

fellow; and as old as I am, sir, says he, *I insist on immediate satisfaction.*

Mrs. Can.   Ay, that must have been to Charles; for 'tis very unlikely Mr. Surface should fight in his own house.   5

Sir Ben.   Gad's life, ma'am, not at all — *giving me immediate satisfaction.* — On this, ma'am, Lady Teazle, seeing Sir Peter in such danger, ran out of the room in strong hysterics, and Charles after her, calling out for hartshorn and water; then, madam, they began to fight with   10 swords —

Enter CRABTREE.

Crab.   With pistols, nephew, pistols!   I have it from undoubted authority.

Mrs. Can.   Oh, Mr. Crabtree, then it is all true!

Crab.   Too true, indeed, madam, and Sir Peter is dan-   15 gerously wounded —

Sir Ben.   By a thrust in segoon quite through his left side.

Crab.   By a bullet lodged in the thorax.

Mrs. Can.   Mercy on me!   Poor Sir Peter!   20

Crab.   Yes, madam; though Charles would have avoided the matter, if he could.

Mrs. Can.   I told you who it was; I knew Charles was the person.

Sir Ben.   My uncle, I see, knows nothing of the matter.   25

Crab.   But Sir Peter taxed him with the basest ingratitude —

Sir Ben.   That I told you, you know —

Crab.   Do, nephew, let me speak! — and insisted on immediate —   30

323

Sir Ben. Just as I said —

Crab. Odds life, nephew, allow others to know something too! A pair of pistols lay on the bureau (for Mr. Surface, it seems, had come home the night before late from Salthill, where he had been to see the Montem with a friend, who has a son at Eton), so, unluckily, the pistols were left charged.

Sir Ben. I heard nothing of this.

Crab. Sir Peter forced Charles to take one, and they fired, it seems, pretty nearly together. Charles's shot took effect, as I tell you, and Sir Peter's missed; but, what is very extraordinary, the ball struck against a little bronze Shakespeare that stood over the fire-place, grazed out of the window at a right angle, and wounded the postman, who was just coming to the door with a double letter from Northamptonshire.

Sir Ben. My uncle's account is more circumstantial, I confess; but I believe mine is the true one, for all that.

Lady Sneer. (*Aside.*) I am more interested in this affair than they imagine, and must have better information. [*Exit.*

Sir Ben. Ah! Lady Sneerwell's alarm is very easily accounted for.

Crab. Yes, yes, they certainly do say — but that's neither here nor there.

Mrs. Can. But, pray, where is Sir Peter at present?

Crab. Oh! they brought him home, and he is now in the house, though the servants are ordered to deny him.

Mrs. Can. I believe so, and Lady Teazle, I suppose, attending him.

Crab. Yes, yes; and I saw one of the faculty enter just before me.

Sir Ben. Hey! who comes here?

Crab. Oh, this is he: the physician, depend on't.

Mrs. Can. Oh, certainly! it must be the physician; 5 and now we shall know.

Enter SIR OLIVER SURFACE.

Crab. Well, doctor, what hopes?

Mrs. Can. Ay, doctor, how's your patient?

Sir Ben. Now, doctor, isn't it a wound with a small-sword? 10

Crab. A bullet lodged in the thorax, for a hundred!

Sir Oliv. Doctor! a wound with a small-sword! and a bullet in the thorax! — Oons! are you mad, good people?

Sir Ben. Perhaps, sir, you are not a doctor? 15

Sir Oliv. Truly, I am to thank you for my degree, if I am.

Crab. Only a friend of Sir Peter's, then, I presume. But, sir, you must have heard of his accident?

Sir Oliv. Not a word! 20

Crab. Not of his being dangerously wounded?

Sir Oliv. The devil he is!

Sir Ben. Run through the body —

Crab. Shot in the breast —

Sir Ben. By one Mr. Surface —

Crab. Ay, the younger.

Sir Oliv. Hey! what the plague! you seem to differ strangely in your accounts: however, you agree that Sir Peter is dangerously wounded.

Sir Ben.   Oh, yes, we agree in that.

Crab.   Yes, yes, I believe there can be no doubt of that.

Sir Oliv.   Then, upon my word, for a person in that situation, he is the most imprudent man alive; for here he ₅ comes, walking as if nothing at all was the matter.

Enter Sir Peter Teazle.

Odds heart, Sir Peter! you are come in good time, I promise you; for we had just given you over!

Sir Ben.   (*Aside to* Crabtree.)   Egad, uncle, this is the most sudden recovery!

₁₂ *Sir Oliv.*   Why, man! what do you out of bed with a small-sword through your body, and a bullet lodged in your thorax?

Sir Pet.   A small-sword and a bullet!

Sir Oliv.   Ay; these gentlemen would have killed you ₁₅ without law or physic, and wanted to dub me a doctor, to make me an accomplice.

Sir Pet.   Why, what is all this?

Sir Ben.   We rejoice, Sir Peter, that the story of the duel is not true, and are sincerely sorry for your other mis-₂₀ fortune.

Sir Pet.   So, so; all over the town already!

[*Aside.*

Crab.   Though, Sir Peter, you were certainly vastly to blame to marry at your years.

Sir Pet.   Sir, what business is that of yours?

Mrs. Can.   Though, indeed, as Sir Peter made so good husband, he's very much to be pitied.

Sir Pet.   Plague on your pity, ma'am! I desire none it.

Sir Ben. However, Sir Peter, you must not mind the laughing and jests you will meet with on the occasion.

Sir Pet. Sir, sir! I desire to be master in my own house.

Crab. 'Tis no uncommon case, that's one comfort.   5

Sir Pet. I insist on being left to myself : without ceremony, I insist on your leaving my house directly!

Mrs. Can. Well, well, we are going; and depend on't, we'll make the best report of it we can.   [*Exit.*

Sir Pet. Leave my house!   10

Crab. And tell how hardly you've been treated. [*Exit.*

Sir Pet. Leave my house!

Sir Ben. And how patiently you bear it.   [*Exit.*

Sir Pet. Fiends! vipers! furies! Oh! that their own venom would choke them!   15

Sir Oliv. They are very provoking indeed, Sir Peter.

Enter ROWLEY.

Row. I heard high words: what has ruffled you, sir?

Sir Pet. Pshaw! what signifies asking? Do I ever pass a day without my vexations?

Row. Well, I'm not inquisitive.   20

Sir Oliv. Well, Sir Peter, I have seen both my nephews in the manner we proposed.

Sir Pet. A precious couple they are!

Row. Yes, and Sir Oliver is convinced that your judgment was right, Sir Peter.   25

Sir Oliv. Yes, I find Joseph is indeed the man, after all.

Row. Ay, as Sir Peter says, he is a man of sentiment.

Sir Oliv. And acts up to the sentiments he professes.

Row. It certainly is edification to hear him talk.

Sir Oliv. Oh, he's a model for the young men of the age! — but how's this, Sir Peter? you don't join us in your friend Joseph's praise, as I expected.

Sir Pet. Sir Oliver, we live in a wicked world, and the fewer we praise the better.

Row. What! do you say so, Sir Peter, who were never mistaken in your life?

Sir Pet. Pshaw! plague on you both! I see by your sneering you have heard the whole affair. I shall go mad among you!

Row. Then, to fret you no longer, Sir Peter, we are indeed acquainted with it all. I met Lady Teazle coming from Mr. Surface's so humbled, that she deigned to request me to be her advocate with you.

Sir Pet. And does Sir Oliver know all this?

Sir Oliv. Every circumstance.

Sir Pet. What, of the closet and the screen, hey?

Sir Oliv. Yes, yes, and the little French milliner. Oh, I have been vastly diverted with the story! ha! ha! ha!

Sir Pet. 'Twas very pleasant.

Sir Oliv. I never laughed more in my life, I assure you: ha! ha! ha!

Sir Pet. Oh, vastly diverting! ha! ha! ha!

Row. To be sure, Joseph with his sentiments! ha! ha! ha!

Sir Pet. Yes, yes, his sentiments! ha! ha! ha! Hypocritical villain!

Sir Oliv. Ay, and that rogue Charles to pull Sir Peter out of the closet: ha! ha! ha!

Sir Pet. Ha! ha! ha! 'twas devilish entertaining, to be sure!

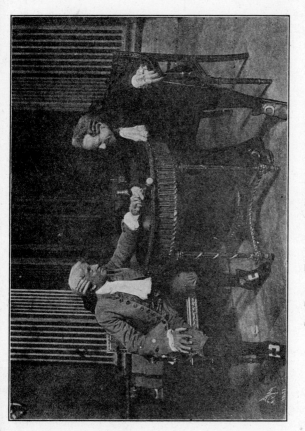

SIR PETER TEAZLE AND SIR OLIVER SURFACE

"Sir Oliver, we live in a wicked world, and the fewer we praise the better."

Sir Oliv. Ha! ha! Egad, Sir Peter, I should like to have seen your face when the screen was thrown down: ha! ha!

Sir Pet. Yes, yes, my face when the screen was thrown down: ha! ha! ha! Oh, I must never show my head 5 again!

Sir Oliv. But come, come, it isn't fair to laugh at you neither, my old friend; though, upon my soul, I can't help it.

Sir Pet. Oh, pray don't restrain your mirth on my 10 account: it does not hurt me at all! I laugh at the whole affair myself. Yes, yes, I think being a standing jest for all one's acquaintance a very happy situation. Oh, yes, and then of a morning to read the paragraphs about Mr. S—, Lady T—, and Sir P—, will be so entertaining! 15

Row. Without affectation, Sir Peter, you may despise the ridicule of fools. But I see Lady Teazle going towards the next room; I am sure you must desire a reconciliation as earnestly as she does.

Sir Oliv. Perhaps my being here prevents her coming 20 to you. Well, I'll leave honest Rowley to mediate between you; but he must bring you all presently to Mr. Surface's, where I am now returning, if not to reclaim a libertine, at least to expose hypocrisy.

Sir Pet. Ah, I'll be present at your discovering your- 25 self there with all my heart; though 'tis a vile unlucky place for discoveries.

Row. We'll follow. [*Exit* Sir Oliver Surface.

Sir Pet. She is not coming here, you see, Rowley.

Row. No, but she has left the door of that room open, 30 you perceive. See, she is in tears.

Sir Pet. Certainly a little mortification appears very becoming in a wife. Don't you think it will do her good to let her pine a little?

Row. Oh, this is ungenerous in you!

5 *Sir Pet.* Well, I know not what to think. You remember the letter I found of hers evidently intended for Charles?

Row. A mere forgery, Sir Peter! laid in your way on purpose. This is one of the points which I intended 10 Snake shall give you conviction of.

Sir Pet. I wish I were once satisfied of that. She looks this way. What a remarkably elegant turn of the head she has! Rowley, I'll go to her.

Row. Certainly.

15 *Sir Pet.* Though, when it is known that we are reconciled, people will laugh at me ten times more.

Row. Let them laugh, and retort their malice only by showing them you are happy in spite of it.

Sir Pet. I' faith, so I will! and, if I'm not mistaken, 20 we may yet be the happiest couple in the country.

Row. Nay, Sir Peter, he who once lays aside suspicion —

Sir Pet. Hold, Master Rowley! if you have any regard for me, never let me hear you utter any thing like a 25 sentiment: I have had enough of them to serve me the rest of my life. [*Exeunt.*

SCENE III. THE LIBRARY IN JOSEPH SURFACE'S HOUSE.

Enter JOSEPH SURFACE *and* LADY SNEERWELL.

Lady Sneer. Impossible! Will not Sir Peter immediately be reconciled to Charles, and of course no longer oppose his union with Maria? The thought is distraction to me.

Jos. Surf. Can passion furnish a remedy? 5

Lady Sneer. No, nor cunning either. Oh, I was a fool, an idiot, to league with such a blunderer!

Jos. Surf. Sure, Lady Sneerwell, I am the greatest sufferer; yet you see I bear the accident with calmness.

Lady Sneer. Because the disappointment doesn't 10 reach your heart; your interest only attached you to Maria. Had you felt for her what I have for that ungrateful libertine, neither your temper nor hypocrisy could prevent your showing the sharpness of your vexation. 15

Jos. Surf. But why should your reproaches fall on me for this disappointment?

Lady Sneer. Are you not the cause of it? Had you not a sufficient field for your roguery in imposing upon Sir Peter, and supplanting your brother, but you must en- 20 deavour to seduce his wife? I hate such an avarice of crimes; 'tis an unfair monopoly, and never prospers.

Jos. Surf. Well, I admit I have been to blame. I confess I deviated from the direct road of wrong, but I don't think we're so totally defeated neither. 25

Lady Sneer. No!

Jos. Surf. You tell me you have made a trial of Snake

since we met, and that you still believe him faithful to
us?

Lady Sneer. I do believe so.

Jos. Surf. And that he has undertaken, should it be
5 necessary, to swear and prove, that Charles is at this time
contracted by vows and honour to your ladyship, which
some of his former letters to you will serve to support.

Lady Sneer. This, indeed, might have assisted.

Jos. Surf. Come, come; it is not too late yet. —
10 (*Knocking at the door.*) But hark! this is probably my
uncle, Sir Oliver: retire to that room; we'll consult
farther when he is gone.

Lady Sneer. Well, but if he should find you out too?

Jos. Surf. Oh, I have no fear of that. Sir Peter will
15 hold his tongue for his own credit's sake — and you may
depend on it I shall soon discover Sir Oliver's weak side!

Lady Sneer. I have no diffidence of your abilities:
only be constant to one roguery at a time.

Jos. Surf. I will, I will! — (*Exit* LADY SNEERWELL.)
20 So! 'tis confounded hard, after such bad fortune, to be
baited by one's confederate in evil. Well, at all events,
my character is so much better than Charles's, that I certainly — hey! — what — this is not Sir Oliver, but old
Stanley again. Plague on't that he should return to tease
25 me just now! I shall have Sir Oliver come and find him
here — and —

Enter SIR OLIVER SURFACE.

Gad's life, Mr. Stanley, why have you come back to plague
me at this time? You must not stay now, upon my word.

Sir Oliv. Sir, I hear your uncle Oliver is expected here,

332

and though he has been so penurious to you, I'll try what he'll do for me.

Jos. Surf.   Sir, 'tis impossible for you to stay now, so I must beg — Come any other time, and I promise you, you shall be assisted.   5

Sir Oliv.   No : Sir Oliver and I must be acquainted.

Jos. Surf.   Zounds, sir ! then I insist on your quitting the room directly.

Sir Oliv.   Nay, sir —

Jos. Surf.   Sir, I insist on't ! — Here, William ! show 10 this gentleman out.   Since you compel me, sir, not one moment — this is such insolence.

> [*Going to push him out.*

Enter CHARLES SURFACE.

Chas. Surf.   Heyday ! what's the matter now?   What the devil, have you got hold of my little broker here? Zounds, brother, don't hurt little Premium.   What's the 15 matter, my little fellow?

Jos. Surf.   So! he has been with you too, has he?

Chas. Surf.   To be sure, he has.   Why, he's as honest a little — But sure, Joseph, you have not been borrowing money too, have you?   20

Jos. Surf.   Borrowing ! no !   But, brother, you know we expect Sir Oliver here every —

Chas. Surf.   O Gad, that's true !   Noll mustn't find the little broker here, to be sure.

Jos. Surf.   Yet Mr. Stanley insists —   25

Chas. Surf.   Stanley ! why his name's Premium.

Jos. Surf.   No, sir, Stanley.

Chas. Surf.   No, no, Premium.

Jos. Surf.   Well, no matter which — but —

Chas. Surf.   Ay, ay, Stanley or Premium, 'tis the same thing, as you say; for I suppose he goes by half a hundred names, besides A. B. at the coffee-house.   [*Knocking.*

5 *Jos. Surf.*   'Sdeath! here's Sir Oliver at the door. — Now I beg, Mr. Stanley —

Chas. Surf.   Ay, ay, and I beg, Mr. Premium —

Sir Oliv.   Gentlemen —

Jos Surf.   Sir, by Heaven you shall go.

10 *Chas. Surf.*   Ay, out with him, certainly!

Sir Oliv.   This violence —

Jos. Surf.   Sir, 'tis your own fault.

Chas. Surf.   Out with him, to be sure.

[*Both forcing* Sir Oliver *out.*

Enter Sir Peter *and* Lady Teazle, Maria, *and* Rowley.

Sir Pet.   My old friend, Sir Oliver — hey! What in 15 the name of wonder — here are dutiful nephews — assault their uncle at a first visit!

Lady Teaz.   Indeed, Sir Oliver, 'twas well we came in to rescue you.

Row.   Truly it was; for I perceive, Sir Oliver, the 20 character of old Stanley was no protection to you.

Sir Oliv.   Nor of Premium either: the necessities of the former could not extort a shilling from that benevolent gentleman; and with the other I stood a chance of faring worse than my ancestors, and being knocked down 25 without being bid for.

Jos. Surf.   Charles!

Chas. Surf.   Joseph!

334

Jos. Surf. 'Tis now complete!

Chas. Surf. Very.

Sir Oliv. Sir Peter, my friend, and Rowley too — look on that elder nephew of mine. You know what he has already received from my bounty; and you also know how gladly I would have regarded half my fortune as held in trust for him: judge then my disappointment in discovering him to be destitute of truth, charity, and gratitude!

Sir Pet. Sir Oliver, I should be more surprised at this declaration, if I had not myself found him to be mean, treacherous, and hypocritical.

Lady Teaz. And if the gentleman pleads not guilty to these, pray let him call me to his character.

Sir Pet. Then, I believe, we need add no more: if he knows himself, he will consider it as the most perfect punishment, that he is known to the world.

Chas. Surf. If they talk this way to Honesty, what will they say to me, by and by? [*Aside.*

[SIR PETER, LADY TEAZLE, *and* MARIA *retire.*

Sir Oliv. As for that prodigal, his brother, there —

Chas. Surf. Ay, now comes my turn: the family pictures will ruin me! [*Aside.*

Jos. Surf. Sir Oliver — uncle, will you honour me with a hearing?

Chas. Surf. Now, if Joseph would make one of his long speeches, I might recollect myself a little. [*Aside.*

Sir Oliv. (*To* JOSEPH SURFACE.) I suppose you would undertake to justify yourself?

Jos. Surf. I trust I could.

Sir Oliv. (*To* CHARLES SURFACE.) Well, sir! — and you could justify yourself too, I suppose?

335

Chas. Surf.   Not that I know of, Sir Oliver.

Sir Oliv.   What! — Little Premium has been let too much into the secret, I suppose?

Chas. Surf.   True, sir; but they were family secrets,
5 and should not be mentioned again, you know.

Row.   Come, Sir Oliver, I know you cannot speak of Charles's follies with anger.

Sir Oliv.   Odds heart, no more I can; nor with gravity either.   Sir Peter, do you know the rogue bargained with
10 me for all his ancestors; sold me judges and generals by the foot, and maiden aunts as cheap as broken china.

Chas. Surf.   To be sure, Sir Oliver, I did make a little free with the family canvas, that's the truth on't.   My ancestors may rise in judgment against me, there's no
15 denying it; but believe me sincere when I tell you — and upon my soul I would not say so if I was not — that if I do not appear mortified at the exposure of my follies, it is because I feel at this moment the warmest satisfaction in seeing you, my liberal benefactor.

20 *Sir Oliv.*   Charles, I believe you.   Give me your hand again : the ill-looking little fellow over the settee has made your peace.

Chas. Surf.   Then, sir, my gratitude to the original is still increased.

25 *Lady Teaz.*   (*Advancing.*)   Yet, I believe, Sir Oliver, here is one whom Charles is still more anxious to be reconciled to.   [*Pointing to* MARIA.

Sir Oliv.   Oh, I have heard of his attachment there; and, with the young lady's pardon, if I construe right —
30 that blush —

Sir Pet.   Well, child, speak your sentiments!

Mar. Sir, I have little to say, but that I shall rejoice to hear that he is happy; for me, whatever claim I had to his attention, I willingly resign to one who has a better title.

Chas. Surf. How, Maria! 5

Sir Pet. Heyday! what's the mystery now? While he appeared an incorrigible rake, you would give your hand to no one else; and now that he is likely to reform I'll warrant you won't have him!

Mar. His own heart and Lady Sneerwell know the 10 cause.

Chas. Surf. Lady Sneerwell!

Jos. Surf. Brother, it is with great concern I am obliged to speak on this point, but my regard to justice compels me, and Lady Sneerwell's injuries can no longer be con- 15 cealed. *[Opens the door.*

Enter LADY SNEERWELL.

Sir Pet. So! another French milliner! Egad, he has one in every room in the house, I suppose!

Lady Sneer. Ungrateful Charles! Well may you be surprised, and feel for the indelicate situation your perfidy 20 has forced me into.

Chas. Surf. Pray, uncle, is this another plot of yours? For, as I have life, I don't understand it.

Jos. Surf. I believe, sir, there is but the evidence of one person more necessary to make it extremely clear. 25

Sir Pet. And that person, I imagine, is Mr. Snake. — Rowley, you were perfectly right to bring him with us, and pray let him appear.

Row. Walk in, Mr. Snake.

Enter SNAKE.

I thought his testimony might be wanted: however, it happens unluckily, that he comes to confront Lady Sneerwell, not to support her.

Lady Sneer. A villain! Treacherous to me at last!
5 Speak, fellow, have you too conspired against me!

Snake. I beg your ladyship ten thousand pardons: you paid me extremely liberally for the lie in question; but I unfortunately have been offered double to speak the truth.

10 *Sir Pet.* Plot and counter-plot, egad!

Lady Sneer. The torments of shame and disappointment on you all!   [*Going.*

Lady Teaz. Hold, Lady Sneerwell — before you go, let me thank you for the trouble you and that gentleman
15 have taken, in writing letters from me to Charles, and answering them yourself; and let me also request you to make my respects to the scandalous college, of which you are president, and inform them that Lady Teazle, licentiate, begs leave to return the diploma they granted her, as
20 she leaves off practice, and kills characters no longer.

Lady Sneer. You too, madam! — provoking — insolent! May your husband live these fifty years! [*Exit.*

Sir Pet. Oons! what a fury!

Lady Teaz. A malicious creature, indeed!

25 *Sir Pet.* What! not for her last wish?

Lady Teaz. Oh, no!

Sir Oliv. Well, sir, and what have you to say now?

Jos. Surf. Sir, I am so confounded, to find that Lady Sneerwell could be guilty of suborning Mr. Snake in this
30 manner, to impose on us all, that I know not what to say:

338

however, lest her revengeful spirit should prompt her to injure my brother, I had certainly better follow her directly. For the man who attempts to — [*Exit.*

Sir Pet. Moral to the last drop!

Sir Oliv. Ay, and marry her, Joseph, if you can. Oil and vinegar! — egad, you'll do very well together.

Row. I believe we have no more occasion for Mr. Snake at present?

Snake. Before I go, I beg pardon once for all, for whatever uneasiness I have been the humble instrument of causing to the parties present.

Sir Pet. Well, well, you have made atonement by a good deed at last.

Snake. But I must request of the company, that it shall never be known.

Sir Pet. Hey! what the plague! are you ashamed of having done a right thing once in your life?

Snake. Ah, sir, consider — I live by the badness of my character; and, if it were once known that I had been betrayed into an honest action, I should lose every friend I have in the world.

Sir Oliv. Well, well — we'll not traduce you by saying any thing in your praise, never fear. [*Exit* SNAKE.

Sir Pet. There's a precious rogue!

Lady Teaz. See, Sir Oliver, there needs no persuasion now to reconcile your nephew and Maria.

Sir Oliv. Ay, ay, that's as it should be, and, egad, we'll have the wedding to-morrow morning.

Chas. Surf. Thank you, dear uncle.

Sir Pet. What, you rogue! don't you ask the girl's consent first?

339

Chas. Surf.   Oh, I have done that a long time — a minute ago — and she has looked yes.

Mar.   For shame, Charles! — I protest, Sir Peter, there has not been a word —

5 *Sir Oliv.*   Well, then, the fewer the better; may your love for each other never know abatement.

Sir Pet.   And may you live as happily together as Lady Teazle and I intend to do!

Chas. Surf.   Rowley, my old friend, I am sure you con-10 gratulate me; and I suspect that I owe you much.

Sir Oliv.   You do, indeed, Charles.

Sir Pet.   Ay, honest Rowley always said you would reform.

Chas. Surf.   Why, as to reforming, Sir Peter, I'll make 15 no promises, and that I take to be a proof that I intend to set about it.   But here shall be my monitor — my gentle guide. — Ah! can I leave the virtuous path those eyes illumine?

Though thou, dear maid, shouldst waive thy beauty's
        sway,
20 Thou still must rule, because I will obey:
An humble fugitive from Folly view,
No sanctuary near but Love and you :   [*To the audience.*
You can, indeed, each anxious fear remove,
For even Scandal dies, if you approve.   [*Exeunt omnes*

340

EPILOGUE.

BY MR. COLMAN.

SPOKEN BY LADY TEAZLE.

I, who was late so volatile and gay,
Like a trade-wind must now blow all one way,
Bend all my cares, my studies, and my vows,
To one dull rusty weathercock — my spouse!
So wills our virtuous bard — the motley Bayes   5
Of crying epilogues and laughing plays!
Old bachelors, who marry smart young wives,
Learn from our play to regulate your lives:
Each bring his dear to town, all faults upon her —
London will prove the very source of honour.   10
Plunged fairly in, like a cold bath it serves,
When principles relax, to brace the nerves:
Such is my case; and yet I must deplore
That the gay dream of dissipation's o'er.
And say, ye fair! was ever lively wife,   15
Born with a genius for the highest life,
Like me untimely blasted in her bloom,
Like me condemn'd to such a dismal doom?
Save money — when I just knew how to waste it!
Leave London — just as I began to taste it!   20
   Must I then watch the early crowing cock,
The melancholy ticking of a clock;

Epilogue.

In a lone rustic hall for ever pounded,
With dogs, cats, rats, and squalling brats surrounded.
With humble curate can I now retire,
(While good Sir Peter boozes with the squire),
5 And at backgammon mortify my soul,
That pants for loo, or flutters at a vole?
Seven's the main! Dear sound that must expire,
Lost at hot cockles round a Christmas fire;
The transient hour of fashion too soon spent,
10 Farewell the tranquil mind, farewell content!
Farewell the plumèd head, the cushioned tête,
That takes the cushion from its proper seat!
That spirit-stirring drum! — card drums I mean,
Spadille — odd trick — pam — basto — king and queen!
15 And you, ye knockers, that, with brazen throat,
The welcome visitors' approach denote;
Farewell all quality of high renown,
Pride, pomp, and circumstance of glorious town!
Farewell! your revels I partake no more,
20 And Lady Teazle's occupation's o'er!
All this I told our bard; he smiled, and said 'twas clear,
I ought to play deep tragedy next year.
Meanwhile he drew wise morals from this play,
And in these solemn periods stalked away: —
25 "Blessed were the fair like you; her faults who stopped
And closed her follies when the curtain dropped!
No more in vice or error to engage,
Or play the fool at large on life's great stage."

APPENDIX

APPENDIX

OLIVER GOLDSMITH

1728-1774

The Personal Touch.   From time to time in the course
of English literature, writers appear for whom we have a
sort of personal affection.   Fate has used them harshly :
their course has been run with a handicap.   Yet they have
smiled at Fate, and have finished their course in spite of
the handicap.   They have left behind them something
bravely attempted, something finely done.   One of such
men was Charles Lamb ; another was Oliver Goldsmith.
Into our estimate of what they were and what they did
the personal element must always enter.

Goldsmith His Own Worst Enemy.   Lamb fell upon
evil days through no fault of his own.   We sympathize
with Goldsmith in his troubles — of which, as he said,
" God has given my share " — yet for these troubles it
must be confessed that he himself was chiefly responsible.
Born with an unfortunate tendency towards indolence
and procrastination, he did not try to equip himself for
the battle of life.   " He was never asked," says a recent
biographer, " to do a stroke of work towards the earning
of his own living until he had arrived at man's estate."
He was maintained at college ; he was, more than once
or twice, supplied with money for a fitting start in the
world.   But each time he threw away the opportunity.

Appendix.

During the closing period of his career he was earning enough to keep him in moderate comfort, yet he died poor and in debt. He seems, indeed, to have been one of those unfortunates who are their own worst enemies.

Early Education. Oliver Goldsmith was born at the village of Pallas, in Ireland, on November 10, 1728. His father, the Reverend Charles Goldsmith, was the rector of the parish. Long afterwards the son wrote of him,

> "A man he was to all the country dear,
> And passing rich on forty pounds a year."

While Oliver was still an infant, the family removed to the village of Lissoy, where the father had secured a somewhat better living. Here the boy received his early education. He learned his A B C at home from one of the servants; his " three R's " at the village school. He was a shy and sensitive lad — small of build, awkward of movement, and slow at his lessons. It is not on record that he showed any signs either of interest in literature or of the capacity to write. He suffered then, as he did all through his life, from a lack of self-confidence. It was woefully easy for his schoolmates to raise, at his expense, " the loud laugh that spoke the vacant mind."

" **Sweet Auburn.**" There is no reasonable doubt that the " Sweet Auburn " of his most beautiful poem, *The Deserted Village*, is Lissoy seen through the golden haze of memory. The details are touched in with a loving hand; the picture is more kindly than accurate. But in the main it is a true picture. A few lines will show how vividly the old days came back to him long after, when he " in populous city pent endured the fading years ":

OLIVER GOLDSMITH

"Sweet Auburn! loveliest village of the plain;
  Where health and plenty cheer'd the labouring swain,
  Where smiling spring its earliest visit paid,
  And parting summer's lingering blooms delayed;
  Dear lovely bowers of innocence and ease,
  Seats of my youth when every sport could please,
  How often have I loiter'd o'er thy green,
  Where humble happiness endear'd each scene!
  How often have I paus'd on every charm,
  The shelter'd cot, the cultivated farm,
  The never-failing brook, the busy mill,
  The decent church that topt the neighbouring hill,
  The hawthorn bush, with seats beneath the shade,
  For talking age and whispering lovers made!"

Trinity College, Dublin. From the rural quiet of Lissoy, Goldsmith plunged into the excitements of student life, at Trinity College, Dublin. As the family funds were small, he was entered as a " Sizar " — that is, he had to wait on table and to do other menial offices in return for his education. At first he objected to the arrangement; but, largely through the persuasion of his good uncle Contarine, he was led to consent. He passed the necessary examination, and began the new life in 1745.

College Life. Of the details of his career at Trinity College we know little enough. He seems to have been a poor student, but a boon companion. His father died while he was still in residence, and he became more than ever dependent upon the kindness of his uncle. It was a happy-go-lucky sort of life that he led. Sometimes he borrowed money from a friend; sometimes he wrote street ballads, which he sold for five shillings apiece. On one occasion he was publicly reprimanded by the College authorities for " sedition and insurrection " — in other words, for joining in a student riot. Another time he won a small money prize and on the strength of it gave an uproarious supper party in his rooms. For this he received a severe overhauling from his tutor, who was " an ill-conditioned brute." Smarting under the disgrace, he ran away. He turned up at Lissoy half-starved; but his brother persuaded him to go back, and the matter was smoothed over. He left Trinity in 1749, hopeful and irresponsible as always, but at least with a degree.

Trying to Get Started. For a considerable period after leaving college, the young graduate lived with his mother at Ballymahon. The relations between them were not very cordial, and the blame seems to rest chiefly upon Oliver himself. The mother was strong-willed and somewhat hot-tempered; at times she must have been made nearly frantic by the shiftlessness of her son. It is said that Tony Lumpkin, at the Three Jolly Pigeons, represented one side of the writer's tastes; it is certain, at least, that he was quite content to enjoy the present hour and to let the world go by. But his relatives grew tired of such things. The young man was first stirred up to try to enter the church. Perfectly good-natured always, he presented himself; but " the church was denied the aid of the young man's eloquence and erudition." Next he became tutor in a wealthy family, survived for a time, and then once more found himself at loose ends.

Emigration. He next thought of emigrating to America, and actually got as far as Cork. Here, however, something mysterious happened, and his ship sailed without him. He paved the way for his return by some highly interesting letters, and finally arrived home again, penni-

less. "If the good Uncle Contarine believed those letters," says Thackeray, "if Oliver's mother believed that
story which the youth related of his going to Cork, with
the purpose of embarking for America; of his having paid
his passage-money, and having sent his kit on board; of
the anonymous captain sailing away with Oliver's luggage,
in a nameless ship, never to return; if Uncle Contarine
and the mother at Ballymahon believed his stories, they
must have been a very simple pair; as it was a very simple
rogue indeed who cheated them."

The Law, and Medicine. The good uncle, however,
was ready to help the young scapegrace again — this time
as a law-student. Oliver reached Dublin with fifty
pounds, spent it almost immediately, and once more
wandered back to Ballymahon. At this point a certain
Canon Goldsmith — a person of influence, apparently —
appears on the scene, with the proposal that the young
man study medicine. The project was eagerly seized
upon; the generous uncle again opened his purse; and
in 1752 Oliver left Ireland — as it turned out, forever.

Edinburgh and Leyden. At Edinburgh he remained
for a year and a half, finding life pleasant, if not profitable.
Then he dropped certain hints to his uncle as to the need
of studying medicine abroad at the famous University of
Leyden. The uncle replied with his customary generosity
and Goldsmith actually went to Leyden. The nature of
his studies is not recorded; it is safe to suppose that they
were not of a very burdensome nature. A characteristic
anecdote is told of this period. He had borrowed money
to leave Leyden, when he saw in a florist's window some
rare and expensive bulbs. Knowing that his uncle was an

enthusiast in such things, he forgot all but the desire to give pleasure to this kind old friend. The bulbs were bought, and sent off to Ireland. Goldsmith, with a single guinea in his pocket, started on a tour of the Continent.

The Grand Tour. Both *The Traveller* and *The Vicar of Wakefield* show some traces of Goldsmith's experiences during his " grand tour " of Europe. But as a matter of fact we know nothing certain about what he really did, or where he really went. That he was on the Continent for about a year and during this time wandered pretty much all over Europe; that somewhere he picked up a medical degree; that he was back in England by February, 1756 — these are the only sureties in the story.

We must not assume too readily that the charming pictures in the poem and the novel reflect what actually occurred. It is more probable that the thing is largely a product of his imagination, and that whatever happened, it did not take place in the charmingly idyllic and pastoral fashion reflected in the poem and the novel. The truth is that we have not enough evidence to construct any detailed account of his journeying. The end of the tale is plain enough, however. The generosity of Uncle Contarine had reached a limit, and Goldsmith found himself in London, hard put to it to earn his bread and butter.

" Grub Street." He now entered on a somber period. The London of the mid-eighteenth century was not kind to those who came there with neither money nor influence. Goldsmith had a struggle to live; his threadbare coat and his uncouth person caused him to meet with repeated rebuffs. After some experience in a chemist's shop, he managed to engage himself as proof-reader to Samuel Richardson, who was then at the height of his fame as the author of the first great English novel, *Pamela*. Thence he drifted into school-teaching, and at length into the work of writing for the booksellers. " Hack-work," they called it ; and it was a miserably paid business. The time was inauspicious for the man who would win his living by authorship ; " the patron was going, and the public had not yet come." Goldsmith " lived on Grub Street," as the cant phrase went ; he wrote critical articles and reviews in their nature superficial and controversial, and managed for some time to eke out an existence. He " compiled with a flowing pen " histories of Greece, Rome, and England ; biographies of Nash and Voltaire.

Futile Schemes. He had not yet found his place in the world. He broke away from his first employer, and tried teaching again. Then an opportunity came for a medical appointment to the Coromandel Coast, on the east side of India. The better to enforce his case, Goldsmith began a work to be called *An Enquiry into the Present State of Polite Learning in Europe*. He did actually obtain the appointment ; but for some reason the project fell through. It is probable that the candidate, in spite of his medical degree, was found to be unqualified for the post. Shortly afterwards (1758) he tried for a position in a London hospital, but failed to pass the examinations.

A Definite Path. Finally, however, a definite path opened before him. The publication of the *Enquiry* in 1759 committed him to the life of a man of letters. This, his first considerable publication, was a treatise on

Appendix.

the arts of Europe. It contained an attack upon the professional literary critics: they are men, he said, "whose trade is a bad one, and who are bad workmen in the trade." But Goldsmith himself had been a critic, and the inconsistency of his position soon brought reprisals from those whom he attacked. The chief enemy thus raised was one Kenrick, who lost no opportunity of abusing him then and afterwards.

"**The Bee**." Of higher quality than the *Enquiry* was a new venture which was next put through. A bookseller in London asked him to become sole contributor to a weekly magazine of the *Spectator* type. This work Goldsmith readily undertook, and the first issue of *The Bee*, as the periodical was called, came out on October 6, 1759. But it was not destined to succeed — principally through the lack of a definite aim and policy. The work that Goldsmith did for it showed in no small degree the charm of style which he later brought to perfection. Here are a few lines from No. 4, called *City Night Piece*.

"The clock has just struck two, the expiring taper rises and sinks in the socket, the watchman forgets the hour in slumber, the laborious and the happy are at rest, and nothing wakes but meditation, guilt, revelry, and despair. The drunkard fills once more the destroying bowl, the robber walks his midnight round, and the suicide lifts his guilty arm against his own sacred person. . . .

"What a gloom hangs all around! The dying lamp feebly emits a yellow gleam; no sound is heard but of the chiming clock, or the distant watch-dog. All the bustle of human pride is forgotten; an hour like this may well display the emptiness of human vanity.

"There will come a time, when this temporary solitude may be made continual, and the city itself, like its inhabitants, fade away and leave a desert in its room."

From the painting by Sir Joshua Reynolds.

DOCTOR SAMUEL JOHNSON

" **The Citizen of the World.**" This passage suggests the method of the " familiar essay," which Goldsmith was presently to handle in a manner peculiarly his own. His mastery of the form, and his command of delicate satire, are seen in a series published originally in a London newspaper and reissued under the title of *The Citizen of the World*. The writer imagines a philosopher from China, who visits England and writes home letters commenting on the characteristic features of the national life. Such a setting, while not new, afforded ample scope for amusing criticism. After a time there appears a mysterious " Man in Black." Under a rough exterior this character conceals a keen intellect and a kindly heart, and acts as guide, counselor, and friend to the stranger from China. Like the Philosophic Vagabond in *The Vicar of Wakefield*, he reflects something of Goldsmith's experience of life; he is, all in all, a person whose acquaintance it is well to make.

Dr. Johnson. The quality of Goldsmith's writing won for him some friends whose fellowship was great gain to him. Most interesting and most prominent of them all was Doctor Samuel Johnson. The sane and vigorous personality of this man dominates the literature of the time; his wonderful goodness of heart is writ large in the story of his life. Sometime in 1761, he sought out Goldsmith. This action was taken before the appearance of any of the work by which Goldsmith's name is familiar to us to-day; it is convincing proof both of his literary ability and of the good Doctor's critical judgment. Their meeting took place before James Boswell began those records of Johnson's life which were eventually to form the most remarkable biography in the English language;

hence we know nothing of how their acquaintance actually was brought about.

A pleasant anecdote has come down to us, however, which casts an amusing light upon their early friendship. A mutual friend called to accompany Doctor Johnson to dinner at Goldsmith's lodgings. He found Johnson gorgeously arrayed — quite contrary to his usual careless fashion. On being asked the reason for this transformation, Johnson said: "Why, sir, I hear that Goldsmith, who is a very great sloven, justifies his disregard of cleanliness and decency by quoting my practise: and I am desirous this night to show him a better example."

Boswell and Goldsmith. With the great Doctor is inseparably connected the name of Boswell, his life-long admirer and very capable biographer. Boswell was impressed by Goldsmith's reference to Johnson's sympathy for the wretched:

> "He had increased my admiration of Johnson's goodness of heart by incidental remarks in the course of conversation, such as, when I mentioned Mr. Levett, whom he entertained under his roof, 'He is poor and honest, which is recommendation enough to Johnson'; and when I wondered that he was very kind to a man of whom I had heard a very bad character, 'He is now become miserable, and that ensures the protection of Johnson.'"

But Boswell seems never to have fully appreciated Goldsmith; he was jealous, for one thing; he had, moreover, little sense of humor, and was quite incapable of understanding the whimsical speeches of which Goldsmith was so fond. Thus, he called him a blunderer, a feather-brain, and made fun of his personal appearance. Goldsmith, for his part, could not resist a telling hit at the pertinaceous

Scotchman. "Who *is* this Scotch cur that follows at Johnson's heels?" somebody asked. His answer was pointed: "He is not a cur: you are too severe — he is a bur. Tom Davies flung him at Johnson in sport, and he has the faculty of sticking."

The Club. Johnson showed his friendship for Goldsmith in a very practical way by advocating his admission to the Club. This was a famous group of brilliant men, among whom were Sir Joshua Reynolds, the great painter, Burke, and several others of eminence in various walks of life. It met once a week to dine and talk, and over its choice fellowship Johnson presided, as of right. " Dr. Goldsmith," said he, " is one of the first men we have now as an author, and he is a very worthy man, too. He has been loose in his principles, but he is coming right." The relation between the two was very close. We may think of the good Doctor as the constant champion of his friend; and as for Goldsmith, it is only necessary to read the beautiful Dedication to *She Stoops to Conquer*.

There was, of course, an occasional falling-out. Once they had a hot dispute at dinner, and Goldsmith received a sharp rebuke. He felt this keenly and at the Club afterwards sat apart, silent and depressed. Johnson perceived this, and said aside to some of the party, " I'll make Dr. Goldsmith forgive me." Then he called to him in a loud voice: " Dr. Goldsmith, something passed between us today where you and I dined. I ask your pardon." Very quickly came the warm-hearted response: " It must be much from you, sir, that I take ill."

" **The Traveller.**" The work in which Goldsmith first showed his true poetic gifts appeared in 1764. *The*

Appendix.

Traveller is a fine bit of modified classicism; which is to say that it follows the general technique of Pope and his school, but with a difference. Johnson extended a friendly hand; he read the proof sheets and reviewed the poem. He was frankly of the opinion that there had not been anything so fine since Pope's time. His judgment, as usual, was sound: the diction of *The Traveller* is as choice and as concise as any of its predecessors; it commands, at the same time, a genuine pathos such as Pope himself could not compass. Goldsmith had an opportunity to advance his own interests when a nobleman who professed himself " much delighted " with the poem offered to do him a kindness. " I could say nothing," remarked the honest bard, " except that I had a brother, a clergyman, who stood in need of help." This was his brother Henry, to whom he pays a touching tribute in his opening lines:

> "Remote, unfriended, melancholy, slow,
> Or by the lazy Scheldt, or wandering Po . . .
> Where'er I roam, whatever realms to see,
> My heart untravell'd fondly turns to thee;
> Still to my brother turns, with ceaseless pain,
> And drags at each remove a lengthening chain.
> Eternal blessing crown my earliest friend,
> And round his dwelling guardian saints attend."

The poem has much quiet beauty of description and much music of expression; the charm of its presentation hides the didactic element, which after all is not very profound. It brought him, as Johnson remarked, " into high reputation." Long after his death, the same kindly critic listened impatiently to some rather supercilious comment on *The Traveller*. " Goldsmith," he broke in,

Dr. Johnson Reading the Manuscript of Goldsmith's "Vicar of Wakefield"

" was a man who, whatever he wrote, did it better than any other man could do. He deserved a place in Westminster Abbey; and every year he lived would have deserved it better."

The Vicar of Wakefield. The fine quality of Goldsmith's greatest work, *The Vicar of Wakefield*, still further substantiates Johnson's defense. This novel, the literary reputation of which stands even higher to-day than when it first appeared, was published in 1766. The manuscript had actually been completed two years before. Johnson sold it for him when his debts were very pressing.

"I received one morning a message from poor Goldsmith that he was in great distress, and, as it was not in his power to come to me, begging that I would come to him as soon as possible. I sent him a guinea, and promised to come to him directly. I accordingly went as soon as I was dressed, and found that his landlady had arrested him for his rent, at which he was in a violent passion. I perceived that he had already changed my guinea, and had got a bottle of Madeira and a glass before him. I put the cork in the bottle, desired him to be calm, and began to talk of the means by which he might be extricated. He then told me that he had a novel ready for the press, which he produced to me. I looked into it, and saw its merit; told the landlady I should soon return; and having gone to a bookseller, sold it for £60. I brought Goldsmith the money, and he discharged his rent, not without rating his landlady in a high tone for having used him so ill."

The price received seems absurdly inadequate; but we must remember that the author was as yet known to the public only as a bookseller's hack. Johnson himself thought that it was " a sufficient price, too, when it was sold; for then the fame of Goldsmith had not been elevated, as it afterwards was, by his *Traveller;* and the bookseller had such faint hopes of profit by his bargain,

Appendix.

that he kept the manuscript by him a long time, and did not publish it till after the *Traveller* had appeared. Then, to be sure, it was accidentally worth more money."

The Story. One of Goldsmith's biographers says that the novel, considered structurally, follows the plan of the Book of Job. A good man is taken as the hero. He is overwhelmed with misfortunes, maintains his beauty of soul in all his trials and tribulations, and in the end is rewarded by receiving back all and more than he had lost. This is true enough; but the reader of to-day is interested rather in the character of the Vicar than in the plot of the novel — which, it must be confessed, is somewhat shadowy and unreal. The true charm of the tale lies in the manner of the telling; the Vicar speaks just as we know such a man ought to speak. He is simple-hearted, pious, and not without a touch of dry humor. One of the best passages in the book is the good man's attempt to reclaim the thieves and robbers in the prison, where he has been unjustly confined. Not often in literature has an author handled a difficult scene — one which might have so easily been spoiled by sentimentality — with a method at once so sure and so delicate.

The Personal Element. It has been said that Goldsmith put into the novel not a little of his own experiences. The point, however, should not be pressed too closely. Like all writers of fiction, he adapted to his purposes that which he knew well; but there is no need to read Goldsmith himself into George Primrose, or the " Philosophic Vagabond." The matter is an interesting field for speculation — nothing more.

For the rest, one should note the beautiful little lyric,

" When lovely woman stoops to folly," the clever " Elegy on a Mad Dog," and the amusing episode of Moses and the green spectacles. Goldsmith said of his work, " There are an hundred faults in this Thing "; but posterity has not endorsed this opinion.

" **The Good-Natur'd Man.**" The next important step in Goldsmith's career was the production of his first comedy, *The Good-Natur'd Man*, at Covent Garden Theatre in 1768. We shall have more to say of this piece, as of eighteenth century comedy in general, elsewhere. At the time he was in his usual condition of impecuniosity, and completed the play in the midst of a mass of other work, chiefly compilations of various sorts. Johnson very kindly wrote a Prologue; the play itself after some exasperating delays was put on and achieved success. It ushered in a more prosperous period of Goldsmith's life, both in respect of the money it gained and the fame which it brought him. There is not yet evident the sure touch and the confident vivacity of *She Stoops to Conquer*, but the play " went " well and was a pleasant relief from the sentimental absurdities of the contemporary drama.

" **The Deserted Village.**" In the "manufactured stuff" which he turned out to order for the booksellers, Goldsmith was a rapid writer; but in the works in which he " struck for fame " he was a slow and conscientious worker. During the halcyon days which followed *The Good-Natur'd Man*, he was deeply engaged with a new poem. A friend of his, calling one day, found that he had just completed the ten lines beginning,

"Dear lovely bowers of innocence and ease,"

Appendix.

"Come," said the poet, "let me tell you this is no bad morning's work; and now, my dear boy, if you are not better engaged, I should be glad to enjoy a shoemaker's holiday with you." This was his name for a day of festival, innocent enough in itself, but leading sometimes to other pleasures less innocent and more expensive. The money that came from his play was too freely spent; he became involved in heavy debts. With the object of shaking himself clear, he went into the country not far from London. Here he worked hard on a *History of Animated Nature*, of which Johnson predicted that it would be as interesting as a Persian tale, though not remarkable for accurate information. But his chief care in his "Shoemaker's Paradise," as he named the little cottage at Edgeware, was the composition of his best poem — *The Deserted Village*. It was published in 1770.

Opinions of the Poem. Anything Goldsmith now wrote was eagerly read; *The Deserted Village* won immediate success. He dedicated the poem to Reynolds; in return the great artist painted a picture which he inscribed: "This attempt to express a character in the *Deserted Village* is dedicated to Dr. Goldsmith by his sincere friend and admirer, Sir Joshua Reynolds." The descriptive passages are marked by sincere beauty and truth, finding expression in verse that is singularly musical. At the same time we must admit that the destruction of the "loveliest village of the plain" is dictated by the needs of poetry and not by those of political economy. But, as with Longfellow's *Evangeline*, we forget historical inaccuracy and economic falsifying when we read the charming lines, steeped as they are in love of nature and in kindly sentiment.

From the painting by Sir Joshua Reynolds.

RESIGNATION.

"But on he moves to meet his latter end,
  Angels around befriending virtue's friend:
Bends to the grave with unperceived decay,
While resignation gently slopes the way."

The Deserted Village, lines 106-110.

The essayist Macaulay held an unfavorable opinion of the poem:

"It is made up of incongruous parts. The village in its happy days is a true English village. The village in its decay is an Irish village. . . . He had assuredly never seen in England the inhabitants of such a paradise turned out of their homes in one day and forced to emigrate in a body to America. The hamlet he had probably seen in Kent; the ejectment he had probably seen in Munster: but, by joining the two, he has produced something which never was and never will be seen in any part of the world."

The judgment of Thackeray, on the other hand, was more kindly, and conceived in a juster spirit of criticism. He was not troubled by any anachronisms or exaggerations which may have got themselves into the poem. He was interested in the broad humanity of the thing, its fine literary quality. " I need not say," he wrote, " with what touching truth, with what exquisite beauty of comparison, the whole theme of the poem is wrought out." He was doubtless thinking of lines like these:

"In all my wanderings round this world of care,
    In all my griefs — and God has given my share —
    I still had hopes, my latest hours to crown,
    Amidst these humble bowers to lay me down. . . .
    And, as an hare whom hounds and horns pursue
    Pants to the place from whence at first she flew,
    I still had hopes, my long vexations past,
    Here to return — and die at home at last."

" **She Stoops to Conquer.**" When Goldsmith was a youth, he once had occasion to ride home from school — a journey of two or more days. On the way he was benighted in a village. Upon asking the way to " the best house " he was directed by some joker to the house of

Appendix.

the village squire. Arriving there, he played the high-handed man of the world, ordered supper, and invited the squire and his family to share it. The incident stuck in his mind, and years afterwards became the groundwork of his greatest comedy. It is no derogation of this excellent work to point out that he was driven to its composition by the pressure of debt, which bore hard upon him during the years 1771-1773. *The Good-Natur'd Man* had been a financial success; turning once more to the same field, he brought out *She Stoops to Conquer; or, The Mistakes of a Night*.

The author had to surmount some irritating delays. The "sentimental comedy" was then in fashion; the actor-manager Colman, who had accepted the play for Covent Garden, felt that anything contrary to the fashionable vogue was a hazardous undertaking. Goldsmith points out this fact in his dedication. But he was determined to produce a comedy that was faithful to nature, for "he hated the sentimentalists and all their works." He remained firm; the varied difficulties were overcome; and the new play was produced on March 15, 1773.

On the fateful night, Johnson determined to be present to lead the applause, and took with him a congenial party. Goldsmith himself ate no dinner, and wandered about disconsolately until the beginning of the fifth act. As he entered the stage door, he heard a hiss — the only mark of disfavor, as it happened, during the whole evening. He hurried up to Colman with an agitated question. Colman's reply was a cruel one: "Pshaw! Doctor, don't be afraid of a squib, when we have been sitting these two hours on a barrel of gunpowder." But Colman and the sentimentalists were wrong; the play was an immense success. The unkind words of the actor were paid for when the whole town was laughing at his lack of judgment in foretelling the failure of the comedy.

Situations. The hiss which so terrified Goldsmith was caused by the improbability of Mrs. Hardcastle's dilemma in the fifth act when, safe in her own garden, she thinks herself forty miles from home. The episode is a little crude; but we should remember that this was a period when highwaymen and other such night terrors were no mere figments of the imagination. The general excellence of the other situations would enable the comedy to carry off a much worse defect. The scene at the Three Jolly Pigeons; the elaborate joke evolved by Tony Lumpkin; the old squire's lecture to his servants; the conversations between Marlow and Miss Hardcastle, — all these are humorously conceived and competently executed. The whole thing is permeated with fun that is at once wholesome and good-natured. The first scene conveys the necessary information in free and brisk conversational form; the last closes the action naturally and effectually.

Characters. The characters, too, show the same firm hand. If some critics are disposed to question the probability of Tony Lumpkin writing the clever song which he sang at the inn, we may say that the young squire is not such a fool as he looks; if they criticize the exaggerated diffidence of Marlow, it may be replied that even to-day such a characteristic is not altogether unknown. In any case, a comedy of manners, written purely to amuse, should not be dealt with like a play of Shakespeare. Mr. and Mrs. Hardcastle are felicitously true to the life

Appendix.

of the day — the former the bluff country squire, especially amusing when he drills his servants as to how they shall behave in company; the latter, the typical country lady, "ambitious of the town." Hastings and Marlow are a pair of normal young men upon whom Fate, in the person of Tony Lumpkin, plays some scurvy tricks. Miss Hardcastle and Miss Neville are sketched in lightly, but sufficiently. We do not look, in a play of this description, for strongly marked characters; the touch should be deft and sure, the manner easy; and all this Goldsmith has achieved. The chief end which he had in view was to amuse; Johnson said: "I know of no comedy for many years that has so much exhilarated an audience; that has answered so well the great end of comedy, making the audience merry."

Closing Years. The money which his new comedy brought in did not permanently relieve Goldsmith from his difficulties. And now, to add to these difficulties, he began to suffer from ill-health. Fits of depression came upon him; he seemed to lose the power of rising above his cares in the old buoyant way. He was forty-five when *She Stoops to Conquer* appeared; an old disease fastened upon him, and he could not shake it off. Still he struggled on. He completed two volumes of a *History of Greece*, and projected a *Popular Dictionary of Arts and Sciences*. He offered to alter *The Good-Natur'd Man* so that Garrick could act in it; but that astute though kindly person evaded the issue by a countersuggestion for a new comedy, and even advanced money for the purpose. With this money, Goldsmith paid a last visit to some dear friends in the country.

"**Retaliation**." In spite of the gloom which was fast settling down, there were some flashes of the old brilliancy. Chief of these was a bright and humorous poem called *Retaliation*. It was never finished and was printed after his death. One evening at St. James's Coffee-house, some of his friends diverted themselves by writing comic epitaphs on Goldsmith, to which he was supposed to reply. Garrick produced the well-known lines:

> "Here lies Nolly Goldsmith, for shortness called Noll,
>   Who wrote like an angel, but talked like poor Poll."

Goldsmith's reply was delayed, but finally took shape in a series of amusing character sketches which hit off very cleverly the personal traits of Burke, Garrick, Reynolds, and others. One or two quotations will show the quality of this " last scintillation of the bright and happy genius." On Burke:

> "Here lies our good Edmund, whose genius was such,
>   We scarcely can praise it or blame it too much;
>   Who, born for the universe, narrowed his mind,
>   And to party gave up what was meant for mankind. . . .
>   Who, too deep for his hearers, still went on refining,
>   And thought of convincing, while they thought of dining. . . .
>   For a patriot too cool, for a drudge disobedient,
>   And too fond of the *right* to pursue the *expedient*."

On Garrick:

> "Here lies David Garrick, describe him who can,
>   An abridgment of all that was pleasant in man;
>   As an actor, confess'd without rival to shine;
>   As a wit, if not first, in the very first line:
>   Yet with talents like these, and an excellent heart,
>   The man had his failings, a dupe to his art. . . :

Appendix.

> Though secure of our hearts, yet confoundedly sick
> If they were not his own by finessing and trick :
> He cast off his friends, as a huntsman his pack,
> For he knew when he pleased he could whistle them back."

On Reynolds :

> "Here Reynolds is laid, and, to tell you my mind,
> He has left not a wiser or better behind :
> His pencil was striking, resistless, and grand,
> H's manners were gentle, complying, and bland :
> Still born to improve us in every part,
> His pencil our faces, his manners our heart."

Death. The lines on Reynolds were the last ever written by Goldsmith. He died on April 4, 1774, at the age of forty-six. To his friends the news came as a personal shock ; Burke is said to have burst into tears ; Reynolds laid aside his brush for that day. He was buried privately in the Temple Church in London. He died heavily in debt — " was ever poet so trusted before ! " was the kindly-humorous remark of Johnson. The great man was asked, two years later, to write an epitaph for a monument to be erected by Goldsmith's friends in West-minster Abbey. He composed the famous Latin inscription containing the lines " Nullum fere scribendi genus non tetigit, nullum quod tetigit non ornavit " — " There was almost no kind of writing which he did not attempt, and he attempted nothing which he did not adorn." It was a just estimate.

Personality. — Of Goldsmith's character much has been written, and not a little has been said which is of a contradictory nature. A great deal depends upon the point of view. It is true that he was, as Macaulay says, a spendthrift, vain, frivolous, profuse, improvident. But it is also true that his " sweet and friendly nature bloomed in the midst of a life's storm and rain and bitter weather." Among his friends he numbered some of the best men of the day. It was honest friendship as well as critical appreciation which led Johnson to say: " He has raised money and squandered it, by every artifice of acquisition and folly of expense. But let not his frailties be remembered ; he was a very great man."

Best of all the comments upon Goldsmith, because of its broad humanity, was the estimate written by Thackeray. We may close this sketch with a brief quotation :

"Think of him reckless, thriftless, vain if you like — but merciful, gentle, generous, full of love and pity. He passes out of our life, and goes to render his account beyond it. Think of the poor pensioners weeping at his grave; think of the noble spirits that admired and deplored him; think of the righteous pen that wrote his epitaph — and of the wonderful and unanimous response of affection with which the world has paid back the love he gave it. His humor delighting us still; his song fresh and beautiful as when first he charmed with it; his words in all our mouths; his very weaknesses beloved and familiar — his benevolent spirit still seems to smile upon us ; to do gentle kindnesses : to succor with sweet charity; to soothe, caress, and forgive; to plead with the fortunate for the unhappy and the poor "

RICHARD BRINSLEY SHERIDAN

1751–1816

An Extraordinary Figure. The career of Richard Brinsley Sheridan is one of the most extraordinary in the course of English literature. At the age of thirty-five he had written two of the greatest comedies ever produced on the English stage. A few years later he astonished the nation with a speech that placed him in the front rank of parliamentary orators. His friends included all the leaders of the day. But as time went on he moved from the blaze of popular admiration into the shadows of sorrow and affliction. Poverty and sickness fixed their hold upon him, and in his misery his friends fell away. Yet no sooner was he dead than all alike hastened to bear witness to his greatness, as of a man whom they delighted to honor. He died neglected and alone; but he received the high tribute of burial in Westminster Abbey.

Birth and Parentage. Sheridan was born in Dublin, Ireland, in September, 1751. His ancestry doubtless had some influence upon his character. His grandfather, Dr. Thomas Sheridan, was an extravagant and hot-headed parson, with a " ready wit and a flow of humor." He was a favorite companion of Dean Swift; it is said, indeed, that *Gulliver's Travels* was written at his house. His father, Thomas Sheridan, early took to the stage and made some considerable reputation. Boswell spoke of his

366

RICHARD BRINSLEY SHERIDAN

"well-informed, animated, and bustling mind"; Dr. Johnson remarked, in his dogmatic way: "There is to be seen in Sheridan something to reprehend, and everything to laugh at; but, sir, he is not a bad man. No, sir; were mankind to be divided into good and bad, he would stand considerably within the ranks of the good." He seems to have been one of those who live by their wits, and to have possessed brilliant parts without the powers of concentration or perseverance. In this, as in other respects, Richard resembled his father.

Education. There were three children in the family, — two boys and a girl. The early education of the boys was undertaken by their mother. As they grew older, however, she handed them over to a Dublin schoolmaster, with a rather despairing letter — "they will teach you patience," she said, "for two such impenetrable dunces I never met with." In 1762 the family went to London, and the boys entered Harrow School.

At School. The elder brother, Charles, passed his schooldays in the colorless fashion of the model boy; we hear nothing about him, one way or the other. Richard, on the contrary, moved along with a kind of cheerful indolence. Liked — even admired — by his mates, he kept on the safe side of punishment and the comfortable side of scholarship. "I do not remember," said one of his masters, "one instance in which he distinguished himself in Latin or English composition, either in prose or verse." Yet the genius was there. "All the while," the same master added, "we saw in him signs of a superior intellect. His eye, his countenance, his general manner, were striking; his answers to any common question were prompt and acute. All boys and all masters were pleased with him." As it stood, the case was a familiar one; it remained to be seen what this brilliant but unscholastic youth, moving lightly and gayly through the school, would do with his talents.

A Picture. To his little sister at this time he appeared as a sort of hero. The family had been in France, where cheaper living expenses made it easier to provide for the boys at Harrow. On their reunion, she wrote:

"He was handsome, not merely in the eyes of a partial sister, but generally allowed to be so. His cheeks had the glow of health, his eyes — the finest in the world — the brilliancy of genius, and were soft as a tender and affectionate heart could render them. The same playful fancy, the same sterling and innoxious wit that was afterwards shown in his writings, cheered and delighted the family circle. I admired — I almost adored him!"

Bath. In 1770 the family moved to Bath. This little town was then known throughout Europe as a health resort and was a center of the fashionable and artistic life of England. A very interesting society was to be found there. The sick came to drink the waters; the wealthy and aristocratic gathered to amuse themselves in the intervals of the London season; artists, actors, and musicians found plenty to do; and on the outskirts hung a motley crowd of gamblers and fortune-seekers. Into this busy world the Sheridans entered. Charles worked faithfully with his father; Richard seems to have done little but enjoy the fascinations of Bath society. His experiences were to bear ample fruit. The whole background of *The Rivals* reflects that youthful environment; Sir Lucius O'Trigger is typical of the unscrupulous adventurer; and Captain Jack Absolute is pleasantly reminiscent of the young author himself.

Marriage. The romance of Sheridan's courtship and marriage is as dramatic as any situation in his plays. Although a piece of real life, the whole thing works out like a drama, where the hero vanquishes the villain, wins the heroine, and "lives happily ever after." There was living in Bath at this time a family by the name of Linley. The father was a composer and musician of note, and there were two beautiful daughters whose fame as singers was more than merely local. The elder, in particular, had many admirers. Among these was a certain Captain Matthews — the "villain of the piece." His designs — which included the desperate plan of carrying off the lady by force — were discovered by Sheridan.

With a fine if quixotic chivalry, he offered to take her to France out of all danger, and to place her with the nuns of St. Quentin at Dunkirk, where his sister had been brought up. The scheme was put into effect, the wife of one of the family servants being taken with them as a chaperon, and the youth delivered his charge in safety. It is a pretty and romantic little tale. The young lovers, for lovers of course they were, were married at Calais in order that no scandal should be unearthed against them, and Richard at once returned to Bath to face the worst.

The second act found the youthful hero called upon to guard his own good name against the attacks of the villain. Captain Matthews, furious at the success of his boyish rival, sent a letter to a newspaper in which he referred to Sheridan as "a L— and a treacherous S—," with more to the same effect. On being taxed in London with the

Appendix.

authorship, Matthews denied all knowledge of it and accused Charles Sheridan. Richard hastened to Bath, and there learned the truth. The brothers returned post-haste to London. In strict accordance with the prevailing custom, a duel was fought. Richard triumphed, and made his antagonist apologize. Later, they fought again; this time Sheridan was badly wounded and had to lie by for a time. At last, in 1773, he married the heroine in the light of day.

Early Attempts. Romantic as the situation of the young couple undoubtedly was, they had to have something to live on. Already Sheridan had shown signs of his ruling passion. At school he had begun, with a fellow Harrovian, the composition of a farce called *Jupiter*, the only merit of which was its forecast of certain qualities in his later play, *The Critic*. At Bath he had made a few stray notes which afterwards were put to good use in *The School for Scandal*. But nothing very definite appears until we come upon a reference to " a comedy of mine in rehearsal at Covent Garden within a few days."

" The Rivals." This comedy was *The Rivals*, which was produced at Covent Garden on January 17, 1775. The first night was not a success. The play was withdrawn and vigorously revised, however, and then it achieved even more than its author had hoped for. The interest of the setting, the cleverness of the dialogue, the bustling action, constituted elements which were sure to win the applause of any audience.

Characters and Situations. The plot in itself is slight; few plays so full of life have been built upon a simpler foundation. Captain Absolute is his own rival, as well as

From the painting by Sir Joshua Reynolds.

MRS. SHERIDAN
As Saint Cecilia

that of Bob Acres, and is a fine dashing sketch of the young gentleman of the time. Bob Acres, the country squire new to the society of town, eagerly brushing up his behavior and his clothes in order to make the best impression, stands out as a highly original figure. The duel scene, when his valor begins to ooze out at the palms of his hands, is the best thing in the play. Sir Lucius O'Trigger, the fire-eater, is a vivid piece of character-work. Sir Anthony is in some respects a caricature of the elder Sheridan, with whom the son was at variance both before and after his marriage. Faulkland, a lover of fine speeches, is redeemed from mere sentimentality by his absurdly exaggerated jealousy and doubt.

Mrs. Malaprop is perhaps the most thoroughly satisfying person in the comedy. Her " nice derangement of epitaphs " keeps the audience in pleased expectation as to what she will say next; her " allegory on the banks of the Nile " is a literary gem. At the same time, her large and gracious personality is sufficiently true to nature; we feel that Sheridan must have drawn her from the life at some phase of his experiences at Bath. Lydia, with her pretty and romantic ideas and her impatience with ordinary routine, was somewhat new to the theater of the day. Julia must be regarded as a concession to the popular taste for sentimental comedy; the only parts of the play which at all lack vigor are the scenes between her and Faulkland. But this is immaterial. The whole is admirably managed — plot, dialogue, character, and all. The general effect is one of extraordinary ease and lightness. The author evinces no effort — the play " must have amused his own fancy when he wrote, as it has amused his audience ever since."

Other Plays.   The skillful interpretation of the part of Sir Lucius O'Trigger was one of the chief factors in the first success of *The Rivals*.   To show his gratitude to the actor who took this rôle, Sheridan wrote expressly for him a farce called *St. Patrick's Day; or, The Scheming Lieutenant*.   It enjoyed only a local and temporary success. He next tried his hand at an opera, *The Duenna*, the music for which was composed by his father-in-law.   "The run of this opera," said the poet Moore, in his biography of Sheridan, "has, I believe, no parallel in the annals of the drama."   Byron termed it "the best comic opera in English."   But the cooler judgment of posterity has set upon it a different value; *The Duenna* has not survived, except for "the forced resurrection of an occasional performance."

Drury Lane Theatre.   In the year 1775, David Garrick, the greatest actor of his day and one of the most successful of theater managers, retired from active work.   He was the chief proprietor of Drury Lane Theatre, the rival of Covent Garden.   When *The Duenna* made its hit with London play-goers, Sheridan conceived the idea of acquiring Garrick's shares in Drury Lane.   After various negotiations, the plan was actually carried out in 1776.   An enormous responsibility was thus thrown upon his shoulders.   It was necessary to convince the public that Drury Lane under the new management would maintain its high reputation.   For a time the city waited in vain, but at last, in May, 1777, the young dramatist silenced all criticism by producing *The School for Scandal*.

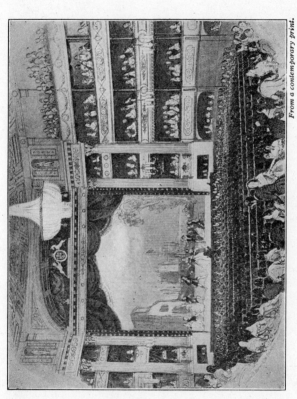

INTERIOR OF DRURY LANE THEATRE

"**The School for Scandal.**" The new play showed a marked advance over *The Rivals*. Sheridan had gained complete mastery of the principles of his art. The dialogue of *The School for Scandal* is more brilliant, the characters are more firmly handled, the situations arise more naturally out of the plot, than is the case with the earlier play. Such competent writing does not come by chance. Sheridan himself was not averse to having the impression prevail that his work was produced off-hand — in a flash of genius, as it were. His method, indeed, gave some support to the idea; the last act of *The School*, for instance, did not reach the actors until five days before the actual performance. It is probably true that he worked rapidly, and " waited upon inspiration." But both of his greatest plays show a highly polished diction, an attainment of fine dramatic effects, which could only be the result of hard work.

The Plot. There are two distinct stories in *The School for Scandal*. One is the " school " itself, built up around Lady Sneerwell and Snake. The germ of this " scandalous circle " had long been in his mind. It had even been jotted down under the name of *The Slanderer: A Pump-Room Scene*. The other story is concerned with Sir Peter Teazle and his young wife, and the two brothers, Joseph and Charles Surface. Sheridan's experience told him that neither plot singly was enough to hold an audience. The stories, therefore, were very skillfully combined, and the spectator is conscious only of unity of purpose and brilliant artistry.

The Screen Scene. Sheridan had a keen instinct for an effective situation. This faculty is admirably illustrated

Appendix.

by the episode in the third scene of the fourth act, where Lady Teazle hides behind the screen. The dramatic elements are developed with consummate ability. The successive visitors — the increasing embarrassment of Joseph Surface — his attempts to avoid the inevitable exposure — the exciting moment when Charles throws down the screen — the skill by which the *dénouement* is made to suggest a means of reconciliation between Sir Peter and Lady Teazle — all these are combined to create a total effect which has scarcely a parallel upon the stage.

The Picture Scene. Only less effective is the scene where Charles Surface refuses to sell the picture of his old uncle. In some respects Charles is merely the conventional spendthrift — the spirited young gallant of the stage. By the device of the picture, however, he is made to reveal a kind of essential good-heartedness, a " reckless gratitude." This at once satisfies the dramatic sense in a new way, and forms a perfectly legitimate contrast to the hypocritical policy of Joseph. Like Sir Oliver, we are ready to forgive him much.

Garrick. Garrick showed a deep personal interest in the new manager and his play. The old actor attended some of the rehearsals, besides the performance; a letter of his indicates his practical point of view: " A gentleman who is as mad as myself about the *School* remarked that the characters upon the stage at the falling of the screen stand too long before they speak. I thought so too the first night: he said it was the same on the second and was remarked by others: tho' they should be astonished and a little petrified, yet it may be carried to too great a length." The Prologue which he wrote for the play reveals an almost paternal feeling, in its reference to Sheridan as " our young bard," and " our young Don Quixote." He was right in his praise and sound in his judgment. The comedy had a really phenomenal success. Two years later the Drury Lane records said " *The School for Scandal* damped the new pieces." It proved to possess qualities of perennial value, since it keeps its hold on the stage down to our own time.

The Critic. In the same year as *The School for Scandal* appeared, Sheridan produced a new play called *The Critic.* It has a special interest as the climax of a long series of " burlesques " which began in Shakespeare's time with *The Knight of the Burning Pestle.* The essential feature of all these plays was that in some way they poked fun at the dramatic tradition of the day. The *Knight* satirized the plays which were written to please the London 'prentices. *The Rehearsal* burlesqued the so-called heroic dramas of the late seventeenth century. Fielding's *History of Tom Thumb* attacked certain pretentious dramatic theories of his time. Gay's inimitable *Beggar's Opera*, in voicing its criticism, took Newgate Prison for a setting and a highwayman for hero.

In Sheridan's play, Mr. Puff invites some friends to a rehearsal of his new tragedy, *The Spanish Armada*. The humor of the piece lies not only in the absurd dialogues and situations of the play rehearsed, but even more in the conversation of the critics who look on. All the faults and foibles of contemporary drama are brought under fire; Sheridan holds the attention of the audience by none of the customary methods of the stage; it is not the plot, but the dialogue which works for success. Nothing in its way has ever been better done than the light-handed mockery of everything pretentious and ungenuine in dramatic composition. *The Critic* was the last of Sheridan's original dramatic compositions. He retained, indeed, the managership of Drury Lane, and preserved a general interest in the stage, but a new field was now opening before him.

Political Tastes. The work of Sheridan as a dramatist occupied a comparatively short period of his life. At the age of twenty-nine he entered on the Parliamentary career which satisfied more completely than did the theatre, his restless and brilliant genius. His tastes first took definite direction when, through the influence of some of his old Harrow schoolmates, he met Charles James Fox. This powerful statesman was then high in the affairs of the nation, and with him Sheridan was destined to be long associated. The two men were mutually attracted; the latter said, after their first meeting, that he " was quite lost in his admiration of Fox "; while Fox declared that " an evening at Sheridan's is worth a week's waiting for." It was about the same time that Dr. Johnson proposed him for the Club, observing that " he who has written the two best comedies of his age is surely a considerable man." At the Club he met Edmund Burke.

In Parliament. Sheridan entered Parliament in 1780. The times were troublous. The American war was drawing to a disastrous conclusion; kept up, indeed, against the better judgment of England by the obstinacy of the King. In Ireland there existed a " sort of chronic semi-rebellion." In India difficulties were arising, through the activities of the East India Company, which began to press for solution. His first speech gave no indication that he was fitted to cope with these great matters. "I am sorry to say," remarked a candid friend, "I do not think this your line. You had much better have stuck to your former pursuits." Sheridan replied with characteristic vehemence: "It is in me, however; and, by Heaven, it shall come out!"

Speech on Warren Hastings. It "came out" in 1787, when a motion to impeach Warren Hastings was brought up in the House of Commons. Hastings had been for twelve years Governor of the Province of Bengal, under the direction of the East India Company, and was accused of extortion and tyranny. As the Company possessed great power and influence, the impeachment of one of its most important officers was a matter of national significance. Burke originated the idea of impeachment; Sheridan was chosen to make the speech setting forth the reasons for the action of the House.

It was a coldly critical audience with which the orator had to deal; the House was composed of hard-headed, unsentimental politicians; difficult to convince — difficult even to move. But Sheridan carried the day. His opportunity had come. He seized it and won a triumph as decided as those upon the narrower arena of the stage. The power of the speech is vividly shown by its effect upon a prominent member of the House who had written a defense of Hastings and who was naturally prejudiced against his accuser.

"At the expiration of the first hour he said to a friend, 'All this is declamatory accusation without proof;' when the second was finished,

'This is a most wonderful oration.' At the close of the third, 'Mr. Hastings has acted most unjustifiably;' the fourth, 'Mr. Hastings is a most atrocious criminal;' and at last, 'Of all monsters of iniquity, the most enormous is Warren Hastings!'"

Another member declared that it was " the most excellent and astonishing performance I ever heard. . . . This is the *universal* sense of all who heard it. . . . The moment he sat down there was a universal shout; every man was on the floor, and all his friends throwing themselves on his neck in raptures of joy and admiration. This account is not at all exaggerated. The effects it produced were proportioned to its merits."

He spoke once more at the actual trial in Westminster Hall. As to the quality of this second oration, the opinions of his friends were divided; some thought that he surpassed his first speech, to others it seemed almost a failure. Macaulay's *Warren Hastings* contains a description of the occasion, which ranks among the noblest passages of English prose.

Sorrows and Losses. In the Impeachment and Trial Speeches Sheridan reached the highest point of his career. The rest of his life can here be touched on only in the briefest way. With all his brilliant gifts of mind and heart, he lacked self-control and steadiness of purpose. Troubles came; the loss of his wife and his little daughter intensified his natural restlessness of soul. His extravagance and want of business ability injured his prospects alike in the theatrical and the political world. Debts and duns harassed him. He formed a friendship with the Prince Regent which, however helpful to the Prince, was not fortunate for Sheridan.

The Prince Regent. One of the most prominent figures of the latter part of the century was the Prince of Wales. The mental breakdown of his father, George III, made it apparent even as early as 1792 that he might at any time be called upon to assume the duties of Regent. He was not a pleasing character. Thoughtless and self-indulgent, he possessed none of the sound qualities of his father, who at least was clean of life and firm of disposition. Occupying this peculiar position, the Prince needed a confidential adviser, in order that he might keep in touch with Parliament. This place was for many years filled by Sheridan. It is a curious circumstance that he showed in his relations with the Prince a ready decision and a business capacity which all too seldom appeared in his own affairs. Yet the fast-living company of which the Prince was the leader was only too congenial to the adviser, and very injurious to his own best interests.

Burning of Drury Lane. Through all these years Sheridan retained the managership of Drury Lane, as well as his seat in Parliament. His public life, slowly sinking to lower levels, was checquered by occasional bursts of recovery — by " a faculty prompt and eager and practical." But a stroke of ill-fortune finally took from him both his available money and his power to earn more. Early in 1809, the theater, which had recently been redecorated and was still barely completed, was burned to the ground. Sheridan was in the House at the time; when he reached the scene of the disaster he realized that all was lost. His entire fortune was wiped out, and the resources of many friends seriously involved.

He showed a brave spirit. The glare of the burning

theater lighted up the House of Commons, where a debate was in progress. One of the members proposed that the House should adjourn out of sympathy for a man who had been so prominent. But Sheridan would not have it. "Whatever may be the extent of the calamity," he said before leaving the assembly, "I hope that it will not interfere with the public business of the country." Later, one of the actors found him in a coffee-house near the ruined building, "swallowing port by the tumblerful." The newcomer made some sympathetic exclamation. "Surely," said Sheridan, "a man may be allowed to take a glass of wine by his own fireside."

The Final Scenes. The closing years were sad. Drury Lane was rebuilt, and Sheridan, though he sold out his shares, expected to act in some sort as manager. But the new committee passed him over. He was growing old; his unreliability and extravagance were proverbial. These weaknesses might be overlooked in a brilliant young manager, or could be redeemed by personal magnetism. They were regarded with scant consideration when the years had bowed him down. To crown all, he lost his seat in Parliament. While a member of the House, he was at least safe from arrest for debt; now, like jackals round a wounded lion, enemies arose all about him. Of his friends, Fox was dead, Burke long estranged; the Prince Regent conveniently forgot him.

One friend who was faithful — probably the poet, Tom Moore — wrote a letter to the *Morning Post* newspaper, which reveals the straits to which he was reduced. "Delay not," it ran, "to draw aside the curtain within which that proud spirit hides its sufferings. Prefer min-

From a contemporary print.

EXTERIOR OF DRURY LANE THEATRE

istering in the chamber of sickness to mustering at

'The splendid sorrows that adorn the hearse,'

I say *life* and *succor* against Westminster Abbey and a funeral."

The Irony of Fate. But it was too late. Sheridan died on July 7, 1816. And then came a touch of dramatic irony which was like the studied effect of a play. No sooner was he dead, than those who had neglected him in his evil days hastened to honor his memory. He was buried in Westminster Abbey, and was followed to his grave by men who represented all that was noble and powerful in the land. It was a fine thing that this occurred; yet one must ask with Moore: " Where were they those royal and noble persons who now crowded to ' partake the yoke ' of Sheridan's glory; where were they all while any life remained in him? Where were they all but a few weeks before, when the zeal now wasted on the grave might have soothed and comforted the deathbed? "

His Achievement. Sheridan is remembered to-day as the writer of the only old plays since Shakespeare which really give pleasure. To his contemporaries he was not only a great dramatist but a great orator. He was, moreover, brilliant in conversation, charming in society, and sincere in friendship. His career was diversified by flashes of the most extraordinary genius and descents into the lowest depths. He stepped aside at the highest period of his political life to squander his wonderful powers in a friendship with the Prince Regent and his school. His greatest work was all done while he was still young; his later life was " bound in shallows and in miseries," without the power to " take the current when it serves."

SOME FEATURES OF LONDON LIFE IN THE EIGHTEENTH CENTURY

The City. The Comedy of Manners, the type to which belong the three plays in this book, reflects the conditions of its time. A brief glance at eighteenth-century London will therefore help us to appreciate these plays. The city may be thought of as containing about 500,000 inhabitants, extending for several miles along both sides of the river, and embracing within itself the extremes of riches and poverty. In its narrow streets the gilded chariot of the nobleman splashed mud on the tradesman or the country fellow who had come in to see the sights. Alongside the docks below London Bridge lay ships freighted with merchandise from all the world. Out of the city ran roads to every part of the kingdom; roads that were hub-deep in mire and infested with highwaymen.

Contemporary Pictures. The life of the time is vividly pictured in the essays of Addison and Steele, and London in particular is the subject of Gay's *Trivia*, a poem which should be read by anyone who would know how men lived then and what they did. The great novels, too, contain many descriptions of the vanished period. In *Pamela*, *Tom Jones*, *Humphrey Clinker*, and *The Vicar of Wakefield* the strange contrasts of the day are faithfully recorded.

Amusements. Life was full and vigorous. Among the amusements were cricket and football, rowing and ballooning, cock-fighting, bear-baiting, and prize-fighting.

382

Huge fairs were held in or near the city. On the outskirts lay the great resorts of Vauxhall and Ranelegh Gardens, much frequented by the wealthier classes. For the use of the general populace there was a kind of "vast metropolitan gymnasium" in Finsbury Fields. It was the centre of attraction for runners, boxers, archers, wrestlers, and athletes of all sorts.

Gambling. Gambling was carried on to an almost incredible extent. It was a national passion. "Society was one huge casino. On whatever pretext and under whatever circumstances half a dozen people of fashion found themselves together — whether for music, or dancing, or politics, or for drinking the waters or each other's wine — the box was sure to be rattling, and the cards being cut and shuffled." That fashionable lounger and well-known man of the world, Horace Walpole, says in one of his letters that Whist "has spread a universal opium over the whole nation; it makes courtiers and patriots sit down to the same pack of cards." There were great gaming clubs — White's, Brooks's, Almack's. At the card tables in these places fortunes were won and lost. One of the "deepest" players was the famous Charles James Fox. "Charles Fox," runs a letter of the period, "sat down to cards last Tuesday after dinner, played all night and next morning, and in that time lost 12,000 pounds : by five that afternoon, he had lost 11,000 more."

Outside of London the principal center for gambling was Bath, whither speculators of all sorts flocked during the summer. A few of the more strong-minded players were able to overcome the fascination of deep play. George

Appendix.

Selwyn, an intimate friend of Horace Walpole, thus shook himself free; "it was," said he, "too great a consumer of four things — time, health, fortune, and thinking." William Pitt used to join in "with intense earnestness," but "perceived the increasing fascination," and presently abandoned gaming for ever. The custom was by no means confined to gentlemen of fashion. The ladies, too, played heavily; the references in *The School for Scandal* and *The Rivals* would find a ready echo in the minds of the audience for whom the plays were written.

Dueling. Dueling and hard drinking were prevalent. The former practice is referred to by a contemporary writer as "the reigning curse" of the age. Duels were fought upon the slightest pretext; the excuse made by Sir Lucius O'Trigger in *The Rivals* is scarcely an exaggeration:

"Pray, sir, be easy; the quarrel is a very pretty quarrel as it stands; we should only spoil it by trying to explain it."

In fact, the whole duel episode in this play owed its success to its faithful portrayal of a familiar custom. The offense, real or imaginary, once taken, "satisfaction" must be given; a false code of honor (but a very strict one) made no other attitude possible.

A very interesting defense of the custom is found in some remarks of Dr. Johnson. He was dining on one occasion, in company with Goldsmith and Boswell, with the "brave old general" Oglethorpe, the founder of the colony of Georgia. The subject of dueling came up, and the general said that "undoubtedly a man has a right to defend his honor." Johnson's views show so well the best opinion of the day that they may be quoted in full:

"Sir, as men become in a high degree refined various causes of offence arise, which are considered to be of such importance, that life must be staked to atone for them, though in reality they are not so. A body that has received a very fine polish may be easily hurt. Before men arrive at this artificial refinement, if one tells his neighbour — he lies, his neighbour tells him — he lies; if one gives his neighbour a blow, his neighbour gives him a blow; but in a state of highly polished society, an affront is held to be a serious injury. It must, therefore, be resented, or rather a duel must be fought upon it; as men have agreed to banish from their society one who puts up with an affront without fighting a duel. Now, Sir, it is never unlawful to fight in self-defence. He, then, who fights a duel, does not fight from passion against his antagonist, but out of self-defence; to avert the stigma of the world, and to prevent himself from being driven out of society. I could wish there were not that superfluity of refinement; but while such notions prevail, no doubt a man may lawfully fight a duel."

Coffee-houses. A pleasanter feature of eighteenth-century London may be seen in the " coffee-houses " which played so important a part in the social life of the capital. The London coffee-houses resembled in many respects the clubs of the present time. People in all walks of life frequented them, not so much to drink " the black and bitter drink called coffee " as to meet friends, to discuss business, or to exchange the news of the day. Familiar to most of us is the picture of Sir Roger de Coverley at a coffee-house — it comes in Number 49 of *The Spectator:*

"I waited on him to the coffee-house, where his remarkable figure drew upon us the eyes of the whole room. He had no sooner seated himself at the upper end of the high table but he called for a clean pipe, a paper of tobacco, a wax candle, and the Supplement, with such an air of cheerfulness and good-humour that all the boys in the coffee-room (who seemed to take a pleasure in serving him) were at once employed on his several errands, insomuch that nobody else could come at a dish of tea until the knight had got all his conveniences about him."

"**The Spectator**." The favorite coffee-house of Addison was one kept by a man named Button. This was, it will be remembered, the meeting-place of the Spectator Club. The Spectator himself may be seen, as he says, "thrusting my head into a round of politicians at Will's, and listening with great attention to the narrations that are made in those little circular audiences. Sometimes I smoke a pipe at Child's. I appear on Sunday nights at St. James's coffee-house . . . my face is likewise very well known at the Grecian, the Cocoa-Tree, and in the assembly of stock-jobbers at Jonathan's."

Famous Resorts. Towards the middle of the century there were about 2000 coffee-houses in the metropolis. They afforded meeting-places for all sorts and conditions of men. Child's was frequented by the clergy and university men; Nando's by the legal profession. Army officers met at Old Man's Coffee-house. Politicians favored several places, chief among them being the Cocoa-Tree for Whigs, and St. James's for Tories. Merchants went to Lloyd's, or Jonathan's; literary men and "wits" to Button's, John's, and the Chapter Coffee-house. The Grecian had a high reputation; it was used on occasion by the Fellows of the Royal Society. Here, too, Goldsmith delighted to gather round him a band of congenial souls, whom he would entertain as far as his precarious means permitted.

The expenses, apparently, were not very great. On payment of one penny, the visitor was admitted to a long room partitioned off into rows of "boxes," where privacy was assured. A dish of coffee or tea cost twopence, a modest sum which included the right to read the chief newspapers and periodicals. Smoking was usually allowed; letters could be written, and there is even record of a clergyman who was seen in a box hastily penning his Sunday sermon.

Johnson and Goldsmith. Dr. Johnson was in the habit of patronizing the Turk's Head Coffee-house, " on purpose," in his kindly way, " to encourage the hostess, who was a good civil woman, and had not too much business." It was at the St. James that Goldsmith used frequently to dine with his friends — David Garrick, Edmund Burke, Sir Joshua Reynolds, and others. It was here too that occasion was given for the composition of his poem *Retaliation*, which was his reply to some humorous epigrams directed against him by the witty company. The poem was never finished, but contains some brilliant " epitaphs " on the humorists. " Let me sit while I'm able," says the poet, " Till all my companions sink under the table." The epitaphs are edged with some pretty keen satire, as may be seen in the passages quoted on page 363.

Clubs. The spirit of conviviality and good-fellowship, which was widespread at this time, led to the formation of many " clubs. " They met at coffee-houses or taverns. So numerous were they, that any man could find a " little nocturnal assembly " to suit his own peculiar tastes. There was, for instance, a " rattle-brained society of mechanic worthies, " who named themselves Knights of the Order of the Golden Fleece in Cornhill, and who may have suggested Dickens's Prentice Knights in *Barnaby Rudge*. The titles of other clubs indicate a pleasing

Appendix.

variety. Here are some of them: The No-Nose Club, the Surly Club, the Atheistical Club, the Split-Farthing Club, the Mock Heroes, the Beau's, the Lying Club, the Beggars' Club, the Small Coalmen's Music Club, and the Man-Hunters' Club — an organization which was quite as grim as the name implies.

"**The Club**." The most famous of them all was " The Club, " founded by Sir Joshua Reynolds and Dr. Johnson. The latter was essentially a " clubbable " man, and in his famous Dictionary defined " club " as " an assembly of good fellows meeting under certain conditions." The first meeting of this notable organization was held at the Turk's Head Tavern in 1763. The original members were Sir Joshua Reynolds, Johnson, Oliver Goldsmith, Dr. Nugent, Bennet Langton, and Topham Beauclerk — two brilliant men about town — Sir J. Hawkins, and M. Chaumier, secretary in the War Office. Other famous men who later were added to the roll were, David Garrick, Edward Gibbon the historian, and James Boswell, Johnson's biographer. Sheridan was elected on the strong recommendation of Johnson. He himself was the leading spirit and presided at those meetings of whose intellectual brilliancy we have, unfortunately, too few records. On the death of Garrick the name was changed to " The Literary Club." It lasted until well into the nineteenth century.

Divided Membership. Most of the fine gentlemen of the day belonged to half a dozen clubs. Goldsmith, a genial soul, so far followed the prevailing custom as to frequent at least two others, besides The Club. He was a member of the Whist Club, and of the Free and Easy

Wednesday Club; at both of which his unfailing good humor made him always welcome. Nor were clubs confined to the upper classes of society. The workingmen also had their assemblies. " Friends' Clubs, " " Smoking Clubs, " or " Lottery Clubs " met regularly at taverns all over London. Typical of these was the gathering at the Three Pigeons, where Tony Lumpkin " knocked himself down " for his famous song.

Vitality of the Age. One is impressed, in reading the annals of the eighteenth century — especially its last fifty years — by the superabundant vitality of the times. It was an age of great men and great achievements. There was much that was harsh, cruel, and bad ; but there was also much that was noble, true, and of good report. A list of those who won honor in all walks of life would be tedious in the mere enumeration. To instance but a few, we have Wolfe and Anson in military and naval affairs ; Burke, Pitt, Fox, and Sheridan in statecraft ; Reynolds and Gainsborough in art ; Jenner in medical science ; Johnson, Gibbon, Goldsmith, and Sheridan in literature. One would give not a little to see these men, and many others only less renowned, in their familiar haunts of old London.

Origin and Growth of Bath. The little town of Bath, where the action of *The Rivals* takes place, was of very ancient origin. Early in their occupation of Britain, the Romans discovered medicinal springs in the middle of a beautiful valley, near a river, and established there a health resort which they named Aquae Solis — "Baths of the Sun." The Saxons destroyed the place in the sixth century, but several of the old Roman baths remain to this day. The city was well known in the seventeenth century, was made popular by a visit of Queen Anne shortly after 1700, and reached the peak of its prosperity during the middle and latter parts of the eighteenth century, under Beau Nash and his successors.

Beau Nash. With Bath is inseparably connected the name of Richard Nash, or " Beau Nash, " as he is known to history. Educated at Oxford and trained as a lawyer, he organized a band under his own control about 1720, and became Master of Ceremonies for the Assemblies. Through a natural adaptability and a large stock of self-assurance he came to be recognized as the social leader of the place — indeed, a kind of uncrowned king. His powers were exercised autocratically, but with more wisdom than usually is found in such cases.

He dictated reforms in dress; he banished from the Assembly " high boots, riding dress, and white aprons." He forbade extortionate charges on the part of lodging-house keepers, and was instrumental in having the roads kept in some degree of proper repair. He restrained the insolence of "chairmen." He even went to the extent of checking the evil of dueling; under his régime it was forbidden to wear swords in the streets. This prohibition is noted in *The Rivals*: " A sword seen in the streets of Bath," says Jack Absolute, " would raise as great an alarm as a mad dog." Nash not only enforced rigidly the customary laws of good society but insisted on the observance of his own Rules of Behaviour, which were posted in the Pump Room.

The laws and customs which he had established long outlived him, and are to be traced as late as the time of Dickens's account in *The Pickwick Papers*. His own end was rather melancholy. His money was derived from a " silent " partnership in certain gaming-houses; when laws against gambling were passed, he lost his income. His ultimate fate was to be pensioned off by the Corporation of Bath, and to wander like an uneasy ghost among the scenes of his former triumphs.

Fashionable Routine. When Bath was at its height as a center of fashion, there was a regular routine for the upper classes. It began with the medicinal bath, which was supposed to be completed by nine in the morning. Then everyone who was anyone assembled at the Pump Room to drink the waters. Doubtless Sheridan here gathered many a suggestion both for the delightful vagaries of Mrs. Malaprop, and the biting scandal of Lady Sneerwell and her friends. Afterwards came walks on the North and South Parades, formal breakfasts, visits to the various circulating libraries, and concerts. The afternoon was usually occupied with a second visit to the Pump Room, followed by tea at the Assembly Rooms. The evening was taken up with card parties, concerts, or the theater. Balls, according to the strict rule established by Nash, began at six and ended at eleven. " The regular hours stupefy me," complains Fag, in the first scene of *The Rivals*, " not a fiddle nor a card after eleven! " If we add to what has been said the brilliant and changing costumes, the life and movement of the time, we shall see that Bath had plenty to offer the fashionable seeker after amusement.

Dress. The fashions of the eighteenth century were always striking and decorative, and were of course seen at their best among the social leaders at Bath. Men wore short wigs, powdered and curled, embroidered coats and waistcoats, silk knee-breeches and stockings, and shoes with huge glittering buckles. For women, the following is an account from a magazine article of 1775:

"The fashionable dress for February, as established at St. James's and Bath. FULL DRESS: The ladies in general still wear their hair dressed high, broad at top, with large flys. Negligees of rich plain colored silks or satins, very much trimmed with chenille, and gauze fancy trimming, ornamented with tassels of different colors and no flounce to the petticoat. Large hoops and drop ear-rings. Colored shoes, and small rose buckles."

Descriptions. The interesting little city occupied an important place of its own in the life of the eighteenth century, as may be gathered from the numerous descriptions, in novels, magazines, and letters. Two of Smollett's novels — *Peregrine Pickle* and *Roderick Random* — contain some vivid passages. A highly humorous picture of Bath society appears in *The New Bath Guide*, a satirical poem of 1766. Goldsmith's *Life of Richard Nash* is a most readable biography of that notorious character. Horace Walpole wrote some brilliant letters on the occasion of his visit there; letters which are more clever than complimentary. Frances Burney, in *The Diary and Letters of Madame d'Arblay*, wrote entertainingly of what she saw. Jane Austen, a native of Bath, placed there the scene of *Northanger Abbey*. For a later description, a picture of a rather faded society living on the memory of past grandeur, one should read Chapters XXXV, XXXVI, and XXXVII of Dickens's *Pickwick Papers*. Here is an amusing sketch of the Bath which he knew:

"The great pump-room is a spacious saloon, ornamented with Corinthian pillars, and a music gallery, and a Tompion clock, and a statue of Nash, and a golden inscription, to which all water-drinkers should attend, for it appeals to them in the cause of a deserving charity. There is a large bar with a marble vase, out of which the pumper gets the water; and there are a number of yellow-looking tumblers, out of which the company get it; and it is a most edifying and satisfactory sight to see the perseverance and gravity with which they swallow it. There are baths near at hand, in which a part of the company wash themselves; and a band plays afterwards, to congratulate the remainder on their having done so. There is another pump-room, into which infirm ladies and gentlemen are wheeled, in such an astonishing variety of chairs and chaises, that any adventurous individual who goes in with the regular number of toes, is in imminent danger of coming out without them; and there is a third into which the quiet people go, for it is less noisy than either. There is an immensity of promenading, on crutches and off: with sticks and without: and a great deal of conversation, and liveliness and pleasantry.

"Every morning, the regular water-drinkers . . . met each other in the pump-room, took their quarter of a pint, and walked consti-

Appendix.

tutionally. At the afternoon's promenade . . . all the great people met in grand assemblage. After this, they walked out, or drove out, or were pushed in Bath chairs, and met one another again. After this, the gentlemen went to the reading-rooms and met divisions of the mass. After this, they went home. If it were theatre night, perhaps they met at the theatre; if it were assembly night, they met at the rooms; and if it were neither, they met the next day — a very pleasant routine, with perhaps a slight touch of sameness."

EIGHTEENTH-CENTURY COMEDY

Drama of the Eighteenth Century. The stage history of the Eighteenth Century begins with the " Queen Anne Drama " and ends with the plays of Richard Brinsley Sheridan. Within this period is placed the rise and fall of the Comedy of Sentiment and the perfecting of the Comedy of Manners. The latter reached its highest development in the three plays included in this book. The story of dramatic literature is, of course, continuous; there are in reality no definite breaks whereby the subject may be neatly separated into exact divisions. But certain tendencies appear during certain periods, and these clearly set off various phases of the drama. Thus, we may say that a distinct epoch in the history of the English stage falls within the period 1700-1779, the last being the year of Sheridan's *Critic*.

The " Restoration Drama." To understand eighteenth-century comedy we must first turn to what is known as the " Restoration Drama." The dramatic history of the Elizabethan Age — the greatest in our annals — ended with the closing of the theaters by the Puritans in 1642. After that the Civil War and the Commonwealth shut out all opportunity for plays or playwrights. But when the " Restoration " took place, — the return of Charles II in 1660 — the theaters were again thrown open, two acting companies were organized, and play-writers found a continuous demand for their work. We can mention here only a few authors, as indicating the general tendencies of the time.

Appendix.

Dramatists. The most successful form of drama was the Comedy of Manners. It had been originated by Ben Jonson, Shakespeare's friend, and limited its subject-matter to the treatment of the superficial behavior of society. With the Restoration dramatists it enters upon a period of extraordinary brilliancy, but also of marked licentiousness. The most notable names are those of Congreve, Vanbrugh, and Farquhar. All showed ease of presentation and a sustained vivacity of dialogue and action; but they manifested also an unsound morality. " The heroes and heroines," says Macaulay, " have a moral code of their own, an exceedingly bad one . . . a code actually received and obeyed by great numbers of people." Goldsmith and Sheridan revived the traditional brilliancy of these writers, while avoiding the elements of coarseness.

John Dryden (1631–1700), " Glorious John," was the representative dramatist of the period, writing fine tragedy in *All for Love*, and excellent comedy in *The Spanish Friar*. The more pretentious side of his work was attacked in a most interesting burlesque called *The Rehearsal*, written by the Duke of Buckingham and others, and acted in 1671. This play is full of " local hits," and unsparingly ridicules the dramatists of the time.

Jeremy Collier. The coarseness of the Restoration comedy presently aroused protest. In 1698 Jeremy Collier published *A Short View of the Immorality and Profaneness of the English Stage*. His attack, ill-balanced though it was, coincided with an awakening public sentiment and gave a strong impetus to the moral regeneration of the theater. Hence, the sound qualities of the Restoration comedy — the wit, the vigor, the conversational brilliancy — remained, while the unhealthy moral atmosphere died with the environment which it reflected.

The " Queen Anne Drama." The reign of Queen Anne (1702–1714) was marked by some interesting dramatic work. Nicholas Rowe, the compiler (in 1709) of the first critical edition of Shakespeare's plays, tried to follow the example of the master-dramatist and " hold the mirror up to nature." But the principal tendencies were decidedly classical ; that is, chiefly in the direction of careful rule and regularity. The foremost example of the type is seen in the *Cato* of Joseph Addison (1672–1719). On this play, influential in its time, Dr. Johnson made his usual sane comment :

"It is rather a poem in dialogue than a drama, rather a succession of just sentiments in elegant language than a representation of natural affections, or of any state probable or possible in human life. . . . The events are expected without solicitude, and are remembered without joy or sorrow."

The same great critic said that the vogue of *Cato* resulted in " the use of dialogue too declamatory, of unaffecting elegance, and chill philosophy." That it was a success is a striking sign of the artificiality of the age.

Reaction. A reaction against artificiality was not long in coming. It found strong expression in the " pantomime," long familiar to the stage but now taking on new glory under the skillful hand of one John Rich. His work was extremely popular and possessed features which were cleverly satirized by Pope in his *Dunciad :*

Appendix.

"He look'd, and saw a sable Sorc'rer rise,
Swift to whose hand a winged volume flies:
All sudden, Gorgons hiss, and Dragons glare,
And ten-horned fiends and Giants rush to war.
Hell rises, Heav'n descends, and dance on Earth,
Gods, imps, and monsters, music, rage, and mirth,
A fire, a jig, a battle, and a ball,
Till one wide conflagration swallows all.
Thence a new world, to Nature's laws unknown,
Breaks out refulgent, with a heav'n its own . . . "

"**The Beggar's Opera**." The reaction was even better illustrated by *The Beggar's Opera*, written by John Gay and produced in 1728. The Italian opera had become popular in London early in the century and Gay used its machinery to develop an idea of his own. In his opera the author is supposed to be an inmate of Newgate, the famous London prison. The hero is Captain Macheath, a highway robber. Other characters are jailers, turnkeys, and various representatives of low life. The author appears on the stage from time to time with advice and suggestions. "I have introduced," he says, "the similes that are in all your celebrated operas: the *Swallow*, the *Moth*, the *Bee*, the *Ship*, the *Flower*, etc. I have a prison scene which the ladies always reckon charmingly pathetic." The close amusingly satirizes the conventional "happy ending" so popular on the stage. Captain Macheath has been captured and is about to be hanged. But, as a Player tells the Beggar, "this is a downright deep Tragedy. The Catastrophe is manifestly wrong, for an Opera must end happily." This objection, the Beggar replies,

"is very just; and is easily removed. For you must allow, that in this kind of Drama, 'tis no matter how absurdly things are brought

398

about. So — you Rabble there — run and cry a Reprieve — let the
prisoner be brought back to his Wives in Triumph."

The success of *The Beggar's Opera* was phenomenal.
Dean Swift wrote from Dublin: " We are as full of it as
London can be ; continually acting, and Houses crammed,
and the Lord Lieutenant several times there laughing his
heart out." Gay's work has enjoyed a more than temporary fame. It has proved well adapted for revival, and
with its charming music and amusing situations has won
marked success of recent years both in England and
America.

Burlesques. Clever writers were not slow to seize the
opportunity of attacking the stilted tragedy of the day.
Henry Fielding had a long dramatic career before he
became a novelist. In 1730 he wrote an amusing burlesque with an elaborate title : — *The Tragedy of Tragedies,
or The Life and Death of Tom Thumb the Great . . . with
the Annotations of H. Scriblerus Secundus.* The " annotations " were directed in a serio-comic vein against the
critical controversies of the day. Another good burlesque
was that of Henry Carey — *Chrononhotonthologos: Being
the Most Tragical Tragedy ever Tragediz'd by any Company of Tragedians.* The mock heroic note may be
illustrated by the opening lines :

> "Aldiborontophoscophornio !
> Where left you Chrononhotonthologos?"

A second burlesque by Fielding was named *Pasquin.* Here
the author introduced rehearsals of both a mock tragedy
and a mock comedy. It was a " satire on the times, "
and hit out right and left at political corruption, contemporary manners, and contemporary taste in the

drama. Fielding's reckless satire caused the passing of
the Licensing Act in 1738. By this the extravagance of
the burlesques was in some degree checked; but they had
served a useful purpose in promoting dramatic sanity.

The Novel. About the middle of the century the
vitality of the theater was threatened by a new literary
art. *Robinson Crusoe* and *Gulliver's Travels* had whetted
the public taste for a different form of mental entertainment. Richardson's *Pamela* in 1740 marked the beginning
of the English novel. Fielding, after his apprenticeship
in the drama, entered the fresh field with *Joseph Andrews*.
His masterpiece *Tom Jones* followed, together with the
only less notable work of Smollett and Sterne. The
drama came to a period of eclipse. It was to be saved
from extinction by a great actor and two great playwrights.

The Garrick Era. That period of English dramatic
history from 1741 to 1779 has been well named "the
Garrick Era." David Garrick, one of the greatest actor-
managers who ever lived, dominated the activities of the
stage. Born in 1741, he made his first appearance in
Shakespeare's *King Richard III*. His success caused an
older actor to remark: "If the young fellow is right, I,
and the rest of the players, have been all wrong." Garrick
possessed great versatility, performing with equal skill
in every field of dramatic art. The famous painting by
Sir Joshua Reynolds, showing him hesitating between the
Muse of Comedy and the Muse of Tragedy, interprets
justly enough the attitude of the man.

Shakespeare Revivals. A marked feature of the
eighteenth-century drama was the reawakened interest
in Shakespeare. The Restoration dramatists treated him

From the painting by Sir Joshua Reynolds.

GARRICK BETWEEN THE COMIC AND TRAGIC MUSES

with little courtesy; Dryden tried to smooth what he termed his " rude and unrefined genius " by altering *The Tempest*. Another writer revamped *King Lear* with a happy ending; still another mangled *Macbeth* into a sort of opera, " with singing and dancing in it." Samuel Pepys, a representative theater-goer, found *A Midsummer Night's Dream* " insipid, " and *Othello* a " mean thing." To them, Shakespeare was " untaught, unpractised, in a barbarous age."

But with the eighteenth century appeared the great critical editions of Shakespeare's plays by Rowe, Pope, Theobald, and others, and with Garrick came a notable series of revivals. Even before him, the comedies began to enjoy their own again, but he set the seal of his approval upon comedies and tragedies alike. More than a score of the plays were produced under his management, and in most he acted a leading rôle. He made alterations, indeed — some of them indefensible. But in the main he was careful to preserve the original form and spirit. A rival of his put on *King Lear* at Covent Garden while Garrick was giving the same play at Drury Lane. The following epigram shows the popular point of view:

> "A King — nay, *every inch a king;*
>   Such Barry doth appear:
> But Garrick's quite a different thing;
>   He's *every inch King Lear*."

Garrick received from his own generation a sort of worship; his reputation is permanent with theater-lovers. He was buried in Westminster Abbey; it was not in mere flattery that Johnson said, "his death eclipsed the gaiety of nations."

Appendix.

The Sentimental Comedy. Not a few of Garrick's triumphs were won in what is known as the "comedy of sentiment." This dramatic type arose as a protest against the immorality of the Restoration drama; and in it sentiment and morality superseded coarseness. Steele, the essayist and friend of Addison, may be regarded as the first to express this new spirit. But it was not long before sentiment became mere sentimentality, and morality changed into high-flown moralizing. The condition finally reached was excellently epitomized by Goldsmith in an article written in 1772. "A new species of drama has been introduced," he said, "under the name of *Sentimental* comedy, in which the virtues of private life are exhibited, rather than the vices exposed; and the distresses rather than the faults of mankind make our interest in the piece."

He goes on to point out that these comedies have had a great success both because they are new, and because they seem to flatter the favorite weaknesses of the average audience. All the characters are good, and generous to a fault; they have little humor, but abound in sentiment. Any faults they may possess are forgiven because of their goodness of heart; their follies are not ridiculed, but commended. There is one argument in its favor, he concludes, which will keep it on the stage:

"It is, of all others, the most easily written. . . . It is only sufficient to raise the characters a little; to deck out the heroine with a riband, and give the hero a title; then to put an insipid dialogue, without character or humour, into their mouths, give them mighty hearts, very fine clothes, furnish a new set of scenes, make a pathetic situation or two, with a sprinkling of tender melancholy conversation through the whole, and there is no doubt but all the ladies will cry, and all the gentlemen applaud."

The Revival of Comedy. Such false conditions — and instances might be multiplied — caused a return to the principles of true comedy. Goldsmith himself was the first to make a practical protest. In his comedy, *The Good-Natur'd Man*, he aimed at the delineation of character, rather than the "refinement" which had driven humor from the stage. The play was not especially successful, because Garrick not only refused to have it at Drury Lane, but put on in opposition the highly sentimental *False Delicacy*. Moreover, the actor Colman, who took the principal part at Covent Garden, showed little enthusiasm.

But the action was now fairly joined. Shortly after the appearance of his first comedy, Goldsmith published his *Essay on the Theatre: or A Comparison between Laughing and Sentimental Comedy*. He asked whether true comedy could not give more amusement than " the kind of false tragedy called sentimental comedy," and whether audiences really delight in weeping at comedy. Samuel Foote, a highly successful burlesque writer, came into the fight against the prevailing taste with an absurd play, *The Handsome Housemaid, or Piety in Pattens*. He lamented that authors seemed all to have agreed that " it was highly improper to show any signs of joyful satisfaction; and that creating a laugh was forcing the higher order of an audience to a vulgar and mean use of their muscles." In his play, he declared, " not a single expression comes from our mouths that can wound the nicest ear, or produce a blush on the most transparent skin."

" She Stoops to Conquer." The victory was won by Goldsmith's second play, *She Stoops to Conquer*. The cheerful naturalness and hearty laughter of this effective comedy of manners decided once for all the return of real humor to the stage. " The fresh air of out-of-doors sweeps through the windows of the old Hardcastle mansion." The opposition, however, died hard. Horace Walpole, statesman and critic (who ought to have known better), made a characteristic remonstrance.

"Dr. Goldsmith has written a comedy — no, it is the lowest of farces. It is not the subject I condemn, though very vulgar, but the execution. The drift tends to no moral, no edification of any kind. The situations, however, are well imagined, and make one laugh, in spite of the grossness of the dialogue, the forced witticisms, and total improbability of the whole plan and conduct. But what disgusts me most is, that though the characters are low, and aim at low humour, not one of them says a sentence that is natural, or marks any character at all."

The criticism was unfortunate for the critic, because Goldsmith had ridiculed the affectation of the word " low " in the Alehouse Scene. Never again was the place of " laughing Comedy " seriously challenged.

Sheridan. The highest achievement of the English Comedy of Manners is found in the work of Sheridan. Against the falsity of the " weeping muse " he delivered blows even more telling than the irony of Goldsmith. And while he directed the weapon of his satire against the false taste that disfigured dramatic composition, he brought back the brilliant dialogue to which the stage had long been a stranger. He was a master of dramatic art. It is the special merit of his dramas, as Hazlitt pointed out, that everything *tells;* nothing is written in vain.

" **The Rivals.**" When *The Rivals* was first produced, it was a failure. It was too long, several of the actors were careless or incompetent, and there was some objection to the part of Sir Lucius O'Trigger, to whom one newspaper referred as "a villainous portrait of an Irish gentleman." Sheridan withdrew the play, revised it, and put it on again a week later. This time it was a triumph. True, there were traces of the sentimental comedy in the Julia-Faulkland episodes, obviously introduced as a concession to the popular taste. These have been cut from the acting version of Joseph Jefferson without, it must be confessed, any great loss. But Sheridan proved, in this his first play, that a comedy which relied upon wit and humor, upon ingenious plot and rapid dialogue, could delight an audience brought up in a very different school.

"**The School for Scandal.**" Garrick's withdrawal from Drury Lane led to Sheridan taking control. The greatest thing he did as manager — probably the greatest thing ever done there — was the production of *The School for Scandal* in 1777. The success of the play can be gauged by the admiring comment of the cynical Horace Walpole.

"To my great astonishment, there were more parts performed admirably in *The School for Scandal* than I almost ever saw in any play. It seemed a marvellous resurrection of the stage. Indeed, the play had as much merit as the actors."

It is justly considered to be a masterpiece, whether we consider the dialogue, the effective handling of dramatic situations, or the clean-cut character work. He does not go deep; nor is there any need that he should do so — the fine-spun analysis of motives, the portrayal of the deeper passions, would be entirely out of place in a comedy of manners. Hence, following the stage traditions of the playwrights who preceded him, he labels his people Lady

Appendix.

Sneerwell, Snake, Sir Benjamin Backbite, and so forth. But the real spirit is finer than anything of the kind in its own field. He wished to amuse, and he wished to laugh out of court the false and the sentimental. These things, therefore, are ridiculed throughout in the character of that young hypocrite Joseph Surface. He is laughed off the stage, and "with him, moralizing sentiment retires baffled and discountenanced."

The Critic. The most direct attack made by Sheridan upon the popular dramatic fallacies is seen in *The Critic; or A Tragedy Rehearsed*. In form it derives from *The Rehearsal* and *Tom Thumb;* in power, it surpasses them both. A writer invites some critical friends to a rehearsal of his tragedy; the humor is supplied by the absurdities of the tragedy, the running comment of the critics, and the delightful explanations of the author. Its purpose was readily understood and enjoyed at the time, as may be gathered from a newspaper review: "The two leading objects of this witty stage satire appear to be these: first, to expose the mock comments of newspaper and other minor writers; and next, to ridicule the false taste and brilliant follies of modern dramatic composition." Some of the satire is specific and directed against local subjects. But the main attack sweeps on with a power of irony which has preserved its stage vitality down to the present day.

The Close of a Period. With Sheridan, the eighteenth-century drama comes to a close. Under him it had reached its finest manifestation. He had restored all the brilliancy of the Restoration drama, while purging it of its objectionable features. He banished false sentiment and unreal moralizing from the English stage. His plays have been produced more often and more successfully than those of any dramatist since Shakespeare. Modern opinion may well be summarized in the words of Sir Henry Irving, the greatest actor-manager of recent times.

"Sheridan brought the comedy of manners to the highest perfection, and *The School for Scandal* remains to this day the most popular comedy in the English language. Some of the characters both in this play and *The Rivals* have become so closely associated with our current speech that we may fairly regard them as imperishable. No farce of our time has so excellent a chance of immortality as *The Critic*."

ACTING THE PLAYS IN SCHOOL

Importance of Acting. Plays were written to be acted; not read. The three comedies which are included in this volume did not appear in book form until after they had been produced on the stage. The audience for which Goldsmith and Sheridan wrote would never have dreamed of reading the plays before seeing them acted. We, unfortunately, are compelled to reverse the method; many of us cannot see them on the stage at all. This much to be regretted; the full excellence of a play cannot be judged from the printed page alone. It is within the power of the average teacher — as it is certainly within his province — to vitalize the comedies by having his pupils act them.

School Value of the Plays. These plays offer an exceptionally valuable field for school dramatics. In the first place, they are all of a fine literary quality. Again, they present — especially *The School for Scandal* — most interesting problems in stagecraft. They are distinguished, moreover, by amusing situations and rapid dialogue. And not least of their attractions is the opportunity for beautiful costuming and effective settings.

In the Class-room. If the school is not in a position to command a " real " stage, a great deal can be done in the class-room. Mark off the front third of the room, and let this space be sacred to the actors. Young people do not ask for much in the way of staging if they know that they are to interpret parts before their classmates. They will quickly realize that " the play's the thing," and that Tony Lumpkin, or Mrs. Malaprop, or Charles Surface, can be made to live again during the recitation period. For the enthusiastic teacher the hour becomes one of sheer delight; he will probably find in himself unsuspected abilities of stage management; he is sure to make some remarkable histrionic discoveries among his pupils. Learning through acting affords the most direct and practical method of mastering the plays, while at the same time it offers a very rational means of training in posture and voice production. There is no doubt, moreover, that in these days of careless speech an additional value may be found in the enforced familiarity with work which combines ease of style with purity of diction.

The " Real " Stage. Many schools are fortunate enough to have a stage where the plays may be put on before an audience. If this be done, the class work takes on a new interest and value, because everything tends towards a definite climax. All things considered, there are no comedies better adapted for the " school play " than those which we are discussing. They are well within the capacities of boys and girls, and they hold the audience. It may be helpful to indicate briefly some of the more important matters that naturally engage the attention of a class which plans to stage any of the plays.

Setting. The formal " set " scene is not absolutely necessary; thoroughly good effects can be secured by employing background material in solid color — green, or dark blue, for example. Burlap of a neutral tint may also be used to advantage. If it is at all possible, however, the set scene should be provided. The plays were written for elaborate staging, and the best results are obtained by observing the condition. After all, there is nothing that cannot be arranged for in the Art and Manual Training Departments of the average high school. The exteriors, of which there are not many, may be presented simply. The Garden in *She Stoops to Conquer* requires only a few potted shrubs, with a " practicable " tree in the background for Mrs. Hardcastle to hide behind. The North and South Parades in *The Rivals* may be treated as streets; King's Mead Fields as open country.

The interiors present more difficulty, but at the same time offer more opportunity for effective design. The Hardcastle mansion is a comfortable country house of the period — " a very well-looking house," Hastings calls it, " antique but creditable." The furniture and the fittings should be solid and substantial. The room at The Three Pigeons Inn can be studied from some of the well-known prints that are readily available. For the interiors in *The Rivals* and *The School for Scandal* a more elaborate plan may be followed. It should be borne in mind that the fashion of the time was ornate; furniture and pictures were designed upon highly ornamental principles. There should be nothing approaching bareness in these settings; it is better to err on the side of over-elaboration. These interiors, too, are to serve as background for costume of the most brilliant description. The plays picture the fashionable London society of the day; the dress of this society was in the highest degree rich and colorful. A study of eighteenth-century furniture can be made in such a book as Quennell's *History of Everyday Things in England*.

Costume. In general, the costumes in *She Stoops to Conquer* should be planned to bring out some degree of contrast between town and country fashions; those of the Sheridan plays to reflect the fashionable styles of the late eighteenth century. They express a note of grace and elegance; they are associated with powder and patches, with sweeping bows and low curtsies — all the elaborate formal politeness which characterized the time. The illustrations in this book have been made with a special view to the needs of young actors. With suitable modifications, the designs for the characters indicated may be used for other characters of the same general type. Thus, Mr. Hardcastle gives suggestions for Sir Anthony Absolute and Sir Peter Teazle; Mrs. Malaprop, for Lady Sneerwell. The young men Marlow and Hastings may follow the costume of Charles Surface. Lady Teazle forms a good model for Lydia and Julia.

Individuality of costume should be provided for in some cases. Tony Lumpkin, as his name suggests, is a boorish young country squire, who may be supposed to know little and to care less about the niceties of dress. In *The Rivals*, Bob Acres and Sir Lucius O'Trigger are to be differentiated from the conventional attire of the others. Sir Lucius is an adventurer, a dashing cavalier of a somewhat rakish description. Bob Acres first appears in riding costume; but as he has come to town to make an impression, his appearance in the succeeding scenes is vivid and exaggerated. Joseph Surface should be dressed with a sort of ostentatious plainness — he affects a modest attire as in keeping with his assumed character.

Acting. The prime requisite for good acting is clear

enunciation. Every effort should be made to avoid slovenly phrasing, bad accentuation, or muffled voice. No amount of histrionic skill can make up for the harsh tones and the careless slurring of words and syllables which mar so many amateur performances.

Next to good enunciation come ease and rapidity of utterance. Especially in these comedies of manners, which are so full of clever repartee, is it necessary that the dialogue be carried on with vivacity. Any self-consciousness, anything at all labored, will ruin the light grace of the conversation. To the young players this quick interchange of wit must come as naturally as if they themselves were the persons involved. Here, of course, we meet the whole problem of "interpretation." A word or two may be said on this point.

"**She Stoops to Conquer**." Goldsmith's comedy has been called "an incomparable farce in five acts." We may interpret this by saying that the fun is continuous throughout, the characters are true to life, and the author never allows himself to lapse into sentimentality — a weakness to which Sheridan yielded more than once. The chief personage of the play is Tony Lumpkin. Because of the danger of over-doing his peculiarities, the part is not easy to act. He is crude and uneducated, but he has a certain amount of broad humor and a sound sense of justice, as may be seen from his behavior in the last act. A theatrical critic of the day spoke of him as "a most diverting portrait of ignorance, rusticity, low cunning, and obstinacy."

Mr. and Mrs. Hardcastle are typical members of the "landed gentry." The Squire is proud of his house, his kitchen, and his wife. She, for her part, lacks his enthusiasm; perhaps because she is conscious that her charms are not what once they were. She is open to flattery, and her partiality for Tony is strongly emphasized. Diggory, one of the most original of stage servants, must not be spoiled by over-acting; with the proper interpretation he has unusual farcical possibilities. Marlow and Hastings are fashionable young gentlemen of leisure. They form a good contrast to the boorish Tony. Miss Neville and Miss Hardcastle should be lightly touched in; a heavy hand will injure the parts. The scenes between the latter and Marlow, in particular, can be made very attractive if the amusing features are intelligently rendered.

"**The Rivals.**" The chief difference between this sparkling comedy and *She Stoops to Conquer* lies in its brilliant dialogue. The efforts of the players should be directed towards bringing out its fine points in the most capable manner. There is also plenty of fun in the situations, culminating in the delightful Duel Scene, when all the characters are brought together on the stage.

Mrs. Malaprop is the most important character — indeed, one of the great figures of the theater. Her part needs very careful casting; her wonderful " derangement of epitaphs " possess their full charm only when spoken by an actress of more than usual ability. The problem is to combine Mrs. Malaprop's complete satisfaction with her own conversational powers, and the absurdity of the expressions which she employs. Sir Lucius O'Trigger tempts the young actor to over-emphasize a popular stage type — the Irish soldier of fortune. The temptation must be resisted. He is " sudden and quick in quarrel; " but he has a saving quality of humor which enables him to extricate himself from a rather humiliating situation with some degree of credit.

Bob Acres is one of Sheridan's best creations. He is a coward, yet we do not despise him; a conceited fop, yet we like him in spite of all. He is more of a personality, less of a type, than Sir Anthony or Captain Jack. A great deal can be made of him on the stage. The acting version of Joseph Jefferson — himself an admirable interpreter of the part — introduced several exaggerations of his conversation. These are better avoided. The best version is the one that Sheridan left.

It was the custom of Joseph Jefferson to omit the Julia-Faulkland episodes. These, as we have seen, are a frank concession to the popular taste for sentimental comedy. They may be " cut " without injuring the development of the plot; but nevertheless if they are left in they can be made interesting. The secret is to take them as seriously as Sheridan meant them, and as his audience received them. The excellent scenes which show Faulkland's jealous and suspicious nature are shorn of their full dramatic value if we leave out the passages which directly reveal his attitude towards Julia.

Captain Jack and his father present no special difficulty. Jack is the stage lover-hero — a dashing handsome fellow, with an inventive genius and plenty of self-confidence. Sir Anthony dominates the scenes in which he appears. He is irascible, obstinate, and has a touch of the gout.

Lydia makes an interesting heroine; quite unconventional in her highly romantic ideas, and her very human

fit of the sulks when she learns the truth about Beverley.
Lucy, the maid, has a small part with distinct coloring.
The two servants who open the play talk as cleverly as
their betters; this conversation needs adequate handling
because it contains so much important "antecedent
information."

"**The School for Scandal.**" In this, the greatest comedy
of manners, the vivid qualities of *The Rivals* are preserved,
while a greater dramatic power is everywhere apparent.
The characters are remarkably clean-cut; the play moves
with a surety and ease which makes its performance a
delight to the actors. In putting it on the stage, the
youthful players should aim at a twofold accomplishment:
to keep up the unflagging energy of the dialogue, and to
interpret the dramatic vigor of the various incidents.
The "scandal scenes" require a mastery of expression;
there must be a complete understanding of their malicious
import — hurtful suggestion, pretended candor, false
good-heartedness, combined with perfect balance of details.

Lady Teazle is introduced with surprising effect. The
veterans in the art of scandal are beaten at their own game
by this quick-witted newcomer. She determines to do as
they do, and even a little more; to the horror of Sir Peter,
she completely succeeds. The moment of sincere feeling
shown by her in the Screen Scene is a masterly touch.
Sir Peter is an honest old fellow, and hears the malicious
talk of the group at Lady Sneerwell's with amazed indig-
nation — "Mercy on my life! — a person they dine with
twice a week!" His attitude in Joseph's library — especially the revelation of his affection for Lady Teazle —
demands the actor's utmost skill.

Appendix.

The two brothers, Charles and Joseph, form a contrast that presents a valuable dramatic problem. Charles is a familiar figure on the stage — the dissipated, careless spendthrift, with good qualities hidden somewhere within him. The strong point in the treatment of his character is the manner in which they are suddenly brought out. His real kindness to the supposed money-lender, his faithfulness to the " little nabob," are both original and effective; they are worked up into a scene of distinct originality; the action and dialogue in Act III, Scene 3 and Act IV, Scene 1 are surpassed only by the Screen Scene. They go with a rush and to do them well is the best possible test of histrionic ability. Joseph is perhaps a little more difficult character — the kind that " can smile and smile and be a villain still." His smooth hypocrisy is veneered with good breeding; as Sir Peter says, he is " moral to the last drop." His carefully-framed " sentiments " are always appropriate, always skillfully introduced; they may well be prefaced with a little affected cough, or a momentary pause.

The minor characters are hit off accurately, and afford sound opportunity for acting. Maria is a pretty figure-head, yet with the courage of her convictions. Careless matches Charles as Snake is aligned with the ladies of the " scandalous college." None of these parts should be neglected. The play is like a fine engraving, where every touch — even the seemingly unimportant — has something to do with the perfection of the whole.

The Songs. One more point. *She Stoops to Conquer* and *The School for Scandal* each has a good song in it, and *The Rivals* would have had one, but for the fact that the actress who was to have it could not sing. These songs must be rendered well. Tony's effusion and the rollicking ditty sung by Careless and his friends are too good to be slighted. Appropriate settings for Tony's song are to be found in the second volume of *Popular Music of the Olden Time*, by W. Chappell, pages 456 and 494. The words and music of "Here's to the maiden of bashful sixteen" come on page 744 of the same volume. Rendered by a competent singer, these will add distinctly to the total effect of the performance.

EXTRA READING

The following books will be found useful for those students who wish to enlarge their general knowledge, or to take up special fields of study.

BIOGRAPHIES

Life and Adventures of Oliver Goldsmith. John Forster. 4 volumes. 1848. An exhaustive and entertaining work.

Life of Goldsmith. Washington Irving. 1849.

Goldsmith. William Black. (English Men of Letters Series.) 1878.

Life of Oliver Goldsmith. Austin Dobson. (Great Writers Series.) 1888.
These two books are the best short accounts.

Memoirs of the Life of the Right Honourable Richard Brinsley Sheridan. Thomas Moore. 2 volumes. 1825. The most important of the earlier biographies.

Sheridan. Mrs. Oliphant. (English Men of Letters Series.) 1884.

Life of Richard Brinsley Sheridan. Lloyd C. Sanders. (Great Writers Series.) 1890. A sound critical study.

Sheridan, a Biography. W. Fraser Rae. 2 volumes. 1906. A very valuable recent biography.

Goldsmith. Thomas Babington Macaulay. 1856.

Sterne and Goldsmith. In *The English Humourists of the Eighteenth Century.* William Makepeace Thackeray. 1853.
These two essays should be read in the order given.

MISCELLANEOUS

Shakespeare to Sheridan. Alwin Thaler.

English Drama of the Restoration and Eighteenth Century. George Henry Nettleton.

Social England.   Volume V.   H. D. Traill.
The Four Georges.   William Makepeace Thackeray.
The Virginians.   William Makepeace Thackeray.
Boswell's *Life of Samuel Johnson* should be consulted for its pictures
    of men and manners, no less than for its exact records of the
    great Doctor himself.   *Trivia*, a delightfully amusing poem by
    John Gay, published in 1716, tells of "the art of walking the
    streets of London."

EXPLANATORY NOTES

EXPLANATORY NOTES.

SHE STOOPS TO CONQUER.

(Throughout these notes, boldface figures refer to pages; lightface, to lines.)

TITLE.

Among the names at first suggested for the play were: *The Mistakes of a Night, The Belle's Stratagem,* and *The Old House a New Inn.* Goldsmith's final choice, *She Stoops to Conquer; or, The Mistakes of a Night,* was prompted by his memory of a line in a play by Dryden: " But kneels to conquer, and but stoops to rise."

DEDICATION.

Doctor Samuel Johnson recognized the genius of Goldsmith before he had written any of the work by which we remember him to day. This Dedication records Goldsmith's sincere friendship for the great scholar and man of letters. Johnson was born in 1709 and died in 1784; he is very familiar to us through the admirable biography written by James Boswell. For the last thirty years of his life he was a kind of " literary dictator," whose judgment was generally accepted as final. Among his works should be mentioned the essays in the *Rambler, Rasselas,* the *Lives of the English Poets,* and the famous *Dictionary.*

sentimental: Goldsmith refers to the type of comedy then in vogue. Its leading characters were invariably persons of rank and fashion; its language was stilted and affected.

Colman: The manager of Covent Garden Theatre from 1764–1774. He held the manuscript of *She Stoops to Conquer* for a long time, and was only persuaded to produce it by Dr. Johnson.

421

Explanatory Notes.

late in the season: The actual date of production was March 15, 1773 — the season closed in May.

PROLOGUE.

The " Prologue " was indispensable to the drama of the eighteenth century. Garrick, like Colman, was doubtful about the play. He wrote the Prologue, however, because he saw certain indications that the public taste was beginning to change, and wished to connect himself with Goldsmith in case the comedy should prove a success.

4. Mr. Woodward: Harry Woodward, the actor, had taken a part in the *Good-Natur'd Man*, but refused that of Tony Lumpkin, for which he was cast. But he delivered the prologue admirably.

4, 3. " **'Tis not alone this mourning suit.**" See *Hamlet*, I. 2. 77:

> " 'Tis not alone my inky cloak, good mother,
> Nor customary suits of solemn black . . .
> That can denote me truly . . . "

12. Shuter: Edward Shuter, another actor — called " poor Ned " below. He was one of the most successful players in *The Good-Natur'd Man*.

13. a mawkish drab: a silly woman, fond of sickly sentiment.

14. succeed: here, " follow."

21. be moral: indulge in moral reflections.

5, 3. " **all is not gold that glitters** ": Note the succession of meaningless platitudes, the stock-in-trade of the sentimental drama.

12. A Doctor: Goldsmith, whose play is to cure the sick " comic muse."

14. Five Draughts: the five acts.

22. within: behind the scenes.

23. The College you, etc.: you form the college which must support him. The line is too condensed for clearness.

DRAMATIS PERSONÆ.

This was the original company of performers. Of one or two of them a word may be said. Lewes had previously been Harlequin in the pantomime. His success as Young Marlow caused Goldsmith to show his gratitude by writing an epilogue for his "benefit" performance on May 7, 1773. Quick, who had taken a part in *The Good Natur'd Man*, made a great hit as Tony Lumpkin. Goldsmith prepared a special sketch for his Benefit on May 8. A song, beginning "Ah, me! when shall I marry me?", originally written for Miss Hardcastle, had to be omitted because Mrs. Bulkley could not sing.

ACT I.

Scene 1.

7, 10. **they travel faster than a stage-coach**: At this time the stage-coach was the most rapid means of conveyance.

12. **basket**: a large wicker-work structure attached to the rear axle-tree of a coach. It was used for carrying baggage.

15. **rumbling**: rambling.

looks for all the world like an inn: This suggestion gives an air of probability to the error of Marlow and Hastings.

19. **Prince Eugene and the Duke of Marlborough**: Two great generals of the early eighteenth century. Prince Eugene was the ally of the Duke at the battle of Blenheim in 1704. It might be interesting to read, in this connection, Southey's poem *After Blenheim*.

8, 4. **an old wife**: Note Hardcastle's essential good-heartedness, as indicated by this speech.

7. **Darby . . . Joan**: the old couple in the familiar ballad, whose married happiness has become proverbial.

> " Darby, dear, we are old and gray,
> Fifty years since our wedding day. . . .
> Always the same, Darby my own,
> Always the same to your old wife Joan."

Explanatory Notes.

9. **make money of that**: make what you can of that.

21. **quotha!** : a contemptuous expression — " learning, indeed ! "

29. **fastened my wig**: The use of the wig was common at the time. Goldsmith once had this trick played on him.

9, 5. **A cat and fiddle**: Mr. Hardcastle is impatient with his wife's partiality for Tony.

21. **this raw evening**: a remark which fixes the time of the action. Note that the whole is confined to one evening — as indicated in the sub-title.

23. **The Three Pigeons**: There were several inns of this name at the time. A small hostelry at Lissoy was afterwards so named in honor of Goldsmith.

27. **low**: This word was much used by the sentimentalists to brand anything that was not in accordance with what they considered good taste on the stage. Goldsmith turns their own weapon against them; see, especially, the next scene.

29. **exciseman**: a collector of inland revenue.

10, 1. **music-box**: barrel-organ.

16. **French frippery**: tawdry finery.

21. **the indigent world could be clothed**, etc.: Goldsmith has a similar thought in *The Vicar of Wakefield*, where the good Vicar rebukes his daughters for undue attention to dress :

" I do not know whether such flouncing and shredding is becoming even in the rich, if we consider, upon a moderate calculation, that the nakedness of the indigent world might be clothed from the trimmings of the vain."

23. **our agreement**: This " agreement " helps to confirm Marlow in his mistake.

12, 15. **set my cap**: make myself attractive.

13, 2. **in face** : looking my best.

30. **monster** : The term was used of any exaggeration in character or appearance.

31. **pink of perfection** : height of excellence. In *The Rivals*, Mrs. Malaprop confuses the expression in her customary way: " He is the very pine-apple of politeness." See page 159.

14, 17. **the improvements**: a term used of gardens improved by cultivation and so forth.

Allons! " Come on ! "

19. **would it were bed-time and all well**: a mock-tragic adaptation of Falstaff's remark in *I King Henry IV*, V. 1. 125:

" I would it were bed-time, Hal, and all well."

QUESTIONS AND TOPICS FOR DISCUSSION.

1. What " antecedent information " do we gain from this scene?

2. How is our interest aroused in the characters?

3. What hints do we gain as to the personality of Tony?

4. Do you note anything looking to the further development of the plot?

ACT I.

Scene 2.

Goldsmith introduces the " shabby " scene both to indicate the tastes of Tony Lumpkin and as a deliberate attack on the sentimental drama.

14, 22. **knock himself down for a song**: The chairman at such gatherings called for a song by tapping on the table with a hammer.

24. **a song I made**: Some critics have said that an uneducated boor like Tony, who was unable even to read a letter, could never have written such a good song. But it is probable that we are not supposed to take his claims to authorship too seriously. In any case, the spirit of the song is quite in accordance with Tony's opinions.

15, 4. **genus**: " genius ".

Lethes . . . Styxes: Lethe was the River of Forgetfulness, Styx the River of Hate, in the Lower World of the ancients. Stygian is the adjective formed from Styx.

7. **Their qui's, etc.**: That is, their education and learning, as shown by the use of Latin words.

8. **pigeons**: The pigeon was supposed to be a foolish bird.

10. **Methodist**: a name first applied about 1730 to the followers of Wesley and Whitefield.

19. **jorum**: a large drinking-bowl.

16, 2. **spunk**: spirit.

4. **low**: "used of the natural, unaffected language and habits of the common people, as contrasted with the mincing, sentimental comedy then in vogue, which dealt only with what was 'genteel,' and in which a stilted kind of polished dialogue was used." Goldsmith's satire is made doubly effective by being placed in the mouth of a "low" character. Note the fine irony of the whole passage.

8. **in a concatenation accordingly**: The speaker probably means "if he behaves like a gentleman." But it is well not to force too much meaning into this amusing dialogue.

11. **obligated**: obliged.

14. **"Water Parted"**: a song in an opera called *Artaxerxes*, published in 1762.

minuet: a stately dance to slow music.

Ariadne: an opera by Handel.

17. **publicans**: inn-keepers.

19. **Ecod**: an oath, common at the time.

23. **winding the straight horn**: sounding a horn while hunting. Pronounce "winding" with a long "i."

31. **Stingo**: nickname for a landlord.

17, 7. **woundily**: exceedingly.

12. **the squeezing of a lemon**: for brewing punch. Tony means "at once."

14. **father-in-law**: step-father — often so used in the eighteenth century.

16. **grumbletonian**: grumbler.

18, 14. **We wanted no ghost to tell us that**: Cf. *Hamlet*, I. 5. 125:

> "There needs no ghost, my lord, come from the grave,
> To tell us that."

25. **trapesing**: wandering about idly, "loafing."

trolloping: untidy, slatternly.

426

19, 27. **Zounds!** A common expletive of the day.

as soon find out the longitude: The determination of the longitude at sea had long caused much difficulty. An accurate method was finally worked out in 1773, the year of the comedy.

20, 9. **your three chairs:** "Your" is here used colloquially, as frequently in Shakespeare.

16. **as an inn:** Goldsmith in his youth had suffered from a joke like that which Tony played on the travelers.

26. **saving your presence:** a phrase used as an apology for an incredible remark, or for a coarse expression.

30. **old blade:** old fellow.

QUESTIONS AND TOPICS FOR DISCUSSION.

1. Can you account for an ignoramus like Tony writing such a clever song?

2. Discuss the satire intended by Goldsmith in the first part of the scene.

3. Why does Tony play his trick on the two travelers?

4. Why did the landlord think the newcomers looked like Frenchmen?

ACT II.

Scene 1.

22, 9. **warren:** a preserve for rabbits, a piece of ground where rabbits are bred.

23, 19. **ould grouse in the gun-room:** This story unfortunately has not been traced.

24, 4. **wauns:** a rustic mock oath.

12. **by the elevens:** a meaningless expression — perhaps Diggory's clumsy way of saying "by the heavens." Note the crude pronunciation of the servants throughout.

26, 5, 6. **comet . . . burning mountain:** This remark would catch the attention of the audience; a brilliant comet had appeared in 1769, and in 1767 there had been an eruption of Vesuvius.

6. **bagatelle:** trifle.

427

Explanatory Notes.

27, 12. **prepossessing**: causing an unfavorable impression. To-day the term has the opposite signification.

14. **duchesses of Drury-lane**: slang phrase for women of the street.

28, 11. **Denain**: a town in northeast France. Mr. Hardcastle's memory is at fault, as the Duke of Marlborough was not present on this occasion.

12. **ventre d'or**: gold-embroidered.

29, 6. **cup**: wine, flavored in a special way, and usually spiced.

26. "**for us that sell ale**": Mr. Hardcastle here makes a quotation, which the young men, of course, understand literally.

29. **the mistakes of government**: At the time of the play this reference would be quickly grasped. Lord North was Prime Minister and the "troubles" under his administration were serious. The difficulties in India are alluded to below, and in America the government was facing the war with the colonies which actually began in 1775.

30, 2. **Heyder Ally**: Haider Ali, Sultan of Mysore, in Madras. He was a dangerous enemy of the East India Company.

Ally Cawn: Ali Khan, Nawab of Bengal, brought the British rule there into confusion until the appointment of Warren Hastings as Governor in 1772.

Ally Croaker: the hero of a popular Irish song.

11. **Westminster-hall**: The Law Courts were held here until 1882.

24. **Belgrade**: in Servia, then Turkish territory.

32, 12. **your pig**, etc.: See note to page **20**, 9.

17. **Let your brains be knocked out**: Hastings gives a double meaning to the words.

26. **Florentine**: a dish not unlike our modern mince pie.

27. **taffety cream**: whipped cream, artificially colored.

28. **made dishes**: fancy dishes.

29. **a green and yellow dinner**: Horace Walpole, in one of his amusing letters, refers to such a dinner: "instead of substantials, there was nothing but a profusion of plates striped red, green, and yellow, gilt plates, blacks, and uniforms!"

33, 3. **Why, really, sir,** etc.: Marlow thinks they have carried their criticism a little too far with the supposed inn-keeper, and offers a word of praise for the fare which he has offered them. He thinks the landlord is offended, and tries to soothe him.

34, 29. **the India director**: Director in the East India Company.

35, 22. **our mistresses**: our lady-loves.

38, 22. **a man of sentiment**: of good taste and fine feelings.

40, 12. **I'm certain he scarce look'd in my face**: This remark gives a reason for Marlow failing to recognize Miss Hardcastle as the " bar-maid."

20. **engaging**: persistent.

27. **coquetting him**: flirting with him.

41, 6. **Ranelegh, St. James's, or Tower Wharf**: Hastings takes advantage of Mrs. Hardcastle's ignorance of London. Ranelegh Gardens and St. James' Park were highly fashionable resorts; Tower Wharf was frequented by much less desirable people.

11. **The Pantheon, the Grotto Gardens, the Borough**: Mrs. Hardcastle reveals her own ignorance in her reply. The Pantheon was a place of amusement intended to rival Ranelegh; the Grotto and the Borough were both in very unfashionable quarters of the city.

14. **The Scandalous Magazine**: an allusion to *The Town and Country Magazine*. See Charles Lamb, *On Books and Reading*:

" Coming in to an inn at night, — having ordered your supper, — what can be more delightful than to find lying in the window-seat, left there time out of mind by the carelessness of some former guest, two or three numbers of the old *Town and Country Magazine*, with its amusing *tête-à-tête* pictures — ' The Royal Lover and Lady G —,' ' The Melting Platonic and the Old Beau,' — and such-like antiquated scandal? "

17. **this head**: this way of arranging my hair. She seats herself, while Hastings stands behind her.

18. **dégagée**: with unstudied ease. Throughout this conversation, the delightful irony of Hastings is quite lost on Mrs. Hardcastle.

Explanatory Notes.

19. **friseur**: hair-dresser.

21. **Ladies' Memorandum-Book**: a magazine of fashions.

25. **inoculation**: for the small-pox, at this time a terrible scourge. Dr. Jenner announced his discovery of vaccination in 1798. There was a practice in vogue long before this, however, by which inoculation with the virus of small-pox was used to give immunity from infection. It proved more or less successful; but was both more dangerous and less certain in its results than the wonderful discovery of Jenner.

42, 9. **Gothic vivacity**: barbarous humor.

10. **tête**: false hair.

23. **samplers**: embroidery work for children, to teach them the various stitches. "Samples" of letters and figures were chiefly used. To-day they are preserved as heirlooms in many of our older families.

43, 12. **crack**: lie. Tony changes the word just in time.

44, 3. **Complete Housewife**: a medical handbook of the time, for use in households.

4. **Quincy**: John Quincy wrote a *Complete English Dispensatory* (1719) which was very popular.

12. **dinging**: "rubbing it in." The word survives in our modern "it was dinned into him."

45, 20. **as a hog in a gate**: *i.e.*, as a hog stuck in a gate. Tony's similes are not elegant.

46, 3. **anon!** an expression of scornful disbelief — "ah, get out!"

QUESTIONS AND TOPICS FOR DISCUSSION.

1. Can you explain the dramatic value of the scene between Hardcastle and his servants, besides its amusing qualities?

2. Does Marlow's lack of "assurance" seem to you exaggerated? Discuss the question.

3. Point out the touches by which the mistake of Hastings and Marlow is made to appear reasonable in their conversation with Mr. Hardcastle.

4. How does Hastings find out their error? Why was Marlow kept in ignorance of the true state of affairs?

5. How would you manage the position and action of Hastings during his talk with Mrs. Hardcastle?

6. What can you say of Mrs. Hardcastle as a hostess? as a mother?

7. How is the development of the plot set forward in the closing part of the scene?

ACT III.

Scene 1.

48, 13. **mauvaise honte**: bashfulness, awkward shyness.

18. **rally**: jest. The two are talking at cross purposes.

21. **Bully Dawson**: a notorious ruffian and card-sharper of the early century. We are told, in Number 2 of *The Spectator*, that Sir Roger De Coverley " kicked Bully Dawson in a coffee-house for calling him youngster."

49, 5. **Marlborough . . . Eugene**: See note to page **7**, 19.

50, 10. **bobs**: ear-rings, pendants.

12. **my genus**: clever fellow — for " genius."

14. **amused**: deluded, deceived.

17. **bear your charges**: meet your expenses.

51, 11. **bounce of a cracker**: bursting of a fire-cracker.

12. **Morrice!** " Get out of here!"

14. **Such a girl as you want jewels!** We begin to see, in the course of this dialogue, some excuse for the expression in Hastings' letter referring to " the hag your mother " — see IV. 1. 420.

24. **paste**: imitation jewelry.

marcasites: imitation gold and silver ornaments.

52, 8. **rose and table-cut things**: " rose cut," having a smooth rounded surface; "table cut," with a flat upper surface, showing facets only at the sides. Both designs, of course, were extremely beautiful.

10. **King Solomon at a puppet show**: That is, they would make you look too gaudily arrayed.

53, 14. **garnets**: green stones, of no very great value.

25. **spark**: lover.

30. **catherine-wheel**: revolving fire-work.

54, 2. **undone**: ruined.

55, 16. **your present dress**: she has changed into her "house dress," in accordance with the agreement with her father. See page 10, lines 23–6.

22. **Cherry**: the landlord's daughter in *The Beaux' Stratagem*, a comedy by George Farquhar, produced in 1707.

56, 3. **my bonnet**: evidently a large bonnet which overshadowed the face, such as was fashionable at the time.

18. **bar cant**: slang talk of the inn.

18, 19. **Lion . . . Lamb . . . Angel**: It was customary to designate rooms at an inn by fanciful names, instead of numbers.

25. **the gallery**: a long room, common in old English country-houses, serving to connect two other apartments. It was used as a "picture-gallery," and for the exhibition of statues, armor, and so on.

27. **recollection**: "collecting myself."

57, 13. **parcel**: lot.

58, 22. **obstropalous**: rude, obstreperous.

23. **dash'd**: subdued, bashful.

29. **rallied her**: joked with her.

59, 5. **Ladies' Club**: There was a famous club of this kind in London — the Albermarle Club.

14. **old Miss Biddy Buckskin**: Miss Rachel Lloyd, foundress of the Albermarle Club. In the play as first acted, the name actually appeared, but Goldsmith changed it when the comedy was printed.

20. **chit**: mere child, little girl.

28. **Odso!** One of the queer expletives which were so plentiful in the eighteenth century.

60, 5. **I never nicked seven**, etc.: A reference to dice-throwing. To "nick seven" was to throw seven with the dice — a great piece of luck. To follow this by "ames ace" — two aces in succession, the lowest possible throw — was to follow good luck by the worst luck possible.

QUESTIONS AND TOPICS FOR DISCUSSION.

1. Trace the "dramatic irony" in the conversation between Miss Hardcastle and her father.

2. Mrs. Hardcastle before and after she knows the jewels are lost. Comment upon Tony's attitude in the matter.

3. How is Marlow's mistake in the identity of Miss Hardcastle made credible to the audience?

4. Miss Hardcastle says: "Give me that hour, then." Explain the dramatic significance of the remark.

ACT IV.

Scene 1.

62, 8. **discover**: reveal.

17. **amuse**: occupy, deceive.

63, 1. **post-coach**: traveling carriage.

64, 23. **To the landlady!** Hastings finds himself in a difficult situation. Note how his concealed agitation is contrasted with the frank manner of Marlow, who is conscious only of having done a helpful deed. We have here one of the most successful minor episodes of the play.

66, 20. **Liberty and Fleet Street**: a political "slogan" of the day. The servant, of course, means nothing by it. The phrase arose about 1763 in connection with the prosecution of John Wilkes for criticizing the government in No. 45 of the *North Briton*. Wilkes, who was personally a somewhat objectionable character, became a sort of martyr in the cause of free speech and the right of the press to discuss public affairs. Fleet Street was the center of journalism in London.

68, 2. **the Rake's Progress**: a series of pictures by the famous artist William Hogarth. It was published in 1735 and illustrated the various steps in the downward career of a young man of fashion. Note the bitter sarcasm of Mr. Hardcastle's remarks.

69, 13. **The Dullissimo-Macaroni**: "Macaroni" means "dandy," and was a familiar term at the time of the play. The Macaronis copied foreign fashions in dress, affected foreign cookery and in general tried to make themselves conspicuous in society. The picture-shops often exhibited caricatures of well-known men, with such titles as "the Southwark Macaroni," "the Martial Macaroni," etc. It was about this same time that the term was sarcastically applied to some troops in the colony of Maryland who wore a showy uniform.

> " Yankee Doodle came to town
>   Riding on a pony;
> He stuck a feather in his cap,
>   And called him Macaroni."

71, 13. **Whistle-jacket**: a famous race-horse.

72, 15. **haspicholls**: Tony means the "harpsichord," an early form of piano.

bobbins: cylinders for holding thread in weaving or lace-making. They moved rapidly to and fro as the work was being done.

19. **incontinently**: immediately.

29. **mun**: rustic for "must."

73, 11. **your print hand**: colloquial usage. See note to page **20**, 9.

29. **izzard**: old name for the letter "z."

74, 7. **feeder**: tamer of game-cocks.

10. **Shake-bag**: large game-cock.

75, 3. **pink of courtesy**: highest example of courtesy. See note to page **13**, 31.

circumspection: prudence, thoughtfulness.

23. **nice**: ingenious, clever.

76, 4. **old Bedlam**: "a regular old lunatic asylum." "Old" has the sense of "thorough," "downright"; as in our modern slang, "a great old time." **Bedlam** was the hospital of St. Mary of Bethlehem for the insane, in London.

17. **baskets**: short ash sticks, known as "single-sticks," with basket-work hand-guards.

QUESTIONS AND TOPICS FOR DISCUSSION.

1. Why did Hastings give the casket to Marlow? Trace the complications following this interchange.

2. Show how Marlow is made to realize his mistake about the inn.

3. What is gained by Marlow's change of attitude towards the supposed bar-maid? How is this brought about?

4. Why does Tony pretend to be in love with his cousin?

5. Show how the letter hastens the *dénouement* of the play.

6. What is it that causes Tony to decide to help the lovers?

7. Note that this Act, like Acts II and III, contains only one scene. Explain the methods by which, in each case, continuity of action is provided for.

ACT V.

Scene 1.

79, 11. **fruitless**: useless.

14. **peremptory**: imperious, authoritative.

80, 6. **competence**: sufficient fortune.

26. **You take me?** you understand me? "you get me?"

83, 10. **forward, canting, ranting**: impudent, slangy, boisterous.

QUESTIONS AND TOPICS FOR DISCUSSION.

1. Explain how the complications are intensified in this scene.

2. What is the dramatic reason for introducing Sir Charles at this point in the play?

3. Explain: "And if you don't find him what I describe — I fear my happiness must never have a beginning."

ACT V.

Scene 2.

84, 6. **basket**: See note to page **7**, 12.

10. **smoked**: sweated.

11. **rabbit me**: a meaningless expletive.

12. **varment**: vermin — the horses, in Tony's opinion, were feeble creatures. The early settlers called the Indians "varmin."

Explanatory Notes.

18. **riddle me this**: solve this riddle for me.

85, 3. **circumbendibus**: roundabout journey.

8. **She thinks herself forty miles off**: This remark caused the single hiss which so worried Goldsmith. See page 360.

9. **cattle**: slang for horses.

27. **quickset hedge**: hedge of hawthorn or box; so-called because it was set out with living (" quick ") shrubs.

86, 12. **kept here**: resorted to this place, made it their headquarters.

89, 4. **There's morality . . . reply**: " There's a lesson in what he says."

QUESTIONS AND TOPICS FOR DISCUSSION.

1. Set the stage for this scene.

2. The audience on the first night found this situation incredible. Do you agree with the judgment? Discuss the question.

3. What is the point of Mr. Hardcastle's remark — " There's morality, however, in his reply."

4. Why does Miss Neville decide to appeal to Mr. Hardcastle?

ACT V.

Scene 3.

90, 7. **explicit**: outspoken, plain.

18. **improves upon me**: makes a more favorable impression.

92, 6. **assiduities**: attentions.

levity: frivolousness, fun-making.

13. **secure admirer**: one who is sure of himself, who has no doubt that he will succeed.

94, 24. **levity**: thoughtlessness.

95, 14. **Witness all men, by these presents**: The usual form of beginning a legal declaration. Tony makes his renouncement in a humorously formal and legal manner.

25. **arbitrary**: self-willed, exacting.

QUESTIONS AND TOPICS FOR DISCUSSION.

1. How would you arrange the action of Marlow and Miss Hardcastle while Sir Charles and Mr. Hardcastle are talking?

2. Trace the steps by which Marlow has been gradually undeceived. Show how the final revelation makes a climax.

3. Explain how the various complications in the plot are cleared up in this scene.

4. Note that all the characters are on the stage. How would you place them so as to produce the best " tableau " at the fall of the curtain?

EPILOGUE.

Goldsmith had a good deal of trouble with his Epilogue. At first, he proposed to write one to be sung; but Mrs. Bulkley, who could not sing, threatened to drop out of the play. He then wrote another in dialogue form for Mrs. Bulkley and Miss Catley, her theatrical rival. Neither lady favored this idea. He then prepared a third, to which the manager, Colman, objected. Finally, he composed the present Epilogue, and it was spoken by Mrs. Bulkley.

97, 8. " **We have our exits and our entrances** ": See *As You Like It*, II. 7. 139:

> " All the world's a stage,
> And all the men and women merely players.
> They have their exits and their entrances;
> And each man in his time plays several parts,
> His acts being seven ages."

15. **caters**: bargains.

16. **coquets**: note to page **40**, 27.

18. **chop-house**: eating-house.

connoisseurs: judges of beauty.

19. **cits**: citizens.

98, 5. **pretends to taste**: claims that she has taste.

caro: a cry of approval — " fine ! ", " splendid ! "

6. **Nancy Dawson**: a popular song of the day.

Explanatory Notes.

Che faro : the opening words of an air in an opera called *Orfeo et Eurydice*, first produced in 1767.

8. **swims** : moves gracefully; especially applied to dancing.

Heinel : a famous Bavarian dancer.

11. **Spadille** : ace of spades — the highest card in the popular games of Ombre and Quadrille.

15. **Bayes** : a character in *The Rehearsal*, supposed to be a caricature of the poet Dryden. There is a pun on the word " bays," or laurels, used as the crown of a successful poet.

EPILOGUE BY TONY LUMPKIN.

Cradock : Joseph Cradock, a friend of Goldsmith. He wrote this Epilogue, but it was rejected as too crude for the stage. Goldsmith, however, good-naturedly printed it with the play, and added the footnote to save Cradock's feelings : " This came too late to be spoken."

99, 2. **nonly** : only.

13. **hoiks** : a cry of the hunting-field.

15. **Sadler's Wells** : a pleasure-resort near London.

16. **roratorio** : for " oratorio.'

THE RIVALS.

PREFACE.

The reason for this Preface, written for the printed edition of the play, is clear enough. Sheridan explains that his Preface is prepared for " the cooler tribunal of the study." He takes the opportunity to point out that Mr. Harris, the proprietor and manager of Covent Garden Theatre, gave him very practical assistance in redeeming the comedy from its failure on the first night — a failure due primarily to the fact that " it was at that time double the length of any acting comedy." He then criticizes some unprovoked attacks which were made on the play, and clears himself from the charge of intending any national reflection in the character of Sir Lucius O'Trigger. He closes with a graceful tribute to the "striking and uncontroverted merit" of the actors who had done so much to insure the success of his work.

PROLOGUE.

108, *Stage Direction:* **Serjeant-at-Law**: member of a grade of lawyer with special rights and privileges, appointed by special process. The term is now no longer employed.

Attorney: a " solicitor." Barristers, in English usage, can receive work only from solicitors. Note that legal phraseology is used throughout.

1. **cramp**: illegible, cramped.

5–10. After the withdrawal of the play on the first night, a new passage was written, which took the place of the lines here printed. The Serjeant says: " How's this? the poet's brief *again?* " and a humorous explanation follows as to why the brief is thus presented once more.

6. **a poet's brief**: the play. A " brief " is a summary of the case drawn up for the guidance of the lawyer conducting the case.

Explanatory Notes.

11. **Sons of Phœbus**: Phœbus was another name for Apollo, the god of poetry. "Some lawyers are poets."

12. **the Fleet**: the famous Debtors' Prison. The latter part of Dickens's *Pickwick Papers* contains some striking pictures of the place.

13–14. **a sprig of bays**: Bays, or laurel, was used to crown poets.

14. **his legal waste of wig**: All lawyers wore large wigs.

15. **Full-bottomed heroes**: Judges wore "full-bottomed" wigs on special occasions; *i.e.*, wigs that descended to their shoulders.

signs: sign-boards.

109, 8. flourish: use high-flown language.

16. **no writ of error lies – - to Drury-lane**: A "writ of error" was a legal term for permission to have a new trial on the ground of some error. The Serjeant, appealing to the audience as the "court," says the judgment given here is final; "we cannot escape by trickery or flaw."

18. **costs of suit**: the winner of a law-suit usually gains the costs of the action from his opponent.

19. **spleen**: anger, ill-nature.

transportation: punishment for a crime by being "transported" to a penal colony. It was abolished in 1853.

24. **right of challenge**: A man sued at law has the right to "challenge," or object to, any juryman, and on sufficient ground to have him struck off the list.

25. **newsman**: newspaper reporter.

PROLOGUE.

(Spoken on the tenth night.)

110, 1. Granted our cause: The poet has won his "case"; the lawyer is no longer needed.

111, 2. The Sentimental Muse: This passage is a hit at the popular type of comedy, to which *The Rivals* was altogether opposed.

3. **The Pilgrim's Progress**, etc.: emblematic of the severe morality of the sentimental comedy.

7. **her sister**: Melpomene, the Muse of Tragedy.

10. **Harry Woodward**, etc.: These characters are all in the cast of the play. The sentimental comedy will end, says the poet, by encroaching on tragedy.

DRAMATIS PERSONÆ.

Note that, in accordance with Sheridan's custom, the names are appropriate to the characters. Suggestive nomenclature had been typical of the drama ever since the time of Ben Jonson. See note on page 230.

ACT I.

Scene 1.

113, 3. **Odd's life!** one of the modified oaths so common in eighteenth-century drama.

9. **Harry, Mrs. Kate**: servants of Sir Anthony.

10. **postilion**: the man who rode one of the horses in a post-chaise. See the illustration facing page 84.

18. **Odd!** an expletive.

20. **Why sure!** an exclamation of surprise.

114, 10. **Ensign**: commissioned officer of the lowest grade. The special duty of an ensign was to carry the flag.

19. **as you may get read to you**: a neat touch — Thomas is unable to read.

20. **Masquerader . . . Jupiter**: Jupiter, king of the Gods, changed himself into various forms in his pursuit of mortal women. You may read in any mythological dictionary the stories of Leda, Danaë, or Europa, which tell of such affairs.

27. **half-pay ensign**: An officer not on service or with his regiment was placed on half pay.

115, 1. **the stocks**: Loans to the government had recently been consolidated into a single stock, bearing uniform interest. The technical name was "stocks."

Explanatory Notes.

5. **thread-papers**: narrow strips of paper in which skeins of thread were rolled up.

7. **a set of thousands**: a set of horses worth thousands of pounds.

draw . . . with: "Does she pull well with him?" "Do they pull well together?" The coachman naturally uses the terms of his profession.

19. **mort**: a great deal, "lots."

21. **pump-room**: the room where people assembled to drink the medicinal waters, which were pumped from reservoirs.

25. **not a fiddle or a card after eleven**: a rule originally made by Beau Nash, the dictator of fashionable society. See page 390.

26. **gentleman**: valet, servant. For an amusing account of the life of these "gentlemen" of Bath at a later date, read Dickens's *Pickwick Papers*, Chapter XXXVII.

116, 2. **wig**: Early in the eighteenth century the wig had become a distinctive feature of costume. The fashion remained in vogue for a long time, and no gentleman who pretended to understand the niceties of dress could appear without his wig. The extravagance in this article of attire is shown by the fact that the finest qualities of hair cost as high as three guineas (about fifteen dollars) an ounce; some wigs are known to have cost £140. Towards the end of the century a gradual change came in, and the wig began to be superseded by the natural hair worn in a queue with powder.

3. **ton**: style.

6. **took to their own hair**: ceased wearing wigs.

7. **Odd rabbit it!** a meaningless oath.

when the fashion, etc.: Note the pun. The "Bar" means both the Law and also the carriage bar on which one stepped when mounting to the "Box" — the coachman's seat.

14. **thoff**: though.

15. **the exciseman**: a revenue officer, one of whose duties was to gauge, or measure, the contents of barrels of liquor.

ta'en to his carrots: taken to wearing his own hair, which was red.

16. **bob**: slang for "wig."

442

17. **the college**: The term here means "the highest authorities."

19. **Mark!** Look there!

29. **Gyde's Porch**: one of the Assembly Rooms, kept by
Mr. Gyde.

QUESTIONS AND TOPICS FOR DISCUSSION.

1. In what respects is this scene a definite introduction to the
movement of the plot?

2. Do you consider that Fag and Thomas converse too cleverly
for what they are supposed to be?

3. What is suggested about Bath; about fashions of the day?

ACT I.

Scene 2.

117, 2. **circulating library**: the equivalent of our modern
public library. Sheridan here makes an amusing attack upon
the prevailing taste in sentimental novels. Later, Sir Anthony
Absolute refers to the circulating library as " an evergreen tree
of diabolical knowledge." Twenty books are mentioned all together; among them the undeniably excellent works of Smollett
and Sterne.

4. **The Reward of Constancy**: *Female Constancy; or, The History of Miss Arabella Waldegrave*, 1767.

6. **The Fatal Connexion**: Published in 1765, by Mrs. Fogarty.

8. **The Mistakes of the Heart**: in three volumes, by Treyssac
de Vergy, 1772.

9. **Mr. Bull**: a bookseller of Bath.

11. **The Delicate Distress**: written by Mrs. Elizabeth Griffith,
as a companion volume to her husband's *The Gordian Knot*.

13. **The Memoirs of Lady Woodford**: " Tenderness and
simplicity," says a review of 1771, " are the characteristics of this
novel."

15. **Mr. Frederick**: a Bath bookseller who flourished from
1745-1772.

Explanatory Notes.

25. **Peregrine Pickle**; etc.: *The Adventures of Peregrine Pickle*, and *The Expedition of Humphrey Clinker* were written by Tobias Smollett, the famous eighteenth-century novelist. With the former was included *The Memoirs of a Lady of Quality*.

The Tears of Sensibility: a group of four novels translated from the French in 1773.

118, 2. **The Sentimental Journey**: written by Laurence Sterne; published in 1768.

4. **The Whole Duty of Man**: a very popular religious work, originally issued in 1659. Within two hundred years more than forty editions were published.

5. **blonds**: lace made of unbleached silk.

6. **sal volatile**: smelling salts.

24. **Mrs. Malaprop**: The name of this famous character, as so often in Sheridan's plays, indicates her prevailing trait. It is formed from the French *mal à propos*, — "not to the purpose," "inappropriate." The idea of her peculiarity is derived from the character of Mrs. Tryfort (" try for it ") in an unpublished comedy by Sheridan's mother, called *A Journey to Bath*.

119, 6. **a tall Irish baronet**: " tall " means " dashing," " adventurous."

8. **rout**: a large evening party.

12–13. **a Delia or a Celia**: conventional poetic names, much used in love letters and poems of the time.

120, 21. **tax me with caprice**: accuse me of whimsicality, or changeableness.

24. **apropos**: " to return to the point."

122, 13. **with her select words**: Mrs. Malaprop is careful to use words which sound well — their actual meaning does not matter. Sometimes her words bear a general resemblance to the right expression — as " illiterate " for " obliterate "; sometimes they are brilliant examples of misapprehension — as " allegory " for " alligator "; sometimes they are merely high-sounding, with no discoverable significance, as in " the last criterion of my affection." The general effect, because of her honest pride in her verbal powers, is a triumph of comedy.

16. **coz**: " cousin."

22. **Roderick Random**: a novel by Smollett.

The Innocent Adultery: a translation of a novel by the French writer Scarron.

23. **Lord Aimworth**: a three-volume novel in the form of letters. It appeared in *The Gentleman's Magazine*, 1773.

24. **Ovid**: Translations of the love stories of Ovid, the Roman poet, were very popular.

25. **The Man of Feeling**: written by the Scotch novelist Henry Mackenzie, in 1771.

26. **Mrs. Chapone**, a book of essays, entitled *Letters on the Improvement of the Mind*, 1773.

Fordyce's Sermons: a collection of *Sermons for Young Women*, by James Fordyce, a Presbyterian minister.

123, 1. **torn away**: to be used for curl-papers.

4. **Lord Chesterfield's Letters**: This very widely read series of letters, containing advice as to the proper qualifications and behavior of a " man of the world," was written by Lord Chesterfield to his son. They were long regarded as models of epistolary correspondence. Mr. Chester, in Dickens's *Barnaby Rudge*, was based upon the character of Lord Chesterfield.

13. **illiterate**: obliterate.

26. **extirpate**: exculpate.

27. **controvertible**: incontrovertible.

124, 20. **intricate**: obstinate — possibly " impertinent."

24. **the black art**: magic.

26. **misanthropy**: misanthrope.

29–30. **half-bound volumes, with marble covers**: the backs and corners bound in leather; the sides of marbled paper.

125, 3. **evergreen tree**: always springing fresh.

8. **laconically**: ironically.

12. **progeny**: prodigy.

15. **simony, or fluxions, or paradoxes**: Mrs. Malaprop has picked up these words somewhere, and thinks they refer to branches of learning. **Simony** is the crime of selling church offices for money; **fluxions**, a mathematical term; **paradoxes**, unexpected turns of speech. The whole passage is an excellent example of her love for big words, of which she has great store.

Explanatory Notes.

18. **diabolical**: She thinks this a good expression to go with the others.

21. **supercilious**: superficial.

22. **geometry**: geography.

23. **contagious**: contiguous.

25. **orthodoxy**: orthography.

27. **reprehend**: apprehend, comprehend.

29. **superstitious**: superfluous.

126, 25. **invocations**: She probably means " proposals."

26. **illegible**: ineligible.

127, 2. **come about**: come round.

4. **intuition**: tuition — perhaps she means " observation."

8. **artificial**: artful.

23. **malevolence**: benevolence.

25. **locality**: loquacity.

128, 11. **paduasoy**: a species of cloth, manufactured in Padua, Italy.

14. **pocket-pieces**: pieces of money carried in the pocket for luck.

16. **Hibernian**: Irishman — from the Latin name for Ireland, *Hibernia*.

QUESTIONS AND TOPICS FOR DISCUSSION.

1. From the books which she mentions, what should you gather about Lydia's tastes in reading?

2. Point out the necessary information supplied by the conversation between Lydia and Julia.

3. How does Julia excuse the " imperfections " of Faulkland?

4. Why does Sir Anthony object to circulating libraries?

5. What do you infer as to Mrs. Malaprop's character from her conversation in this scene?

ACT II.

Scene 1.

129, 7. **interjectural**: " parenthetical " — thrown in, as it were.

15. **curious**: inquisitive.

130, 9. **chairmen**: carriers of sedan chairs. The sedan chair was a conveyance very common at this time. It was constructed to hold one person, seated, and was carried by two men by means of long poles thrust through holders at the sides.

10. **minority waiters**: This term has caused some discussion. " Waiters " were persons employed by the Customs authorities. They were sometimes known as " tide waiters " and, like the " ticket porters " of Dickens's time, were employed on odd jobs. These were the " minority waiters " of the play.

billiard-markers: employed to keep score in a public billiard-room.

14. **whenever I draw**, etc.: Under this financial metaphor, Fag points out that he is a skillful liar.

16. **take care you don't hurt your credit**, etc.: Carrying out the figure, Captain Absolute warns him not to make his lies too elaborate.

22. **gentleman**: See note to page **115,** 26.

131, 26 **reversion**: right of succession to the estate.

132, 9. **farrago**: medley, mixture.

30. **aspiration**: breath.

134, 8. **Odds whips and wheels!** The system of " oaths referential," on which Acres prides himself, is best explained in his own words. See page 139.

9. **the Mall**: a famous road in London. In the eighteenth century it was a fashionable promenade; to-day it is used frequently for state processions.

15. **solicit your connexions**: " beg the honor of your acquaintance." Note how, quite unconsciously, Acres plays upon Faulkland's jealousy as the conversation goes on. Captain Absolute stands aside and enjoys the situation.

25. **the German Spa**: " Spa " was a name for a health resort. The original Spa, in Belgium, was noted for its mineral springs.

135, 16. **Odds crickets!** Cf. the familiar expression, "as merry as a cricket."

136, 8. **harpsichord**: an early form of the piano.

9–10. **squallante, rumblante, and quiverante**: words made up on the spur of the moment in imitation of the musical term

447

Explanatory Notes.

"andante." Probably Acres shows what he means by the sound of his voice.

11. **minims and crotchets**: half-notes and quarter-notes.

16. "**music the food of love**": the opening lines of Shakespeare's *Twelfth Night*:

> "If music be the food of love, play on."

22. **purling-stream airs**: sentimental tunes, sounding like a babbling brook.

23. "**When absent from my soul's delight**": probably a song found in *Calliope; or, The Vocal Enchantress*.

25. "**Go, gentle gales**": a familiar song of the day, published in a collection of 1762. It begins:

> "Go, gentle gales,
>   Go, bear my sighs away,
>   And to my love,
>   The tender notes convey."

27. "**My heart's my own, my will is free**": a song from *Love in a Village*, by Isaac Bickerstaffe. The first verse would not be calculated to soothe Faulkland's agitation:

> "My heart's my own, my will is free,
>   And so shall be my voice;
> No mortal man shall wed with me,
>   Till first he's made my choice."

137, 26. **minuet**: a slow, stately dance for four couples.

29. **country-dancing**: dances of rural origin. Any number of couples stand up opposite each other, as in the dance known as "Sir Roger de Coverley."

138, 5. **cotillon**: a dignified dance of French origin.

8. **palming**: "squeezing hands."

9. **a managed filly**: young horse taught in a riding-school.

18. **impregnate**: contaminate.

22. **looby**: lout, lubber.

139, 9–10. **odds frogs and tambours**: "Frogs" were ornamental fastenings on a military coat. "Tambours" were frames for embroidering silk, or the fabric made on them.

11. **ancient madam**: his mother, who apparently kept him under strict control.

448

12. **cashier**: dismiss from service, do away with. A military officer dishonorably discharged was said to be cashiered.

13. **incapable**: useless.

16. **thoff**: though.

20. **flints**: In the "flint-lock" pistol of the eighteenth century, the hammer was fitted with a piece of flint. This truck against a steel disk and made sparks which set off the charge.

26. **militia**: Each county in England was required to raise a body of citizens who were called on to do fourteen days' military training during the year.

140, 20. **bumpers**: brimming glasses of wine, to "drink her health."

141, 15. **I am sensible**: "I know very well."

143, 27. **the Crescent**: the Royal Crescent in Bath.

28. **Cox's Museum**: a popular exhibition of mechanical curiosities.

144, 31. **lodge a five-and-threepence**: similar to the phrase, "cut off with a shilling."

145, 2. **I'll unget you**: "I'll cease to be your father."

16. **turnspit**: a small dog, placed in a sort of treadmill which turned the spit for roasting meat.

QUESTIONS AND TOPICS FOR DISCUSSION.

1. What can you say of Fag's theory of serving his master?
2. Does the jealousy of Faulkland seem to you exaggerated? Discuss the question.
3. What is Captain Absolute's attitude towards Faulkland?
4. Explain the system of "sentimental swearing."
5. Wherein does Sir Anthony seem to be most unreasonable?

ACT II.

Scene 2.

146, 10. **till my purse . . . form**: till I have been sufficiently bribed.

147, 16. **incentive**: instinctive.

Explanatory Notes.

17. **induction**: seduction.

18. **combination**: connection.

commotion: emotion.

19. **superfluous**: superficial.

20. **punctuation**: punctilio.

21. **infallible**: ineffable.

22. **criterion**: Of this a critic wrote in 1828: "This word has no business here; but it is not easy to hit upon any one sounding something like it with a meaning any way suitable. Our readers will observe that Mrs. Malaprop knows a great many hard words; but has not a very correct ear in applying them."

148, 2. **pressed**: To "press" a man was to seize him by force for service in the Navy. The "press-gang" was a familiar institution in Sheridan's day.

3. **get their habeas corpus**: be set at liberty. The "Habeas Corpus Act" forbade holding any one in prison without due inquiry into his alleged offense.

12. **nice**: particular, delicate.

22. **gemman**: "gentleman."

29. **baggage**: familiar colloquialism — "sly girl."

call him out: challenge him to a duel.

QUESTIONS AND TOPICS FOR DISCUSSION.

1. How does Lucy explain the peculiarities of Mrs. Malaprop's letter?

2. What complications are indicated in this scene?

3. Why is Fag so eager to tell his master what Lucy has found out?

ACT III.

Scene 1.

150, 18. **for me**: as far as I'm concerned.

152, 7. **don't she?**: for "doesn't she?"; a common colloquialism.

153, 18. **phlegmatic**: cold, unenthusiastic.

19. **anchorite**: hermit, vowed never to marry.

stock: stick, or wooden block.

20. **block**: a wooden "dummy" on which uniforms were stretched to be dusted.

154, 9. **be the Promethean torch to you**: that is, inspire you with new life. In the old Greek myth, Prometheus stole fire from Heaven to give life to men that he had made out of clay.

QUESTIONS AND TOPICS FOR DISCUSSION.

1. Why does Captain Absolute make peace with his father? How does he accomplish it?

2. Why does he pretend indifference to Lydia?

3. "Not to please your father, Sir?" Point out the humor of this remark.

ACT III.

Scene 2.

This is one of the "sentimental" parts of the play that were cut out by Joseph Jefferson in his acting version. As you can see, the excision can be made without serious injury to the general movement of the plot. On the other hand, it illustrates so clearly the eccentric and irritating jealousy of Faulkland, that it may very well be retained in any production of the comedy.

156, 16. **veering but a point**: changing in the slightest degree. A "point" is one of the thirty two divisions of the compass.

29. **nice attention**: discriminating care.

157, 5. **Æthiop**: Ethiopian, negro.

158, 6. **pressing**: tending, aiming.

28. **virago**: violent old woman.

29. **spleen**: spite.

QUESTIONS AND TOPICS FOR DISCUSSION.

1. Comment upon this scene as an example of "sentimental comedy." In what respects does it seem unnatural?

2. Give reasons for, and against, the removal of this scene in producing the play with an amateur company.

3. Indicate the method by which the character of Faulkland is brought out.

Explanatory Notes.

ACT III.

Scene 3.

159, 2. **accommodation**: recommendation.

3. **ingenuity**: ingenuousness.

13. **ineffectual**: intellectual.

23. **the orange-tree** often bears blossoms and fruit at the same time.

25. **pine-apple**: perhaps, "pinnacle." Mrs. Malaprop means that he is the "pink of politeness."

160, 1. **strolling**: vagabond, idle.

8. **exploded**: exposed — perhaps she means "discovered."

9. **conjunctions**: injunctions.

10. **preposition**: proposition.

12. **particle**: article — perhaps "particular."

14. **hydrostatics**: hysterics.

15. **persisted**: desisted.

16. **interceded**: intercepted.

161, 22. **reprehend**: comprehend.

23. **oracular**: vernacular.

24. **nice derangement of epitaphs**: choice arrangement of epithets.

30. **coxcomb**: conceited fool.

31. **harridan**: bad-tempered old woman.

162, 11. **in the nick**: "in the nick of time."

laid by the heels: captured and overthrown. Literally, "put in the stocks."

15. **perpetrated**: perhaps "planned."

163, 9. **wait on her**: call on her.

165, 12. **deports**: comports, *i.e.*, behaves.

166, 1. **contain**: restrain myself.

10. **allegory**: alligator.

QUESTIONS AND TOPICS FOR DISCUSSION.

1. Discuss a few of the more remarkable "Malapropisms" in this scene.

2. Point out the irony in some of Captain Absolute's remarks.

3. What was the plan to " have the fellow laid by the heels "?

4. " My persecution is not yet come to a crisis." Explain this remark in the light of Lydia's general attitude towards Captain Absolute.

5. Dramatic irony in the closing portion of the scene.

ACT III.

Scene 4.

167, 7. **an**: if.

8. **monkerony**: for " macaroni," or dandy. See note to page **69**, 13.

11. **Clod-hall**: Acres' country place.

16. **I'll hold a gallon**: I'll bet a gallon.

22. **Mr. De-la-Grace**: the French dancing-master.

23. **balancing, and chasing, and boring**: movements in dancing.

168, 6. **sink, slide, coupée**: dancing steps.

11. **tabours**: drums.

valued: thought difficult.

12. **cross-over to couple**: movement in a country-dance.

14. **allemandes**: German dances.

18. **pas . . . paws**: Note Acres' thoroughly English pronunciation.

19. **Antigallican**: anti-French.

26. **Jack-a-Lantern**: " will-o'-the-wisp " — the burning marsh-gas which often led travelers astray.

169, 20. **We wear no swords here**: The wearing of swords had originally been forbidden by Beau Nash, to check dueling in Bath. See page 390.

170, 8. **Achilles**: the Greek hero in Homer's *Iliad*.

9. **Alexander the Great**: king of Macedon, the greatest warrior of his time.

15. **pans**: in old-fashioned pistols, the part of the lock which held the powder. It was exploded by sparks from the flint, and set off the charge in the barrel.

19. **the new room**: the new Assembly Rooms, built in 1771

Explanatory Notes.

27. **the milk of human kindness**: See *Macbeth*, I. 5. 17–19:
> " . . . yet do I fear thy nature;
> It is too full o' the milk of human kindness
> To catch the nearest way."

29. **I could do such deeds**: See *Hamlet*, III. 2. 399–401
> " Now could I drink hot blood,
> And do such bitter business as the day
> Would quake to look on."

171, 15. **addressing**: paying attention to.

23. **King's-Mead-Fields**: on the southwest of the city; originally a " royal domain."

QUESTIONS AND TOPICS FOR DISCUSSION.

1. Does David admire his master's dress, or not?
2. The views of Acres on dancing.
3. The etiquette of dueling, according to Sir Lucius.
4. How is Acres persuaded to send the challenge?

ACT IV.

Scene 1.

173, 4. **the old lady**: Acres' mother.

8. **cormorants**: the cormorant is a large sea-bird, proverbial for its fierce voracity.

10. **quarter-staff, or short-staff**: the " quarter-staff " was a stout pole, about eight feet long, formerly much used by the English peasantry as a weapon. The " short staff," or " single-stick," was a short stick with a hand-guard of basket-work. For an excellent account of a fight with quarter-staffs, read Scott's *Ivanhoe*, Chapter II.

21–22. **this honour seems to me . . . false friend**: Read Falstaff's amusing dissertation on honor in *I King Henry IV*, V. 1. 143 ff.

176, 7. **St. George**: the patron saint of England. He was the center of many legends, the most familiar of which was his fight with the Dragon.

28. **my second**: The "second" in a duel was the friend selected by the challenger to arrange all preliminaries. In this case, Captain Absolute cannot act, because he is supposed to be a friend of Beverley, the man challenged.

QUESTIONS AND TOPICS FOR DISCUSSION

1. David's views on dueling.
2. The effect of these views on his master.
3. How does Captain Absolute help Acres in his plan?

ACT IV.

Scene 2.

178, 6. **caparisons**: comparisons.

10-11. **alacrity and adulation**: Another instance of Mrs. Malaprop's love of high-sounding words used for their own sake. Perhaps she means "sagacity and penetration."

12. **grammatical**: perhaps "symmetrical."

14. **what Hamlet says**: What Hamlet really says may be found in the play, Act III, Scene 4, lines 56–59:

> "Hyperion's curls, the front of Jove himself;
> An eye like Mars, to threaten and command;
> A station, like the herald Mercury
> New lighted on a heaven-kissing hill."

19. **similitude**: simile.

180, 2. **affluence**: influence.

181, 8. **quinsy**: inflammation of the throat.

182, 7. **Bedlam**: the famous London hospital for the insane. See note to page 76, 4.

183, 19. **compilation**: appellation.

26. **clever**: her., "agreeable," "satisfactory."

30. **anticipate . . . future**: Note the typical confusion.

184, 6. **Youth's the season made for joy**: The first line of a song in the second act of *The Beggar's Opera*, by John Gay (see page 398):

> "Youth's the season made for joys,
> Love is then our duty,

455

Explanatory Notes.

> She who that alone employs
> Well deserves her beauty.
>> Let's be gay
>> While we may,
> Beauty's a flower despised in decay."

186, 24. **analysed**: paralyzed.

187, 2. **Cerberus**: the three-headed dog of mythology that guarded the entrance to the Lower World.

QUESTIONS AND TOPICS FOR DISCUSSION.

1. How is the identity of Beverley discovered?

2. What is the effect upon Lydia? Sir Anthony? Mrs. Malaprop?

3. Why does Lydia turn against Captain Absolute?

4. How does Sir Anthony account for her change of attitude?

ACT IV.
Scene 3.

188, 8. **the old serpent**: the Devil. See Genesis III.

9. **caught, like vipers**, etc.: It was an old belief that vipers could be safely caught by holding out to them a piece of red cloth. This they would attack furiously, expending all their venom. The "bit of red cloth" here refers to the scarlet uniform of army officers.

189, 27. **Spring Gardens**: a pleasure resort near the river.

190, 1. **pother**: fuss, bother.

10. **small sword**: light sword, or rapier, used for fencing.

192, 23. **captious sceptic**: complaining doubter.

30. **touchstone**: test. "Touchstone" was a kind of mineral applied to test the value of alloys of gold and silver.

31. **sterling**: of standard value; "sterling ore," pure gold.

QUESTIONS AND TOPICS FOR DISCUSSION.

1. Describe the plan of Sir Lucius to pick a quarrel with Captain Absolute.

2. Why does Captain Absolute accept the challenge?

3. Explain his annoyance with Faulkland.

ACT V.

Scene 1.

The opening portion of this scene forms another " sentimental " episode. It was " cut " by Jefferson in his acting version. The conversation offers, however, an interesting illustration of Faulkland's ridiculous " touchstone " idea, and of Julia's sound common sense.

194, 12. **untoward** : unfortunate, ill-omened.

197, 12. **probation** : test, proof.

19. **licensed power** : legal right ; *i.e.*, by marrying him.

198, 13–15. **moon's** ; . . . **idiot** . . . **madness** : an allusion to the old superstition that madness was caused by the influence of the moon. The word " lunatic " is derived from the Latin *Luna*, the moon. We still speak of " mooning about," to express stupid aimlessness.

199, 13. **a mere Smithfield bargain** : a reference to the Smithfield cattle market in London.

16. **conscious** : in the sense, as often in eighteenth-century literature, of " sharing in."

four horses — Scotch parson : At the time, minors could not be married in England without their parents' consent. Many young couples therefore ran away to Scotland, where the only formality required was the statement of intention to marry and the presence of witnesses. The Scotch village nearest the border was Gretna Green. It is recorded that the toll-keeper here married two hundred couples in one year.

21. **a bishop's license** : legal permission to marry.

23. **cried three times** : This was the formality which frequently took the place of a license, and was known as " publishing the banns of marriage." The names of the contracting parties were announced publicly at three consecutive church services.

200, 16. **suicide, parricide** : Mrs. Malaprop seizes on dangerous-sounding words, with no attention to their meaning.

simulation : perhaps " dissimulation " — but we must not insist on a definition.

17. **antistrophe** : catastrophe.

Explanatory Notes.

22. **enveloped**: developed — she means revealed. Possibly there is a humorous hidden reference to Fag's way of enveloping what he has to say in a mist of fine language. Note his remarks throughout.

25. **forms**: distinguishes, characterizes.

201, 2. **flourishing on**: enlarging on. See note to page **109**, 7.

8. **perpendiculars**: particulars.

16. **We have lived much together**, etc.: Fag does not like to admit that he is only the servant of Captain Absolute.

29. **firearms**, etc.: In his excitement, David takes any compound of " fire " to express his fear. A " firelock " was a flint-lock gun or pistol, a " fire office " was a fire insurance office.

30. **crackers**: fireworks.

31. **angry savour**: dangerous appearance.

202, 4. **was**: note the significance of the past tense.

9. **participate**: precipitate.

11. **given**: disposed.

12. **Philistine**: a term used in the eighteenth century of any violent character, or of drunkards, etc. In the nineteenth century, Matthew Arnold originated the use of the word in the sense of " unenlightened," " uncultured."

16. **putrifactions**: petrifactions. The limestone rocks in Derbyshire contain the remains of fossilized animals.

18. **felicity**: velocity.

23. **exhort**: escort.

24. **envoy**: convoy.

25. **precede**: The mistake is typical of Mrs. Malaprop.

QUESTIONS AND TOPICS FOR DISCUSSION.

1. What is the outcome of Faulkland's plan to test the affection of Julia?

2. Lydia's ideas on elopement.

3. Discuss Fag's method of breaking the news of the duel.

4. Compare the manner of speech used by Fag and by Mrs. Malaprop. How does David add to the general effect of the situation?

ACT V.

Scene 2.

203, 1. **A sword seen**, etc.: See page 391.

206, 14. **beadles**: inferior officers of a parish, employed to keep order in church, and to guard against minor offenses outside. The beadle survived until well on into the nineteenth century. Read Dickens's account of the type in " Our Parish," in *Sketches by Boz*, and by all means make the acquaintance of Mr. Bumble in the same author's *Oliver Twist*.

16. **Give me your shoulder**: Sir Anthony is lame from the gout. See page **113**, 12.

QUESTIONS AND TOPICS FOR DISCUSSION.

1. Captain Absolute's method of quieting his father's suspicions.

2. By what device is the time provided for Captain Absolute to get out of the hearing of David and Sir Anthony?

3. Show how this scene provides the dramatic element of suspense.

ACT V.

Scene 3.

This scene forms a most amusing and interesting climax. The conversation between Sir Lucius and Acres is especially well worked out. It was here, in the part of Bob Acres, that Joseph Jefferson achieved his greatest success in the field of comedy.

207, 21. **a quietus**: discharge, release. A legal term, meaning a quittance given on the settlement of an account.

25. **pickled**: slang for " embalmed."

26. **the Abbey**: the Abbey Church at Bath.

27. **very snug lying**: comfortable corners to be buried in.

208, 5. **Odds files**: The " Oath referential " here evidently has a military significance. A " file " in a military formation is a row of soldiers forming a line from front to rear.

15. **of its own head**: of its own accord.

459

Explanatory Notes.

29. **just as lieve**: just as soon.

209, 24. **doubt**: fear.

212, 23. **I serve his majesty**: as an officer in the army, Captain Absolute could not refuse a challenge.

213, 14. **delusions**: allusions.

214, 13. **dissolve**: resolve, reveal.

15. **illuminate**: elucidate.

24. **Vandyke**: Vandal. The Vandals were barbarians who plundered Rome in the fifth century; Vandyke was a noted Dutch painter.

216, 14. **the New Rooms**: See note, page **170**, 19.

16. **we single lads**: Evidently Sir Anthony was a widower — or he may be merely taking advantage of his wife's absence.

18. **are stolen**: have stolen away — the two girls have moved up stage and are talking together.

QUESTIONS AND TOPICS FOR DISCUSSION.

1. Discuss the dueling arrangements as suggested by Sir Lucius. What is the effect of his ideas upon Acres?

2. How does Acres escape the duel?

3. What complications are cleared up in the closing scene?

4. How would you place the various characters at the fall of the curtain?

EPILOGUE.

This Epilogue received high praise from contemporary critics. One writer referred to it as " one of the most excellent and poetical prologues we ever remember to have heard "; another said that it " runs to the conclusion in as beautiful lines as ever did credit to our language." The neat phraseology, with the touches of humor and the vein of moralizing, were thoroughly satisfying to the taste of the day.

218, 5. **damned**: condemned.

9. **cit**: slang for citizen.

17. **chides**, etc.: scolds those who do not drink fast enough.

20. **Chloe**: conventional name in poetry.

460

219, 3. **various face** : changes of expression.

20. **fairly** : justly, honorably, rightly.

220, 8. **beaux** : dandies — plural of the French *beau*, a term used of the man of fashion.

GENERAL QUESTIONS.

1. Sketch the development of the plot.

2. Cite a scene which appears to you especially effective, and comment upon Sheridan's methods as revealed in it.

3. The " sentimental scenes."

4. The speech of Mrs. Malaprop.

5. Instances of wit in the dialogue.

6. What were the functions of the Prologue and the Epilogue?

THE ACTING VERSION OF JOSEPH JEFFERSON.

There are several modern versions of *The Rivals* which differ in more or less degree from the text that Sheridan left. To American audiences the best-known is that prepared by Joseph Jefferson. This famous actor gave an interpretation of the part of Bob Acres which was little less successful than his memorable rendering of Rip Van Winkle. Jefferson was strongly attracted to *The Rivals*. "This comedy," he says, "kept running in my head with almost the same persistence that 'Rip Van Winkle' did in the old time.

"*Bob*, too, was an attractive fellow to contemplate. Sheridan had filled him with such quaintness and eccentricity that he became to me irresistible. I would often think of him in the middle of the night. . . . The variety of situations in which the author had placed him ; his arrival in town with his shallow head full of nonsense and his warm heart overflowing with love for an heiress who could not endure him in the country because he used to dress so badly ; a nature soft and vain, with a strong mixture of goose and peacock ; his aping of the fashion of the town, with an unmistakable survival of rural manners ; his swagger and braggadocio while writing the challenge ; and above all the abject fright that falls upon him when he realizes what he has done — could the exacting heart of a comedian ask for more than these?".

461

Explanatory Notes.

Jefferson condensed the play to three acts, his most important excision being the omission of the Julia-Faulkland episodes. A statement of his changes will be interesting to students of the original. The general plan was as follows:

Act I. Scene 1 was the second scene of Sheridan's first act, with the part of Julia omitted. Sheridan's first scene was left out.

Scene 2 was the first scene of Sheridan's second act, ending with the angry departure of Sir Anthony.

Act II. Scene 1. A combination of Sheridan's II. 2 and III. 1.

Scene 2. Sheridan's III. 3. The original III. 2 was omitted.

Act III. Scene 1. A combination of Sheridan's III. 4 and IV. 1.

Scene 2. Sheridan's IV. 2. The original IV. 3 was omitted.

Scene 3. Sheridan's V. 1, beginning with the entrance of Mrs. Malaprop and David.

Scene 4. Sheridan's V. 2.

Scene 5. Sheridan's V. 3. The play ended with the words of Mrs. Malaprop: "O, Sir Anthony! Men are all deceivers."

These changes, of course, were made by a veteran actor and were arranged with a single eye to effectiveness on the modern stage. Jefferson's friends were divided in their opinion of the fitness of such alterations. One said: "It reminded me of that line in Buchanan Read's poem, 'And Sheridan twenty miles away.'" Another remarked that Jefferson was sacrilegious and deserved to be haunted by Sheridan's ghost. Others, again, approved what had been done. To the reader and the student, any such modifications of a literary masterpiece are of secondary importance. The prime interest will always lie in the text as it came from the hand of the author.

THE SCHOOL FOR SCANDAL.

A PORTRAIT.

This poem was first sent round in manuscript among Sheridan's friends. Mrs. Crewe was a famous beauty of the day, a close friend of the writer's family, and often entertained Sheridan himself, as well as Burke, Sir Joshua Reynolds, and other prominent men, at her country estate of Crewe Hall. The reason for printing the poem with the play is obvious from the opening passage and the last ten lines.

223, 18. **inuendos**: hints, veiled suggestions.

224, 5. **Amoret**: for Mrs. Crewe. In the third Book of Spenser's *Faerie Queene*, Amoret was the personification of grace and beauty.

6. **In worthier verse**: referring to a poem written by Charles James Fox, also in praise of Mrs. Crewe.

16. **Reynolds**: Sir Joshua Reynolds, the famous portrait-painter.

19. **Granby . . . Devon**: The Marchioness of Granby and the Duchess of Devonshire, both painted by Reynolds.

226, 14. **Greville**: Mrs. Greville, mother of Mrs. Crewe. To her Sheridan dedicated *The Critic*.

17. **Millar**: Lady Millar, or Miller, was a prominent member of Bath society who used to preside over literary and artistic entertainments.

24. **science**: knowledge, learning.

227, 4. **conviction**: realization of evil-doing.

6. **blistered tongue**: alluding to the old belief that lying caused a blister on the tongue.

Explanatory Notes.

PROLOGUE.

Garrick was intensely interested in Sheridan's play, which was frankly designed to restore the former glories of Drury-lane. See page 372 ff.

228, 2. **modish**: fashionable.

5. **vapours**: a more or less imaginary nervous ailment, very common among ladies of fashion in the eighteenth century. To-day, we should call such an attack "a fit of the blues."

8. **quantum sufficit**: plenty, enough to satisfy any one.

15. **sal volatile**: smelling salts.

18. **poz**: slang for "positive."

20. **dash and star**: In these "bold and free" items, the names of the persons concerned were not printed in full, but indicated by the first letter of the name followed by a dash, or a row of asterisks.

22. **Grosvenor Square**: pronounced "Grov'nor"; a fashionable residential section of London.

229, 12. **Proud of your smiles**, etc.: *i.e.*, in *The Rivals*.

13. **Don Quixote**: The hero of the great story written by Cervantes. Don Quixote went out to slay the "hydra" of the exaggerated romance of chivalry; in the same way Sheridan attacked the sentimental novel in *The Rivals*. "Our young Don Quixote" now goes forth, says Garrick, to slay the hydra, Scandal.

17. **cavallerio**: cavalier, knight.

DRAMATIS PERSONÆ.

230. Sheridan's nomenclature forms an interesting study. His method was common in the drama of the eighteenth century, but perhaps had never been so successfully adopted. It is, in a word, to suggest the characteristic of each person by means of the name. The following list will indicate his skill in this regard: Lady Teazle, Joseph Surface, Lady Sneerwell, Snake, Mrs. Candour, Backbite, Crabtree, Careless, Miss Verjuice, the Widow Ochre, Miss Evergreen, Miss Simper, Miss Prim, Mrs. Pursey, Miss Gadabout, Sir Filigree Flirt, Captain Boastall, Mrs. Clackitt, Mr. and Mrs. Honeymoon, Sir Harry Bouquet, Mr. Nicket, Mrs. Drowzie, Lady Betty Curricle.

ACT I.

Scene 1.

231, 8. **fine a train**: excellent state of development.

18–19. **separate maintenance**: a "separation," in which the husband was bound to support his wife.

20. **a tête-à-tête in the Town and Country Magazine**: This magazine began publication in 1769. Each month it printed a "tête-à-tête"— a sketch of some fashionable intrigue. "We flatter ourselves," wrote the editor in the first number, "the anecdotes which we shall be able to furnish will be a means of handing down to posterity a lively idea of the beauties, and their most zealous admirers, of this era." The titles of the articles were clear enough to any one interested; for example, *Miss R— and the Libertine Macaroni, Miss P—m and the Hibernian hero.* The intention, as announced in the magazine, was to reform "the fashionable vices of the age"; but as a matter of fact the articles were in many cases merely scurrilous and insulting.

232, 8. **wants**: lacks.

235, 9. **execution**: forced sale of personal property to pay his debts.

239, 6. **York Mail**: the mail-coach running from London to York. This was, of course, the fastest means of conveyance.

240, 25. **rebus**: a puzzle in which words are represented by pictures.

241, 2. **extempore**: offhand, on the spur of the moment.

3. **conversazione**: an entertainment where conversation was confined chiefly to literary and artistic subjects.

19. **Petrarch's Laura**: Laura was the subject of a "sonnet sequence" by the Italian poet Petrarch, who lived in the fourteenth century.

Waller's Saccharissa: Edmund Waller was an English poet of the seventeenth century, who sang the praises of Lady Dorothy Sidney under the name of Saccharissa.

21. **quarto page**: a square-shaped page.

Explanatory Notes.

243, 10. **Old Jewry**: a street in London, near the Bank of England. It was chiefly inhabited by Jewish money-lenders at this period.

13. **Irish Tontine**: A system of life insurance devised by Tonti, an Italian banker of the seventeenth century. By his scheme, a fund was subscribed, usually as a government loan, and the income was divided among the subscribers. The principal was eventually paid to the last survivor. Stevenson's story, *The Wrong Box*, tells of the struggles of two such legatees to obtain the payment of a valuable tontine.

244, 4. **penchant**: weakness — here, a decided liking for Charles.

QUESTIONS AND TOPICS FOR DISCUSSION.

1. What do we learn, in the conversation between Snake and Lady Sneerwell, (*a*) of the general situation which the play is to develop, (*b*) of the activities of Lady Sneerwell?

2. The character of Joseph Surface, as indicated in this scene.

3. The attitude of Maria towards scandal.

4. How is the leading trait of Mrs. Candour suggested?

5. Explain how the general conversation in the latter part of the scene connects itself with the movement of the plot.

ACT I.

Scene 2.

245, 10. **gall**: ill-temper.

21. **humours**: fancies.

246, 1. **Master Rowley**: a type of the faithful old family servant. He is the confidant of his master and is in general a privileged person because of his long service.

2. **crosses**: annoyances, perplexities.

247, 12. **bounty**: generosity.

27. **enjoin us**: direct us, make us promise.

QUESTIONS AND TOPICS FOR DISCUSSION

1. Old Rowley.
2. The conflict of opinion as to Charles and Joseph.
3. Sir Peter's troubles, as revealed by himself.

ACT II.

Scene 1.

249, 21. **Pantheon**: a large hall in London, used for concerts and other entertainments. See note to page 41, 11.

22. **fête champêtre**: open-air festival.

250, 14. **tambour**: embroidery-frame.

16. **fruits in worsted**: embroidery work.

25. **ruffles**: frills, sewed on the front of a shirt.

26. **Pope Joan**: a simple game of cards.

31. **vis-à-vis**: literally, "face to face." The larger type of coach was arranged to seat four persons.

251, 2. **white cats**: slang for horses.

Kensington Gardens: a London Park, a fashionable center of the day.

4. **docked**: with mane and tail cropped close.

21. **elegant expense**: the expenditure proper for a lady of fashion.

252, 13. **rid on a hurdle**: ridden to execution on a hurdle. The "hurdle" was a rough cart on which criminals were taken to the gallows.

14. **utterers of forged tales**: the figures of speech are drawn from terms applied to the crimes of forging ("uttering") money and clipping the edges of coins. The latter was a common practice, and to prevent it the device was adopted of milling the edges of gold and silver coins. Macaulay points out the prevalence of these practices: "Hurdles, with four, five, six wretches convicted of counterfeiting or mutilating the coin of the realm, were dragged month after month up Holborn Hill." Sir Peter means that the scandal-mongers deserve a worse punishment than the counterfeiters.

467

Explanatory Notes.

QUESTIONS AND TOPICS FOR DISCUSSION.

1. Account for the attitude of Lady Teazle.
2. Comment upon the last speech of Sir Peter.

ACT II.

Scene 2.

253, 15. **taking the dust**: slang for "driving."

16. **Hyde Park**: a large and beautiful park in London.

duodecimo phaëton: tiny carriage — "duodecimo" was a name for books of the smallest size. "Phaëton" was a low, four-wheeled carriage, drawn by one or two horses.

21. **macaronies**: See note to page **69**, 13.

254, 1. **Phœbus**: or Apollo, was the god of poetry.

9. **piquet**: a gambling card-game. There were two players, using thirty-two cards.

255, 16. **caulks**: stops up.

256, 5. **poor's-box**: a box, usually placed at the church door, to receive money for the poor.

29. **small whey**: water drawn off from curdled milk. "Small" means weakened.

257, 2. **drummer's**: bandsmen in the army wore their hair in a queue.

3. **the Ring**: a circular path for driving, laid out in Hyde Park by Charles II.

258, 18. **à la Chinoise**: in the Chinese fashion.

19. **table d'hôte**: hotel dinner-table.

20. **Spa**: a health resort in Belgium. See note, page **134**, 15.

259, 6. **allow**: acknowledge.

17–18. **manors . . . fame**: note the play on words for "manners" and "game."

28. **law merchant**, etc.: mercantile law; "slander currency" should be under the law just as much as real currency.

30. **drawer**: here, "originator."

31. **indorsers**: the "indorser" of a note is responsible if the original drawer fails to pay.

468

262, 10. **cicisbeo** : an Italian word meaning " one who plays the gallant to a married woman."

23. **politics** : careful arrangements.

QUESTIONS AND TOPICS FOR DISCUSSION.

1. Compare the methods of Mrs. Candour and Lady Teazle in retailing scandal.

2. What comments are made by Sir Peter upon the proceedings? How are they received?

3. Can you draw a distinction between malice and wit, as shown by the conversation in this scene?

4. How does Joseph quiet Lady Teazle's suspicions? Do you gain any further insight into his character?

ACT II.

Scene 3.

263, 24. **compound** : make an arrangement to pay his debts.
264, 16. **cross** : troublesome, annoying.
265, 25. **Allons!** Come on!

QUESTIONS AND TOPICS FOR DISCUSSION.

1. Why is Sir Oliver introduced at this stage of the plot?

2. What is the significance of Old Rowley's remark: " Take care, pray, sir "?

3. Discuss Sir Oliver's views about his two nephews.

ACT III.

Scene 1.

266, 3. **jet** : point, " gist."
267, 3. **our immortal bard** : Shakespeare.
5. **a heart to pity** : See *II King Henry IV*, IV. 4. 31–2:
" He hath a tear to pity, and a hand
Open as day for melting charity."
268, 19. **Crutched Friars** : a street in London, near the Tower. The name is derived from an old monastery of " Crossed Friars " (Latin, *Fratres Sanctae Crucis*).

Explanatory Notes.

269, 18. **cant**: slang.

270, 12. **unconscionable**: hard-hearted, conscienceless.

19. **run out**: complain.

Annuity Bill: an act of Parliament to safeguard persons under age (" minors ") by providing that contracts made with them for annuities should be legally void.

272, 17. **crossed**: thwarted, checked.

QUESTIONS AND TOPICS FOR DISCUSSION.

1. Describe the plan of Sir Oliver to test the character of Charles.

2. Why does Sir Peter send for Maria?

3. Do you find Sir Peter or Lady Teazle the more to blame for the failure of their attempted reconciliation?

4. Do you find any touch of pathos in this scene? What is its dramatic value?

ACT III.

Scene 2.

277, 22. **in arrear**: owing.

23. **bags**: a special kind of wig.

bouquets: frequently carried by footmen when on duty.

26. **à propos**: " to come to the point."

278, 1. **distresses**: forced sales.

18. **capital**: important.

20. **equity of redemption**: the right to redeem the clothes.

21. **reversion**: a future claim on the French velvet suit.

22. **post-obit**: " a bond given for the purpose of securing to the lender a sum of money on the death of some specified individual from whom the borrower has expectations." *Century Dictionary*.

23. **point**: fine lace.

QUESTIONS AND TOPICS FOR DISCUSSION.

1. Comment on Trip as a " gentleman's gentleman."

2. Sir Oliver's views on the subject.

ACT III.

Scene 3.

279, 9. **Burgundy** : a French wine.

10. **Spa-water** : mineral water.

16. **a hazard regimen** : a special diet for the game of hazard — see the first part of the remark.

280, 7. **give a round of her peers** : propose in turn the health of ladies who are her equals in beauty.

9. **canonised vestals** : sainted maidens.

19. **never study** : " Don't bother to think of anything else."

20. **want** : lack.

24. **Here's to the maiden**, etc. : Sheridan had a knack of writing clever songs, as may be seen by reading some of those in his opera *The Duenna*. This song was set to a very striking air.

283, 8. **Mr. Premium's a stranger** : A touch of real good-heartedness on Charles's part. He will not allow the stranger to be made uncomfortable.

284, 22. **bough-pots** : flower-pots, or large vases for holding shrubs.

285, 13. **post-obit on Sir Oliver's life** : *i.e.*, money raised on the security of what Charles is to receive when Sir Oliver dies.

27. **too good a life** : too healthy — a post-obit would not be a profitable investment.

286, 12. **mends** : improves.

31. **race-cups** : gold or silver cups won in horse-racing.

287, 1. **corporation-bowls** : bowls presented by the corporation of a city.

28. **no bowels** : no feeling.

288, 17. **you shall be appraiser** : you shall estimate the value.

QUESTIONS AND TOPICS FOR DISCUSSION.

1. How does the scene show Charles's tastes and friendships?
2. Why does he interfere in behalf of " little Premium " ?
3. How does Sir Oliver carry out his part?
4. What is his opinion of Charles at this point? Why?

Explanatory Notes.

ACT IV.

Scene 1.

289, 2. **the Conquest**: the Norman Conquest of England in 1066 A.D.

5. **volontière grace**: natural ease.

6. **Raphaels**: Raphael was a great Italian painter of the Renaissance period.

10. **inveterate**: unquestionable.

290, 3. **no common bit of mahogany**: According to the usual fashion, the "genealogy" was written out on a large sheet of parchment and mounted on a heavy mahogany roller. Careless rolls up the parchment and uses the whole thing as an auctioneer's hammer.

7. **ex post facto**: retrospective. An "ex post facto" law is one which provides a penalty for an act done before the law was passed.

16. **the Duke of Marlborough's wars**: See note to page **7**, 19.

17. **Malplaquet**: a battle won by Marlborough in 1708.

19. **not cut out of his feathers**: Charles points to the military uniform, which in Marlborough's day was highly elaborate.

31. **Kneller**: Sir Godfrey Kneller, a famous portrait painter of German birth. He spent most of his life in England, and died in 1723. He painted many pictures of kings and queens, and was especially renowned for his portraits of ladies of the Court.

291, 10. **beaux**: gentlemen.

21. **more respect for the woolsack**: Charles means that he ought to have more respect for a high legal dignitary. The "woolsack" is the cushion of the Lord Chancellor's seat in the House of Lords. "In the reign of Queen Elizabeth, an Act of Parliament was passed to prevent the exportation of wool; and, that this source of our national wealth might be kept constantly in mind, *woolsacks* were placed in the House of Peers, whereon the Judges sat." Brewer, *Dictionary of Phrase and Fable.*

28. **bought or sold**: Note Charles's pun.

292, 4. **Norwich**: A town about a hundred miles northeast of London.

472

7. **make it guineas**: A "guinea" was worth twenty-one shillings; a pound, twenty shillings.

28. **inveterate**: hardened.

293, 20. **Here's a draught for your sum**: "Here's a check for your total."

26. **I beg pardon, sir**, etc.: Sir Oliver suddenly remembers that he is playing a part.

294, 5. **the little nabob**: "Nabob" was a name applied to a man who had amassed his wealth in India and returned to spend it in England. The type is well described in Macaulay's *Lord Clive;* an excellent example of the nabob in fiction is Jos Sedley, in Thackeray's *Vanity Fair.*

295, 7. **splenetic**: ill-tempered.

QUESTIONS AND TOPICS FOR DISCUSSION.

1. The " picture scene " possesses much dramatic effect. Explain in detail how this is brought about.

2. Charles's views on paying his debts.

3. How does the author manage that we shall sympathize with Charles, rather than blame him?

ACT IV.

Scene 2.

296, 7. **games so deep**: gambles so heavily.

15. **necessitous**: needy, poverty-stricken.

17. **hosier**: one who deals in stockings, and in knitted wear generally.

20. **benevolence**: charity.

297, 11. **with the gloss on**: "brand new."

QUESTIONS AND TOPICS FOR DISCUSSION.

1. Can you account for the appearance of Old Rowley?

2 This short scene has a definite dramatic object. What is this object?

ACT IV.

Scene 3.

297, 16. **I wish**: I hope.

24. **her chair**: her private sedan-chair.

298, 3. **curious**: inquisitive.

300, 10. **faux pas**: false step.

301, 1. **Don't you think**, etc.: Lady Teazle is disgusted with Joseph's hypocrisy.

19. **Now, Mr. Logic**: sarcastic — " can your logic get me out of this situation? " The sentence is interrupted before she can finish.

302, 4. **a coxcomb in**: conceited about.

303, 24. **frail**: wicked.

305, 13. **sensibly**: decidedly.

306, 10. **trepan**: deceive.

307, 7. **tax him**: accuse him.

309, 25. **incog.**: for *incognito; i.e.*, in disguise, or unseen.

312, 4. **Charles Surface throws down the screen**: This is really the climax of the play. The whole scene affords an excellent study in dramatic methods. In no play is better use made of the elements of suspense, dramatic irony, and brilliant dialogue. See page 374.

QUESTIONS AND TOPICS FOR DISCUSSION.

1. This scene is generally considered the most effective in the comedy. Make an analysis of its development, indicating the various steps which lead to the climax.

2. Cite some instances of dramatic irony.

3. Comment upon Lady Teazle's speech beginning, " No, sir; she has recovered her senses." What indication is therein afforded as to the future?

4. Set the stage, and place the characters, for the moment when Charles throws down the screen.

ACT V.

Scene 1.

315, 12. **policy**: clever scheming.

316, 10. **speculative benevolence**: kindness expressed only in fine words.

20. **doubt**: fear.

27. **complaisance**: smoothness, self-satisfaction.

318, 1. **bullion**: cash.

2. **rupees**: silver coins of India, worth about two shillings, or fifty cents.

pagodas: gold coins of India, stamped on the reverse side with the figure of a pagoda, or temple. Their value was about eight shillings, or two dollars.

5. **avadavats**: small song-birds from India, with red and black plumage.

Indian crackers: small fire-crackers, not unlike the modern " Chinese crackers."

319, 17. **French plate**: a cheap imitation of silver.

QUESTIONS AND TOPICS FOR DISCUSSION.

1. Sir Oliver's plan to test Joseph.

2. Summarize Joseph's conversation with the supposed **Mr.** Stanley.

3. What part is played by Rowley?

ACT V.

Scene 2.

323, 9. **hartshorn**: smelling-salts.

17. **segoon**: in fencing, a thrust delivered downward and to the left, directed toward the heart. The term is from the French *Seconde,* and designates the second of the four basic movements in fencing.

324, 5. **Salthill**, etc.: The boys of Eton, the old and famous school, used to go every third year on Whitsun-Tuesday to a place called Salt-Hill, near the school. There they would levy contributions (" salt money ") on the passers-by, for the benefit of the captain of the school. The custom was known as " processus ad Montem " — going to the Mount.

15. **double letter**: a letter on which a double charge was made. Before the days of postage stamps, letters were paid for by the recipient.

28. **deny him**: prevent any one from seeing him.

325, 1. **one of the faculty**: a doctor.

327, 26. **Yes, I find Joseph is indeed the man**: Note the deep irony of this remark.

328, 19. **vastly diverted**: highly amused.

329, 25. **discovering**: revealing.

QUESTIONS AND TOPICS FOR DISCUSSION.

1. Separate the stories told respectively by Mrs. Candour, Sir Benjamin Backbite, and Crabtree.

2. Discuss the effect produced by the entrance of Sir Oliver; of Sir Peter.

3. What is revealed in the conversation between Sir Oliver and Sir Peter after the others leave?

ACT V.

Scene 3.

331, 21. **avarice**: greediness.

332, 17. **diffidence of**: lack of faith in, distrust of.

21. **baited**: scolded, chided.

334, 4. **A. B. at the coffee-house**: an allusion to the custom of making appointments at a coffee-house with intentional concealment of the name.

335, 25. **recollect myself**: " pull myself together," make up some story.

336, 21. **the ill-looking fellow over the settee**: See page **292**, line 19.

338, 18. **Lady Teazle, licentiate**, etc.: Lady Teazle says that although she has received one diploma from the " scandalous college," she will now return it and will take no higher degree. A " licentiate " was one who had a license to practice medicine, but who had not yet been admitted to the final degree.

29. **suborning**: bribing.

339, 22. **traduce you**: take away your character.

QUESTIONS AND TOPICS FOR DISCUSSION.

1. Why does Lady Sneerwell come to see Joseph?

2. Explain why the brothers unite in trying to get rid of " Mr. Stanley."

3. Comment upon the behavior of Joseph and Charles, respectively, after Sir Oliver is made known to them.

4. Why does Joseph summon Lady Sneerwell? With what result?

5. The dramatic value of Snake's intervention.

6. Is the closing speech of Charles appropriate to his character? In what respects does it form a fitting end to the play? Discuss fully.

7. Explain the devices by which all is made to end happily.

GENERAL QUESTIONS.

1. Analyze the course of the plot, noting act and scene divisions.

2. In what respects does this play show an advance over *The Rivals?*

3. Write a note on the names of the characters.

4. " The play is notable for the ease and charm of the dialogue, for the brilliancy of its sketches of character, for the truth of its observation of limited phases of life; but not for depth of treatment." Discuss this criticism.

EPILOGUE.

341, Mr. Colman: George Colman, manager of the Hay-market Theatre.

1. **volatile**: frivolous.

5. **motley Bayes**: Bayes here means " poet "; he is termed

Explanatory Notes.

" motley " because he writes " crying epilogues " and " laughing plays." Bayes was the character in *The Rehearsal* intended for a caricature of Dryden. See page 396.

342, 1. **pounded** : imprisoned, shut in. The village " pound " was an inclosure where strayed animals were confined.

6. **loo** : a popular card game.

vole : the winning of all the tricks ; cf. " grand slam," in the modern game of Bridge.

7. **Seven's the main!** : a throw of dice. The caster called the " main " by naming any number from five to nine, and then threw the dice. If his number turned up, he won his stake.

8. **hot cockles** : a parlor game played in the country. Read the amusing account in *The Vicar of Wakefield*, Chapter VII.

10–20. **farewell the tranquil mind**, etc.: The whole passage is an amusing parody of *Othello*, III. 3. 347–357 :

> " O, now for ever
> Farewell the tranquil mind ! farewell content !
> Farewell the plumèd troop and the big wars
> That made ambition virtue ! O, farewell,
> The spirit-stirring drum, the ear-piercing fife,
> The royal banner and all quality.
> Pride, pomp and circumstance of glorious war !
> And, O your mortal engines, whose rude throats
> The immortal Jove's dread thunders counterfeit,
> Farewell ! Othello's occupation's gone ! "

11. **plumèd head** : alluding to the elaborate headdress of the day.

cushioned tête : hair fancifully built up. See Mrs. Hard-castle's remark in *She Stoops to Conquer*, I. 1. : " He said I only wanted him to throw off his wig to convert it into a *tête* for my own wearing ! "

8. **drum** : fashionable card-party.

9. **Spadille** : the ace of spades.

pam : the knave of clubs.

basto : the ace of clubs. Read Pope's description of the game of Ombre in *The Rape of the Lock*, Canto III.

15. **knockers**: door-knockers were used instead of bells, which did not appear until a considerably later period.

24. **in these solemn periods**: with these solemn lines.

28. **life's great stage**: See *As You Like It*, II. 7. 139–140:
    " All the world's a stage,
    And all the men and women merely players."

SUBJECTS FOR INVESTIGATION.

1. A Visit to Bath.
2. Going to the Play.
3. Sheridan as a Statesman.
4. Goldsmith and Doctor Johnson.
5. The Trial of Warren Hastings.
6. The Friends of Goldsmith.
7. The First Performance of *The Rivals*.
8. The Rise of the " Comedy of Manners."
9. The " Sentimental Muse."
10. " Sentiment " in Modern Plays.
11. Dramatic Gains and Losses in the "Comedy of Manners," as compared with Shakespeare's Comedies.
12. Dangers of the London Streets.
13. Coffee-houses in the Eighteenth Century.
14. Clubs — with Special Reference to " The Club."
15. The Triumphs of David Garrick.
16. Garrick in his Relations with Goldsmith and Sheridan.
17. Satire in *The Critic*.
18. The Function of the Prologue in the Plays of Goldsmith and Sheridan.
19. Indications of the Comedy of Sentiment in Sheridan's Plays.
20. Joseph Jefferson's Acting Version of *The Rivals*.